MODERN WORLD
LITERATURE

1866

HOLT, RINEHART AND WINSTON

Harcourt Brace & Company

Austin • New York • Orlando • Atlanta • San Francisco • Boston • Dallas • Toronto • London

REVIEWERS

The following educators reviewed the Twentieth Century *unit for* World Literature.

James Aune
St. Olaf College
Northfield, Minnesota

Abena P. A. Busia
Rutgers University
New Brunswick, New Jersey

Dore J. Levy
Brown University
Providence, Rhode Island

Fernando Operé
University of Virginia
Charlottesville, Virginia

Gretchen Polnac
Reagan High School
Austin, Texas

John R. Williamson
Johnson Central Senior
 High School
Paintsville, Kentucky

Cover: ACC: 74.138
Andre Derain
The Turning Road, L'Estaque, 1906
The Museum of Fine Arts, Houston

ACKNOWLEDGMENTS

For permission to reprint copyrighted material, grateful acknowledgment is made to the following sources:

African Universities Press: "Telephone Conversation" by Wole Soyinka from *Reflections: Nigerian Prose and Verse,* edited by Frances Ademola.

Copyright © 1962 by African Universities Press Ltd. Lagos.
The Asia Society: "Thoughts of Hanoi" by Nguyen Thi Vinh, translated by Nguyen Ngoc Bich. Copyright © 1975 by The Asia Society.

(See page iii, which is an extension of the copyright page.)

(continued on page 346, which is an extension of the copyright page.)

CONTENTS

Africa and the Middle East

Asia

THE
WORLD
IN THE
TWENTIETH
CENTURY

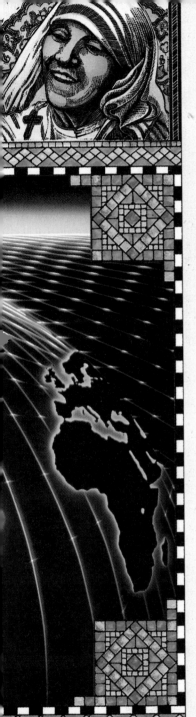

THE TWENTIETH CENTURY

▼ **Time** ▼
1900s

▼ **Place** ▼
The World

▼ **Literary Significance** ▼

In an age of stunning technological advances, widespread warfare, and global communication, humans have gained an increased awareness of the impact they have on their world. Twentieth-century writers have taken on the age-old challenge of finding new ways to express themselves, to understand their places in a constantly—often volatilely—changing world, and to understand the workings of their own minds. The result has been a vibrant array of literary movements ranging from modernism to existentialism, from absurdism to magical realism.

The literature of the twentieth century spans many forms: poetry, fiction, drama, autobiography, and journalism. It has raised new questions and presented new responses to eternal problems such as war, the limitation of personal, political, and intellectual freedoms, and the expression of personal experience. The writings of the twentieth century represent a mosaic of experiences at once bizarre and familiar, at once global and personal.

TIME LINE
The Twentieth Century

British Prime Minister Winston Churchill (left), American President Franklin Roosevelt (center), and Soviet Marshal Joseph Stalin led the Allies to victory over the Axis Powers in World War II.

The Granger Collection, New York

LITERARY EVENTS

▼

Modernism, **c. 1890–1940**

Selma Lagerlöf is awarded the Nobel Prize, **1909**

James Joyce, *Dubliners*, **1914**

Franz Kafka, *The Metamorphosis*, **1915**

Anna Akhmatova, "Lot's Wife," **early 20s**

T.S. Eliot, *The Waste Land*, **1922**

Isak Dinesen, *Out of Africa*, **1937**

Aimé Césaire coins the term *négritude* and becomes one of the founders of the Negritude movement, **1939**

Gabriela Mistral is awarded the Nobel Prize, **1945**

1900	1910	1920	1930	1940

Great Britain defeats Boers of South Africa in Boer War, **1902**

Wright brothers develop the first aircraft, **1903**

Russo-Japanese War, **1904–1905**

Albert Einstein proposes the theory of relativity, **1905**

Chinese Revolution forces led by Sun Yat-sen overthrow the Manchu dynasty, **1911**

World War I, **1914–1918**

Russian Revolution; V.I. Lenin comes to power in Russia, **1917**

Nineteenth Amendment to U.S. Constitution gives women the vote, **1920**

Rise of Adolf Hitler in Germany and Benito Mussolini in Italy, **1920s**

Josef Stalin replaces Lenin as leader of the USSR, **1924**

Worldwide economic depression begins, **1929**

Adolf Hitler becomes chancellor of Germany, **1933**

The Holocaust— Nazis murder over twelve million Jews, Gypsies, and other "undesirables," **1938–1945**

Spanish Civil War, **1936–1939**

Japan invades China, **1937**

World War II begins in Europe; Germany invades Poland, **1939**

Japanese bomb Pearl Harbor, **1941**

U.S. drops atomic bombs on Japan; World War II ends; United Nations founded; Cold War begins, **1945**

European decolonialization, **1945–1970s**

State of Israel is proclaimed, **1948**

People's Republic of China is established, **1949**

▲

CULTURAL AND HISTORICAL EVENTS

Library of Congress

The Wright brothers and their aircraft, 1903.

Mohandas K. Gandhi.

Wide World Photos

Santha Rama Rau, *Gifts of Passage*, **1951**

Albert Camus is awarded the Nobel Prize, **1957**

Elie Wiesel, *Night,* **1958**

Postmodernism movement; magical realism develops in Latin America, **1960s**

Léopold Sédar Senghor is elected first president of Senegal, **1960**

Barbara Kimenye, *Kalasanda*, **1965**

Margaret Atwood, *The Animals in That Country,* **1968**

Pablo Neruda is awarded the Nobel Prize, **1971**

Yehuda Amichai, *Laments on the War Dead,* **1974**

Chinese students protested for democratic reforms at Tiananmen Square, Beijing, 1989.

Reuters/Bettmann Newsphotos

Gabriel García Márquez is awarded the Nobel Prize, **1982**

Jamaica Kincaid, *Annie John,* **1983**

Wole Soyinka is awarded the Nobel Prize, **1986**

Derek Walcott is awarded the Nobel Prize, **1992**

Octavio Paz is awarded the Nobel Prize, **1990**

Naguib Mahfouz, *The Time and the Place,* **1991**

| **1950** | **1960** | **1970** | **1980** | **1990** |

Korean War, **1950–1953**

Soviets launch the first satellite into outer space, **1957**

NASA

An American astronaut on a spacewalk above the earth.

Berlin Wall is built, **1961**

Cuban missile crisis; U.S. troops go to South Vietnam, **1962**

President John F. Kennedy is assassinated, **1963**

Cultural Revolution in People's Republic of China, **1966–1969**

Six-Day War between Israel and Arab nations, **1967**

Assassination of Martin Luther King, Jr.; USSR invades Czechoslovakia, **1968**

U.S. astronauts land on the moon, **1969**

OPEC oil embargo leads to energy crisis, **1973**

Watergate scandal causes President Nixon to resign, **1974**

Vietnam War ends, **1975**

Shah deposed in Iran; Ayatollah Khomeini comes to power, **1979**

Solidarity trade union is founded in Poland, **1980**

Mikhail Gorbachev becomes premier of USSR and establishes policy of glasnost (openness), **1985**

Berlin Wall is dismantled; Communist regimes are replaced by democratic ones in Poland, Czechoslovakia, etc.; Chinese hardliners crack down on pro-democracy students in Tiananmen Square, **1989**

East and West Germany are reunited, **1990**

U.S. and allies wage war against Iraq and liberate Kuwait; USSR dissolves, **1991**

Nelson Mandela becomes President of South Africa, **1994**

This time line border contains international symbols and contemporary letter forms from a variety of alphabets worldwide.

Time Line   3

THE TWENTIETH CENTURY

At the beginning of the twentieth century, the colonies of the European empires covered most of the earth. But Europe's long period of exploration, conquest, and colonization was coming to an end. Much of the twentieth century would be marked by periods of widespread warfare with interim periods of uneasy peace. Colonies' demands for independence become increasingly intense, and many European countries that began the century as world powers found their once seemingly limitless resources dwindling. Throughout the world, artists, writers, and poets sought new forms to express the monumental changes they witnessed during this turbulent century.

World War I

Intense competition among the European powers for overseas colonies and markets was a major cause of **World War I** (1914–1918). Germany, Turkey, and Bulgaria joined Austria-Hungary to fight the Allies, who included Great Britain, France, Russia, Italy, and the United States. The conflict was a brutal exercise in trench warfare.

The peace that followed World War I was short-lived. In 1929, an economic downturn known as the **Great Depression** devastated economies throughout the world. The legacy of war and dire economic circumstances was great change and continued aggression in some parts of the world. The **Russian Revolution**, for example, caused the downfall of the monarchy and established Communist rule in Russia. In the Far East, Japan began invading China and other neighboring countries. In Europe, dictators such as Hitler, Mussolini, and Franco came into power, thus planting the seeds for further destruction in World War II.

American troops in France, 1918. *The use of poisoned gas in World War I added a devastating new dimension to warfare.*

World War II

World War II began in 1939, when Nazi Germany invaded Poland. The main participants in the war were the **Axis powers**—Germany, Italy, and Japan—and the **Allies**—Great Britain, France, the U.S.S.R., China, the United States, and others.

In May 1945, Germany surrendered to the Allies, but it wasn't until August, when President Harry Truman ordered the atomic bombings of the Japanese cities of Hiroshima and Nagasaki, that the war finally ended. The jubilation of the victorious allies was tempered as the world became aware of two horrors: the destructive power of the atomic bomb, and the Nazi attempt to exterminate all European Jews and others they considered "undesirable." In Hiroshima and Nagasaki, over 300,000 people, mostly civilians,

> **❝** The people, and the people alone, are the motive force in the making of world history. **❞**
> —Quotations of Chairman Mao, *Mao Tse Tung*

World War II in Europe, 1939–1945

Axis Powers   Area of Axis Control
Allied Nations   Area of Allied Control
Neutral Nations

Poster for Hitler's National Student Organization during World War II; the caption reads, "The German student fights for leader and land." *Nazi propaganda helped rally the support Hitler needed to carry out his diabolical objectives.*

66 Nonviolence is the first article of my faith. It is also the last article of my creed. **99**

—*Speech, March 23, 1922, Mohandas K. Gandhi*

were burned or irradiated to death by the two bombs. In the German death camps of Auschwitz, Dachau, and elsewhere, the Nazis killed over twelve million people. Altogether, over twelve million soldiers and twenty million civilians were killed during World War II.

The Cold War

The end of World War II marked the beginning of the nuclear age. The United States and the Soviet Union emerged as antagonistic superpowers, and the **Cold War** began. From the end of World War II until the period of *glasnost* ("openness" in Russian) ushered in by Mikhail Gorbachev in the mid-1980s, the U.S. and U.S.S.R. were involved in a stupendous arms race. At the height of the Cold War, both sides had stockpiled enough nuclear weapons to kill every man, woman, and child on the planet twelve times.

New Nations Emerge

More significant in the long run than the Cold War was the decline of the Western imperial powers and its result—the emergence of dozens of newly independent states in Africa and Asia, as well as the political redefinition of older nations

> The end of World War II ushered in a new era of politics with new players: the U.S. and Soviet superpowers and newly independent nations in Africa, Asia, and Latin America.

there and in Latin America. These nations and others began to assert their own identities and reclaim territories. This process of self-determination, however, was seldom achieved without conflict. For example, war has broken out several times in the Middle East over the establishment of Jewish and Arab states in former British Palestine. Despite much mediation, many Arabs have opposed the creation of a Jewish homeland by the United Nations. Countries like Korea and Vietnam, once freed from foreign rule, were torn apart

UPI/Bettmann Newsphotos

Victims of the war in Vietnam, 1965.

by internal factions trying to impose their own rule. Both the Korean and Vietnam wars were, in simplest terms, conflicts between supporters of Communist and democratic governments. South Africa, Northern Ireland, and Central America are some other regions of the globe where violence is a common experience due to the conflicts of race, religion, and political beliefs.

Science and Technology

The twentieth century has seen amazing developments in science and technology—telephones, phonographs, televisions, automobiles, airplanes, computers, space technology, and medical advances such as antibiotics. Particularly important advances have been made in communication and transportation. Not everyone has enjoyed the benefits of these advances, however. The majority of the world's less-industrialized nations still suffers from the effects of poverty and disease. Nor have technological advances in themselves

" Perfection of means and confusion of goals seem, in my opinion, to characterize our age. "
—Out of My Later Years, *Albert Einstein*

always been a boon to humanity—many of these advances have produced dangerous side effects. For example, technological progress contributed to the massacres in the

> **The twentieth century has seen remarkable advances in science and technology. But accompanying these advances have been large-scale disasters.**

trenches of World War I, the Holocaust in World War II, nuclear weapons, and ecological disasters such as the nuclear accident at the Chernobyl power plant in the Soviet Union.

Artistic Responses to the Twentieth Century

For many, the nineteenth-century belief that human history was a record of slow but certain progress died in the aftermath of World War I. Traditional values came under attack, and art forms of the past were seen as inadequate to express the experiences of the modern world. By rejecting the old forms, writers, painters, musicians, and other creative artists were free to experiment with new themes and styles.

Film, Art, and Music

Most twentieth-century painters rejected the styles of previous centuries. For example, Pablo Picasso and Georges Braque, who were influenced by African sculpture and by concepts of geometry, developed a style called *cubism*, which reduced objects and figures to their basic geometric forms. In 1937 Picasso painted *Guernica* in reaction to the brutal German bombing of the village of Guernica during the Spanish Civil War. Shortly after he painted this large mural, the German secret police began harassing him at his studio in Nazi-occupied Paris. One officer, noticing a photograph of *Guernica* lying on a table, asked "Did you do that?" "No," Picasso replied, "you did."

After the invention of the motion picture around the turn of the century, films quickly became a new popular art

Mushroom cloud resulting from the atomic bombing of Nagasaki, Japan, by the U.S. in World War II.

❝ He: You saw nothing in Hiroshima. Nothing.
She: I saw everything. Everything. ❞

—Hiroshima, Mon Amour,
Marguerite Duras

GUERNICA, PABLO PICASSO (1881–1973).

form. Most films were escapist—adventures, comedies, or romantic dramas—but others reflected the pessimism of the postwar era. Charlie Chaplin, an early cinematic master, wrote, directed, and acted in many films that took an ironic look at war, industry, and other important issues of the day.

A determination to break new ground was also apparent in popular music. Two of the most innovative popular musical forms of the century were developed by African Americans: jazz and the blues. During the 1950s, rock-and-roll burst on the scene, causing fans to scream and swoon over their new heroes—Buddy Holly, Chuck Berry, Elvis Presley, and Little Richard. Then, in the 1960s, superstar groups such as the Beatles and the Rolling Stones gained adulation. Since then, hard rock, punk rock, new wave, reggae, and rap music have evolved.

Literature in the Twentieth Century

In literature, a broad movement called **modernism** flourished between 1890 and 1940. In general, modernists were concerned with the loss of traditional values brought on by the major advances and disasters of the early twentieth century. Modernist literature usually reflects the fragmentation and uncertainty that writers and poets perceived all around them. Many modernists emphasized psychological exploration over direct social commentary. Some, like **James**

Jazz great Dizzy Gillespie has helped revolutionize the sound of music in the U.S. and abroad.

Joyce (see page 73), turned to experimental techniques such as **stream of consciousness**. In *Ulysses*, Joyce used this technique to describe everything that happens to a man in a single day—including all his thoughts, both conscious and unconscious. Other writers, such as **Franz Kafka** (see page 20) and **Akutagawa Ryunosuke** (see page 259), used nightmarish settings and situations to express the alienation of the individual in modern society.

Poets such as T. S. Eliot and **Rainer Maria Rilke** (see page 14) broke with traditional forms to express their own personal visions. In his most famous poem, *The Waste Land*, Eliot describes a world without faith, incapable of restoring its spiritual and moral values. Many other poets of this time abandoned traditional rhyme and meter. Their free-verse poems also experimented with punctuation and the physical appearance of the poem on the page.

Sigmund Freud (1856–1939), the founder of modern psychology. *Freud's psychoanalytic theories greatly influenced the works of many twentieth-century artists.*

The Key of the Country, René Magritte, 1948. *Surrealism is a literary and artistic movement that rejects the division between rational and irrational thought and instead expresses the play of the unconscious mind. The movement had a profound effect on the development of post-World War II artistic movements, such as abstract expressionism in painting and absurdism in literature.*

Responses to War

While many modernists wrote elaborate, inward-looking "studies" of human consciousness, other twentieth-century authors turned their pens to direct and blistering accounts of the wars that raged on nearly every continent of the world. Erich Maria Remarque's *All Quiet on the Western Front* and Ernest Hemingway's *A Farewell to Arms* are two novels, written from opposite sides of the battle line, that reveal the tragedy of World War I. **Elie Wiesel** wrote an autobiography of his own imprisonment in a Nazi concentration camp during World War II in *Night* (see page 98).

In the period of general disenchantment following the world wars, literature increasingly focused on themes of alienation, uncertainty, and despair.

Absurdism and Existentialism

To reflect a world in which human existence is seemingly unreasonable and incoherent, playwrights such as Eugène Ionesco, Samuel Beckett, and Harold Pinter created dramas with characters that speak only in banalities and with plots that go nowhere. At the end of Beckett's *Waiting for Godot*, one tramp says, "Well? Shall we go?" and the other responds, "Yes, let's go." The final stage direction, however, is "*They do not move.*"

While the **theater of the absurd** tried to dramatize the "facts" of human existence, some writers began searching for a philosophy that would allow them to understand and accept the apparent senselessness of existence. Simone de Beauvoir, Jean-Paul Sartre, **Albert Camus** (see page 110), and others developed one such philosophy, which they called **existentialism**. Existentialism takes its name from the idea that a person's physical existence precedes his or her "essence," or meaning. This means that there are no preexisting meanings, values, or guidelines for human beings. But since we want and need clarity and rationality in our lives, the existentialists concluded that each person must create his or her own meaning, or essence, in life. Existentialism had a deep impact on Christian and Jewish thought, and theologians of both faiths developed their own brands of existentialism, which emphasized a reexamination of humanity's relationship with God.

> **❝** I, a stranger and afraid
> In a world I never made. **❞**
>
> —Last Poems,
> A. E. Housman

Simone de Beauvoir and Jean-Paul Sartre, two founders of the literary and philosophical movement existentialism.

AP/Wide World Photos

The Fantastic

Some writers responded to the increasingly hostile and confusing world by creating fantasy or **science-fiction** stories. Although the earliest examples of science fiction in literature can be traced back to the 1600s, the genre did not reach its present form until the late 1800s. In the twentieth century, science fiction has developed in two basic directions: an infatuation with technology (Isaac Asimov and others), or an exploration of humanity's precarious place in the universe (H. G. Wells and others). The novels of William Burroughs, Kurt Vonnegut, and **Stanislaw Lem** (see page 137) often use the conventions of science fiction to make serious comments about our world.

Cultural Identity and Literature

Twentieth-century writers from less-industrialized nations often address the problems of cultural identity. They have seen their local cultures uprooted by colonialism or foreign influence, and they have had to ask themselves whether they are to celebrate their native traditions, imitate foreign models, or create new modes of expression.

In Latin America, artists have responded in different ways. The Argentinian author **Jorge Luis Borges** (see page 164), one of the central figures in the Latin American literary "Boom" that followed World War II, devoured nearly everything European libraries had to offer, yet his brand of fiction, which blends fantastic events and philosophical inquiry, is strikingly unique and much imitated today by writers around the world. Chilean poet **Pablo Neruda** (see page 160) was greatly influenced by the modernist movement, but his epic work, *Las Alturas de Machu Picchu* (*The Heights of Machu Picchu*), reconciles the poet with his country's ancient Indian heritage.

The 1960s saw the development of **magical realism**, which contains elements of both the real world and the world of fantasy. Magical realists such as Colombia's **Gabriel García Márquez** (see page 173) were influenced by **surrealism**, which encouraged the free association of ideas as a means of exploring the unconscious mind. But they were just as much influenced by the rich folklore traditions of Latin America.

NASA

American astronaut on the moon.

HBJ Photo

Buenos Aires, Argentina, the center of Latin America's literary "Boom."

In Africa, there was much controversy over the literary movement known as **négritude**, which asserted the value of African traditions. Some writers believed that négritude was a necessary response to years of imperialism, while others, like **Chinua Achebe** (see page 209) and **Wole Soyinka** (see page 217), felt that négritude tended to idealize Africa's precolonial past and that African literature must instead examine that past more critically.

African writers have also debated the question of which language they should write in: that of the colonizers, which in many cases has become the only common language for the descendants of different tribes, or their native tongues. Kenyan author **Ngũgĩ wa Thiong'o** (see page 293) has taken the latter position, turning to his native language Kikuyu after much success writing in English. Achebe, Soyinka, and others feel that by writing in English they reach a wider audience.

Twentieth-century women writers also struggled to establish a cultural identity, for until the early twentieth century, most women had virtually no political voice and little representation in literature. As the twentieth century unfolded, more and more women writers addressed the plight of their sex in a world controlled by men. In her work *The Second Sex*, Simone de Beauvoir analyzed women's secondary status in society and denounced the male middle class for perceiving women as objects. Colette, **Margaret Atwood** (see page 182), and **Jamaica Kincaid** (see page 186), among many others, have also helped define the politics and culture of the women's movement of the twentieth century.

Diversity of World Literatures

In literature, as in history, many different stories are proceeding at once. As we approach the year 2000, both the end of a century and the end of a millennium, we look back on cataclysmic changes that cannot be easily reduced to some clear shape or significance. Very few people could have predicted the reunification of East and West Germany or the dissolution of the Soviet Union. We know only that challenges to our understanding and imagination remain. "The only certain thing about the future," historian Eric Hobsbawm writes in *The Age of Empire*, "is that it will surprise even those who have seen furthest into it."

> ❝ A great writer is, so to speak, a second government in his country. And for that reason no regime has ever loved great writers, only minor ones. ❞
> —The First Circle, *Aleksandr Solzhenitsyn*

Reuters/Bettmann Newsphotos

In November of 1989, the Berlin Wall, which divided Communist East Berlin and democratic West Berlin, came down, heralding the end of Communism in Eastern Europe.

Rainer Maria Rilke
1875–1926, Austria/Czechoslovakia

The German-language poet Rainer Maria Rilke (rī′nər mä·rē′ä ril′kə) thought that the monotonous routines of everyday life functioned as a husk that prevented new ideas from entering people's minds and souls. To prevent the husk from forming, Rilke spent his life on the road—wandering from nation to nation, stopping briefly wherever admirers provided food and shelter.

Rilke was born to a German-speaking family in Prague, now the capital of Czechoslovakia, when the area was still part of the Austrian empire. During childhood, he was torn between his mother, who dressed him as a girl, and his father, who sent him to military academies. In 1892, Rilke's wealthy uncle came to the rescue by offering to pay for his nephew's studies in philosophy, art, and German literature. Rilke liked these subjects and continued to study them in Munich, Germany. In 1901, Rilke married the German sculptor Clara Westhoff. But he soon discovered that married life did not suit him, and he abandoned his wife and baby daughter so that he could travel and write.

One of the greatest influences on Rilke and his work was the French sculptor Auguste Rodin (rô·da n′), with whom Rilke worked. Rodin showed the young poet that art was hard work, not merely an outpouring of emotion.

After leaving Rodin, Rilke revised much of his earlier verse and composed some of his finest poetry. Soon after this burst of creativity, however, Rilke entered a dry period. Seeking inspiration, he visited northern Africa and then lived in the Italian city of Trieste. Here he began a series of philosophical poems, the *Duino Elegies* (1923). The project was interrupted by World War I, in which he served briefly in the Austrian military. After the war, Rilke settled in Switzerland, completed the *Duino Elegies*, and wrote his complex *Sonnets to Orpheus* (1923). Plagued by ill health since the war, Rilke died of a blood disease when he was only fifty-one. By this time his poems, with their meticulously chiseled images, had already established him as one of the most original poets of the twentieth century.

Reader's Guide

BLACK CAT
THE SWAN

Background

When Rilke was working for Auguste Rodin, he confided to the sculptor that he was suffering from writer's block. Rodin advised him to go to the zoo and look at an animal until he could "see" it, adding that it might take as long as two or three weeks, possibly more. Rilke took this strange advice. He went to the zoo, concentrated on a panther, and then wrote the first of his *Dinggedichte* (ding'gə·dikh't), or "thing poems." What Rilke most admired about Rodin's sculptures was their ability to capture not only the outward appearance of a person, animal, or object, but also its inner vitality and spirit. Each of Rilke's "thing poems," like Rodin's sculptures, seeks to communicate both external reality and the "inward nature of things."

Writer's Response

Choose a person, animal, or thing that you can observe closely. In your journal, write a paragraph describing it in as much detail as you can. Try to also describe what it makes you think of and how it makes you feel. Does it make you feel happy or sad, calm or excited, or something else?

Literary Focus

Figurative language describes one thing in terms of another, usually very different, thing. Figurative language, which includes similes and metaphors, is not meant to be understood on a literal level. A **simile** compares two seemingly unlike things by using a connective word such as *like* or *as* ("My feet are as cold as two chunks of ice"). A **metaphor** compares two seemingly unlike things without the connective ("My feet are chunks of ice"). When the comparison is developed over several lines, it is called an **extended metaphor**. Many writers, for example, have compared life to a journey through a maze: We often make wrong turns or run into dead ends, and we can never know exactly how things will turn out.

BLACK CAT

Rainer Maria Rilke

translated by

STEPHEN MITCHELL

*In describing the cat, Rilke avoids such clichés as "black as coal" or "black as night." Keep track of the unusual **similes** and **metaphors** he uses to describe the cat, and decide which you find the most effective.*

Elaine Tin Nyo

A ghost, though invisible, still is like a place
your sight can knock on, echoing; but here
within this thick black pelt, your strongest gaze
will be absorbed and utterly disappear:

5   just as a raving madman, when nothing else
can ease him, charges into his dark night
howling, pounds on the padded wall, and feels
the rage being taken in and pacified.

She seems to hide all looks that have ever fallen
10   into her, so that, like an audience,
she can look them over, menacing and sullen,
and curl to sleep with them. But all at once

as if awakened, she turns her face to yours;
and with a shock, you see yourself, tiny,
15   inside the golden amber of her eyeballs
suspended, like a prehistoric fly.°

15–16. amber . . . prehistoric fly:
Small, prehistoric creatures
such as flies are sometimes
perfectly preserved for millions
of years in amber, or fossilized
tree sap. The color amber
takes its name from the trans-
lucent yellow or brownish yellow color of this sap.

THE SWAN
Rainer Maria Rilke

translated by

ROBERT BLY

 There is an extended comparison in this poem. What things are being compared?

This clumsy living that moves lumbering
as if in ropes through what is not done
reminds us of the awkward way the swan walks.

And to die, which is a letting go
5 of the ground we stand on and cling to every day,
is like the swan when he nervously lets himself down

into the water, which receives him gaily
and which flows joyfully under
and after him, wave after wave,
10 while the swan, unmoving and marvelously calm,
is pleased to be carried, each minute more fully grown,
more like a king, composed, farther and farther on.

First Thoughts

Which of these poems best expresses the "inward nature" of its subject? Why do you say so?

Identifying Facts

1. According to the first stanza of "Black Cat," why is it easier to "see" a ghost than the black cat?
2. What does the first stanza of "The Swan" compare the swan's walk to? What does the rest of the poem compare the swan's swimming to?

Interpreting Meanings

1. Do you think the **simile** in the second stanza of "Black Cat" is effective? How does it help you to understand the cat's inner nature? Find three other **similes** in the poem, and explain how they contribute to the meaning of the poem.
2. In the last stanza of "Black Cat," the speaker is shocked to see himself reflected in the cat's eyes as if he were a fly suspended in amber. How does this **simile** reveal how the speaker views himself or humanity in general?

3. Explain the **extended metaphor** in "The Swan." How might it refer to a religious or spiritual concept of death and the afterlife?

Applying Meanings

In "The Swan," Rilke says that death is one kind of "letting go / of the ground we stand on and cling to every day." What are other things we "cling to"? Have you ever "let go" of any of these things? Were you nervous at first, like the swan? Think of examples of "letting go" from your own life.

Creative Writing Response

1. **Writing a "Thing Poem" About an Animal.** Choose an animal that you are familiar with or one that you feel strongly about. You may even choose a mythical animal if you like. Then, like Rilke, try to capture the essential spirit of the creature by describing its outward appearance. Use **imagery** and **figurative language** to describe the animal and to convey your feelings about it. If you wrote about an animal in the Writer's Response (see page 15), you may use this paragraph as the starting point for your poem.

2. **Writing from Another Point of View.** Imagine yourself being seen from the **point of view** of another person, or even an animal. Think of a characteristic action that reveals your inner nature. For example, imagine someone (or something) observing you as you perform some task that you do well and enjoy—or a task that you do poorly and hate. How would the onlooker see you?

Write a brief prose passage or poem describing yourself as seen from this other point of view.

Language and Vocabulary
German and English

German, like English, belongs to the **Germanic branch** of the Indo-European family of languages. German and English went their separate ways long ago, but in modern times, English has borrowed many words from German. Some of these words entered English in Europe; others were introduced to American English by German-speaking immigrants in the New World. On a separate piece of paper, match each English word listed in the left-hand column with the right-hand column's information about the word's origin. Check your answers in a dictionary.

1. blitz
   a. from a German term going back to medieval Latin for "small biscuit with crossed arms"

2. delicatessen
   b. from the German compound of "bell" + "play"

3. glockenspiel
   c. from the German words for "garden of children"

4. kindergarten
   d. shortened from the German words for "lightning war"

5. pretzel
   e. from the German words for "choice foods"

PRIMARY SOURCES

Rilke's Letters to a Young Poet

Early in the twentieth century, an aspiring young poet named Franz Xaver Kappus wrote to Rilke for advice. The two corresponded for several years. After Rilke died, Kappus published Rilke's letters in Letters to a Young Poet *(1929). The following excerpt is from Rilke's first letter to Kappus.*

You ask whether your verses are any good. You ask me. You have asked others before this. You send them to magazines. You compare them with other poems, and you are upset when certain editors reject your work. Now (since you have said you want my advice) I beg you to stop doing that sort of thing. You are looking outside, and that is what you should most avoid right now. No one can advise or help you— no one. There is only one thing you should do. Go into yourself. Find out the reason that commands you to write; see whether it has spread its roots into the very depths of your heart; confess to yourself whether you would have to die if you were forbidden to write. This most of all: ask yourself in the most silent hour of your night: *must* I write? Dig into yourself for a deep answer. And if this answer rings out in assent, if you meet this solemn question with a strong, simple *''I must,''* then build your life in accordance with this necessity; your whole life, even into its humblest and most indifferent hour, must become a sign and witness to this impulse. Then come close to Nature. Then, as if no one had ever tried before, try to say what you see and feel and love and lose. Don't write love poems; avoid those forms that are too facile and ordinary: they are the hardest to work with, and it takes a great, fully ripened power to create something individual where good, even glorious, traditions exist in abundance. So rescue yourself from these general themes and write about what your everyday life offers you; describe your sorrows and desires, the thoughts that pass through your mind and your belief in some kind of beauty—describe all these with heartfelt, silent, humble sincerity and, when you express yourself, use the Things around you, the images from your dreams, and the objects that you remember. If your everyday life seems poor, don't blame *it*; blame yourself; admit to yourself that you are not enough of a poet to call forth its riches; because for the creator there is no poverty and no poor, indifferent place. And even if you found yourself in some prison, whose walls let in none of the world's sounds— wouldn't you still have your childhood, that jewel beyond all price, that treasure house of memories? Turn your attention to it. Try to raise up the sunken feelings of this enormous past; your personality will grow stronger, your solitude will expand and become a place where you can live in the twilight, where the noise of other people passes by, far in the distance.—And if out of this turning-within, out of this immersion in your own world, *poems* come, then you will not think of asking anyone whether they are good or not.

Franz Kafka
1883–1924, Austria/Czechoslovakia

The Granger Collection, New York

Franz Kafka once wrote that literature should be an axe that smashes through the "frozen sea" inside every person. The "frozen sea" is, in part, the alienation and despair that Kafka and many others felt in the unstable years of the early twentieth century. Kafka's grotesque tales often do strike the reader with the force of an axe. In *The Metamorphosis* (1915), for instance, a man transforms into a giant insect and is treated as a vermin by his family. In *The Trial* (1925), a man is arrested, convicted, tried by a mysterious court, and executed without ever knowing his crime. In *The Castle* (1926), the hero is not allowed to communicate with his employer in a castle.

Like many of his characters, Kafka was lonely and insecure. His insecurities stemmed in part from social frictions in his native Prague, now the capital of Czechoslovakia, which for most of Kafka's life was under Austrian control. Although Kafka was educated in Prague's elite German-language academy and became part of a group of German-speaking Jewish intellectuals known as the Prague Circle, he was keenly aware of his status as an outsider in the Czech population. In fact, as a Czech Jew, Kafka was doubly an outsider: He was distrusted by the Czechs because he spoke German and despised by the Germans because he was a Jew.

Kafka had a distant relationship with his father, a stern man who treated his son with indifference and even contempt. Kafka expressed his feelings of dislike and fear, as well as his continued search for approval, in *Letter to His Father*, a one-hundred-page document that was never actually sent to his father.

Kafka was rarely satisfied with his literary efforts, and before his death from tuberculosis he asked his friend and editor Max Brod (1884–1968) to burn his manuscripts. Fortunately for future readers, Brod ignored the request and published the manuscripts. Kafka's works have had an enormous impact on modern literature. They are so famous that they have given rise to the English word *Kafkaesque*, which is used to describe any situation or setting that is characterized by spiritual anxiety, isolation, surreal distortion, or senselessness.

Reader's Guide

THE METAMORPHOSIS

Background

Nearly every culture has myths and folktales about people, animals, or objects that undergo startling transformations. Fairy tales often include such metamorphoses: A frog turns into a prince; a pumpkin turns into Cinderella's coach. One of the world's first story collections, *Metamorphoses* by the Roman poet Ovid, retells famous transformation stories from Greek and Roman mythology. While Kafka's story draws on traditions from mythology and folklore, it belongs not to the wonderful, magical world of myth, but to the bizarre world of **surrealism**—art or literature that goes beyond realism to portray the irrational events of dreams or nightmares. *The Metamorphosis* begins with a transformation that plunges us immediately into Kafka's world, where extraordinary events are commonplace.

Although it would be a mistake to reduce Kafka's fiction to its autobiographical elements, tensions in his life can be seen in all of his works, perhaps especially in *The Metamorphosis*. Some scholars have pointed out that *Samsa,* the family name of the characters in the story, is a cryptogram (code version) of *Kafka.* Gregor Samsa, the main character, is like Kafka himself in that he has a boring job, wants to spend more time in artistic pursuits, and has mixed feelings toward his family. Sometimes called a novella, *The Metamorphosis* was the longest work that Kafka published in his lifetime.

Writer's Response

Recall a dream you have had that involved bizarre events that could never happen in real life. In a paragraph or two, describe those events and your reaction to them.

Literary Focus

A **symbol** is a person, place, thing, or event that stands both for itself and something beyond itself. Some symbols are widely recognized: a heart is a symbol for love; a snake is a symbol for evil. Sometimes writers create less obvious symbols. For example, a shark may function as the animal itself while it also stands for something else—cruelty or power or nature. A symbol usually represents an abstract idea or a range of related ideas.

THE METAMORPHOSIS
Franz Kafka
translated by
STANLEY CORNGOLD

> *Some readers view the transformation that occurs at the beginning of this story as a literalization of the hostile expression "You vermin!" which Kafka's father had once used to deride one of Kafka's friends. As you read* **The Metamorphosis,** *decide whether the transformation could be a* **symbol.** *If so, what does it symbolize?*

1

When Gregor Samsa woke up one morning from unsettling dreams, he found himself changed in his bed into a monstrous vermin. He was lying on his back as hard as armor plate, and when he lifted his head a little, he saw his vaulted brown belly, sectioned by arch-shaped ribs, to whose dome the cover, about to slide off completely, could barely cling. His many legs, pitifully thin compared with the size of the rest of him, were waving helplessly before his eyes.

"What's happened to me?" he thought. It was no dream. His room, a regular human room, only a little on the small side, lay quiet between the four familiar walls. Over the table, on which an unpacked line of fabric samples was all spread out—Samsa was a traveling salesman—hung the picture which he had recently cut out of a glossy magazine and lodged in a pretty gilt frame. It showed a lady done up in a fur hat and a fur boa,[1] sitting upright and raising up against the viewer a heavy fur muff in which her whole forearm had disappeared.

Gregor's eyes then turned to the window, and the overcast weather—he could hear raindrops hitting against the metal window ledge—completely depressed him. "How about going back to sleep for a few minutes and forgetting all this nonsense," he thought, but that was completely impracticable, since he was used to sleeping on his right side and in his present state could not get into that position. No matter how hard he threw himself onto his right side, he always rocked onto his back again. He must have tried it a hundred times, closing his eyes so as not to have to see his squirming legs, and stopped only when he began to feel a slight, dull pain in his side, which he had never felt before.

"Oh God," he thought, "what a grueling job I've picked! Day in, day out—on the road. The upset of doing business is much worse than the actual business in the home office, and, besides, I've got the torture of traveling, worrying about changing trains, eating miserable food at all hours, constantly seeing new faces, no relationships that last or get more intimate. To the devil with it all!" He felt a slight itching up on top of his belly; shoved himself slowly on his back closer to the bedpost, so as to be able to lift his head

better; found the itchy spot, studded with small white dots which he had no idea what to make of; and wanted to touch the spot with one of his legs but immediately pulled it back, for the contact sent a cold shiver through him.

He slid back again into his original position. "This getting up so early," he thought, "makes anyone a complete idiot. Human beings have to have their sleep. Other traveling salesmen live like harem women.[2] For instance, when I go back to the hotel before lunch to write up the business I've done, these gentlemen are just having breakfast. That's all I'd have to try with my boss; I'd be fired on the spot. Anyway, who knows if that wouldn't be a very good thing for me. If I didn't hold back for my parents' sake, I would have quit long ago, I would have marched up to the boss and spoken my piece from the bottom of my heart. He would have fallen off the desk! It is funny, too, the way he sits on the desk and talks down from the heights to the employees, especially when they have to come right up close on account of the boss's being hard of hearing. Well, I haven't given up hope completely; once I've gotten the money together to pay off my parents' debt to him—that will probably take another five or six years—I'm going to do it without fail. Then I'm going to make the big break. But for the time being I'd better get up, since my train leaves at five."

And he looked over at the alarm clock, which was ticking on the chest of drawers. "God Almighty!" he thought. It was six-thirty, the hands were quietly moving forward, it was actually past the half-hour, it was already nearly a quarter to. Could it be that the alarm hadn't gone off? You could

---

1. **boa** (bō′ə): long scarf worn around the neck.

2. **live like harem women:** that is, lead pampered, leisurely lives.

see from the bed that it was set correctly for four o'clock; it certainly had gone off, too. Yes, but was it possible to sleep quietly through a ringing that made the furniture shake? Well, he certainly hadn't slept quietly, but probably all the more soundly for that. But what should he do now? The next train left at seven o'clock; to make it, he would have to hurry like a madman, and the line of samples wasn't packed yet, and he himself didn't feel especially fresh and ready to march around. And even if he did make the train, he could not avoid getting it from the boss, because the messenger boy had been waiting at the five-o'clock train and would have long ago reported his not showing up. He was a tool of the boss, without brains or backbone. What if he were to say he was sick? But that would be extremely embarrassing and suspicious because during his five years with the firm Gregor had not been sick even once. The boss would be sure to come with the health-insurance doctor, blame his parents for their lazy son, and cut off all excuses by quoting the health-insurance doctor, for whom the world consisted of people who were completely healthy but afraid to work. And, besides, in this case would he be so very wrong? In fact, Gregor felt fine, with the exception of his drowsiness, which was really unnecessary after sleeping so late, and he even had a ravenous appetite.

Just as he was thinking all this over at top speed, without being able to decide to get out of bed—the alarm clock had just struck a quarter to seven—he heard a cautious knocking at the door next to the head of his bed. "Gregor," someone called—it was his mother—"it's a quarter to seven. Didn't you want to catch the train?" What a soft voice! Gregor was shocked to hear his own voice answering, unmistakably his own voice, true,

but in which, as if from below, an insistent distressed chirping intruded, which left the clarity of his words intact only for a moment really, before so badly garbling them as they carried that no one could be sure if he had heard right. Gregor had wanted to answer in detail and to explain everything, but, given the circumstances, confined himself to saying, "Yes, yes, thanks, Mother, I'm just getting up." The wooden door must have prevented the change in Gregor's voice from being noticed outside, because his mother was satisfied with this explanation and shuffled off. But their little exchange had made the rest of the family aware that, contrary to expectations, Gregor was still in the house, and already his father was knocking on one of the side doors, feebly but with his fist. "Gregor, Gregor," he called, "what's going on?" And after a little while he called again in a deeper, warning voice, "Gregor! Gregor!" At the other side door, however, his sister moaned gently, "Gregor? Is something the matter with you? Do you want anything?" Toward both sides Gregor answered: "I'm all ready," and made an effort, by meticulous pronunciation and by inserting long pauses between individual words, to eliminate everything from his voice that might betray him. His father went back to his breakfast, but his sister whispered, "Gregor, open up, I'm pleading with you." But Gregor had absolutely no intention of opening the door and complimented himself instead on the precaution he had adopted from his business trips, of locking all the doors during the night even at home.

First of all he wanted to get up quietly, without any excitement; get dressed; and, the main thing, have breakfast, and only then think about what to do next, for he saw clearly that in bed he would never think things through to a rational conclusion. He remembered how even in the past he had often felt some kind of slight pain, possibly caused by lying in an uncomfortable position, which, when he got up, turned out to be purely imaginary, and he was eager to see how today's fantasy would gradually fade away. That the change in his voice was nothing more than the first sign of a bad cold, an occupational ailment of the traveling salesman, he had no doubt in the least.

It was very easy to throw off the cover; all he had to do was puff himself up a little, and it fell off by itself. But after this, things got difficult, especially since he was so unusually broad. He would have needed hands and arms to lift himself up, but instead of that he had only his numerous little legs, which were in every different kind of perpetual motion and which, besides, he could not control. If he wanted to bend one, the first thing that happened was that it stretched itself out; and if he finally succeeded in getting this leg to do what he wanted, all the others in the meantime, as if set free, began to work in the most intensely painful agitation. "Just don't stay in bed being useless," Gregor said to himself.

First he tried to get out of bed with the lower part of his body, but this lower part—which by the way he had not seen yet and which he could not form a clear picture of—proved too difficult to budge; it was taking so long; and when finally, almost out of his mind, he lunged forward with all his force, without caring, he had picked the wrong direction and slammed himself violently against the lower bedpost, and the searing pain he felt taught him that exactly the lower part of his body was, for the moment anyway, the most sensitive.

He therefore tried to get the upper part of his body out of bed first and warily turned his head toward the edge of the bed. This worked easily, and in spite of its width and weight, the mass of his body finally followed, slowly, the movement of his head. But when at last he stuck his head over the edge of the bed into the air, he got too scared to continue any further, since if he finally let himself fall in this position, it would be a miracle if he didn't injure his head. And just now he had better not for the life of him lose consciousness; he would rather stay in bed.

But when, once again, after the same exertion, he lay in his original position, sighing, and again watched his little legs struggling, if possible more fiercely, with each other and saw no way of bringing peace and order into this mindless motion, he again told himself that it was impossible for him to stay in bed and that the most rational thing was to make any sacrifice for even the smallest hope of freeing himself from the bed. But at the same time he did not forget to remind himself occasionally that thinking things over calmly—indeed, as calmly as possible—was much better than jumping to desperate decisions. At such moments he fixed his eyes as sharply as possible on the window, but unfortunately there was little confidence and cheer to be gotten from the view of the morning fog, which shrouded even the other side of the narrow street. "Seven o'clock already," he said to himself as the alarm clock struck again, "seven o'clock already and still such a fog." And for a little while he lay quietly, breathing shallowly, as if expecting, perhaps, from the complete silence the return of things to the way they really and naturally were.

But then he said to himself, "Before it strikes a quarter past seven, I must be completely out of bed without fail. Anyway, by that time someone from the firm will be here to find out where I am, since the office opens before seven." And now he started rocking the complete length of his body out of the bed with a smooth rhythm. If he let himself topple out of bed in this way, his head, which on falling he planned to lift up sharply, would presumably remain unharmed. His back seemed to be hard; nothing was likely to happen to it when it fell onto the carpet. His biggest misgiving came from his concern about the loud crash that was bound to occur and would probably create, if not terror, at least anxiety behind all the doors. But that would have to be risked.

When Gregor's body already projected halfway out of bed—the new method was more of a game than a struggle, he only had to keep on rocking and jerking himself along—he thought how simple everything would be if he could get some help. Two strong persons—he thought of his father and the maid—would have been completely sufficient; they would only have had to shove their arms under his arched back, in this way scoop him off the bed, bend down with their burden, and then just be careful and patient while he managed to swing himself down onto the floor, where his little legs would hopefully acquire some purpose. Well, leaving out the fact that the doors were locked, should he really call for help? In spite of all his miseries, he could not repress a smile at this thought.

He was already so far along that when he rocked more strongly he could hardly keep his balance, and very soon he would have to commit himself, because in five minutes it would be a quarter past seven—when the doorbell rang. "It's someone from the firm," he said to himself and almost froze, while his little legs only danced more quickly. For a moment everything remained quiet. "They're not going to answer," Gregor said to himself, captivated by some senseless

hope. But then, of course, the maid went to the door as usual with her firm stride and opened up. Gregor only had to hear the visitor's first word of greeting to know who it was—the office manager himself. Why was only Gregor condemned to work for a firm where at the slightest omission they immediately suspected the worst? Were all employees louts without exception, wasn't there a single loyal, dedicated worker among them who, when he had not fully utilized a few hours of the morning for the firm, was driven half-mad by pangs of conscience and was actually unable to get out of bed? Really, wouldn't it have been enough to send one of the apprentices to find out—if this prying were absolutely necessary—did the manager himself have to come, and did the whole innocent family have to be shown in this way that the investigation of this suspicious affair could be entrusted only to the intellect of the manager? And more as a result of the excitement produced in Gregor by these thoughts than as a result of any real decision, he swung himself out of bed with all his might. There was a loud thump, but it was not a real crash. The fall was broken a little by the carpet, and Gregor's back was more elastic than he had thought, which explained the not very noticeable muffled sound. Only he had not held his head carefully enough and hit it; he turned it and rubbed it on the carpet in anger and pain.

"Something fell in there," said the manager in the room on the left. Gregor tried to imagine whether something like what had happened to him today could one day happen even to the manager; you really had to grant the possibility. But, as if in rude reply to this question, the manager took a few decisive steps in the next room and made his patent leather boots creak. From the room on the right his sister whispered, to inform Gregor, "Gregor, the manager is here." "I know," Gregor said to himself; but he did not dare raise his voice enough for his sister to hear.

"Gregor," his father now said from the room on the left, "the manager has come and wants to be informed why you didn't catch the early train. We don't know what we should say to him. Besides, he wants to speak to you personally. So please open the door. He will certainly be so kind as to excuse the disorder of the room." "Good morning, Mr. Samsa," the manager called in a friendly voice. "There's something the matter with him," his mother said to the manager while his father was still at the door, talking. "Believe me, sir, there's something the matter with him. Otherwise how would Gregor have missed a train? That boy has nothing on his mind but the business. It's almost begun to rile me that he never goes out nights. He's been back in the city for eight days now, but every night he's been home. He sits there with us at the table, quietly reading the paper or studying timetables. It's already a distraction for him when he's busy working with his fret saw.[3] For instance, in the span of two or three evenings he carved a little frame. You'll be amazed how pretty it is; it's hanging inside his room. You'll see it right away when Gregor opens the door. You know, I'm glad that you've come, sir. We would never have gotten Gregor to open the door by ourselves; he's so stubborn. And there's certainly something wrong with him, even though he said this morning there wasn't." "I'm coming right away," said Gregor slowly and deliberately, not moving in order not to miss a word of the conversation. "I haven't any other explanation myself," said the manager. "I hope it's nothing serious. On the other hand, I must say that we businessmen—fortunately or unfortunately, whichever you prefer—very often simply have to overcome a slight indisposition for business reasons." "So can the manager come in now?" asked his father, impatient, and knocked on the door again. "No," said Gregor. In the room on the left there was an embarrassing silence; in the room on the right his sister began to sob.

Why didn't his sister go in to the others? She had probably just got out of bed and not even started to get dressed. Then what was she crying about? Because he didn't get up and didn't let the manager in, because he was in danger of losing his job, and because then the boss would start hounding his parents about the old debts? For the time being, certainly, her worries were unnecessary. Gregor was still here and hadn't the slightest intention of letting the family down. True, at the moment he was lying on the carpet, and no one knowing his condition could seriously have expected him to let the manager in. But just because of this slight discourtesy, for which an appropriate excuse would easily be found later on, Gregor could not simply be dismissed. And to Gregor it seemed much more sensible to leave him alone now than to bother him with crying and persuasion. But it was just the uncertainty that was tormenting the others and excused their behavior.

"Mr. Samsa," the manager now called, raising his voice, "what's the matter? You barricade yourself in your room, answer only 'yes' and 'no,' cause your parents serious, unnecessary worry, and you neglect—I mention this only in passing—your duties to the firm in a really shocking manner. I am speaking here in the name of your parents and of

---

3. **fret saw:** saw with a long narrow blade and fine teeth, used to cut scrolls and other curved patterns in boards or metal plates.

your employer and ask you in all seriousness for an immediate, clear explanation. I'm amazed, amazed. I thought I knew you to be a quiet, reasonable person, and now you suddenly seem to want to start strutting about, flaunting strange whims. The head of the firm did suggest to me this morning a possible explanation for your tardiness—it concerned the cash payments recently entrusted to you—but really, I practically gave my word of honor that this explanation could not be right. But now, seeing your incomprehensible obstinacy, I am about to lose even the slightest desire to stick up for you in any way at all. And your job is not the most secure. Originally I intended to tell you all this in private, but since you make me waste my time here for nothing, I don't see why your parents shouldn't hear, too. Your performance of late has been very unsatisfactory; I know it is not the best season for doing business, we all recognize that; but a season for not doing any business, there is no such thing. Mr. Samsa, such a thing cannot be tolerated."

"But sir," cried Gregor, beside himself, in his excitement forgetting everything else, "I'm just opening up, in a minute. A slight indisposition, a dizzy spell, prevented me from getting up. I'm still in bed. But I already feel fine again. I'm just getting out of bed. Just be patient for a minute! I'm not as well as I thought yet. But really I'm fine. How something like this could just take a person by surprise! Only last night I was fine, my parents can tell you, or wait, last night I already had a slight premonition. They must have been able to tell by looking at me. Why didn't I report it to the office! But you always think that you'll get over a sickness without staying home. Sir! Spare my parents! There's no basis for any of the accusations that you're making against me now; no one has

ever said a word to me about them. Perhaps you haven't seen the last orders I sent in. Anyway, I'm still going on the road with the eight o'clock train; these few hours of rest have done me good. Don't let me keep you, sir. I'll be at the office myself right away, and be so kind as to tell them this, and give my respects to the head of the firm."

And while Gregor hastily blurted all this out, hardly knowing what he was saying, he had easily approached the chest of drawers, probably as a result of the practice he had already gotten in bed, and now he tried to raise himself up against it. He actually intended to open the door, actually present himself and speak to the manager; he was eager to find out what the others, who were now so anxious to see him, would say at the sight of him. If they were shocked, then Gregor had no further responsibility and could be calm. But if they took everything calmly, then he, too, had no reason to get excited and could, if he hurried, actually be at the station by eight o'clock. At first he slid off the polished chest of drawers a few times, but at last, giving himself a final push, he stood upright; he no longer paid any attention to the pains in his abdomen, no matter how much they were burning. Now he let himself fall against the back of a nearby chair, clinging to its slats with his little legs. But by doing this he had gotten control of himself and fell silent, since he could now listen to what the manager was saying.

"Did you understand a word?" the manager was asking his parents. "He isn't trying to make fools of us, is he?" "My God," cried his mother, already in tears, "maybe he's seriously ill, and here we are, torturing him. Grete![4] Grete!" she then cried. "Mother?" called his sister from the other side. They

---

4. **Grete** (grē'tə)

communicated by way of Gregor's room. "Go to the doctor's immediately. Gregor is sick. Hurry, get the doctor. Did you just hear Gregor talking?" "That was the voice of an animal," said the manager, in a tone conspicuously soft compared with the mother's yelling. "Anna!" "Anna!" the father called through the foyer into the kitchen, clapping his hands, "get a locksmith right away!" And already the two girls were running with rustling skirts through the foyer—how could his sister have gotten dressed so quickly?—and tearing open the door to the apartment. The door could not be heard slamming; they had probably left it open, as is the custom in homes where a great misfortune has occurred.

But Gregor had become much calmer. It was true that they no longer understood his words, though they had seemed clear enough to him, clearer than before, probably because his ear had grown accustomed to them. But still, the others now believed that there was something the matter with him and were ready to help him. The assurance and confidence with which the first measures had been taken did him good. He felt integrated into human society once again and hoped for marvelous, amazing feats from both the doctor and the locksmith, without really distinguishing sharply between them. In order to make his voice as clear as possible for the crucial discussions that were approaching, he cleared his throat a little—taking pains, of course, to do so in a very muffled manner, since this noise, too, might sound different from human coughing, a thing he no longer trusted himself to decide. In the next room, meanwhile, everything had become completely still. Perhaps his parents were sitting at the table with the manager, whispering; perhaps they were all leaning against the door and listening.

Gregor slowly lugged himself toward the door, pushing the chair in front of him, then let go of it, threw himself against the door, held himself upright against it—the pads on the bottom of his little legs exuded a little sticky substance—and for a moment rested there from the exertion. But then he got started turning the key in the lock with his mouth. Unfortunately it seemed that he had no real teeth—what was he supposed to grip the key with?—but in compensation his jaws, of course, were very strong; with their help he actually got the key moving and paid no attention to the fact that he was undoubtedly hurting himself in some way, for a brown liquid came out of his mouth, flowed over the key, and dripped onto the floor. "Listen," said the manager in the next room, "he's turning the key." This was great encouragement to Gregor; but everyone should have cheered him on, his father and mother, too. "Go, Gregor," they should have called, "keep going, at that lock, harder, harder!" And in the delusion that they were all following his efforts with suspense, he clamped his jaws madly on the key with all the strength he could muster. Depending on the progress of the key, he danced around the lock; holding himself upright only by his mouth, he clung to the key, as the situation demanded, or pressed it down again with the whole weight of his body. The clearer click of the lock as it finally snapped back literally woke Gregor up. With a sigh of relief he said to himself, "So I didn't need the locksmith after all," and laid his head down on the handle in order to open wide one wing of the double doors.

Since he had to use this method of opening the door, it was really opened very wide while he himself was still invisible. He first had to edge slowly around the one wing of the door, and do so very carefully if he was not to fall flat on his back just before entering. He was still busy with this difficult maneuver and had no time to pay attention to anything else when he heard the manager burst out with a loud "Oh!"—it sounded like a rush of wind—and now he could see him, standing closest to the door, his hand pressed over his open mouth, slowly backing away, as if repulsed by an invisible, unrelenting force. His mother—in spite of the manager's presence she stood with her hair still unbraided from the night, sticking out in all directions—first looked at his father with her hands clasped, then took two steps toward Gregor, and sank down in the midst of her skirts spreading out around her, her face completely hidden on her breast. With a hostile expression his father clenched his fist, as if to drive Gregor back into his room, then looked uncertainly around the living room, shielded his eyes with his hands, and sobbed with heaves of his powerful chest.

Now Gregor did not enter the room after all but leaned against the inside of the firmly bolted wing of the door, so that only half his body was visible and his head above it, cocked to one side and peeping out at the others. In the meantime it had grown much lighter; across the street one could see clearly a section of the endless, grayish black building opposite—it was a hospital—with its regular windows starkly piercing the façade; the rain was still coming down, but only in large, separately visible drops that were also pelting the ground literally one at a time. The breakfast dishes were laid out lavishly on the table, since for his father breakfast was the most important meal of the day, which he would prolong for hours while reading various newspapers. On the wall directly opposite hung a photograph of Gregor from his army days, in a lieutenant's uniform, his hand on his sword, a carefree smile on his lips, demanding respect for his bearing and his rank. The door to the foyer was open, and since the front door was open, too, it was possible to see out onto the landing and the top of the stairs going down.

"Well," said Gregor—and he was thoroughly aware of being the only one who had kept calm—"I'll get dressed right away, pack up my samples, and go. Will you, will you please let me go? Now, sir, you see, I'm not stubborn and I'm willing to work; traveling is a hardship, but without it I couldn't live. Where are you going, sir? To the office? Yes? Will you give an honest report of everything? A man might find for a moment that he was unable to work, but that's exactly the right time to remember his past accomplishments and to consider that later on, when the obstacle has been removed, he's bound to work all the harder and more efficiently. I'm under so many obligations to the head of the firm, as you know very well. Besides, I also have my parents and my sister to worry about. I'm in a tight spot, but I'll also work my way out again. Don't make things harder for me than they already are. Stick up for me in the office, please. Traveling salesmen aren't well liked there, I know. People think they make a fortune leading the gay life. No one has any particular reason to rectify this prejudice. But you, sir, you have a better perspective on things than the rest of the office, an even better perspective, just between the two of us, than the head of the firm himself, who in his capacity as owner easily lets his judgment be swayed against an employee. And you also know very well that the traveling salesman, who is out of the office practically the whole year round, can so easily become the victim of gossip, coincidences, and unfounded accusations, against which he's completely unable to defend himself,

Parois d'Oreines, Jean Dubuffet (1901–1985)

? *What is Gregor's initial reaction to his transformation? Does his reaction surprise you?*

since in most cases he knows nothing at all about them except when he returns exhausted from a trip, and back home gets to suffer on his own person the grim consequences, which can no longer be traced back to their causes. Sir, don't go away without a word to tell me you think I'm at least partly right!"

But at Gregor's first words the manager had already turned away and with curled lips looked back at Gregor only over his twitching shoulder. And during Gregor's speech he did not stand still for a minute but, without letting Gregor out of his sight, backed toward the door, yet very gradually, as if there were some secret prohibition against leaving the room. He was already in the foyer, and from the sudden movement with which he took his last step from the living room, one

might have thought he had just burned the sole of his foot. In the foyer, however, he stretched his right hand far out toward the staircase, as if nothing less than an unearthly deliverance were awaiting him there.

Gregor realized that he must on no account let the manager go away in this mood if his position in the firm were not to be jeopardized in the extreme. His parents did not understand this too well; in the course of the years they had formed the conviction that Gregor was set for life in this firm; and furthermore, they were so preoccupied with their immediate troubles that they had lost all consideration for the future. But Gregor had this forethought. The manager must be detained, calmed down, convinced, and finally won over; Gregor's and the family's future depended on it! If only his sister had been there! She was perceptive; she had already begun to cry when Gregor was still lying calmly on his back. And certainly the manager, this ladies' man, would have listened to her; she would have shut the front door and in the foyer talked him out of his scare. But his sister was not there, Gregor had to handle the situation himself. And without stopping to realize that he had no idea what his new faculties of movement were, and without stopping to realize either that his speech had possibly—indeed, probably—not been understood again, he let go of the wing of the door; he shoved himself through the opening, intending to go to the manager, who was already on the landing, ridiculously holding onto the banisters with both hands; but groping for support, Gregor immediately fell down with a little cry onto his numerous little legs. This had hardly happened when for the first time that morning he had a feeling of physical well-being; his little legs were on firm ground; they obeyed him completely, as he noted to his joy; they even strained to carry him away wherever he wanted to go; and he already believed that final recovery from all his sufferings was imminent. But at that very moment, as he lay on the floor rocking with repressed motion, not far from his mother and just opposite her, she, who had seemed so completely self-absorbed, all at once jumped up, her arms stretched wide, her fingers spread, and cried, "Help, for God's sake, help!" held her head bent as if to see Gregor better, but inconsistently darted madly backward instead; had forgotten that the table laden with the breakfast dishes stood behind her; sat down on it hastily, as if her thoughts were elsewhere, when she reached it; and did not seem to notice at all that near her the big coffeepot had been knocked over and coffee was pouring in a steady stream onto the rug.

"Mother, Mother," said Gregor softly and looked up at her. For a minute the manager had completely slipped his mind; on the other hand at the sight of the spilling coffee he could not resist snapping his jaws several times in the air. At this his mother screamed once more, fled from the table, and fell into the arms of his father, who came rushing up to her. But Gregor had no time now for his parents; the manager was already on the stairs; with his chin on the banister, he was taking a last look back. Gregor was off to a running start, to be as sure as possible of catching up with him; the manager must have suspected something like this, for he leaped down several steps and disappeared; but still he shouted "Agh," and the sound carried through the whole staircase. Unfortunately the manager's flight now seemed to confuse his father completely, who had been relatively calm until now, for instead of running after the manager himself, or at least not hindering Gregor in his pursuit, he

seized in his right hand the manager's cane, which had been left behind on a chair with his hat and overcoat, picked up in his left hand a heavy newspaper from the table, and stamping his feet, started brandishing the cane and the newspaper to drive Gregor back into his room. No plea of Gregor's helped, no plea was even understood; however humbly he might turn his head, his father merely stamped his feet more forcefully. Across the room his mother had thrown open a window in spite of the cool weather, and leaning out, she buried her face, far outside the window, in her hands. Between the alley and the staircase a strong draft was created, the window curtains blew in, the newspapers on the table rustled, single sheets fluttered across the floor. Pitilessly his father came on, hissing like a wild man. Now Gregor had not had any practice at all walking in reverse, it was really very slow going. If Gregor had only been allowed to turn around, he could have gotten into his room right away, but he was afraid to make his father impatient by this time-consuming gyration, and at any minute the cane in his father's hand threatened to come down on his back or his head with a deadly blow. Finally, however, Gregor had no choice, for he noticed with horror that in reverse he could not even keep going in one direction; and so, incessantly throwing uneasy side glances at his father, he began to turn around as quickly as possible, in reality turning only very slowly. Perhaps his father realized his good intentions, for he did not interfere with him; instead, he even now and then directed the maneuver from afar with the tip of his cane. If only his father did not keep making this intolerable hissing sound! It made Gregor lose his head completely. He had almost finished the turn when—his mind continually on this hissing—he made a mistake and even started turning back around to his original position. But when he had at last successfully managed to get his head in front of the opened door, it turned out that his body was too broad to get through as it was. Of course in his father's present state of mind it did not even remotely occur to him to open the other wing of the door in order to give Gregor enough room to pass through. He had only the fixed idea that Gregor must return to his room as quickly as possible. He would never have allowed the complicated preliminaries Gregor needed to go through in order to stand up on one end and perhaps in this way fit through the door. Instead, he drove Gregor on, as if there were no obstacle, with exceptional loudness; the voice behind Gregor did not sound like that of only a single father; now this was really no joke anymore, and Gregor forced himself—come what may—into the doorway. One side of his body rose up, he lay lopsided in the opening, one of his flanks was scraped raw, ugly blotches marred the white door, soon he got stuck and could not have budged any more by himself, his little legs on one side dangled tremblingly in midair, those on the other were painfully crushed against the floor—when from behind his father gave him a hard shove, which was truly his salvation, and bleeding profusely, he flew far into his room. The door was slammed shut with the cane, then at last everything was quiet.

2

It was already dusk when Gregor awoke from his deep, comalike sleep. Even if he had not been disturbed, he would certainly not have woken up much later, for he felt that he had rested and slept long enough, but it seemed to him that a hurried step and a cautious shutting of the door leading to the foyer had awakened him. The light of the electric streetlamps lay in pallid streaks on the ceiling and on the upper parts of the furniture, but underneath, where Gregor was, it was dark. Groping clumsily with his antennae, which he was only now beginning to appreciate, he slowly dragged himself toward the door to see what had been happening there. His left side felt like one single long, unpleasantly tautening scar, and he actually had to limp on his two rows of legs. Besides, one little leg had been seriously injured in the course of the morning's events—it was almost a miracle that only one had been injured—and dragged along lifelessly.

Only after he got to the door did he notice what had really attracted him—the smell of something to eat. For there stood a bowl filled with fresh milk, in which small slices of white bread were floating. He could almost have laughed for joy, since he was even hungrier than he had been in the morning, and he immediately dipped his head into the milk, almost to over his eyes. But he soon drew it back again in disappointment; not only because he had difficulty eating on account of the soreness in his left side—and he could eat only if his whole panting body cooperated—but because he didn't like the milk at all, although it used to be his favorite drink, and that was certainly why his sister had put it in the room; in fact, he turned away from the bowl almost with repulsion and crawled back to the middle of the room.

In the living room, as Gregor saw through the crack in the door, the gas had been lit, but while at this hour of the day his father was in the habit of reading the afternoon newspaper in a loud voice to his mother and sometimes to his sister, too, now there wasn't a sound. Well, perhaps this custom of reading aloud, which his sister was always telling him and writing him about, had recently been discontinued altogether. But in all the other rooms, too, it was just as still, although the apartment certainly was not empty. "What a quiet life the family has been leading," Gregor said to himself, and while he stared rigidly in front of him into the darkness, he felt very proud that he had been able to provide such a life in so nice an apartment for his parents and his sister. But what now if all the peace, the comfort, the contentment, were to come to a horrible end? In order not to get involved in such thoughts, Gregor decided to keep moving, and he crawled up and down the room.

During the long evening first one of the side doors and then the other was opened a small crack and quickly shut again; someone had probably had the urge to come in and then had had second thoughts. Gregor now settled into position right by the living-room door, determined somehow to get the hesitating visitor to come in, or at least to find out who it might be; but the door was not opened again, and Gregor waited in vain. In the morning, when the doors had been locked, everyone had wanted to come in; now that he had opened one of the doors and the others had evidently been opened during the day, no one came in, and now the keys were even inserted on the outside.

It was late at night when the light finally went out in the living room, and now it was easy for Gregor to tell that his parents and his sister had stayed up so long, since, as he could distinctly hear, all three were now retiring on tiptoe. Certainly no one would come in to Gregor until the morning; and so he had ample time to consider undisturbed how best to rearrange his life. But the empty high-ceilinged room in which he was forced to lie flat on the floor made him nervous,

without his being able to tell why—since it was, after all, the room in which he had lived for the past five years—and turning half unconsciously and not without a slight feeling of shame, he scuttled under the couch where, although his back was a little crushed and he could not raise his head any more, he immediately felt very comfortable and was only sorry that his body was too wide to go completely under the couch.

There he stayed the whole night, which he spent partly in a sleepy trance, from which hunger pangs kept waking him with a start, partly in worries and vague hopes, all of which, however, led to the conclusion that for the time being he would have to lie low and, by being patient and showing his family every possible consideration, help them bear the inconvenience which he simply had to cause them in his present condition.

Early in the morning—it was still almost night—Gregor had the opportunity of testing the strength of the resolutions he had just made, for his sister, almost fully dressed, opened the door from the foyer and looked in eagerly. She did not see him right away, but when she caught sight of him under the couch—God, he had to be somewhere, he couldn't just fly away—she became so frightened that she lost control of herself and slammed the door shut again. But, as if she felt sorry for her behavior, she immediately opened the door again and came in on tiptoe, as if she were visiting someone seriously ill or perhaps even a stranger. Gregor had pushed his head forward just to the edge of the couch and was watching her. Would she notice that he had left the milk standing, and not because he hadn't been hungry, and would she bring in a dish of something he'd like better? If she were not going to do it of her own free will, he would rather starve than call it to her attention, although, really, he felt an enormous urge to shoot out from under the couch, throw himself at his sister's feet, and beg her for something good to eat. But his sister noticed at once, to her astonishment, that the bowl was still full, only a little milk was spilled around it; she picked it up immediately—not with her bare hands, of course, but with a rag—and carried it out. Gregor was extremely curious to know what she would bring him instead, and he racked his brains on the subject. But he would never have been able to guess what his sister, in the goodness of her heart, actually did. To find out his likes and dislikes, she brought him a wide assortment of things, all spread out on an old newspaper: old, half-rotten vegetables; bones left over from the evening meal, caked with congealed white sauce; some raisins and almonds; a piece of cheese, which two days before Gregor had declared inedible; a plain slice of bread, a slice of bread and butter, and one with butter and salt. In addition to all this she put down some water in the bowl apparently permanently earmarked for Gregor's use. And out of a sense of delicacy, since she knew that Gregor would not eat in front of her, she left hurriedly and even turned the key, just so that Gregor should know that he might make himself as comfortable as he wanted. Gregor's legs began whirring now that he was going to eat. Besides, his bruises must have completely healed, since he no longer felt any handicap, and marveling at this he thought how, over a month ago, he had cut his finger very slightly with a knife and how this wound was still hurting him only the day before yesterday. "Have I become less sensitive?" he thought, already sucking greedily at the cheese, which had immediately and forcibly attracted him ahead of all the other dishes. One right after the other, and with eyes streaming with tears of contentment, he devoured the cheese, the vegetables, and the sauce; the fresh foods, on the other hand, he did not care for; he couldn't even stand their smell and even dragged the things he wanted to eat a bit farther away. He had finished with everything long since and was just lying lazily at the same spot when his sister slowly turned the key as a sign for him to withdraw. That immediately startled him, although he was almost asleep, and he scuttled under the couch again. But it took great self-control for him to stay under the couch even for the short time his sister was in the room, since his body had become a little bloated from the heavy meal, and in his cramped position he could hardly breathe. In between slight attacks of suffocation he watched with bulging eyes as his unsuspecting sister took a broom and swept up, not only his leavings, but even the foods which Gregor had left completely untouched—as if they too were no longer usable—and dumping everything hastily into a pail, which she covered with a wooden lid, she carried everything out. She had hardly turned her back when Gregor came out from under the couch, stretching and puffing himself up.

This, then, was the way Gregor was fed each day, once in the morning, when his parents and the maid were still asleep, and a second time in the afternoon after everyone had had dinner, for then his parents took a short nap again, and the maid could be sent out by his sister on some errand. Certainly they did not want him to starve either, but perhaps they would not have been able to stand knowing any more about his meals than from hearsay, or perhaps his sister wanted to spare them even what was possibly only a minor torment, for really, they were suffering enough as it was.

Gregor could not find out what excuses had been made to get rid of the doctor and the locksmith on that first morning, for since the others could not understand what he said, it did not occur to any of them, not even to his sister, that he could understand what they said, and so he had to be satisfied, when his sister was in the room, with only occasionally hearing her sighs and appeals to the saints. It was only later, when she had begun to get used to everything—there could never, of course, be any question of a complete adjustment—that Gregor sometimes caught a remark which was meant to be friendly or could be interpreted as such. "Oh, he liked what he had today," she would say when Gregor had tucked away a good helping, and in the opposite case, which gradually occurred more and more frequently, she used to say, almost sadly, "He's left everything again."

But if Gregor could not get any news directly, he overheard a great deal from the neighboring rooms, and as soon as he heard voices, he would immediately run to the door concerned and press his whole body against it. Especially in the early days, there was no conversation that was not somehow about him, if only implicitly. For two whole days there were family consultations at every mealtime about how they should cope; this was also the topic of discussion between meals, for at least two members of the family were always at home, since no one probably wanted to stay home alone and it was impossible to leave the apartment completely empty. Besides, on the very first day the maid—it was not completely clear what and how much she knew of what had happened—had begged his mother on bended knees to dismiss her immediately; and when she said goodbye a quarter of an hour later, she thanked them in tears for the dismissal, as if for the greatest favor that had ever been done to her in this house, and made a solemn vow, without anyone asking her for it, not to give anything away to anyone.

Now his sister, working with her mother, had to do the cooking, too; of course, that did not cause her much trouble, since they hardly ate anything. Gregor was always hearing one of them pleading in vain with one of the others to eat and getting no answer except, "Thanks, I've had enough," or something similar. They did not seem to drink anything either. His sister often asked her father if he wanted any beer and gladly offered to go out for it herself; and when he did not answer, she said, in order to remove any hesitation on his part, that she could also send the janitor's wife to get it, but then his father finally answered with a definite "No," and that was the end of that.

In the course of the very first day his father explained the family's financial situation and prospects to both the mother and the sister. From time to time he got up from the table to get some kind of receipt or notebook out of the little strongbox he had rescued from the collapse of his business five years before. Gregor heard him open the complicated lock and secure it again after taking out what he had been looking for. These explanations by his father were to some extent the first pleasant news Gregor had heard since his imprisonment. He had always believed that his father had not been able to save a penny from the business, at least his father had never told him anything to the contrary, and Gregor, for his part, had never asked him any questions. In those days Gregor's sole concern had been to do everything in his power to make the family forget as quickly as possible the business disaster which had plunged everyone into a state of total despair. And so he had begun to work with special ardor and had risen almost overnight from stock clerk to traveling salesman, which of course had opened up very different moneymaking possibilities, and in no time his successes on the job were transformed, by means of commissions, into hard cash that could be plunked down on the table at home in front of his astonished and delighted family. Those had been wonderful times, and they had never returned, at least not with the same glory, although later on Gregor earned enough money to meet the expenses of the entire family and actually did so. They had just gotten used to it, the family as well as Gregor, the money was received with thanks and given with pleasure, but no special feeling of warmth went with it any more. Only his sister had remained close to Gregor, and it was his secret plan that she, who, unlike him, loved music and could play the violin movingly, should be sent next year to the Conservatory,[5] regardless of the great expense involved, which could surely be made up for in some other way. Often during Gregor's short stays in the city the Conservatory would come up in his conversations with his sister, but always merely as a beautiful dream which was not supposed to come true, and his parents were not happy to hear even these innocent allusions; but Gregor had very concrete ideas on the subject and he intended solemnly to announce his plan on Christmas Eve.

Thoughts like these, completely useless in his present state, went through his head as he stood glued to the door, listening. Sometimes out of general exhaustion he could not listen any more and let his head bump carelessly against the door, but immediately

pulled it back again, for even the slight noise he made by doing this had been heard in the next room and made them all lapse into silence. "What's he carrying on about in there now?" said his father after a while, obviously turning toward the door, and only then would the interrupted conversation gradually be resumed.

Gregor now learned in a thorough way—for his father was in the habit of often repeating himself in his explanations, partly because he himself had not dealt with these matters for a long time, partly, too, because his mother did not understand everything the first time around—that in spite of all their misfortunes, a bit of capital, a very little bit, certainly, was still intact from the old days, which in the meantime had increased a little through the untouched interest. But besides that, the money Gregor had brought home every month—he had kept only a few dollars for himself—had never been completely used up and had accumulated into a tidy principal. Behind his door Gregor nodded emphatically, delighted at this unexpected foresight and thrift. Of course he actually could have paid off more of his father's debt to the boss with this extra money, and the day on which he could have gotten rid of his job would have been much closer, but now things were undoubtedly better the way his father had arranged them.

Now this money was by no means enough to let the family live off the interest; the principal was perhaps enough to support the family for one year, or at the most two, but that was all there was. So it was just a sum that really should not be touched and that had to be put away for a rainy day; but the money to live on would have to be earned. Now his father was still healthy, certainly, but he was an old man who had not worked for the past five years and who in any case

---

5. **Conservatory:** school of music.

could not be expected to undertake too much; during these five years, which were the first vacation of his hard-working yet unsuccessful life, he had gained a lot of weight and as a result had become fairly sluggish. And was his old mother now supposed to go out and earn money, when she suffered from asthma, when a walk through the apartment was already an ordeal for her, and when she spent every other day lying on the sofa under the open window, gasping for breath? And was his sister now supposed to work—who for all her seventeen years was still a child and whom it would be such a pity to deprive of the life she had led until now, which had consisted of wearing pretty clothes, sleeping late, helping in the house, enjoying a few modest amusements, and above all, playing the violin? At first, whenever the conversation turned to the necessity of earning money, Gregor would let go of the door and throw himself down on the cool leather sofa which stood beside it, for he felt hot with shame and grief.

Often he lay there the whole long night through, not sleeping a wink and only scrabbling on the leather for hours on end. Or, not balking at the huge effort of pushing an armchair to the window, he would crawl up to the window sill and, propped up in the chair, lean against the window, evidently in some sort of remembrance of the feeling of freedom he used to have from looking out the window. For, in fact, from day to day he saw things even a short distance away less and less distinctly; the hospital opposite, which he used to curse because he saw so much of it, was now completely beyond his range of vision, and if he had not been positive that he was living in Charlotte Street—a quiet but still very much a city street—he might have believed that he was looking out of his window into a desert where the gray

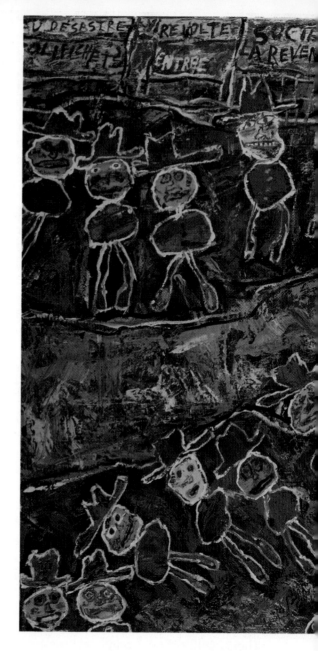

sky and the gray earth were indistinguishably fused. It took his observant sister only twice to notice that his armchair was standing by the window for her to push the chair back to the same place by the window each time she had finished cleaning the room, and from then on she even left the inside casement of the window open.

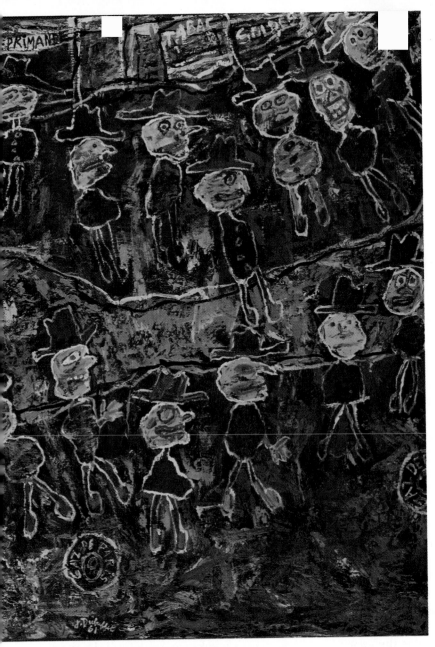

Spinning Round, Jean Dubuffet, 1961.

❓ *How would you describe the tone of Kafka's novella thus far? Comic? Ironic? Tragic? Explain your answer.*

If Gregor had only been able to speak to his sister and thank her for everything she had to do for him, he could have accepted her services more easily; as it was, they caused him pain. Of course his sister tried to ease the embarrassment of the whole situation as much as possible, and as time went on, she naturally managed it better and

better, but in time Gregor, too, saw things much more clearly. Even the way she came in was terrible for him. Hardly had she entered the room than she would run straight to the window without taking time to close the door—though she was usually so careful to spare everyone the sight of Gregor's room—then tear open the casements with

Franz Kafka **39**

eager hands, almost as if she were suffocating, and remain for a little while at the window even in the coldest weather, breathing deeply. With this racing and crashing she frightened Gregor twice a day; the whole time he cowered under the couch, and yet he knew very well that she would certainly have spared him this if only she had found it possible to stand being in a room with him with the window closed.

One time—it must have been a month since Gregor's metamorphosis, and there was certainly no particular reason any more for his sister to be astonished at Gregor's appearance—she came a little earlier than usual and caught Gregor still looking out the window, immobile and so in an excellent position to be terrifying. It would not have surprised Gregor if she had not come in, because his position prevented her from immediately opening the window, but not only did she not come in, she even sprang back and locked the door; a stranger might easily have thought that Gregor had been lying in wait for her, wanting to bite her. Of course Gregor immediately hid under the couch, but he had to wait until noon before his sister came again, and she seemed much more uneasy than usual. He realized from this that the sight of him was still repulsive to her and was bound to remain repulsive to her in the future, and that she probably had to overcome a lot of resistance not to run away at the sight of even the small part of his body that jutted out from under the couch. So, to spare her even this sight, one day he carried the sheet on his back to the couch—the job took four hours—and arranged it in such a way that he was now completely covered up and his sister could not see him even when she stooped. If she had considered this sheet unnecessary, then of course she could have removed it, for it was clear enough that it could not be for his own pleasure that Gregor shut himself off altogether, but she left the sheet the way it was, and Gregor thought that he had even caught a grateful look when one time he cautiously lifted the sheet a little with his head in order to see how his sister was taking the new arrangement.

During the first two weeks, his parents could not bring themselves to come in to him, and often he heard them say how much they appreciated his sister's work, whereas until now they had frequently been annoyed with her because she had struck them as being a little useless. But now both of them, his father and his mother, often waited outside Gregor's room while his sister straightened it up, and as soon as she came out she had to tell them in great detail how the room looked, what Gregor had eaten, how he had behaved this time, and whether he had perhaps shown a little improvement. His mother, incidentally, began relatively soon to want to visit Gregor, but his father and his sister at first held her back with reasonable arguments to which Gregor listened very attentively and of which he wholeheartedly approved. But later she had to be restrained by force, and then when she cried out, "Let me go to Gregor, he is my unfortunate boy! Don't you understand that I have to go to him?" Gregor thought that it might be a good idea after all if his mother did come in, not every day of course, but perhaps once a week; she could still do everything much better than his sister, who, for all her courage, was still only a child and in the final analysis had perhaps taken on such a difficult assignment only out of childish flightiness.

Gregor's desire to see his mother was soon fulfilled. During the day Gregor did not want to show himself at the window, if only out of consideration for his parents, but he couldn't crawl very far on his few square yards of floor space, either; he could hardly put up with just lying still even at night; eating soon stopped giving him the slightest pleasure, so, as a distraction, he adopted the habit of crawling crisscross over the walls and the ceiling. He especially liked hanging from the ceiling; it was completely different from lying on the floor; one could breathe more freely; a faint swinging sensation went through the body; and in the almost happy absent-mindedness which Gregor felt up there, it could happen to his own surprise that he let go and plopped onto the floor. But now, of course, he had much better control of his body than before and did not hurt himself even from such a big drop. His sister immediately noticed the new entertainment Gregor had discovered for himself—after all, he left behind traces of his sticky substance wherever he crawled—and so she got it into her head to make it possible for Gregor to crawl on an altogether wider scale by taking out the furniture which stood in his way—mainly the chest of drawers and the desk. But she was not able to do this by herself; she did not dare ask her father for help; the maid would certainly not have helped her, for although this girl, who was about sixteen, was bravely sticking it out after the previous cook had left, she had asked for the favor of locking herself in the kitchen at all times and of only opening the door on special request. So there was nothing left for his sister to do except to get her mother one day when her father was out. And his mother did come, with exclamations of excited joy, but she grew silent at the door of Gregor's room. First his sister looked to see, of course, that everything in the room was in order; only then did she let her mother come in. Hurrying as fast as he could, Gregor had pulled the sheet down lower still and pleated it more tightly—it really looked just like a sheet accidently thrown over the couch. This time Gregor also refrained from spying from under the sheet; he renounced seeing his mother for the time being and was simply happy that she had come after all. "Come on, you can't see him," his sister said, evidently leading her mother in by the hand. Now Gregor could hear the two frail women moving the old chest of drawers—heavy for anyone—from its place and his sister insisting on doing the harder part of the job herself, ignoring the warnings of her mother, who was afraid that she would over-exert herself. It went on for a long time. After struggling for a good quarter of an hour, his mother said that they had better leave the chest where it was, because, in the first place, it was too heavy, they would not finish before his father came, and with the chest in the middle of the room, Gregor would be completely barricaded; and, in the second place, it was not at all certain that they were doing Gregor a favor by removing his furniture. To her the opposite seemed to be the case; the sight of the bare wall was heartbreaking; and why shouldn't Gregor also have the same feeling, since he had been used to his furniture for so long and would feel abandoned in the empty room. "And doesn't it look," his mother concluded very softly—in fact she had been almost whispering the whole time, as if she wanted to avoid letting Gregor, whose exact whereabouts she did not know, hear even the sound of her voice, for she was convinced that he did not understand the words—"and doesn't it look as if by removing his furniture we were showing him that we have given up all hope of his getting better and are leaving him to his own devices without any consideration? I think the best thing would be to try to keep the room exactly the way it was before, so that when Gregor comes back to us again, he'll find everything unchanged and can forget all the more easily what's happened in the meantime."

When he heard his mother's words, Gregor realized that the monotony of family life, combined with the fact that not a soul had addressed a word directly to him, must have addled his brain in the course of the past two months, for he could not explain to himself in any other way how in all seriousness he could have been anxious to have his room cleared out. Had he really wanted to have his warm room, comfortably fitted with furniture that had always been in the family, changed into a cave, in which, of course, he would be able to crawl around unhampered in all directions but at the cost of simultaneously, rapidly, and totally forgetting his human past? Even now he had been on the verge of forgetting, and only his mother's voice, which he had not heard for so long, had shaken him up. Nothing should be removed; everything had to stay; he could not do without the beneficial influence of the furniture on his state of mind; and if the furniture prevented him from carrying on this senseless crawling around, then that was no loss but rather a great advantage.

But his sister unfortunately had a different opinion; she had become accustomed, certainly not entirely without justification, to adopt with her parents the role of the particularly well-qualified expert whenever Gregor's affairs were being discussed; and so her mother's advice was now sufficient reason for her to insist, not only on the removal of the chest of drawers and the desk, which was all she had been planning at first, but also on the removal of all the furniture with the exception of the indispensable couch. Of course it was not only childish defiance and

the self-confidence she had recently acquired so unexpectedly and at such a cost that led her to make this demand; she had in fact noticed that Gregor needed plenty of room to crawl around in; and on the other hand, as best she could tell, he never used the furniture at all. Perhaps, however, the romantic enthusiasm of girls her age, which seeks to indulge itself at every opportunity, played a part, by tempting her to make Gregor's situation even more terrifying in order that she might do even more for him. Into a room in which Gregor ruled the bare walls all alone, no human being beside Grete was ever likely to set foot.

And so she did not let herself be swerved from her decision by her mother, who, besides, from the sheer anxiety of being in Gregor's room, seemed unsure of herself, soon grew silent, and helped her daughter as best she could to get the chest of drawers out of the room. Well, in a pinch Gregor could do without the chest, but the desk had to stay. And hardly had the women left the room with the chest, squeezing against it and groaning, than Gregor stuck his head out from under the couch to see how he could feel his way into the situation as considerately as possible. But unfortunately it had to be his mother who came back first, while in the next room Grete was clasping the chest and rocking it back and forth by herself, without of course budging it from the spot. His mother, however, was not used to the sight of Gregor, he could have made her ill, and so Gregor, frightened, scuttled in reverse to the far end of the couch but could not stop the sheet from shifting a little at the front. That was enough to put his mother on the alert. She stopped, stood still for a moment, and then went back to Grete.

Although Gregor told himself over and over again that nothing special was happening, only a few pieces of furniture were being moved, he soon had to admit that this coming and going of the women, their little calls to each other, the scraping of the furniture along the floor had the effect on him of a great turmoil swelling on all sides, and as much as he tucked in his head and his legs and shrank until his belly touched the floor, he was forced to admit that he would not be able to stand it much longer. They were clearing out his room; depriving him of everything that he loved; they had already carried away the chest of drawers, in which he kept the fret saw and other tools; were now budging the desk firmly embedded in the floor, the desk he had done his homework on when he was a student at business college, in high school, yes, even in public school—now he really had no more time to examine the good intentions of the two women, whose existence, besides, he had almost forgotten, for they were so exhausted that they were working in silence, and one could hear only the heavy shuffling of their feet.

And so he broke out—the women were just leaning against the desk in the next room to catch their breath for a minute— changed his course four times, he really didn't know what to salvage first, then he saw hanging conspicuously on the wall, which was otherwise bare already, the picture of the lady all dressed in furs, hurriedly crawled up on it and pressed himself against the glass, which gave a good surface to stick to and soothed his hot belly. At least no one would take away this picture, while Gregor completely covered it up. He turned his head toward the living-room door to watch the women when they returned.

They had not given themselves much of a rest and were already coming back; Grete had put her arm around her mother and was practically carrying her. "So what should we take now?" said Grete and looked around. At that her eyes met Gregor's as he clung to the wall. Probably only because of her mother's presence she kept her self-control, bent her head down to her mother to keep her from looking around, and said, though in a quavering and thoughtless voice: "Come, we'd better go back into the living room for a minute." Grete's intent was clear to Gregor; she wanted to bring his mother into safety and then chase him down from the wall. Well, just let her try! He squatted on his picture and would not give it up. He would rather fly in Grete's face.

But Grete's words had now made her mother really anxious; she stepped to one side, caught sight of the gigantic brown blotch on the flowered wallpaper, and, before it really dawned on her that what she saw was Gregor, cried in a hoarse, bawling voice: "Oh, God, Oh, God!"; and, as if giving up completely, she fell with outstretched arms across the couch and did not stir. "You, Gregor!" cried his sister with raised fist and piercing eyes. These were the first words she had addressed directly to him since his metamorphosis. She ran into the next room to get some kind of spirits to revive her mother; Gregor wanted to help, too—there was time to rescue the picture—but he was stuck to the glass and had to tear himself loose by force; then he, too, ran into the next room, as if he could give his sister some sort of advice, as in the old days; but then had to stand behind her doing nothing while she rummaged among various little bottles; moreover, when she turned around she was startled, a bottle fell on the floor and broke, a splinter of glass wounded Gregor in the face, some kind of corrosive medicine flowed around him; now without waiting any longer, Grete grabbed as many little bottles as she could carry and ran with them inside to her mother; she slammed the door behind her with her foot. Now Gregor was cut off from his mother, who was perhaps near death through his fault; he could not dare open the door if he did not want to chase away his sister, who had to stay with his mother; now there was nothing for him to do except wait; and tormented by self-reproaches and worry, he began to crawl, crawled over everything, walls, furniture and ceiling, and finally in desperation, as the whole room was beginning to spin, fell down onto the middle of the big table.

A short time passed; Gregor lay there prostrate; all around, things were quiet, perhaps that was a good sign. Then the doorbell rang. The maid, of course, was locked up in her kitchen and so Grete had to answer the door. His father had come home. "What's happened?" were his first words; Grete's appearance must have told him everything. Grete answered in a muffled voice, her face was obviously pressed against her father's chest; "Mother fainted, but she's better now. Gregor's broken out." "I knew it," his father said. "I kept telling you, but you women don't want to listen." It was clear to Gregor that his father had put the worst interpretation on Grete's all-too-brief announcement and assumed that Gregor was guilty of some outrage. Therefore, Gregor now had to try to calm his father down, since he had neither the time nor the ability to enlighten him. And so he fled to the door of his room and pressed himself against it for his father to see, as soon as he came into the foyer, that Gregor had the best intentions of returning to his room immediately and that it was not necessary to drive him back; if only the door were opened for him, he would disappear at once.

But his father was in no mood to notice such subtleties; "Ah!" he cried as he entered, in a tone that sounded as if he were at once furious and glad. Gregor turned his head away from the door and lifted it toward his father. He had not really imagined his father looking like this, as he stood in front of him now; admittedly Gregor had been too absorbed recently in his newfangled crawling to bother as much as before about events in the rest of the house and should really have been prepared to find some changes. And yet, and yet—was this still his father? Was this the same man who in the old days used to lie wearily buried in bed when Gregor left on a business trip; who greeted him on his return in the evening, sitting in his bathrobe in the armchair, who actually had difficulty getting to his feet but as a sign of joy only lifted up his arms; and who, on the rare occasions when the whole family went out for a walk, on a few Sundays in June and on the major holidays, used to shuffle along with great effort between Gregor and his mother, who were slow walkers themselves, always a little more slowly than they, wrapped in his old overcoat, always carefully planting down his crutch-handled cane, and, when he wanted to say something, nearly always stood still and assembled his escort around him? Now, however, he was holding himself very erect, dressed in a tight-fitting blue uniform with gold buttons, the kind worn by messengers at banking concerns; above the high stiff collar of the jacket his heavy chin protruded; under his bushy eyebrows his black eyes darted bright, piercing glances; his usually rumpled white hair was combed flat, with a scrupulously exact, gleaming part. He threw his cap—which was adorned with a gold monogram, probably that of a bank—in an arc across the entire room onto the couch, and with the tails of his long uniform jacket slapped back, his hands in his pants pockets, went for Gregor with a sullen look on his face. He probably did not know himself what he had in mind; still he lifted his feet unusually high off the floor, and Gregor staggered at the gigantic size of the soles of his boots. But he did not linger over this, he had known right from the first day of his new life that his father considered only the strictest treatment called for in dealing with him. And so he ran ahead of his father, stopped when his father stood still, and scooted ahead again when his father made even the slightest movement. In this way they made more than one tour of the room, without anything decisive happening; in fact, the whole movement did not even have the appearance of a chase because of its slow tempo. So Gregor kept to the floor for the time being, especially since he was afraid that his father might interpret a flight onto the walls or the ceiling as a piece of particular nastiness. Of course, Gregor had to admit that he would not be able to keep up even this running for long, for whenever his father took one step, Gregor had to execute countless movements. He was already beginning to feel winded, just as in the old days he had not had very reliable lungs. As he now staggered around, hardly keeping his eyes open in order to gather all his strength for the running; in his obtuseness not thinking of any escape other than by running; and having almost forgotten that the walls were at his disposal, though here of course they were blocked up with elaborately carved furniture full of notches and points—at that moment a lightly flung object hit the floor right near him and rolled in front of him. It was an apple; a second one came flying right after it; Gregor stopped dead with fear; further running was useless, for his father was determined to bombard him. He had filled his pockets from the fruit bowl on the buffet and was now pitching one apple after another, for the time being without taking good aim. These little red apples rolled around on the floor as if electrified, clicking into each another. One apple, thrown weakly, grazed Gregor's back and slid off harmlessly. But the very next one that came flying after it literally forced its way into Gregor's back; Gregor tried to drag himself away, as if the startling, unbelievable pain might disappear with a change of place; but he felt nailed to the spot and stretched out his body in a complete confusion of all his senses. With his last glance he saw the door of his room burst open as his mother rushed out ahead of his screaming sister, in her chemise,[6] for his sister had partly undressed her while she was unconscious in order to let her breathe more freely; saw his mother run up to his father and on the way her unfastened petticoats slid to the floor one by one; and saw as, stumbling over the skirts, she forced herself onto his father, and embracing him, in complete union with him—but now Gregor's sight went dim—her hands clasping his father's neck, begged for Gregor's life.

3

Gregor's serious wound, from which he suffered for over a month—the apple remained imbedded in his flesh as a visible souvenir since no one dared to remove it—seemed to have reminded even his father that Gregor was a member of the family, in spite of his present pathetic and repulsive shape, who could not be treated as an enemy; that, on the contrary, it was the commandment of family duty to swallow their disgust and endure him, endure him and nothing more.

---

6. **chemise** (shə·mēz′): loose, sliplike undergarment.

And now, although Gregor had lost some of his mobility probably for good because of his wound, and although for the time being he needed long, long minutes to get across his room, like an old war veteran—crawling above ground was out of the question—for this deterioration of his situation he was granted compensation which in his view was entirely satisfactory: every day around dusk the living-room door—which he was in the habit of watching closely for an hour or two beforehand—was opened, so that, lying in the darkness of his room, invisible from the living room, he could see the whole family sitting at the table under the lamp and could listen to their conversation, as it were with general permission; and so it was completely different from before.

Of course, these were no longer the animated conversations of the old days, which Gregor used to remember with a certain nostalgia in small hotel rooms when he'd had

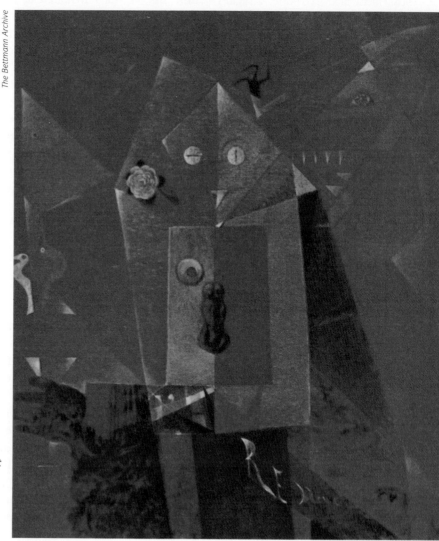

THE BLUE HOUR, MAX ERNST (1891–1976).

❓ *Do you think Gregor might have done anything to deserve—or to make him a likely victim for—his strange transformation; or was it a chance misfortune? Explain your answer.*

to throw himself wearily into the damp bedding. Now things were mostly very quiet. Soon after supper his father would fall asleep in his armchair; his mother and sister would caution each other to be quiet; his mother, bent low under the light, sewed delicate lingerie for a clothing store; his sister, who had taken a job as a salesgirl, was learning shorthand and French in the evenings in order to attain a better position some time in the future. Sometimes his father woke up, and as if he had absolutely no idea that he had been asleep, said to his mother, "Look how long you're sewing again today!" and went right back to sleep, while mother and sister smiled wearily at each other.

With a kind of perverse obstinacy his father refused to take off his official uniform even in the house; and while his robe hung uselessly on the clothes hook, his father dozed, completely dressed, in his chair, as if he were always ready for duty and were waiting even here for the voice of his superior. As a result, his uniform, which had not been new to start with, began to get dirty in spite of all the mother's and sister's care, and Gregor would often stare all evening long at this garment, covered with stains and gleaming with its constantly polished gold buttons, in which the old man slept most uncomfortably and yet peacefully.

As soon as the clock struck ten, his mother tried to awaken his father with soft encouraging words and then persuade him to go to bed, for this was no place to sleep properly, and his father badly needed his sleep, since he had to be at work at six o'clock. But with the obstinacy that had possessed him ever since he had become a messenger, he always insisted on staying at the table a little longer, although he invariably fell asleep and then could be persuaded only with the greatest effort to exchange his armchair for bed. However much mother and sister might pounce on him with little admonitions, he would slowly shake his head for a quarter of an hour at a time, keeping his eyes closed, and would not get up. Gregor's mother plucked him by the sleeves, whispered blandishments into his ear, his sister dropped her homework in order to help her mother, but all this was of no use. He only sank deeper into his armchair. Not until the women lifted him up under his arms did he open his eyes, look alternately at mother and sister, and usually say, "What a life. So this is the peace of my old age." And leaning on the two women, he would get up laboriously, as if he were the greatest weight on himself, and let the women lead him to the door, where, shrugging them off, he would proceed independently, while Gregor's mother threw down her sewing and his sister her pen as quickly as possible so as to run after his father and be of further assistance.

Who in this overworked and exhausted family had time to worry about Gregor any more than was absolutely necessary? The household was stinted more and more; now the maid was let go after all; a gigantic bony cleaning woman with white hair fluttering about her head came mornings and evenings to do the heaviest work; his mother took care of everything else, along with all her sewing. It even happened that various pieces of family jewelry, which in the old days his mother and sister had been overjoyed to wear at parties and celebrations, were sold, as Gregor found out one evening from the general discussion of the prices they had fetched. But the biggest complaint was always that they could not give up the apartment, which was much too big for their present needs, since no one could figure out how Gregor was supposed to be moved. But Gregor understood easily that it was not only consideration for him which prevented their moving, for he could easily have been transported in a suitable crate with a few air holes; what mainly prevented the family from moving was their complete hopelessness and the thought that they had been struck by a misfortune as none of their relatives and acquaintances had ever been hit. What the world demands of poor people they did to the utmost of their ability; his father brought breakfast for the minor officials at the bank, his mother sacrificed herself to the underwear of strangers, his sister ran back and forth behind the counter at the request of the customers; but for anything more than this they did not have the strength. And the wound in Gregor's back began to hurt anew when mother and sister, after getting his father to bed, now came back, dropped their work, pulled their chairs close to each other and sat cheek to cheek; when his mother, pointing to Gregor's room, said, "Close that door, Grete"; and when Gregor was back in darkness, while in the other room the women mingled their tears or stared dry-eyed at the table.

Gregor spent the days and nights almost entirely without sleep. Sometimes he thought that the next time the door opened he would take charge of the family's affairs again, just as he had done in the old days; after this long while there again appeared in his thoughts the boss and the manager, the salesmen and the trainees, the handyman who was so dense, two or three friends from other firms, a chambermaid in a provincial hotel—a happy fleeting memory—a cashier in a millinery store,[7] whom he had courted earnestly but too slowly—they all appeared, intermingled with strangers or people he had already forgotten; but instead of helping him and his family, they were all inaccessible, and he was glad when they faded away. At other times he was in no mood to worry about his family, he was completely filled with rage at his miserable treatment, and although he could not imagine anything that would pique his appetite, he still made plans for getting into the pantry to take what was coming to him, even if he wasn't hungry. No longer considering what she could do to give Gregor a special treat, his sister, before running to business every morning and afternoon, hurriedly shoved any old food into Gregor's room with her foot; and in the evening, regardless of whether the food had only been toyed with or—the most usual case—had been left completely untouched, she swept it out with a swish of the broom. The cleaning up of Gregor's room, which she now always did in the evenings, could not be done more hastily. Streaks of dirt ran along the walls, fluffs of dust and filth lay here and there on the floor. At first, whenever his sister came in, Gregor would place himself in those corners which were particularly offending, meaning by his position in a sense to reproach her. But he could probably have stayed there for weeks without his sister's showing any improvement; she must have seen the dirt as clearly as he did, but she had just decided to leave it. At the same time she made sure—with an irritableness that was completely new to her and which had in fact infected the whole family—that the cleaning of Gregor's room remain her province. One time his mother had submitted Gregor's room to a major housecleaning, which she managed only after employing a couple of pails of water— all this dampness, of course, irritated Gregor,

---

7. **millinery store:** store that sells women's hats.

too, and he lay prostrate, sour and immobile, on the couch—but his mother's punishment was not long in coming. For hardly had his sister noticed the difference in Gregor's room that evening than, deeply insulted, she ran into the living room and, in spite of her mother's imploringly uplifted hands, burst out in a fit of crying, which his parents—his father had naturally been startled out of his armchair—at first watched in helpless amazement; until they too got going; turning to the right, his father blamed his mother for not letting his sister clean Gregor's room; but turning to the left, he screamed at his sister that she would never again be allowed to clean Gregor's room; while his mother tried to drag his father, who was out of his mind with excitement, into the bedroom; his sister, shaken with sobs, hammered the table with her small fists; and Gregor hissed loudly with rage because it did not occur to any of them to close the door and spare him such a scene and a row.[8]

But even if his sister, exhausted from her work at the store, had gotten fed up with taking care of Gregor as she used to, it was not necessary at all for his mother to take her place and still Gregor did not have to be neglected. For now the cleaning woman was there. This old widow, who thanks to her strong bony frame had probably survived the worst in a long life, was not really repelled by Gregor. Without being in the least inquisitive, she had once accidentally opened the door of Gregor's room, and at the sight of Gregor—who, completely taken by surprise, began to race back and forth although no one was chasing him—she had remained standing, with her hands folded on her stomach, marveling. From that time on she never failed to open the door a crack every morning and every evening and peek in hurriedly at Gregor. In the beginning she also used to call him over to her with words she probably considered friendly, like, "Come over here for a minute, you old dung beetle!" or "Look at that old dung beetle!" To forms of address like these Gregor would not respond but remained immobile where he was, as if the door had not been opened. If only they had given this cleaning woman orders to clean up his room every day, instead of letting her disturb him uselessly whenever the mood took her. Once, early in the morning—heavy rain, perhaps already a sign of approaching spring, was beating on the window panes—Gregor was so exasperated when the cleaning woman started in again with her phrases that he turned on her, of course slowly and decrepitly, as if to attack. But the cleaning woman, instead of getting frightened, simply lifted up high a chair near the door, and as she stood there with her mouth wide open, her intention was clearly to shut her mouth only when the chair in her hand came crashing down on Gregor's back. "So, is that all there is?" she asked when Gregor turned around again, and she quietly put the chair back in the corner.

Gregor now hardly ate anything anymore. Only when he accidentally passed the food laid out for him would he take a bite into his mouth just for fun, hold it in for hours, and then mostly spit it out again. At first he thought that his grief at the state of his room kept him off food, but it was the very changes in his room to which he quickly became adjusted. His family had gotten into the habit of putting in this room things for which they could not find any other place, and now there were plenty of these, since one of the rooms in the apartment had been

8. **row** (rou): quarrel.

rented to three boarders. These serious gentlemen—all three had long beards, as Gregor was able to register once through a crack in the door—were obsessed with neatness, not only in their room, but since they had, after all, moved in here, throughout the entire household and especially in the kitchen. They could not stand useless, let alone dirty, junk. Besides, they had brought along most of their own household goods. For this reason many things had become superfluous, and though they certainly weren't salable, on the other hand they could not just be thrown out. All these things migrated into Gregor's room. Likewise the ash can and the garbage can from the kitchen. Whatever was not being used at the moment was just flung into Gregor's room by the cleaning woman, who was always in a big hurry; fortunately, Gregor generally saw only the object involved and the hand that held it. Maybe the cleaning woman intended to reclaim the things as soon as she had a chance or else to throw out everything together in one fell swoop, but, in fact, they would have remained lying wherever they had been thrown in the first place if Gregor had not squeezed through the junk and set it in motion, at first from necessity, because otherwise there would have been no room to crawl in, but later with growing pleasure, although after such excursions, tired to death and sad, he did not budge again for hours.

Since the roomers sometimes also had their supper at home in the common living room, the living-room door remained closed on certain evenings, but Gregor found it very easy to give up the open door, for on many evenings when it was opened he had not taken advantage of it, but instead, without the family's noticing, had lain in the darkest corner of his room. But once the cleaning woman had left the living-room door slightly open, and it also remained opened a little when the roomers came in in the evening and the lamp was lit. They sat down at the head of the table where in the old days his father, his mother, and Gregor had eaten, unfolded their napkins, and picked up their knives and forks. At once his mother appeared in the doorway with a platter of meat, and just behind her came his sister with a platter piled high with potatoes. A thick vapor steamed up from the food. The roomers bent over the platters set in front of them as if to examine them before eating, and, in fact, the one who sat in the middle, and who seemed to be regarded by the other two as an authority, cut into a piece of meat while it was still on the platter, evidently to find out whether it was tender enough or whether it should perhaps be sent back to the kitchen. He was satisfied, and mother and sister, who had been watching anxiously, sighed with relief and began to smile.

The family itself ate in the kitchen. Nevertheless, before going into the kitchen, his father came into this room and, bowing once, cap in hand, made a turn around the table. The roomers rose as one man and mumbled something into their beards. When they were alone again, they ate in almost complete silence. It seemed strange to Gregor that among all the different noises of eating he kept picking up the sound of their chewing teeth, as if this were a sign to Gregor that you needed teeth to eat with and that even with the best make of toothless jaws you couldn't do a thing. "I'm hungry enough," Gregor said to himself, full of grief, "but not for these things. Look how these roomers are gorging themselves, and I'm dying!"

On this same evening—Gregor could not remember having heard the violin during the whole time—the sound of violin playing came from the kitchen. The roomers had already finished their evening meal, the one in the middle had taken out a newspaper, given each of the two others a page, and now, leaning back, they read and smoked. When the violin began to play, they became attentive, got up, and went on tiptoe to the door leading to the foyer, where they stood in a huddle. They must have been heard in the kitchen, for his father called, "Perhaps the playing bothers you, gentlemen? It can be stopped right away." "On the contrary," said the middle roomer. "Wouldn't the young lady like to come in to us and play in here where it's much roomier and more comfortable?" "Oh, certainly," called Gregor's father, as if he were the violinist. The boarders went back into the room and waited. Soon Gregor's father came in with the music stand, his mother with the sheet music, and his sister with the violin. Calmly his sister got everything ready for playing; his parents—who had never rented out rooms before and therefore behaved toward the roomers with excessive politeness—did not even dare sit down on their own chairs; his father leaned against the door, his right hand inserted between two buttons of his uniform coat, which he kept closed; but his mother was offered a chair by one of the roomers, and since she left the chair where the roomer just happened to put it, she sat in a corner to one side.

His sister began to play. Father and mother, from either side, attentively followed the movements of her hands. Attracted by the playing, Gregor had dared to come out a little further and already had his head in the living room. It hardly surprised him that lately he was showing so little consideration for the others; once such consideration had been his greatest pride. And yet he would never have had better reason to keep hidden; for now, because of the dust which lay all over his room and blew around at the slightest movement, he, too, was completely covered with dust; he dragged around with him on his back and along his sides fluff and hairs and scraps of food; his indifference to everything was much too deep for him to have gotten on his back and scrubbed himself clean against the carpet, as once he had done several times a day. And in spite of his state, he was not ashamed to inch out a little farther on the immaculate living-room floor.

Admittedly no one paid any attention to him. The family was completely absorbed by the violin-playing; the roomers, on the other hand, who at first had stationed themselves, hands in pockets, much too close behind his sister's music stand, so that they could all have followed the score, which certainly must have upset his sister, soon withdrew to the window, talking to each other in an undertone, their heads lowered, where they remained, anxiously watched by his father. It now seemed only too obvious that they were disappointed in their expectation of hearing beautiful or entertaining violin-playing, had had enough of the whole performance, and continued to let their peace be disturbed only out of politeness. Especially the way they all blew the cigar smoke out of their nose and mouth toward the ceiling suggested great nervousness. And yet his sister was playing so beautifully. Her face was inclined to one side, sadly and probingly her eyes followed the lines of music. Gregor crawled forward a little farther, holding his head close to the floor, so that it might be possible to catch her eye. Was he an animal, that music could move him so? He felt as if the way to the unknown nourishment he longed for were coming to light. He was determined to force himself on until he reached his sister, to pluck at her skirt, and to let her know in this way that she should bring her violin into his room, for no one here appreciated her playing the way he would appreciate it. He would never again let her out of his room—at least not for as long as he lived; for once, his nightmarish looks would be of use to him; he would be at all the doors of his room at the same time and hiss and spit at the aggressors; his sister, however, should not be forced to stay with him, but would do so of her own free will; she should sit next to him on the couch, bending her ear down to him, and then he would confide to her that he had had the firm intention of sending her to the Conservatory, and that, if the catastrophe had not intervened, he would have announced this to everyone last Christmas—certainly Christmas had come and gone?—without taking notice of any objections. After this declaration his sister would burst into tears of emotion, and Gregor would raise himself up to her shoulder and kiss her on the neck which, ever since she started going out to work, she kept bare, without a ribbon or collar.

"Mr. Samsa!" the middle roomer called to Gregor's father and without wasting another word pointed his index finger at Gregor, who was slowly moving forward. The violin stopped, the middle roomer smiled first at his friends, shaking his head, and then looked at Gregor again. Rather than driving Gregor out, his father seemed to consider it more urgent to start by soothing the roomers although they were not at all upset, and Gregor seemed to be entertaining them more than the violin-playing. He rushed over to them and tried with outstretched arms to drive them into their room and at the same time with his body to block their view of Gregor. Now they actually did get a little angry—it was not clear whether because of his father's behavior or because of their dawning realization of having had without knowing it such a next-door neighbor as Gregor. They demanded explanations from his father; in their turn they raised their arms, plucked excitedly at their beards, and, dragging their feet, backed off toward their room. In the meantime his sister had overcome the abstracted mood into which she had fallen after her playing had been so suddenly interrupted; and all at once, after holding violin and bow for a while in her slackly hanging hands and continuing to follow the score as if she were still playing, she pulled herself together, laid the instrument on the lap of her mother—who was still sitting in her chair, fighting for breath, her lungs violently heaving—and ran into the next room, which the roomers, under pressure from her father, were nearing more quickly than before. One could see the covers and bolsters on the beds, obeying his sister's practiced hands, fly up and arrange themselves. Before the boarders had reached the room, she had finished turning down the beds and had slipped out. Her father seemed once again to be gripped by his perverse obstinacy to such a degree that he completely forgot any respect still due his tenants. He drove them on and kept on driving until, already at the bedroom door, the middle boarder stamped his foot thunderingly and thus brought him to a standstill. "I herewith declare," he said, raising his hand and casting his eyes around for Gregor's mother and sister, too, "that in view of the disgusting conditions prevailing in this apartment and family"—here he spat curtly and decisively on the floor—"I give notice as of now. Of course, I won't pay a cent for the days I have been living here, either; on the contrary, I shall consider taking some sort of action against you with claims that—believe me—will be easy to substantiate." He stopped and looked straight in front of him, as if he were expecting something. And, in fact, his two friends at once chimed in with the words, "We, too, give notice as of now." Thereupon he grabbed the doorknob and slammed the door with a bang.

Gregor's father, his hands groping, staggered to his armchair and collapsed into it; it looked as if he were stretching himself out for his usual evening nap, but the heavy drooping of his head, as if it had lost all support, showed that he was certainly not asleep. All this time Gregor had lain quietly at the spot where the roomers had surprised him. His disappointment at the failure of his plan—but perhaps also the weakness caused by so much fasting—made it impossible for him to move. He was afraid with some certainty that in the very next moment a general debacle would burst over him, and he waited. He was not even startled by the violin as it slipped from under his mother's trembling fingers and fell off her lap with a reverberating clang.

"My dear parents," said his sister and by way of an introduction pounded her hand on the table, "things can't go on like this. Maybe you don't realize it, but I do. I won't pronounce the name of my brother in front of this monster, and so all I say is: we have to try to get rid of it. We've done everything humanly possible to take care of it and to put up with it; I don't think anyone can blame us in the least."

"She's absolutely right," said his father to himself. His mother, who still could not catch her breath, began to cough dully behind her hand, a wild look in her eyes.

His sister rushed over to his mother and held her forehead. His father seemed to have been led by Grete's words to more definite thoughts, had sat up, was playing with the cap of his uniform among the plates which were still lying on the table from the roomers' supper, and from time to time looked at Gregor's motionless form.

"We must try to get rid of it," his sister now said exclusively to her father, since her mother was coughing too hard to hear anything. "It will be the death of you two, I can see it coming. People who already have to work as hard as we do can't put up with this constant torture at home, too. I can't stand it anymore either." And she broke out crying so bitterly that her tears poured down onto her mother's face, which she wiped off with mechanical movements of her hand.

"Child," said her father kindly and with unusual understanding, "but what can we do?"

Gregor's sister only shrugged her shoulders as a sign of the bewildered mood that had now gripped her as she cried, in contrast with her earlier confidence.

"If he could understand us," said her father, half questioning; in the midst of her crying Gregor's sister waved her hand violently as a sign that that was out of the question.

"If he could understand us," his father repeated and by closing his eyes, absorbed his daughter's conviction of the impossibility of the idea, "then maybe we could come to an agreement with him. But the way things are——"

"It has to go," cried his sister. "That's the only answer, Father. You just have to try to get rid of the idea that it's Gregor. Believing it for so long, that is our real misfortune. But how can it be Gregor? If it were Gregor, he would have realized long ago that it isn't possible for human beings to live with such a creature, and he would have gone away of his own free will. Then we wouldn't have a brother, but we'd be able to go on living and honor his memory. But as things are, this animal persecutes us, drives the roomers away, obviously wants to occupy the whole apartment and for us to sleep in the gutter. Look, Father," she suddenly shrieked, "he's starting in again!" And in a fit of terror that was completely incomprehensible to Gregor, his sister abandoned even her mother, literally shoved herself off from her chair, as if she would rather sacrifice her mother than stay near Gregor, and rushed behind her father, who, upset only by her behavior, also stood up and half-lifted his arms in front of her as if to protect her.

But Gregor had absolutely no intention of frightening anyone, let alone his sister. He had only begun to turn around in order to trek back to his room; certainly his movements did look peculiar, since his ailing condition made him help the complicated turning maneuver along with his head, which he lifted up many times and knocked against the floor. He stopped and looked around. His good intention seemed to have been recognized; it had only been a momentary scare. Now they all watched him, silent and sad. His mother lay in her armchair, her legs stretched out and pressed together, her eyes almost closing from exhaustion; his father and his sister sat side by side, his sister had put her arm around her father's neck.

Now maybe they'll let me turn around, Gregor thought and began his labors again. He could not repress his panting from the exertion, and from time to time he had to rest. Otherwise no one harassed him, he was left completely on his own. When he had completed the turn, he immediately began to crawl back in a straight line. He was astonished at the great distance separating him from his room and could not understand at all how, given his weakness, he had covered the same distance a little while ago almost without realizing it. Constantly intent only on rapid crawling, he hardly noticed that not a word, not an exclamation from his family, interrupted him. Only when he was already in the doorway did he turn his head—not completely, for he felt his neck stiffening; nevertheless, he still saw that behind him nothing had changed except that his sister had gotten up. His last glance ranged over his mother, who was now fast asleep.

He was hardly inside his room when the door was hurriedly slammed shut, firmly bolted, and locked. Gregor was so frightened at the sudden noise behind him that his little legs gave way under him. It was his sister who had been in such a hurry. She had been standing up straight, ready and waiting, then she had leaped forward nimbly, Gregor had not even heard her coming, and she cried "Finally!" to her parents as she turned the key in the lock.

"And now?" Gregor asked himself, looking around in the darkness. He soon made the discovery that he could no longer move at all. It did not surprise him; rather, it seemed unnatural that until now he had actually been able to propel himself on these thin little legs. Otherwise he felt relatively comfortable. He had pains, of course, throughout his whole body, but it seemed to him that they were gradually getting fainter and fainter and would finally go away altogether. The rotten apple in his back and the inflamed area around it, which were completely covered with fluffy dust, already hardly bothered him. He thought back on his family with deep emotion and love. His conviction that he would have to disappear was, if possible, even firmer than his sister's. He remained in this state of empty and peaceful reflection until the tower clock struck three in the morning. He still saw that outside the window everything was beginning to grow light. Then, without his consent, his head sank down to the floor, and from his nostrils streamed his last weak breath.

When early in the morning the cleaning woman came—in sheer energy and impatience she would slam all the doors so hard although she had often been asked not to, that once she had arrived, quiet sleep was no longer possible anywhere in the apartment—she did not at first find anything out of the ordinary on paying Gregor her usual short visit. She thought that he was deliberately lying motionless, pretending that his feelings were hurt; she credited him with unlimited intelligence. Because she happened to be holding the long broom, she

Toad (Le Crapaud), Pablo Picasso, 1949.

tried from the doorway to tickle Gregor with it. When this too produced no results, she became annoyed and jabbed Gregor a little, and only when she had shoved him without any resistance to another spot did she begin to take notice. When she quickly became aware of the true state of things, she opened her eyes wide, whistled softly, but did not dawdle; instead, she tore open the door of the bedroom and shouted at the top of her voice into the darkness: "Come and have a look, it's croaked; it's lying there, dead as a doornail!"

The couple Mr. and Mrs. Samsa sat up in their marriage bed and had a struggle overcoming their shock at the cleaning woman before they could finally grasp her message. But then Mr. and Mrs. Samsa hastily scrambled out of bed, each on his side, Mr. Samsa threw the blanket around his shoulders, Mrs. Samsa came out in nothing but her nightgown; dressed this way, they entered Gregor's room. In the meantime, the door of the living room had also opened, where Grete had been sleeping since the roomers had moved in; she was fully dressed, as if she had not been asleep at all; and her pale face seemed to confirm this. "Dead?" said Mrs. Samsa and looked inquiringly at the cleaning woman, although she could scrutinize everything for herself and could recognize the truth even without scrutiny. "I'll say," said the cleaning woman, and to prove it she pushed Gregor's corpse with her broom a good distance sideways. Mrs. Samsa made a movement as if to hold the broom back but did not do it. "Well," said Mr. Samsa, "now we can thank God!" He crossed himself, and the three women followed his example. Grete, who never took her eyes off the corpse, said, "Just look how thin he was. Of course he didn't eat anything for such a long time. The food came out again just the

way it went in." As a matter of fact, Gregor's body was completely flat and dry; this was obvious now for the first time, really, since the body was no longer raised up by his little legs and nothing else distracted the eye.

"Come in with us for a little while, Grete," said Mrs. Samsa with a melancholy smile, and Grete, not without looking back at the corpse, followed her parents into their bedroom. The cleaning woman shut the door and opened the window wide. Although it was early in the morning, there was already some mildness mixed in with the fresh air. After all, it was already the end of March.

The three boarders came out of their room and looked around in astonishment for their breakfast; they had been forgotten. "Where's breakfast?" the middle roomer grumpily asked the cleaning woman. But she put her finger to her lips and then hastily and silently beckoned the boarders to follow her into Gregor's room. They came willingly and then stood, their hands in the pockets of their somewhat shabby jackets, in the now already very bright room, surrounding Gregor's corpse.

At that point the bedroom door opened, and Mr. Samsa appeared in his uniform, his wife on one arm, his daughter on the other. They all looked as if they had been crying; from time to time Grete pressed her face against her father's sleeve.

"Leave my house immediately," said Mr. Samsa and pointed to the door, without letting go of the women. "What do you mean by that?" said the middle roomer, somewhat nonplussed, and smiled with a sugary smile. The two others held their hands behind their back and incessantly rubbed them together, as if in joyful anticipation of a big argument, which could only turn out in their favor. "I mean just what I say," answered Mr. Samsa, and with his two companions marched in a straight line toward the roomer. At first the roomer stood still and looked at the floor, as if the thoughts inside his head were fitting themselves together in a new order. "So, we'll go, then," he said and looked up at Mr. Samsa as if, suddenly overcome by a fit of humility, he were asking for further permission even for this decision. Mr. Samsa merely nodded briefly several times, his eyes wide open. Thereupon the roomer actually went immediately into the foyer, taking long strides; his two friends had already been listening for a while, their hands completely still, and now they went hopping right after him, as if afraid that Mr. Samsa might get into the foyer ahead of them and interrupt the contact with their leader. In the foyer all three took their hats from the coat rack, pulled their canes from the umbrella stand, bowed silently, and left the apartment. In a suspicious mood which proved completely unfounded, Mr. Samsa led the two women out onto the landing; leaning over the banister, they watched the three roomers slowly but steadily going down the long flight of stairs, disappearing on each landing at a particular turn of the stairway and a few moments later emerging again; the farther down they got, the more the Samsa family's interest in them wore off, and when a butcher's boy with a carrier on his head came climbing up the stairs with a proud bearing, toward them and then up on past them, Mr. Samsa and the women quickly left the banister and all went back, as if relieved, into their apartment.

They decided to spend this day resting and going for a walk; they not only deserved a break in their work, they absolutely needed one. And so they sat down at the table and wrote three letters of excuse, Mr. Samsa to the management of the bank, Mrs. Samsa to her employer, and Grete to the store owner. While they were writing, the cleaning woman came in to say that she was going, since her morning's work was done. The three letter writers at first simply nodded without looking up, but as the cleaning woman still kept lingering, they looked up, annoyed. "Well?" asked Mr. Samsa. The cleaning woman stood smiling in the doorway, as if she had some great good news to announce to the family but would do so only if she were thoroughly questioned. The little ostrich feather which stood almost upright on her hat and which had irritated Mr. Samsa the whole time she had been with them swayed lightly in all directions. "What do you want?" asked Mrs. Samsa, who inspired the most respect in the cleaning woman. "Well," the cleaning woman answered, and for good-natured laughter could not immediately go on, "look, you don't have to worry about getting rid of the stuff next door. It's already been taken care of." Mrs. Samsa and Grete bent down over their letters, as if to continue writing; Mr. Samsa, who noticed that the cleaning woman was now about to start describing everything in detail, stopped her with a firmly outstretched hand. But since she was not going to be permitted to tell her story, she remembered that she was in a great hurry, cried, obviously insulted, "So long, everyone," whirled around wildly, and left the apartment with a terrible slamming of doors.

"We'll fire her tonight," said Mr. Samsa, but did not get an answer from either his wife or his daughter, for the cleaning woman seemed to have ruined their barely regained peace of mind. They got up, went to the window, and stayed there, holding each other tight. Mr. Samsa turned around in his chair toward them and watched them quietly for a while. Then he called, "Come on now, come over here. Stop brooding over the past. And have a little consideration for me, too." The women obeyed him at once, hurried over to him, fondled him, and quickly finished their letters.

Then all three of them left the apartment together, something they had not done in months, and took the trolley into the open country on the outskirts of the city. The car, in which they were the only passengers, was completely filled with warm sunshine. Leaning back comfortably in their seats, they discussed their prospects for the time to come, and it seemed on closer examination that these weren't bad at all, for all three positions—about which they had never really asked one another in any detail—were exceedingly advantageous and especially promising for the future. The greatest immediate improvement in their situation would come easily, of course, from a change in apartments; they would now take a smaller and cheaper apartment, but one better situated and in every way simpler to manage than the old one, which Gregor had picked for them. While they were talking in this vein, it occurred almost simultaneously to Mr. and Mrs. Samsa, as they watched their daughter getting livelier and livelier, that lately, in spite of all the troubles which had turned her cheeks pale, she had blossomed into a good-looking, shapely girl. Growing quieter and communicating almost unconsciously through glances, they thought that it would soon be time, too, to find her a good husband. And it was like a confirmation of their new dreams and good intentions when at the end of the ride their daughter got up first and stretched her young body.

First Thoughts

Kafka explicitly forbade his publishers to include any illustration of Gregor as an insect. He felt that any literal representation would be meaningless. Do you agree with his view? Did you form a mental image of the metamorphosed Gregor? Draw your image of Gregor after his transformation, then discuss your drawing with the class.

Identifying Facts

1. After discovering that he has changed into a ''monstrous vermin,'' what is Gregor's chief concern?

2. What does Gregor do for a living? What does he dislike about his job? Explain why he feels he cannot resign.

3. Who is Gregor's primary caretaker? In the course of the story, what change takes place in this person's attitude toward Gregor?

4. How does the family's treatment of Gregor deteriorate? What does Gregor's father do that permanently injures Gregor?

5. After Gregor dies, what do his parents plan? What is ''like a confirmation of their new dreams''?

Interpreting Meanings

1. **Irony** is the difference between what one expects to happen and what actually happens. What is ironic about Gregor's family's reaction to his change in form? Identify another example of irony in the story.

2. Gregor's reaction to Grete's violin playing leads to the **climax** of the novel.

How is his entrance into the living room the "final straw"?

3. In your opinion, what does the "monstrous vermin" **symbolize**? In symbolic terms, what is significant about the kind of creature Gregor transforms into—as opposed, say, to a dog or a cat?

4. The word *samsja* in Czech means "being alone." Do you think it was Gregor's change in form or his inability to communicate that contributed more to his isolation? How might things have been different if he had been able to express himself?

5. As Gregor's condition deteriorates, his family's condition improves. Some critics have said that the title of the novel refers not only to Gregor's metamorphosis, but also to his family's. Do you agree? Explain your response.

Applying Meanings

Although Kafka's story takes place more than seventy years ago, we still read about Gregor with fascination and curiosity. Do you think that this story is relevant to life today? You may not wake up tomorrow and find yourself changed into a bug, but do you ever suffer the same feelings and frustrations as Gregor did? Might there be other ways in which people "transform" because of their problems? Discuss your opinions with the class.

Creative Writing Response

1. **Writing from a Different Point of View.** Except for the last part, after Gregor's death, this novella is told from the **limited third-person point of view**: We are limited to Gregor's view of events. Gregor gives a very matter-of-fact account of his metamorphosis, but we can imagine how the other members of the family are reacting. In a few paragraphs, tell about Gregor's metamorphosis from Grete's point of view. You might start with, "One morning, as I whispered through the wall to Gregor, I heard strange chirping noises coming out of his room. . . ."

2. **Describing Another Metamorphosis.** Since ancient times, the **motif** of a metamorphosis has been used in stories. Describe a story in which a metamorphosis takes place—it can be from a myth, a book, or a movie. (Think of all those weird shape changes that take place in science-fiction movies.) You can make up your own metamorphosis story if you like. Does the metamorphosed form reflect any traits of the original being?

Critical Writing Response

1. **Analyzing a Character.** One of the central conflicts in the story is the relationship between Gregor and his father, which some critics see as reflecting Kafka's view of his relationship with his own father. Write a paragraph in which you analyze Mr. Samsa's character. Before you write, consider the following questions:

   a. How does Mr. Samsa view Gregor's metamorphosis? (Is he sympathetic? indifferent?) How does he treat Gregor?

   b. How does Mr. Samsa change after he gets a job and begins to support the family again?

   c. How do you think Gregor views his father? As a symbol of authority? Or does he think his father is weak? Does Gregor like his father?

2. **Responding to a Critic.** Critic Paul L. Landsburg believes that *The Metamorphosis* is an **allegory**, or a story in which each character and event stands for something else. In an allegory, the writer is trying to teach some moral meaning about life. As you read the

quotation below, think about any individuals or groups in society that could suffer the same kind of alienation and treatment that Gregor suffered.

> "To be an exception or in the minority is the original social sin. When in society any group of men characterized by anomalous tastes or racial or social heredity is denounced as 'vermin,' there will always be one group that from then on will see nothing but the other's rottenness, and another fraction within the scorned group that will think and act as if they had truly been transformed into vermin."
> —Paul L. Landsburg

Write two paragraphs in which you discuss how individuals or groups of people can actually begin to act the way they are treated.

Language and Vocabulary

Adjectives from People's Names

The adjective *Kafkaesque* is just one of many English words that come from the names of real people or fictional characters. Such adjectives usually develop when a person's or character's behavior or achievements are so well known that similar behavior or achievements are compared to them.

Choose the correct meaning of each italicized adjective in the phrases below. Check your answers in a dictionary and identify the person or character whose name gave rise to the adjective.

1. a *Herculean* task
   a) arduous   b) tedious
   c) short   d) easy

2. a *Machiavellian* politician
   a) weak   b) idealistic
   c) up-to-date   d) crafty

3. a *platonic* friendship
   a) spiritual or intellectual   b) passionate
   c) deceitful   d) long-standing

4. *quixotic* behavior
   a) mature   b) mysterious
   c) romantic and idealistic   d) fickle

5. *Shakespearean* language
   a) vulgar   b) poetic
   c) redundant   d) puzzling

THE ART OF TRANSLATION

Two Translations of The Metamorphosis

In reading *The Metamorphosis,* you are not simply reading a story by Kafka. You are also reading the work of a skilled translator who has tried to convey the meaning and spirit of Kafka's German in lively, natural English prose.

Whether a translator is faced with a text in French, Russian, Spanish, or Japanese, he or she takes on a difficult task. First of all, a word-for-word translation from the original language into English would probably not make sense. In addition, many foreign words have several possible English equivalents, and some words may have no English equivalents. Furthermore, **idioms**, or expressions specific to a particular language, cannot be translated literally. For example, the idiomatic expression, "He's a wet blanket'' doesn't make much sense when translated to another language, but most languages probably *do* have an equivalent, figurative expression that conveys the same meaning: ''He always manages to bring out the negative aspect of things.'' Translators must find these approximations. Just look at the many ways Gregor's metamorphosed form (*ungeheueres Ungeziefer* in German) has been translated: ''monstrous vermin,'' ''gigantic insect,'' ''enormous bug,'' ''a giant kind of vermin,'' and ''monstrous bug.''

Here are several passages from *The Metamorphosis*. The first passage in each example is from the translation you have just read, by Stanley Corngold. The second passage is from a translation by Willa and Edwin Muir. Read each pair of passages aloud, and discuss how they differ in diction (word choice), naturalness of language, rhythm, and ultimate meaning. Which version do you prefer, and why?

1. **a.** ''Traveling salesmen aren't well liked there, I know. People think they make a fortune leading the gay life. No one has any particular reason to rectify this prejudice.''

   b. ''Travelers are not popular there, I know. People think they earn sacks of money and have a good time. A prejudice there's no particular reason for revising.''

2. **a.** ''In fact, Gregor felt fine, with the exception of his drowsiness, which was really unnecessary after sleeping so late, and he even had a ravenous appetite.''

   b. ''Gregor really felt quite well, apart from a drowsiness that was utterly superfluous after such a long sleep and he was even unusually hungry.''

3. **a.** '' 'That was the voice of an animal,' said the manager, in a tone conspicuously soft compared with the mother's yelling.''

   b. '' 'That was no human voice,' said the chief clerk in a voice noticeably low beside the shrillness of the mother's.''

4. **a.** ''Then, without his consent, his head sank down to the floor, and from his nostrils streamed his last weak breath.''

   b. ''Then his head sank to the floor of its own accord and from his nostrils came the last faint flicker of his breath.''

5. **a.** '' 'Come and have a look, it's croaked; it's lying there, dead as a doornail.' ''

   b. '' 'Just look at this, it's dead; it's lying here dead and done for.' ''

Selma Lagerlöf
1858–1940, Sweden

AP/Wide World Photos

When Selma Lagerlöf (lä′gər·lüf′) was studying to become a schoolteacher, she attended a lecture that was to change her life. The subject of the lecture was Swedish folk ballads. These narrative songs reminded her of the folklore she had learned as a child in Sweden's Värmland district, and of the happy days in the house that her family was forced to sell when her father died. Lagerlöf's bittersweet memories inspired her to begin writing about the legends and folktales of her childhood. The books she wrote became so popular that she was soon able to repurchase her beloved family home with the money she made.

As a child, Lagerlöf listened to her grandmother tell Swedish folktales, and she never tired of reading books from the family library.

Her first novel, *The Story of Gösta Berling* (1891), was set in her childhood home, Värmland. To her surprise, the novel won first prize in a competition. Success followed success as *Invisible Links* (1894), a collection of Swedish legends and other tales, earned her a Swedish Academy writing scholarship and praise from Sweden's king. By now a household name in her homeland, Lagerlöf retired from her teaching career to devote herself to writing. A trip to the Middle East prompted *Jerusalem* (1901–1902), a two-volume novel about Swedes who immigrated to Jerusalem in quest for spiritual fulfillment. Four years later came the children's book, *The Wonderful Adventures of Nils,* which recounts a young boy's adventures as he travels across Sweden on the back of a goose.

In 1909, Lagerlöf became the first woman writer to win the Nobel Prize for literature. By the time she reached seventy, she was so famous that her birthday was celebrated in Sweden and in several neighboring nations. Although she was a committed pacifist and feminist, her social concerns rarely found their way into her novels. In her final years, however, Lagerlöf was outraged to find herself hailed as a "Nordic princess" in Nazi Germany, and began defiantly arranging for German intellectuals to escape Nazi persecution by coming to Sweden—an activity she continued even after World War II broke out and Sweden declared itself neutral.

Reader's Guide

THE RAT TRAP

Background

This story takes place in the Värmland area of Sweden where Selma Lagerlöf spent her childhood. Because the region had many iron ore deposits, it became a center of Sweden's iron industry during the second half of the nineteenth century. Iron ore mined in the district was brought to furnaces called ironworks, where it was smelted to remove impurities and then shaped into bars or sheets. The ironmasters who owned the ironworks became very wealthy and bought vast tracts of land, some of which they leased to tenant farmers and retired ironworkers. While the Industrial Revolution brought prosperity to some, it brought poverty to many others. Many farm laborers lost their jobs and became wandering peddlers or beggars. This story includes such a peddler, as well as an ironmaster, his daughter, and an elderly tenant farmer.

Writer's Response

There is a vast difference between the wealthiest and poorest people in our country today. Write a few sentences contrasting the lifestyles of the wealthiest and poorest people in your community.

Literary Focus

Point of view is the vantage point from which a writer tells a story. The traditional vantage point for storytelling is the **omniscient** (or all-knowing) **point of view**. The omniscient narrator is not a character in the story, but a godlike observer who knows everything that is going on in each character's heart and mind. This narrator can also provide us with information that no character knows. ("Thomas was sailing along effortlessly on his roller blades, unaware that the getaway car would soon burst out of the quiet side street.") Selma Lagerlöf uses the omniscient point of view in "The Rat Trap."

THE RAT TRAP

Selma Lagerlöf

translated by

FLORENCE AND NABOTH HEDIN

> *Read the first three paragraphs of "The Rat Trap" and think about the peddler's "rat trap theory" of the world. Does this theory make sense to you? What does the theory reveal about the peddler's view of life?*

EVENING IN THE KARL JOHAN STREET, EDVARD MUNCH (1863–1944).

Scala/Art Resource, New York

Once upon a time there was a man who went around selling small rat traps of wire. He made them himself at odd moments, from material he got by begging in the stores or at the big farms. But even so, the business was not especially profitable, so he had to resort to both begging and petty thievery to keep body and soul together. Even so, his clothes were in rags, his cheeks were sunken, and hunger gleamed in his eyes.

No one can imagine how sad and monotonous life can appear to such a vagabond, who plods along the road, left to his own meditations. But one day this man had fallen into a line of thought which really seemed to him entertaining. He had naturally been thinking of his rat traps when suddenly he was struck by the idea that the whole world about him—the whole world with its lands and seas, its cities and villages—was nothing but a big rat trap. It had never existed for any other purpose than to set baits for people. It offered riches and joys, shelter and food, heat and clothing, exactly as the rat trap offered cheese and pork, and as soon as anyone let himself be tempted to touch the bait, it closed in on him, and then everything came to an end.

The world had, of course, never been very kind to him, so it gave him unwonted[1] joy to think ill of it in this way. It became a cherished pastime of his, during many dreary ploddings, to think of people he knew who had let themselves be caught in the dangerous snare, and of others who were still circling around the bait.

One dark evening as he was trudging along the road he caught sight of a little gray cottage by the roadside, and he knocked on the door to ask shelter for the night. Nor was he refused. Instead of the sour faces which ordinarily met him, the owner, who was an old man without wife or child, was happy to get someone to talk to in his loneliness. Immediately he put the porridge pot on the fire and gave him supper; then he carved off such a big slice from his tobacco roll that it was enough both for the stranger's pipe and his own. Finally he got out an old pack of cards and played *mjölis*[2] with his guest until bedtime.

The old man was just as generous with his confidences as with his porridge and tobacco. The guest was informed at once that in his days of prosperity his host had been a crofter at Ramsjö Ironworks[3] and had worked on the land. Now that he was no longer able to do day labor, it was his cow which supported him. Yes, that bossy[4] was extraordinary. She could give milk for the creamery every day, and last month he had received all of thirty kronor[5] in payment.

The stranger must have seemed incredulous, for the old man got up and went to the window, took down a leather pouch which hung on a nail in the very window frame, and picked out three wrinkled ten-kronor bills. These he held up before the eyes of his guest, nodding knowingly, and then stuffed them back into the pouch.

The next day both men got up in good season. The crofter was in a hurry to milk his cow, and the other man probably thought he should not stay in bed when the head of the house had gotten up. They left the cottage at the same time. The crofter locked the door and put the key in his pocket. The man with the rat traps said goodbye and thank you, and thereupon each went his own way.

But half an hour later the rat-trap peddler stood again before the door. He did not try to get in, however. He only went up to the window, smashed a pane, stuck in his hand, and got hold of the pouch with the thirty kronor. He took the money and thrust it into his own pocket. Then he hung the leather pouch very carefully back in its place and went away.

As he walked along with the money in his pocket he felt quite pleased with his smartness. He realized, of course, that at first he dared not continue on the public highway, but must turn off the road, into the woods. During the first few hours this caused him no difficulty. Later in the day it

---

1. **unwonted** (un·wän'tid): unaccustomed.
2. **mjölis** (myö'lis): Swedish card game.
3. **crofter at Ramsjö** (räm'shyō) **Ironworks:** tenant farmer on land owned by the Ramsjö Ironworks.
4. **bossy:** colloquial term for a cow.
5. **thirty kronor** (krō'nôr'): about six dollars when the story takes place; the krona is the monetary unit of Sweden; *kronor* is the plural form.

became worse, for it was a big and confusing forest which he had gotten into. He tried, to be sure, to walk in a definite direction, but the paths twisted back and forth so strangely! He walked and walked, without coming to the end of the wood, and finally he realized that he had only been walking around in the same part of the forest. All at once he recalled his thoughts about the world and the rat trap. Now his own turn had come. He had let himself be fooled by a bait and had been caught. The whole forest, with its trunks and branches, its thickets and fallen logs, closed in upon him like an impenetrable prison from which he could never escape.

It was late in December. Darkness was already descending over the forest. This increased the danger, and increased also his gloom and despair. Finally he saw no way out, and he sank down on the ground, tired to death, thinking that his last moment had come. But just as he laid his head on the ground, he heard a sound—a hard, regular thumping. There was no doubt as to what that was. He raised himself. "Those are the hammer strokes from an iron mill," he thought. "There must be people nearby." He summoned all his strength, got up, and staggered in the direction of the sound.

The Ramsjö Ironworks, which is now closed down, was, not so long ago, a large plant, with smelter,[6] rolling mill,[7] and forge.[8] In the summertime, long lines of heavily-loaded barges and scows slid down the canal which led to a large inland lake, and in the wintertime the roads near the mill were black from all the coal dust which sifted down from the big charcoal crates.

During one of the long dark evenings just before Christmas, the master smith and his helper sat in the dark forge near the furnace waiting for the pig iron, which had been put in the fire, to be ready to put on the anvil.[9] Every now and then one of them got up to stir the glowing mass with a long iron bar, returning in a few moments, dripping with perspiration, though, as was the custom, he wore nothing but a long shirt and a pair of wooden shoes.

All the time there were many sounds to be heard in the forge. The big bellows groaned and the burning coal cracked. The fire boy shoveled charcoal into the maw of the furnace with a great deal of clatter. Outside roared the waterfall, and a sharp north wind whipped the rain against the brick-tiled roof.

It was probably on account of all this noise that the blacksmith did not notice that a man had opened the gate and entered the forge, until he stood close up to the furnace.

Surely it was nothing unusual for poor vagabonds without any better shelter for the night to be attracted to the forge by the glow of light which escaped through the sooty panes, and to come in to warm themselves in front of the fire. The blacksmiths glanced only casually and indifferently at the intruder. He looked the way people of his type usually did, with a long beard, dirty, ragged, and with a bunch of rat traps dangling on his chest.

He asked permission to stay, and the master blacksmith nodded a haughty consent without honoring him with a single word.

The tramp did not say anything, either.

---

6. **smelter:** place where iron ore is fused or melted in order to separate out the impurities.

7. **rolling mill:** machine used to roll out metal bars or sheets.

8. **forge:** here, place where metal is heated in a furnace and then hammered or molded into shape.

9. **anvil:** metal block on which objects are hammered into shape.

THE FOUNDRY, EYRE CROWE (1824–1910).

He had not come there to talk but only to warm himself and sleep.

In those days the Ramsjö iron mill was owned by a very prominent ironmaster whose greatest ambition was to ship out good iron to the market. He watched both night and day to see that the work was done as well as possible, and at this very moment he came into the forge on one of his nightly rounds of inspection.

Naturally the first thing he saw was the tall ragamuffin who had eased his way so close to the furnace that steam rose from his wet rags. The ironmaster did not follow the example of the blacksmiths, who had hardly deigned to look at the stranger. He walked close up to him, looked him over very carefully, then tore off his slouch hat[10]

10. **slouch hat:** style of hat with a drooping brim.

to get a better view of his face.

"But of course it is you, Nils Olof!" he said. "How you do look!"

The man with the rat traps had never before seen the ironmaster of Ramsjö and did not even know what his name was. But it occurred to him that if the fine gentleman thought he was an old acquaintance, he might perhaps throw him a couple of kronor. Therefore he did not want to undeceive him all at once.

"Yes, God knows things have gone downhill with me," he said.

"You should not have resigned from the regiment," said the ironmaster. "That was the mistake. If only I had still been in the service at the time, it never would have happened. Well, now, of course, you will come home with me."

To go along up to the manor house and be received by the owner like an old

Selma Lagerlöf **67**

regimental comrade—that, however, did not please the tramp.

"No, I couldn't think of it!" he said, looking quite alarmed.

He thought of the thirty kronor. To go up to the manor house would be like throwing himself voluntarily into the lions' den. He only wanted a chance to sleep here in the forge and then sneak away as inconspicuously as possible.

The ironmaster assumed that he felt embarrassed because of his miserable clothing.

"Please don't think that I have such a fine home that you cannot show yourself there," he said. "Elizabeth is dead, as you may already have heard. My boys are abroad, and there is no one at home except my oldest daughter and myself. We were just saying that it was too bad we didn't have any company for Christmas. Now come along with me and help us make the Christmas food disappear a little faster."

But the stranger said no, and no, and again no, and the ironmaster saw that he must give in.

"It looks as though Captain von Ståhle[11] preferred to stay with you tonight, Stjernström,"[12] he said to the master blacksmith, and turned on his heel.

But he laughed to himself as he went away, and the blacksmith, who knew him, understood very well that he had not said his last word.

It was not more than half an hour before they heard the sound of carriage wheels outside the forge, and a new guest came in, but this time it was not the ironmaster. He had sent his daughter, apparently hoping that she would have better powers of persuasion than he himself.

She entered, followed by a valet,[13] carrying on his arm a big fur coat. She was not at all pretty, but seemed modest and quite shy. In the forge everything was just as it had been earlier in the evening. The master blacksmith and his apprentice still sat on their bench, and iron and charcoal still glowed in the furnace. The stranger had stretched himself out on the floor and lay with a piece of pig iron under his head and his hat pulled down over his eyes. As soon as the young girl caught sight of him she went up and lifted his hat. The man was evidently used to sleeping with one eye open. He jumped up abruptly and seemed to be quite frightened.

"My name is Edla Willmansson," said the young girl. "My father came home and said that you wanted to sleep here in the forge tonight, and then I asked permission to come and bring you home to us. I am so sorry, Captain, that you are having such a hard time."

She looked at him compassionately, with her heavy eyes, and then she noticed that the man was afraid. "Either he has stolen something or else he has escaped from jail," she thought, and added quickly, "You may be sure, Captain, that you will be allowed to leave us just as freely as you came. Only please stay with us over Christmas Eve."

She said this in such a friendly manner that the rat-trap peddler must have felt confidence in her.

"It would never have occurred to me that you would bother with me yourself, miss," he said. "I will come at once."

He accepted the fur coat, which the valet handed him with a deep bow, threw it over his rags, and followed the young lady out to the carriage, without granting the astonished

11. **von Ståhle** (fon stô′lə)
12. **Stjernström** (styern′strôm)
13. **valet** (val′it): personal manservant.

blacksmiths so much as a glance.

But while he was riding up to the manor house he had evil forebodings.

"Why the devil did I take that fellow's money?" he thought. "Now I am sitting in the trap and will never get out of it."

The next day was Christmas Eve, and when the ironmaster came into the dining room for breakfast he probably thought with satisfaction of his old regimental comrade whom he had run across so unexpectedly.

"First of all we must see to it that he gets a little flesh on his bones," he said to his daughter, who was busy at the table. "And then we must see that he gets something else to do than to run around the country selling rat traps."

"It is queer that things have gone downhill with him as badly as that," said the daughter. "Last night I did not think there was anything about him to show that he had once been an educated man."

"You must have patience, my little girl," said the father. "As soon as he gets clean and dressed up, you will see something different. Last night he was naturally embarrassed. The tramp manners will fall away from him with the tramp clothes."

Just as he said this the door opened and the stranger entered. Yes, now he was truly clean and well dressed. The valet had bathed him, cut his hair, and shaved him. Moreover, he was dressed in a good-looking suit of clothes which belonged to the ironmaster. He wore a white shirt and a starched collar and whole shoes.

But although his guest was now so well groomed, the ironmaster did not seem pleased. He looked at him with puckered brow, and it was easy enough to understand that when he had seen the strange fellow in the uncertain reflection from the furnace he might have made a mistake, but that now, when he stood there in broad daylight, it was impossible to mistake him for an old acquaintance.

"What does this mean?" he thundered.

The stranger made no attempt to dissimulate. He saw at once that all the splendor had come to an end.

"It is not my fault, sir," he said. "I never pretended to be anything but a poor trader, and I pleaded and begged to be allowed to stay in the forge. But no harm has been done. At worst I can put on my rags again and go away."

"Well," said the ironmaster, hesitating a little, "it was not quite honest, either. You must admit that, and I should not be surprised if the sheriff would like to have something to say in the matter."

The tramp took a step forward and struck the table with his fist.

"Now I am going to tell you, Mr. Ironmaster, how things are," he said. "This whole world is nothing but a big rat trap. All the good things that are offered you are nothing but cheese rinds and bits of pork, set out to drag a poor fellow into trouble. And if the sheriff comes now and locks me up for this, then you, Mr. Ironmaster, must remember that a day may come when you yourself may want to get a big piece of pork, and then you will get caught in the trap."

The ironmaster began to laugh.

"That was not so badly said, my good fellow. Perhaps we should let the sheriff alone on Christmas Eve. But now get out of here as fast as you can."

But just as the man was opening the door, the daughter said, "I think he ought to stay with us today. I don't want him to go." And with that she went and closed the door.

"What in the world are you doing?" said the father.

The daughter stood there quite embarrassed and hardly knew what to answer. That morning she had felt so happy when she thought how homelike and Christmassy she was going to make things for the poor hungry wretch. She could not get away from the idea all at once, and that was why she had interceded for the vagabond.

"I am thinking of this stranger here," said the young girl. "He walks and walks the whole year long, and there is probably not a single place in the whole country where he is welcome and can feel at home. Wherever he turns he is chased away. Always he is afraid of being arrested and cross-examined. I should like to have him enjoy a day of peace with us here—just one in the whole year."

The ironmaster mumbled something in his beard. He could not bring himself to oppose her.

"It was all a mistake, of course," she continued. "But anyway I don't think we ought to chase away a human being whom we have asked to come here, and to whom we have promised Christmas cheer."

"You do preach worse than a parson," said the ironmaster. "I only hope you won't have to regret this."

The young girl took the stranger by the hand and led him up to the table.

"Now sit down and eat," she said, for she could see that her father had given in.

The man with the rat traps said not a word; he only sat down and helped himself to the food. Time after time he looked at

Early landscape by Wassily Kandinsky (1866–1944).
Do you think that the rat-trap seller has indeed fallen into a trap? What do you predict will happen to him?

the young girl who had interceded for him. Why had she done it? What could the crazy idea be?

After that, Christmas Eve at Ramsjö passed just as it always had. The stranger did not cause any trouble because he did nothing but sleep. The whole forenoon he lay on the sofa in one of the guest rooms and slept at one stretch. At noon they woke him up so that he could have his share of the good Christmas fare, but after that he slept again. It seemed as though for many years he had not been able to sleep as quietly and safely as here at Ramsjö.

In the evening, when the Christmas tree was lighted, they woke him up again, and he stood for a while in the drawing room, blinking as though the candlelight hurt him, but after that he disappeared again. Two hours later he was aroused once more. He then had to go down into the dining room and eat the Christmas fish and porridge.

As soon as they got up from the table he went around to each one present and said thank you and good night, but when he came to the young girl she gave him to understand that it was her father's intention that the suit which he wore was to be a Christmas present—he did not have to return it; and if he wanted to spend next Christmas Eve in a place where he could rest in peace, and be sure that no evil would befall him, he would be welcomed back again.

The man with the rat traps did not answer anything to this. He only stared at the young girl in boundless amazement.

The next morning the ironmaster and his daughter got up in good season to go to the early Christmas service. Their guest was still asleep, and they did not disturb him.

When, at about ten o'clock, they drove back from church, the young girl sat and hung her head even more dejectedly than usual. At church she had learned that one of the old crofters of the ironworks had been robbed by a man who went around selling rat traps.

"Yes, that was a fine fellow you let into the house," said her father. "I only wonder how many silver spoons are left in the cupboard by this time."

The wagon had hardly stopped at the front steps when the ironmaster asked the valet whether the stranger was still there. He added that he had heard at church that the man was a thief. The valet answered that the fellow had gone and that he had not taken anything with him at all. On the contrary, he had left behind a little package which Miss Willmansson was to be kind enough to accept as a Christmas present.

The young girl opened the package, which was so badly done up that the contents came into view at once. She gave a little cry of joy. She found a small rat trap, and in it lay three wrinkled ten-kronor notes. But that was not all. In the rat trap lay also a letter written in large, jagged characters:

Honored and noble Miss:

Since you have been so nice to me all day long, as if I was a captain, I want to be nice to you, in return, as if I was a real captain: for I do not want you to be embarrassed at this Christmas season by a thief; but you can give back the money to the old man on the roadside, who has the money pouch hanging on the window frame as a bait for poor wanderers.

The rat trap is a Christmas present from a rat who would have been caught in this world's rat trap if he had not been raised to captain, because in that way he got power to clear himself.

Written with friendship and high regard,
Captain von Ståhle

Selma Lagerlöf **71**

First Thoughts

Did you think the peddler would return the thirty kronor in the end? Did you find his action believable? Why or why not?

Identifying Facts

1. In the rat-trap peddler's theory of the world, what is the bait? What happens after someone takes the bait?

2. Why does the peddler return to the crofter's cottage? Why does he later feel like a rat in a trap?

3. Why does the ironmaster invite the peddler into his home? What kindnesses does Edla show the peddler?

4. What do Edla and her father learn at church on Christmas morning? What do they discover when they return home?

Interpreting Meanings

1. What effect does Lagerlöf achieve with the opening words of the story? What **point of view** is associated with stories that open with these words?

2. After the peddler steals the thirty kronor, he becomes lost in a forest. The forest is clearly real, but it may also be a **symbol**—something that represents a larger idea or concept. What do you think the forest might **symbolize**? Cite details from the story to support your answer.

3. How does Lagerlöf's use of the **omniscient point of view** help us understand the peddler better than if he were telling the story himself?

4. In the peddler's note to Edla, how does he say he managed to avoid "this world's rat trap"? Why do you think the peddler signed his note "Captain von Ståhle"?

Applying Meanings

This story seems to suggest that if someone, even a criminal, is treated with honor and respect, he or she will become honorable and respectable. Do you think this is generally true, or do you think this theory is too simplistic? Discuss your opinion, giving examples from your own experiences.

Creative Writing Response

Writing a Different Conclusion. This story is about a man who was treated honorably and who then acted honorably. If the ironmaster and his daughter had not been kind to the peddler after they discovered he was not who they thought he was, how do you think the peddler would have reacted? How would the story have ended? Write a different ending to the story, beginning with the ironmaster's words on page 69, "What does this mean?"

James Joyce
1882–1941, Ireland

The Bettmann Archive

James Joyce was the oldest of ten children born to a poor Roman Catholic family in "dear, dirty Dublin." He was an enthusiastic student and eventually enrolled at Dublin's University College. When he was twenty, however, he left Dublin and repressive Irish Catholic society for the cosmopolitan cities of Paris, Trieste, Rome, and Zurich. At the time of his death he had not set foot in his homeland for nearly thirty years. Yet, ironically, all of his writings deal with his childhood home.

In his first major work, a collection of short stories called *Dubliners* (1914), Joyce provides snapshots of the paralyzing world from which he fled. His simple style here contrasts sharply with his later, more revolutionary, works. Joyce's poetic, autobiographical novel *A Portrait of the Artist as a Young Man* (1916) followed. The novel is full of experimental wordplay and was praised in literary circles on both sides of the Atlantic, though it had met with several rejections before an American company agreed to publish it. Joyce had even greater difficulty publishing his next book, *Ulysses* (1922). This novel vividly illustrates Joyce's blend of realism and symbolism, his groundbreaking use of inventive language, and his ability to capture characters' thoughts with the stream-of-consciousness technique. Loosely paralleling Homer's *Odyssey*, it takes place in Dublin on a single day—June 16, 1904—which, not coincidentally, was the day Joyce fell in love with his future wife, Nora Barnacle.

Joyce's last major work was *Finnegans Wake* (1939). This highly experimental novel is so filled with allusions, foreign expressions, and word coinages that no one can read it without guidance. For example, this passage describes Finnegan's fall off a wall and his subsequent death: "The great fall of the offwall entailed at such short notice the pftjschute of Finnegan, erse solid man, that the humptyhillhead of humself promptly sends an unquiring one well to the west in quest of his tumptytumtoes. . . ."

Although Joyce's books were banned, pirated, and often misunderstood, he is now regarded as one of the greatest literary talents of the twentieth century.

Reader's Guide

EVELINE

Background

"Eveline" is the fourth of the fifteen stories in *Dubliners*. Although it is one of the first stories Joyce ever wrote, his characteristic focus on the inner workings of characters' minds is already evident. In all the stories in *Dubliners,* Joyce uses a device he called an **epiphany**. Joyce borrowed the term from theology and used it to mean a sudden remark, symbol, or moment that sums up and clarifies the meaning of a complex experience. Joyce's epiphanies usually occur at or near the end of each story. Sometimes a character achieves a new insight; at other times, only the reader becomes aware of the character's true nature. In either case, the new awareness is not stated directly. Instead, Joyce provides details from which readers must make their own inferences.

Writer's Response

Think of a time when you suddenly changed your opinion, attitude, or behavior. Freewrite about the change and explain what caused it.

Literary Focus

Joyce was one of the first modernists to use **stream of consciousness** as a narrative technique. Early in the century, writers interested in psychology began to recognize that the human mind does not usually operate in a linear fashion; instead, it leaps around from thought to thought and feeling to feeling in what seems to be a random way. For example, eating a cinnamon roll for breakfast may remind a woman of the smell that often filled her grandmother's kitchen. She may then recall a childhood trip to her grandmother's in which the family car broke down, and that may remind her that her own car needs repairs, and so on. Joyce brought stream of consciousness to its highest form in his novels *Ulysses* and *Finnegans Wake,* and we see the beginnings of this technique in "Eveline."

EVELINE

James Joyce

Joyce once wrote that he chose to set his stories in Dublin "because that city seemed to me the center of paralysis." As you read, think about how this famous phrase, "center of paralysis," applies to the character of Eveline.

She sat at the window watching the evening invade the avenue. Her head was leaned against the window curtains and in her nostrils was the odor of dusty cretonne.[1] She was tired.

Few people passed. The man out of the last house passed on his way home; she heard his footsteps clacking along the concrete pavement and afterwards crunching on the cinder path before the new red houses. One time there used to be a field there in which they used to play every evening with other people's children. Then a man from Belfast bought the field and built houses in it—not like their little brown houses but bright brick houses with shining roofs. The children of the avenue used to play together in that field—the Devines, the Waters, the Dunns, little Keogh the cripple, she and her brothers and sisters. Ernest, however, never played: he was too grown up. Her father used often to hunt them in out of the field with his blackthorn stick; but usually little Keogh used to keep *nix*[2] and call out when he saw her father coming. Still they seemed to have been rather happy then. Her father was not so bad then; and besides, her mother was alive. That was a long time ago; she and her brothers and sisters were all grown up; her mother was dead. Tizzie Dunn was dead, too, and the Waters had gone back to England. Everything changes. Now she was going to go away like the others, to leave her home.

Home! She looked round the room, reviewing all its familiar objects which she had dusted once a week for so many years, wondering where on earth all the dust came from. Perhaps she would never see again those familiar objects from which she had never dreamed of being divided. And yet during all those years she had never found out the name of the priest whose yellowing photograph hung on the wall above the broken harmonium[3] beside the colored print of the promises made to Blessed Margaret Mary Alacoque.[4] He had been a school friend of her father. Whenever he showed the photograph to a visitor her father used to pass it with a casual word:

---

1. **cretonne** (krē·tän′): heavy printed cloth used for curtains.
2. **keep *nix***: serve as a lookout.
3. **harmonium:** small organ.
4. **promises . . . Alacoque** (à·là·kôk′): the Lord's promises to Margaret Mary Alacoque (1647–1690), French nun who as a child suffered from self-inflicted paralysis but was miraculously cured when she dedicated herself to a holy life.

DUBLIN FROM THE LIFFEY, engraving.

How does Eveline feel about leaving home?

"He is in Melbourne now."

She had consented to go away, to leave her home. Was that wise? She tried to weigh each side of the question. In her home anyway she had shelter and food; she had those whom she had known all her life about her. Of course she had to work hard both in the house and at business. What would they say of her in the Stores when they found out that she had run away with a fellow? Say she was a fool, perhaps; and her place would be filled up by advertisement. Miss Gavan would be glad. She had always had an edge on her, especially whenever there were people listening.

"Miss Hill, don't you see these ladies are waiting?"

"Look lively, Miss Hill, please."

She would not cry many tears at leaving the Stores.

But in her new home, in a distant unknown country, it would not be like that. Then she would be married—she, Eveline. People would treat her with respect then. She would not be treated as her mother had been. Even now, though she was over nineteen, she sometimes felt herself in danger of her father's violence. She knew it was that that had given her the palpitations. When they were growing up he had never gone for her, like he used to go for Harry and Ernest, because she was a girl; but latterly he had begun to threaten her and say what he would do to her only for her dead mother's sake. And now she had nobody to protect her. Ernest was dead and Harry, who was in the church decorating business, was nearly always down somewhere in the country. Besides, the invariable squabble for money on Saturday nights had begun to weary her unspeakably. She always gave her entire wages—seven shillings[5]—and Harry always sent up what he could but the trouble was to get any money from her father. He said she used to squander the money, that she had no head, that he wasn't going to give her his hard-earned money to throw about the streets, and much more, for he was usually fairly bad of a Saturday night. In the end he would give her the money and ask her had she any intention of buying Sunday's dinner. Then she had to rush out as quickly as she could and do her marketing, holding her black leather purse tightly in her hand as she elbowed her way through the crowds and returning home late under her load of provisions. She had hard work to keep the house together and to see that the two young children who had been left to her charge went to school regularly and got their meals regularly. It was hard work—a hard life—but now that she was about to leave it she did not find it a wholly undesirable life.

She was about to explore another life with Frank. Frank was very kind, manly, openhearted. She was to go away with him by the night boat to be his wife and to live with him in Buenos Aires where he had a home waiting for her. How well she remembered the first time she had seen him; he was lodging in a house on the main road where she used to visit. It seemed a few weeks ago. He was standing at the gate, his peaked cap pushed back on his head and his hair tumbled forward over a face of bronze. Then they had come to know each other. He used to meet her outside the Stores every evening and see her home. He took her to see *The Bohemian Girl* and she felt elated as she sat in an unaccustomed part of the theater with him. He was awfully fond of music and sang a little. People knew that they were courting and, when he sang about the lass that loves a sailor, she always felt pleasantly confused. He used to call her Poppens out of fun. First of all it had been an excitement for her to have a fellow and then she had begun to like him. He had tales of distant countries. He had started as a deck boy at a pound a month on a ship of the Allan Line going out to Canada. He told her the names of the ships he had been on and the names of the different services. He had sailed through the Strait of Magellan and he told her stories of the terrible Patagonians.[6] He had fallen on his feet in Buenos Aires, he said, and had come over to the old country just for a holiday. Of course, her father had found out the affair and had forbidden her to have anything to say to him.

"I know these sailor chaps,"[7] he said.

One day he had quarreled with Frank and after that she had to meet her lover secretly.

The evening deepened in the avenue. The white of two letters in her lap grew indistinct. One was to Harry; the other was to her father. Ernest had been her favorite but she liked Harry, too. Her father was becoming old lately, she noticed; he would miss her. Sometimes he could be very nice. Not long before, when she had been laid up for

---

5. **seven shillings:** A shilling is a former British coin worth five pennies, or one-twentieth of a pound. Seven shillings would have been a low salary.

6. **Patagonians** (pat'ə·gō'nē·ənz): inhabitants of the southern part of Argentina; at the time of the story, Patagonia was still a frontier area, similar to the American West of the last century.

7. **chaps:** fellows.

a day, he had read her out a ghost story and made toast for her at the fire. Another day, when their mother was alive, they had all gone for a picnic to the Hill of Howth. She remembered her father putting on her mother's bonnet to make the children laugh.

Her time was running out but she continued to sit by the window, leaning her head against the window curtain, inhaling the odor of dusty cretonne. Down far in the avenue she could hear a street organ playing. She knew the air. Strange that it should come that very night to remind her of the promise to her mother, her promise to keep the home together as long as she could. She remembered the last night of her mother's illness; she was again in the close dark room at the other side of the hall and outside she heard a melancholy air of Italy. The organ player had been ordered to go away and given sixpence. She remembered her father strutting back into the sickroom saying:

"Damned Italians! coming over here!"

As she mused the pitiful vision of her mother's life laid its spell on the very quick of her being—that life of commonplace sacrifices closing in final craziness. She trembled as she heard again her mother's voice saying constantly with foolish insistence:

"Derevaun Seraun![8] Derevaun Seraun!"

She stood up in a sudden impulse of terror. Escape! She must escape! Frank would save her. He would give her life, perhaps love, too. But she wanted to live. Why should she be unhappy? She had a right to happiness. Frank would take her in his arms, fold her in his arms. He would save her.

She stood among the swaying crowd in the station at the North Wall.[9] He held her hand and she knew that he was speaking to her, saying something about the passage over and over again. The station was full of soldiers with brown baggages. Through the wide doors of the sheds she caught a glimpse of the black mass of the boat, lying in beside the quay wall, with illumined portholes. She anwered nothing. She felt her cheek pale and cold and, out of a maze of distress, she prayed to God to direct her, to show her what was her duty. The boat blew a long mournful whistle into the mist. If she went, tomorrow she would be on the sea with Frank, steaming towards Buenos Aires. Their passage had been booked. Could she still draw back after all he had done for her? Her distress awoke a nausea in her body and she kept moving her lips in silent fervent prayer.

A bell clanged upon her heart. She felt him seize her hand:

"Come!"

All the seas of the world tumbled about her heart. He was drawing her into them: he would drown her. She gripped with both hands at the iron railing.

"Come!"

No! No! No! It was impossible. Her hands clutched the iron in frenzy. Amid the seas she sent a cry of anguish!

"Eveline! Evvy!"

He rushed beyond the barrier and called to her to follow. He was shouted at to go on but he still called to her. She set her white face to him, passive, like a helpless animal. Her eyes gave him no sign of love or farewell or recognition.

---

8. **Derevaun Seraun:** Some scholars suggest that the phrase is corrupt Irish Gaelic for ''the end of song is raving madness'' or ''the end of pleasure is pain.'' Although it does appear to be based on Irish Gaelic, the phrase as it stands is gibberish.

9. **North Wall:** wharf that is part of Dublin Harbor.

Why do you think Eveline decides to stay in Ireland rather than escape to Buenos Aires with Frank? Do you think she made the right decision?

Identifying Facts

1. What are Eveline's responsibilities in the Hill household?
2. What was Mr. Hill's reaction to the relationship between Frank and his daughter?
3. Summarize the final scene at the quay.

Interpreting Meanings

1. Find an example of loosely associated thoughts or memories that illustrate Joyce's use of the **stream-of-consciousness** narrative technique. What do Eveline's thoughts and memories reveal about her character and the kind of life she led before meeting Frank?
2. Around what **internal conflict** do Eveline's thoughts center? In what way is this also an **external conflict** between her and her society?
3. What finally causes Eveline to refuse to leave with Frank? What events or thoughts earlier in the story **foreshadowed**, or hinted at, this decision?

Applying Meanings

Do you think that the desire to assert our independence must always conflict with our responsibilities to others? Discuss this in relation to a time you felt a conflict between your duties to others and your own need for independence.

Creative Writing Response

Capturing Your Own Stream of Consciousness. In a freewriting exercise, try to capture your own **stream of consciousness**. Remember that stream of consciousness attempts to portray the thinking mind directly, without organizing the thoughts. Start with something you are seeing or thinking or feeling right now. Then jot down the flow of thoughts, emotions, memories, and associations that run through your mind. Don't worry about sentence structure or punctuation or even making sense. Just write down whatever enters your mind. If you wish, you may then edit these jottings and organize them so that you can use them later in a sketch or short story.

Critical Writing Response

Writing About an Epiphany. Write a brief essay about the **epiphany** in ''Eveline.'' In your essay, answer these questions:

1. What is the story's epiphany, or moment of awareness, about Eveline's true nature and desires?
2. What do we learn about Eveline at this point? How does this new awareness differ from our earlier impressions and the impressions she had of herself?
3. Would you say that *she* experiences a new awareness? Or is the awareness merely on the reader's part?

Before writing, you may find it helpful to jot down general answers to these questions and then find details in the story that will help you support and explain your answers.

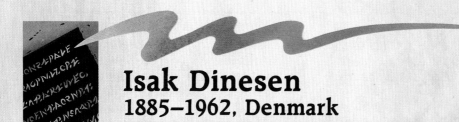

Isak Dinesen
1885–1962, Denmark

The Granger Collection, New York

When the American author Ernest Hemingway accepted the 1954 Nobel Prize for literature, he remarked that the award should instead have gone to Danish writer Isak Dinesen. Hemingway, who loved Africa and set several works there, was especially impressed with Dinesen's *Out of Africa*, an autobiographical account of her years in British East Africa, now Kenya. Although Dinesen is often recognized as the European author who best captured the beauty of the African landscape, she wrote equally well of northern Europe and the Danish upper class.

Born into a family of wealthy aristocrats in coastal Denmark, Dinesen's spirit of adventure was often at odds with her sheltered upbringing. After her father died and the cousin she loved refused to marry her, she defiantly set sail for Africa to marry the cousin's twin brother, Bror Blixen-Finecke. In 1914, the couple established a coffee plantation in what is now Kenya. Blixen's wayward lifestyle, however, left his wife often on her own. After the couple divorced in 1921, Dinesen ran the six-thousand-acre farm by herself for ten years.

Many of Dinesen's stories celebrate the power of women. In *Out of Africa*, Dinesen says that she often visited the Somali women on her property to listen to their stories. "It was a trait common to all these tales," Dinesen wrote, "that the heroine, chaste or not, would get the better of the male characters and come out of the tale triumphant. . . . Within this enclosed women's world . . . I felt the presence . . . of a Millennium when women were to reign supreme in the world."

In 1931, the price of coffee plummeted and Dinesen's plantation went bankrupt. In the same year her lover, the British pilot Denys Finch-Hatton, was killed in a plane crash. These events led Dinesen to return to Denmark and to devote herself to writing. Three years later she published *Seven Gothic Tales*, stories about mysterious events and persecuted heroines in Europe hundreds of years ago. Dinesen's international reputation was cemented with *Out of Africa*, which was published simultaneously in Denmark and Britain in 1937.

Reader's Guide

THE RING

Background

Denmark, Dinesen's homeland and the setting of "The Ring," is a democratic constitutional monarchy. At the time this story takes place, however, the nation was not democratic. The nobility lived in a grand style, while the rest of the population was very poor and sometimes had to turn to crimes such as poaching—trespassing on a landowner's property to hunt game or catch fish—in order to feed themselves and their families. Such crimes were harshly punished; a livestock thief often faced death if he were caught. Upper-class attitudes toward the plight of the poor varied widely. Some members of the upper class— like Sigismund in "The Ring"—held humanitarian views and advocated social, political, and economic reforms. Many others found such ideas dangerous.

As the story opens, we learn that Lise, the main character, has been determined since childhood to marry Sigismund, a landowner who nevertheless comes from a family of lower rank than hers. Lise's parents have finally agreed to the marriage, and the newlyweds are blissfully happy.

Writer's Response

What kind of person do you think that Lise, a newly married young woman from the upper class, will be? Write your predictions in a few sentences.

Literary Focus

Characters are often classified as static or dynamic. A **static character** is one who changes little or not at all in the course of the story. A **dynamic character**, on the other hand, changes in an important way as a result of the action of the story. The **protagonist**, or main character, of a story is almost always a dynamic character. How the protagonist changes or what he or she learns is usually our best clue as to a story's **theme**, or larger meaning.

THE RING

Isak Dinesen

Read until you come to the paragraph on page 85 that begins, "This meeting in the wood from beginning to end passed without a word. . . ." Stop and write down what you think will happen during this encounter. When you finish the story, see if your prediction was correct.

On a summer morning a hundred and fifty years ago a young Danish squire and his wife went out for a walk on their land. They had been married a week. It had not been easy for them to get married, for the wife's family was higher in rank and wealthier than the husband's. But the two young people, now twenty-four and nineteen years old, had been set on their purpose for ten years; in the end her haughty parents had had to give in to them.

They were wonderfully happy. The stolen meetings and secret, tearful love letters were now things of the past. To God and man they were one; they could walk arm in arm in broad daylight and drive in the same carriage, and they would walk and drive so till the end of their days. Their distant paradise had descended to earth and had proved, surprisingly, to be filled with the things of everyday life: with jesting and railleries, with breakfasts and suppers, with dogs, haymaking, and sheep. Sigismund, the young husband, had promised himself that from now there should be no stone in his bride's path, nor should any shadow fall across it. Lovisa,[1] the wife, felt that now, every day and for

the first time in her young life, she moved and breathed in perfect freedom because she could never have any secret from her husband.

To Lovisa—whom her husband called Lise[2]—the rustic atmosphere of her new life was a matter of wonder and delight. Her husband's fear that the existence he could offer her might not be good enough for her filled her heart with laughter. It was not a long time since she had played with dolls; as now she dressed her own hair, looked over her linen press and arranged her flowers, she again lived through an enchanting and cherished experience: one was doing everything gravely and solicitously, and all the time one knew one was playing.

It was a lovely July morning. Little woolly clouds drifted high up in the sky, the air was full of sweet scents. Lise had on a white muslin frock and a large Italian straw hat. She and her husband took a path through the park; it wound on across the meadows, between small groves and groups of trees, to the sheep field. Sigismund was going to show his wife his sheep. For this reason she

---

1. **Lovisa** (lō·vē′sə)

2. **Lise** (lē′sə)

A MOUNTAIN PATH AT CAPEL CURIG, WALES, EBENEZER DOWNARD, 1860.

had not brought her small white dog, Bijou,[3] with her, for he would yap at the lambs and frighten them, or he would annoy the sheep dogs. Sigismund prided himself on his sheep; he had studied sheep breeding in Mecklenburg[4] and England, and had brought back with him Cotswold rams[5] by which to improve his Danish stock. While they

---

3. **Bijou** (bē′zhoo′): ''jewel'' (French).
4. **Mecklenburg:** agricultural region in northern Germany.
5. **Cotswold rams:** the males of a kind of sheep originally bred in the Cotswold Hills of southwestern England.

walked he explained to Lise the great possibilities and difficulties of the plan.

She thought: "How clever he is, what a lot of things he knows!" and at the same time: "What an absurd person he is, with his sheep! What a baby he is! I am a hundred years older than he."

But when they arrived at the sheepfold the old sheepmaster Mathias met them with the sad news that one of the English lambs was dead and two were sick. Lise saw that her husband was grieved by the tidings; while he questioned Mathias on the matter she kept silent and only gently pressed his

Isak Dinesen   **83**

arm. A couple of boys were sent off to fetch the sick lambs, while the master and servant went into the details of the case. It took some time.

Lise began to gaze about her and to think of other things. Twice her own thoughts made her blush deeply and happily, like a red rose, then slowly her blush died away, and the two men were still talking about sheep. A little while after, their conversation caught her attention. It had turned to a sheep thief.

This thief during the last months had broken into the sheepfolds of the neighborhood like a wolf, had killed and dragged away his prey like a wolf, and like a wolf had left no trace after him. Three nights ago the shepherd and his son on an estate ten miles away had caught him in the act. The thief had killed the man and knocked the boy senseless, and had managed to escape. There were men sent out to all sides to catch him, but nobody had seen him.

Lise wanted to hear more about the horrible event, and for her benefit old Mathias went through it once more. There had been a long fight in the sheep house, in many places the earthen floor was soaked with blood. In the fight the thief's left arm was broken; all the same, he had climbed a tall fence with a lamb on his back. Mathias added that he would like to string up the murderer with these two hands of his, and Lise nodded her head at him gravely in approval. She remembered Red Riding Hood's wolf, and felt a pleasant little thrill running down her spine.

Sigismund had his own lambs in his mind, but he was too happy in himself to wish anything in the universe ill. After a minute he said: "Poor devil."

Lise said: "How can you pity such a terrible man? Indeed Grandmamma was right when she said that you were a revolutionary and a danger to society!" The thought of Grandmamma, and of the tears of past days, again turned her mind away from the gruesome tale she had just heard.

The boys brought the sick lambs and the men began to examine them carefully, lifting them up and trying to set them on their legs; they squeezed them here and there and made the little creatures whimper. Lise shrank from the show and her husband noticed her distress.

"You go home, my darling," he said, "this will take some time. But just walk ahead slowly, and I shall catch up with you."

So she was turned away by an impatient husband to whom his sheep meant more than his wife. If any experience could be sweeter than to be dragged out by him to look at those same sheep, it would be this. She dropped her large summer hat with its blue ribbons on the grass and told him to carry it back for her, for she wanted to feel the summer air on her forehead and in her hair. She walked on very slowly, as he had told her to do, for she wished to obey him in everything. As she walked she felt a great new happiness in being altogether alone, even without Bijou. She could not remember that she had ever before in all her life been altogether alone. The landscape around her was still, as if full of promise, and it was hers. Even the swallows cruising in the air were hers, for they belonged to him,[6] and he was hers.

She followed the curving edge of the grove and after a minute or two found that she was out of sight to the men by the sheep

---

6. **him:** that is, Sigismund; in Denmark at the time of the story, birds and other wild animals on an estate were the owner's property and anyone who hunted or caught them without permission would be prosecuted.

house. What could now, she wondered, be sweeter than to walk along the path in the long flowering meadow grass, slowly, slowly, and to let her husband overtake her there? It would be sweeter still, she reflected, to steal into the grove and to be gone, to have vanished from the surface of the earth from him when, tired of the sheep and longing for her company, he should turn the bend of the path to catch up with her.

An idea struck her; she stood still to think it over.

A few days ago her husband had gone for a ride and she had not wanted to go with him, but had strolled about with Bijou in order to explore her domain. Bijou then, gamboling, had led her straight into the grove. As she had followed him, gently forcing her way into the shrubbery, she had suddenly come upon a glade in the midst of it, a narrow space like a small alcove with hangings of thick green and golden brocade, big enough to hold two or three people in it. She had felt at that moment that she had come into the very heart of her new home. If today she could find the spot again she would stand perfectly still there, hidden from all the world. Sigismund would look for her in all directions; he would be unable to understand what had become of her and for a minute, for a short minute—or, perhaps, if she was firm and cruel enough, for five—he would realize what a void, what an unendurably sad and horrible place the universe would be when she was no longer in it. She gravely scrutinized the grove to find the right entrance to her hiding place, then went in.

She took great care to make no noise at all, therefore advanced exceedingly slowly. When a twig caught the flounces of her ample skirt she loosened it softly from the muslin, so as not to crack it. Once a branch took hold of one of her long golden curls; she stood still, with her arms lifted, to free it. A little way into the grove the soil became moist; her light steps no longer made any sound upon it. With one hand she held her small handkerchief to her lips, as if to emphasize the secretness of her course. She found the spot she sought and bent down to divide the foliage and make a door to her sylvan closet. At this, the hem of her dress caught her foot and she stopped to loosen it. As she rose she looked into the face of a man who was already in the shelter.

He stood up erect, two steps off. He must have watched her as she made her way straight toward him.

She took him in in one single glance. His face was bruised and scratched, his hands and wrists stained with dark filth. He was dressed in rags, barefooted, with tatters wound round his naked ankles. His arms hung down to his sides, his right hand clasped the hilt of a knife. He was about her own age. The man and the woman looked at each other.

This meeting in the wood from beginning to end passed without a word; what happened could only be rendered by pantomime. To the two actors in the pantomime it was timeless; according to a clock it lasted four minutes.

She had never in her life been exposed to danger. It did not occur to her to sum up her position, or to work out the length of time it would take to call her husband or Mathias, whom at this moment she could hear shouting to his dogs. She beheld the man before her as she would have beheld a forest ghost: the apparition itself, not the sequels of it, changes the world to the human who faces it.

Although she did not take her eyes off the face before her, she sensed that the alcove had been turned into a covert. On the ground a couple of sacks formed a couch; there were some gnawed bones by it. A fire must have been made here in the night, for there were cinders strewn on the forest floor.

After a while she realized that he was observing her just as she was observing him. He was no longer just run to earth and crouching for a spring, but he was wondering, trying to know. At that she seemed to see herself with the eyes of the wild animal at bay in his dark hiding place: her silently approaching white figure, which might mean death.

He moved his right arm till it hung down straight before him between his legs. Without lifting the hand he bent the wrist and slowly raised the point of the knife till it pointed at her throat. The gesture was mad, unbelievable. He did not smile as he made it, but his nostrils distended, the corners of his mouth quivered a little. Then slowly he put the knife back in the sheath by his belt.

She had no object of value about her, only the wedding ring which her husband had set on her finger in church, a week ago. She drew it off, and in this movement dropped her handkerchief. She reached out her hand with the ring toward him. She did not bargain for her life. She was fearless by nature, and the horror with which he inspired her was not fear of what he might do to her. She commanded him, she besought him to vanish as he had come, to take a dreadful figure out of her life, so that it should never have been there. In the dumb movement her young form had the grave authoritativeness of a priestess conjuring down some monstrous being by a sacred sign.

He slowly reached out his hand to hers, his finger touched hers, and her hand was steady at the touch. But he did not take the ring. As she let it go it dropped to the ground as her handkerchief had done.

For a second the eyes of both followed it. It rolled a few inches toward him and stopped before his bare foot. In a hardly perceivable movement he kicked it away and again looked into her face. They remained like that, she knew not how long, but she felt that during that time something happened, things were changed.

He bent down and picked up her handkerchief. All the time gazing at her, he again drew his knife and wrapped the tiny bit of cambric round the blade. This was difficult for him to do because his left arm was broken. While he did it his face under the dirt

Portrait of the Artist's Sister, Hans Thoma (1839–1924).

Describe Lise's feelings toward her husband: are they wholly loving, or ambivalent?

and suntan slowly grew whiter till it was almost phosphorescent. Fumbling with both hands, he once more stuck the knife into the sheath. Either the sheath was too big and had never fitted the knife, or the blade was much worn—it went in. For two or three more seconds his gaze rested on her face; then he lifted his own face a little, the strange radiance still upon it, and closed his eyes.

The movement was definitive and unconditional. In this one motion he did what she had begged him to do: he vanished and was gone. She was free.

She took a step backward, the immovable, blind face before her, then bent as she had done to enter the hiding place, and glided away as noiselessly as she had come. Once outside the grove she stood still and looked round for the meadow path, found it and began to walk home.

Her husband had not yet rounded the edge of the grove. Now he saw her and helloed to her gaily; he came up quickly and joined her.

The path here was so narrow that he kept half behind her and did not touch her. He began to explain to her what had been the matter with the lambs. She walked a step before him and thought: All is over.

After a while he noticed her silence, came up beside her to look at her face and asked, "What is the matter?"

She searched her mind for something to say, and at last said: "I have lost my ring."

"What ring?" he asked her.

She answered, "My wedding ring."

As she heard her own voice pronounce the words she conceived their meaning.

Her wedding ring. "With this ring"— dropped by one and kicked away by another—"with this ring I thee wed."[7] With this lost ring she had wedded herself to something. To what? To poverty, persecution, total loneliness. To the sorrows and the sinfulness of this earth. "And what therefore God had joined together let man not put asunder."

"I will find you another ring," her husband said. "You and I are the same as we were on our wedding day; it will do as well. We are husband and wife today, too, as much as yesterday, I suppose."

Her face was so still that he did not know if she had heard what he said. It touched him that she should take the loss of his ring so to heart. He took her hand and kissed it. It was cold, not quite the same hand as he had last kissed. He stopped to make her stop with him.

"Do you remember where you had the ring on last?" he asked.

"No," she answered.

"Have you any idea," he asked, "where you may have lost it?"

"No," she answered. "I have no idea at all."

---

7. **With this ring . . . I thee wed:** quotation from the vows exchanged at a wedding ceremony.

First Thoughts

Did you find any character or event in this story confusing or unsettling? If so, describe your thoughts and feelings about it.

Identifying Facts

1. How old is Lise when the story opens? What recent event has made her "wonderfully happy"?
2. What prompts Lise to hide in the clearing in the shrubbery? Summarize the events that take place there.
3. When Sigismund asks if she has any idea where she lost the ring, what does Lise say?

Interpreting Meanings

1. Why do you think Lise says at the beginning of the story that never having secrets from her husband allows her to move and breathe "in perfect freedom"?
2. Why do you think Lise keeps the incident in the glade a secret from her husband?
3. Which of the three main characters are **static**, or unchanging, and which are **dynamic**, or changing? Cite details from the story to support your answer.
4. What might the ring **symbolize**, or represent, in Lise's life? What change in Lise does the loss of the ring represent?
5. What is the **irony** in Sigismund being touched that his wife "should take the loss of his ring so to heart"?
6. Consider the biblical story of the fall of Adam and Eve. Explain how "The Ring" could be seen as a modern version of this story.

Applying Meanings

Do you think married people should never have secrets from each other? Or do you think secrets are inevitable? Discuss.

Creative Writing Response

Writing a Dialogue. If Lise and the stranger had spoken, what do you think they would have said to each other? Write the conversation that you imagine taking place between them. Be sure to punctuate their dialogue correctly.

Critical Writing Response

Analyzing a Dynamic Character. Write an essay analyzing Lise, concentrating on the change that occurred when she encountered the man in the glade. In describing her character before and after this incident, remember to consider **(a)** her appearance, **(b)** her actions, **(c)** what she says, **(d)** the response of other characters, and **(e)** the writer's direct comments about her. Include answers to these questions in your essay: Why did Lise decide to enter the glade? Why did she not speak with the man? Why did she offer him her wedding ring? Why did she not tell her husband about the man in the glade?

Language and Vocabulary

Words from Place Names

Many English words come from the names of cities and other places around the world. For example, the strong sheer cotton fabric known as *muslin* was first made in the city of Mosul in northern Iraq, and the fine thin linen known as *cambric* was first made in the northern French town of Cambrai.

All of the following English words also come from the names of places. Use a dictionary to help you explain the origin of each word and the meanings of any unfamiliar words.

1. chihuahua
2. denim
3. dollar
4. madras
5. mausoleum
6. mecca
7. sardine
8. shanghai
9. tangerine
10. tuxedo

Anna Akhmatova
1889–1966, Russia

The Granger Collection, New York

When writers express political views in their writing, they often run into problems with government authorities. Anna Akhmatova (uk·mät′ə·və), however, was persecuted for many years because she did *not* write on political themes. In the years following the Russian Revolution in 1917, only "socially useful" art was tolerated. Akhmatova was viciously attacked and her poems suppressed because they were too "personal."

Akhmatova grew up just outside St. Petersburg in the suburb that had been for centuries the summer palace of the czars. Here she became part of the thriving artistic community of prerevolutionary St. Petersburg. The poetry that Akhmatova began publishing in 1912 illustrates ideas of **acmeism**, a movement she and her husband, the poet Nikolai Gumilev, helped found. A reaction to French Symbolism (see page 983), which was then fashionable in Russia, acmeism rejected ambiguous symbols and the Symbolists' view of the artist as a mystic. For Akhmatova, the poet was not a visionary but a craftsperson, patiently building poems from words.

Akhmatova's early successes came to an abrupt end with the Russian Revolution in 1917. Five years later, her ex-husband was shot for allegedly plotting against the new Soviet government. Although he and Akhmatova were divorced at this time, she was deemed guilty by association and her poetry suppressed. She was not allowed to publish at all from 1922 to 1940, and in 1946 she was expelled from the Soviet Writers' Union.

In the years of Stalinist terror that followed, Akhmatova watched as friends and colleagues were arrested and sent to prison camps, many never to return. Her own son was imprisoned until Stalin's death in 1953. Akhmatova's long poem "Requiem" captures those dark days in the image of an anonymous woman standing month after month outside a St. Petersburg prison waiting for news of a loved one.

Akhmatova's home became the refuge and meeting place of a younger generation of Russian poets. In her final years, she was recognized officially again and was even allowed to travel to the West.

Reader's Guide

LOT'S WIFE

Background

"Lot's Wife" is based on the biblical incident recounted in Genesis 19 in which God sends angels to punish the city of Sodom for its wickedness. When the angels arrive disguised as men, only a man named Lot treats them justly. As a result, the angels warn him that God will destroy the city. They tell him to flee with his family and not look back. Lot's wife, however, disobeys the command and glances back. She is immediately turned into a pillar of salt. Akhmatova wrote "Lot's Wife," which was originally published in the *Paris Review*, in the early 1920s, shortly after her former husband was executed, but before the worst years of the Stalin era. At that time, many Russian intellectuals had begun to flee the country, but Akhmatova chose to stay.

Writer's Response

In a paragraph or two, describe how you might feel if you lived in a country that you were compelled to leave because of an intolerable situation—politics, war, or famine. Would you need to "look back" on your life there, or would you leave without a backward glance and concentrate on starting anew?

Literary Focus

Akhmatova was a founder of a movement called **acmeism**. Acmeists strove to eliminate ambiguous symbols from their work and instead emphasized the clear communication of ideas through richly textured language. As they saw it, part of the craft of poetry involved organizing thoughts into **stanzas**—line groupings that followed a **rhyme scheme**, or pattern of end-of-line rhymes. In the original Russian, "Lot's Wife" is arranged in **quatrains**, or four-line stanzas, in which the first and third lines always rhyme, as do the second and fourth lines. In this English translation by poet Richard Wilbur, the stanza structure and rhyme scheme match those of the original Russian.

LOT'S WIFE
Anna Akhmatova
translated by
RICHARD WILBUR

> *Read to the end of the second stanza. From the images of the city that the speaker recalls, how do you think she feels about leaving?*

THE STORY OF ABRAHAM AND LOT: THE FLIGHT FROM SODOM, RAPHAEL (1483–1520).

The just man followed then his angel guide
Where he strode on the black highway, hulking
   and bright;
But a wild grief in his wife's bosom cried,
Look back, it is not too late for a last sight

5   *Of the red towers of your native Sodom, the square*
Where once you sang, the gardens you shall mourn,

And the tall house with empty windows where
You loved your husband and your babes were born.

　　She turned, and looking on the bitter view
10　Her eyes were welded shut by mortal pain;
　　Into transparent salt her body grew,
　　And her quick feet were rooted in the plain.

　　Who would waste tears upon her? Is she not
　　The least of our losses, this unhappy wife?
15　Yet in my heart she will not be forgot
　　Who, for a single glance, gave up her life.

First Thoughts

How do you think the speaker feels about Lot's wife? Is she seen as foolish and disobedient, or as passionate and courageous? Do you agree with the speaker's views?

Identifying Facts

1. Whom does Lot follow?
2. What particular places in Sodom does Lot's wife want to see one last time? When she looks back and sees Sodom's destruction, what happens to her eyes and body?
3. According to the last stanza, where will Lot's wife not be forgotten?

Interpreting Meanings

1. What, in general, makes Lot's wife care about Sodom, despite its evils? What does the phrase "mortal pain" (line 10) suggest about how we should view her attitude?
2. Often a **stanza** expresses one unit of thought. Which of these stanzas contain one thought? Which express more than one thought?

3. Do you think that Akhmatova is simply retelling a biblical incident in verse? Reread the biography and background sections and explain how the poem might also relate to Akhmatova's life and to the political situation in Russia at the time she wrote the poem.

Applying Meanings

What events in your past do you look back on with affection or nostalgia? Do you think this is usually a negative or a positive thing to do? Explain, providing examples to illustrate your opinion.

Creative Writing Response

Writing a Rhymed Stanza. Write a four-line stanza imitating the *abab* rhyme scheme of Akhmatova's poem. On a separate sheet of paper, you may write two lines to complete the stanza below, or you may write one or more stanzas that are entirely your own.

(a) I came upon a secret place
(b) Where all the world was far away

(a) _____
(b) _____

Pasternak's Tribute to Akhmatova

Cornell Capa/Magnum Photos, Inc.

**Russian poet and novelist Boris Pasternak
(1890–1960).**

One of Anna Akhmatova's friends and colleagues was Boris Pasternak, a famous poet and novelist (his most famous novel is *Doctor Zhivago*). In this tribute poem, Pasternak compares Akhmatova's composition of poetry to the work of a seamstress. What does Pasternak's final line suggest about the value he found in all of Akhmatova's poetry?

To Anna Akhmatova
Boris Pasternak
translated by
Eugene M. Kayden

It seems I'm choosing the essential words
That I can liken to your pristine power.
And if I err, it's all the same to me,

For I shall cling to all my errors still.

I hear the constant patter on wet roofs,
The smothered eclogue[1] of the wooden pavements.
A certain city[2] comes clear in every line,
And springs to life in every syllable.

The roads are blocked, despite the tide of spring
All round. Your clients are a stingy, cruel lot.
Bent over piles of work, the sunset burns;
Eyes blear and moist from sewing by a lamp.

You long for the boundless space of Ladoga,[3]
And hasten, weary, to the lake for change
And rest. It's little in the end you gain.
The canals smell rank like musty closet-chests.

And like an empty nut the hot wind frets
Across their waves, across the blinking eyelids
Of stars and branches, posts and lamps, and one
Lone seamstress gazing far above the bridge.

I know that eyes and objects vary greatly
In singleness and sharpness, yet the essence
Of greatest strength, dissolving fear, is the sky
At night beneath the gaze of polar light.

That's how I call to mind your face and glance.
No, not the image of that pillar of salt
Exalts me now, in which five years ago
You set in rhymes our fear of looking back.

But as it springs in all your early work,
Where crumbs of unremitting prose grew strong,
In all affairs, like wires conducting sparks,
Your work throbs high with our remembered past.

---

1. **eclogue:** here, dialogue; used figuratively.
2. **A certain city:** St. Petersburg.
3. **Ladoga** (lä′dô·gä′): a large Russian lake.

Federico García Lorca
1898–1936, Spain

Art Resource, New York

On the evening of July 19, 1936, Chilean poet Pablo Neruda (ne·rōō′də) (see page 1294), then living in Spain, went to meet his friend Federico García Lorca (fe′de·rē′kô gär·sē′ä lôr′kä). Neruda waited and waited, but García Lorca never appeared because he had been kidnapped by Fascist supporters of Spanish dictator Francisco Franco. The kidnappers took García Lorca to a Granada cemetery, forced him to dig his own grave, and then shot him. The murder shocked the world, especially since the thirty-eight-year-old writer had never taken an active role in politics. Viewed as a martyr, he became

known as the "Poet of the Blood," and many of his poems about sorrow and death took on additional significance.

Granada, the site of his brutal murder, was also the city near which García Lorca grew up. Born to a well-to-do farm family, García Lorca valued the simple pleasures of rural life and also learned to love music, poetry, and all the arts. In 1919 García Lorca went to Madrid to study at the city's university. Among the talented artists he met there were Juan Ramón Jiménez, already a distinguished poet, and Salvador Dalí, the experimental painter whose surrealism would influence García Lorca's poetry and plays.

His most famous plays are tragedies dealing with thwarted womanhood. *Blood Wedding* (1933) is the story of a bride who runs away with a previous lover and is then murdered by her husband. This play, together with *Yerma* (1934) and *The House of Bernarda Alba* (1936), are considered to be García Lorca's finest dramatic works.

Shortly before his death, García Lorca published *Lament for the Death of a Bullfighter* (1935), considered to be the greatest elegy in modern Spanish poetry and a moving premonition of his own death. García Lorca was at the height of his celebrity when he was murdered by the Fascists. As Pablo Neruda later mourned, "Who could have believed there were monsters on this earth, in his own Granada, capable of such an inconceivable crime?"

Reader's Guide

THE GUITAR

Background

García Lorca often drew inspiration from the Andalusian (an'də·lōō'zhən) area of southern Spain where he grew up. Here there is a rich tradition of Gypsy folk music that includes *cante jondo* (kän'te hōn'dō), literally "deep song." Highly emotional and rhythmic, *cante jondo* is usually performed by colorfully dressed dancers in the passionate style known as flamenco. Many of García Lorca's poems, including "The Guitar," use modernist images to evoke the passionate feelings associated with *cante jondo*.

The guitar, on which *cante jondo* is traditionally played, is a musical instrument long associated with Spain. It arose, probably in sixteenth-century Spain, from the *vihuela* (ve·wā'la), a guitar-shaped instrument that medieval Spanish minstrels played in place of a lute. Later modifications resulted in what is known as the classical or Spanish guitar, whose reputation as a concert instrument was much enhanced by the great Spanish guitarist Andrés Segovia (si·gō'vē·ə).

Writer's Response

Different sounds bring different feelings and emotions to mind. Write a few sentences describing your feelings when you hear a guitar (electric or acoustic) or some other musical instrument.

Literary Focus

Free verse is poetry that is free of traditional rules of meter and form. While it does not have a regular **meter** or **rhyme scheme**, free verse does have a conversational rhythm. It also uses poetic devices such as **imagery**, **alliteration**, **repetition**, **assonance** (repeated vowel sounds), and **onomatopoeia**. Because there is no fixed meter to determine where each line should end, the free-verse poet must carefully decide how to break the poem into lines. In making such decisions, he or she considers both the emphasis in meaning and the sound or rhythm that a particular line break helps create. Translators of free-verse poetry must keep the same considerations in mind. "The Guitar," both in the original Spanish and in the English translation, uses free verse.

Federico García Lorca **95**

GUITAR, PABLO PICASSO, 1920.

THE GUITAR
Federico García Lorca
translated by
RACHEL BENSON AND ROBERT O'BRIEN

 As you read "The Guitar," note the images that convey emotion. What overriding emotion does García Lorca associate with the guitar?

The cry of the guitar
begins.
The crystals of dawn are
breaking.
5 The cry of the guitar
begins.
It's useless to stop it.
It's impossible to
stop it.
10 Its cry monotonous
as the weeping of water,
as the weeping of wind
over the snowfall.
It's impossible to

15 stop it.
It cries for
distant things.
Sand of the scalding South
seeking white camellias.[1]
20 It mourns the arrow without target,
evening without morning, and the first
bird dead upon the branch.
Oh, guitar!
25 Heart wounded by five swords.

---

1. **camellias** (kə·mēl′yəz): the blooms of an evergreen shrub that grows in mild climates; camellia bushes would not thrive in a hot, sandy place.

First Thoughts

What is the main emotion you felt while reading the poem? What is the poem's **tone**? Identify the words or phrases that contributed to this tone.

Identifying Facts

1. What word names the sound of the guitar in lines 1 and 5? What is its sound compared to in lines 11–13?
2. According to lines 20–23, what three things does the guitar mourn?
3. What is the guitar compared to in the last line?

Interpreting Meanings

1. In saying that it is "impossible to stop" the guitar, what might García Lorca be suggesting?
2. What aspects of human experience might the **image** in lines 18–19 represent? Explain your answer.
3. What do the **images** in lines 20–23 suggest about the causes of human sorrow?
4. What do you think the "five swords" represent?

Applying Meanings

Music is often used as a symbol for life itself. What instrument or type of music symbolizes life for you? Compare your answer with those of your classmates.

Critical Writing Response

Comparing Translations. In a brief essay, compare the translation by poet Robert Bly (below) with the translation by Benson and O'Brien that you have just read. Focus on differences in **diction**, or word choice, **imagery**, and the way wording in specific lines contributes to the overall sound or **rhythm**. In your topic sentence, state which translation you prefer. In the body of your paper, give examples to explain your preference. Conclude by restating which translation you like better and why.

The Guitar
Federico García Lorca
translated by
Robert Bly

The crying of the guitar
starts.
The goblets
of the dawn break.
5   The crying of the guitar
starts.
No use to stop it.
It is impossible
to stop it.
10   It cries repeating itself
as the water cries,
as the wind cries
over the snow.
It is impossible
15   to stop it.
It is crying for things
far off.
The warm sand of the South
that asks for white camellias.
20   For the arrow with nothing to hit,
the evening with no dawn coming,
and the first bird of all dead
on the branch.
Guitar!
25   Heart wounded, gravely,
by five swords.

Elie Wiesel
b. 1928, Romania

AP/Wide World Photos

Elie Wiesel (el'ē vē·zel'), a survivor of the Nazi concentration camps, turned to writing as a way to keep alive the memory of the atrocities committed during World War II. Seeking to avert new holocausts, Wiesel has also drawn attention to the plight of Cambodians, Soviet Jews, South African blacks, and other victims of persecution throughout the world.

Wiesel grew up among the devout Hasidic Jews of Sighet, a village in Romania's Carpathian Mountains. News from the outside world rarely filtered into this remote community. When the Nazis arrived in 1944 and rounded up all of the Jews, Wiesel and his family had no idea that they were being sent to Nazi death camps. They ended up in Auschwitz (oush'vits), the most infamous of these camps. Here Elie's mother and youngest sister were among the many Jews who were gassed to death. Meanwhile, Elie and his father were made slave laborers and sent to Buchenwald (bo͞o'k'n·wôld'), another concentration camp, where Elie's father died of starvation and disease.

Finally, on April 11, 1945, the surviving prisoners of Buchenwald were liberated by the United States Third Army. As one of Europe's millions of displaced persons, Wiesel at first settled in France. Always interested in writing, Wiesel began working for a French newspaper while still a student at the Sorbonne in Paris. His friend, the writer François Mariac, encouraged Wiesel to record for humanity the horrors he had endured. But Wiesel waited ten years before writing about his wartime ordeal. "I was afraid that words might betray it," he later explained. What Wiesel finally wrote was his autobiography *Night* (1958), one of the most significant and powerful accounts of Nazi atrocities ever written.

Since then, Wiesel has written many works about the Holocaust—the term he first used for the Nazi policy of systematic mass murder of European Jews. He has also described prewar Hasidic life and published several collections of Jewish folktales.

Reader's Guide

from NIGHT

Background

In the wake of Germany's defeat in World War I, an obscure war veteran named Adolf Hitler wrote a book called *Mein Kampf* that outlined his plan to restore German military might. According to Hitler, Germans were the "master race" and everyone else was inferior. The Jews in particular were made the scapegoat for all the world's evils.

Throughout the 1930s, Hitler's followers, the Nazis, made strong political advances in Germany. After their power was consolidated, they began invading neighboring nations. As more and more Jews fell into Nazi hands with each new German conquest, the Nazis secretly began transporting them to concentration camps like Auschwitz in Poland and Buchenwald in Germany. In these camps, Jews were shot by firing squads, executed in gas chambers, tortured in medical experiments, worked to death as slave laborers, or killed by starvation and disease. The dead were then burned in ditches or ovenlike structures called *crematoria*.

Jews were not the only victims of the Nazi mass murders. A similar fate awaited Gypsies, political opponents, homosexuals, captured Resistance fighters in conquered lands, and others. In all, about twelve million people were killed, nearly six million of them Jews. In Auschwitz alone, about two and a half million people were executed and another half million died of starvation and neglect.

Writer's Response

The horrors of World War II have been recorded in many books, movies, and television programs. Write a paragraph describing what you remember most clearly about such depictions of World War II events. What feelings did these depictions evoke in you?

Literary Focus

An **autobiography** is a written account of a person's own life. People write their autobiographies for a variety of reasons. Some simply want to recapture the events and emotions of their lives, while others want to make some political or philosophical point. Wiesel has said that his purpose in writing *Night* was to "bear witness" to what happened to Jews and other victims of the Nazis.

Elie Wiesel **99**

from NIGHT

Elie Wiesel

translated by

STELLA RODWAY

> *As you read this excerpt from* **Night***, focus on the events that Wiesel witnesses and his growing awareness of what is happening to him. Which details show that Wiesel, for all his emotional involvement, is nevertheless giving a fairly objective portrait of events?*

The train stopped at Kaschau, a little town on the Czechoslovak frontier. We realized then that we were not going to stay in Hungary. Our eyes were opened, but too late.

The door of the car slid open. A German officer, accompanied by a Hungarian lieutenant-interpreter, came up and introduced himself.

"From this moment, you come under the authority of the German army. Those of you who still have gold, silver, or watches in your possession must give them up now. Anyone who is later found to have kept anything will be shot on the spot. Secondly, anyone who feels ill may go to the hospital car. That's all."

The Hungarian lieutenant went among us with a basket and collected the last possessions from those who no longer wished to taste the bitterness of terror.

"There are eighty of you in this wagon," added the German officer. "If anyone is missing, you'll all be shot, like dogs. . . ."

They disappeared. The doors were closed. We were caught in a trap, right up to our necks. The doors were nailed up; the way back was finally cut off. The world was a cattle wagon hermetically sealed.[1]

We had a woman with us named Madame Schächter.[2] She was about fifty; her ten-year-old son was with her, crouched in a corner. Her husband and two eldest sons had been deported with the first transport by mistake. The separation had completely broken her.

I knew her well. A quiet woman with tense, burning eyes, she had often been to our house. Her husband, who was a pious man, spent his days and nights in study, and it was she who worked to support the family.

Madame Schächter had gone out of her mind. On the first day of the journey she had already begun to moan and to keep asking why she had been separated from her family. As time went on, her cries grew hysterical.

On the third night, while we slept, some of us sitting one against the other and some standing, a piercing cry split the silence:

"Fire! I can see a fire! I can see a fire!"

---

1. **hermetically sealed:** airtight; used figuratively here to mean completely sealed off.
2. **Schächter** (shäkh'tər)

Arriving at Auschwitz train station. *Immediately upon arrival at the concentration camp at Auschwitz, prisoners were divided into those who would go directly to the gas chambers and those who would be sent into slave labor.*

Snark/Art Resource, New York

There was a moment's panic. Who was it who had cried out? It was Madame Schächter. Standing in the middle of the wagon, in the pale light from the windows, she looked like a withered tree in a cornfield. She pointed her arm toward the window, screaming:

"Look! Look at it! Fire! A terrible fire! Mercy! *Oh, that fire!*"

Some of the men pressed up against the bars. There was nothing there; only the darkness.

The shock of this terrible awakening stayed with us for a long time. We still trembled from it. With every groan of the wheels on the rail, we felt that an abyss was about

Elie Wiesel   **101**

to open beneath our bodies. Powerless to still our own anguish, we tried to console ourselves:

"She's mad, poor soul. . . ."

Someone had put a damp cloth on her brow, to calm her, but still her screams went on:

"Fire! Fire!"

Her little boy was crying, hanging onto her skirt, trying to take hold of her hands. "It's all right, Mummy! There's nothing there. . . . Sit down. . . ." This shook me even more than his mother's screams had done.

Some women tried to calm her. "You'll find your husband and your sons again . . . in a few days. . . ."

She continued to scream, breathless, her voice broken by sobs. "Jews, listen to me! I can see a fire! There are huge flames! It is a furnace!"

It was as though she were possessed by an evil spirit which spoke from the depths of her being.

We tried to explain it away, more to calm ourselves and to recover our own breath than to comfort her. "She must be very thirsty, poor thing! That's why she keeps talking about a fire devouring her."

But it was in vain. Our terror was about to burst the sides of the train. Our nerves were at breaking point. Our flesh was creeping. It was as though madness were taking possession of us all. We could stand it no longer. Some of the young men forced her to sit down, tied her up, and put a gag in her mouth.

Silence again. The little boy sat down by his mother, crying. I had begun to breathe normally again. We could hear the wheels churning out that monotonous rhythm of a train traveling through the night. We could begin to doze, to rest, to dream. . . .

An hour or two went by like this. Then another scream took our breath away. The woman had broken loose from her bonds and was crying out more loudly than ever:

"Look at the fire! Flames, flames everywhere. . . ."

Once more the young men tied her up and gagged her. They even struck her. People encouraged them:

"Make her be quiet! She's mad! Shut her up! She's not the only one. She can keep her mouth shut. . . ."

They struck her several times on the head—blows that might have killed her. Her little boy clung to her; he did not cry out; he did not say a word. He was not even weeping now.

An endless night. Toward dawn, Madame Schächter calmed down. Crouched in her corner, her bewildered gaze scouring the emptiness, she could no longer see us.

She stayed like that all through the day, dumb, absent, isolated among us. As soon as night fell, she began to scream: "There's a fire over there!" She would point at a spot in space, always the same one. They were tired of hitting her. The heat, the thirst, the pestilential stench, the suffocating lack of air—these were as nothing compared with these screams which tore us to shreds. A few days more and we should all have started to scream, too.

But we had reached a station. Those who were next to the windows told us its name:

"Auschwitz."

No one had ever heard that name.

The train did not start up again. The afternoon passed slowly. Then the wagon doors slid open. Two men were allowed to get down to fetch water.

When they came back, they told us that, in exchange for a gold watch, they had discovered that this was the last stop. We would be getting out here. There was a labor camp. Conditions were good. Families would not be split up. Only the young people would go to work in the factories. The old men and invalids would be kept occupied in the fields.

The barometer of confidence soared. Here was a sudden release from the terrors of the previous nights. We gave thanks to God.

Madame Schächter stayed in her corner, wilted, dumb, indifferent to the general confidence. Her little boy stroked her hand.

As dusk fell, darkness gathered inside the wagon. We started to eat our last provisions. At ten in the evening, everyone was looking for a convenient position in which to sleep for a while, and soon we were all asleep. Suddenly:

"The fire! The furnace! Look, over there! . . ."

Waking with a start, we rushed to the window. Yet again we had believed her, even if only for a moment. But there was nothing outside save the darkness of night. With shame in our souls, we went back to our places, gnawed by fear, in spite of ourselves. As she continued to scream, they began to hit her again, and it was with the greatest difficulty that they silenced her.

The man in charge of our wagon called a German officer who was walking about on the platform, and asked him if Madame Schächter could be taken to the hospital car.

"You must be patient," the German replied. "She'll be taken there soon."

Toward eleven o'clock, the train began to move. We pressed against the windows. The convoy was moving slowly. A quarter of an hour later, it slowed down again. Through the windows we could see barbed wire; we realized that this must be the camp.

We had forgotten the existence of Madame Schächter. Suddenly, we heard terrible screams:

"Jews, look! Look through the window! Flames! Look!"

And as the train stopped, we saw this time that flames were gushing out of a tall chimney into the black sky.

Madame Schächter was silent herself. Once more she had become dumb, indifferent, absent, and had gone back to her corner.

We looked at the flames in the darkness. There was an abominable odor floating in the air. Suddenly, our doors opened. Some odd-looking characters, dressed in striped shirts and black trousers, leapt into the wagon. They held electric torches[3] and truncheons. They began to strike out to right and left, shouting:

"Everybody get out! Everyone out of the wagon! Quickly!"

We jumped out. I threw a last glance toward Madame Schächter. Her little boy was holding her hand.

In front of us flames. In the air that smell of burning flesh. It must have been about midnight. We had arrived—at Birkenau, reception center for Auschwitz.

The cherished objects we had brought with us thus far were left behind in the train, and with them, at last, our illusions.

Every two yards or so an SS man held his Tommy gun[4] trained on us. Hand in hand we followed the crowd.

An SS noncommissioned officer came to meet us, a truncheon in his hand. He gave the order:

"Men to the left! Women to the right!"

Eight words spoken quietly, indifferently, without emotion. Eight short, simple words. Yet that was the moment when I parted

---

3. **electric torches:** flashlights.
4. **Tommy gun:** submachine gun.

from my mother. I had not had time to think, but already I felt the pressure of my father's hand: we were alone. For a part of a second I glimpsed my mother and my sisters moving away to the right. Tzipora held Mother's hand. I saw them disappear into the distance; my mother was stroking my sister's fair hair, as though to protect her, while I walked on with my father and the other men. And I did not know that in that place, at that moment, I was parting from my mother and Tzipora forever. I went on walking. My father held onto my hand.

Behind me, an old man fell to the ground. Near him was an SS man, putting his revolver back in its holster.

My hand shifted on my father's arm. I had one thought—not to lose him. Not to be left alone.

The SS officers gave the order:

"Form fives!"

Commotion. At all costs we must keep together.

"Here, kid, how old are you?"

It was one of the prisoners who asked me this. I could not see his face, but his voice was tense and weary.

"I'm not quite fifteen yet."

"No. Eighteen."

"But I'm not," I said, "Fifteen."

"Fool. Listen to what *I* say."

Then he questioned my father, who replied:

"Fifty."

Victims of the Holocaust.

In what way were Madame Schäcter's visions prophetic?

The other grew more furious than ever.

"No, not fifty. Forty. Do you understand? Eighteen and forty."

He disappeared into the night shadows. A second man came up, spitting oaths at us.

"What have you come here for, you sons of bitches? What are you doing here, eh?"

Someone dared to answer him.

"What do you think? Do you suppose we've come here for our own pleasure? Do you think we asked to come?"

A little more, and the man would have killed him.

"You shut your trap, you filthy swine, or I'll squash you right now! You'd have done better to have hanged yourselves where you were than come here. Didn't you know what was in store for you at Auschwitz? Haven't you heard about it? In 1944?"

No, we had not heard. No one had told us. He could not believe his ears. His tone of voice became increasingly brutal.

"Do you see that chimney over there? See it? Do you see those flames? (Yes, we did see the flames.) Over there—that's where you're going to be taken. That's your grave, over there. Haven't you realized it yet? You dumb bastards, don't you understand anything? You're going to be burned. Frizzled away. Turned into ashes."

He was growing hysterical in his fury. We stayed motionless, petrified. Surely it was all a nightmare? An unimaginable nightmare?

I heard murmurs around me.

"We've got to do something. We can't let ourselves be killed. We can't go like beasts to the slaughter. We've got to revolt."

There were a few sturdy young fellows among us. They had knives on them, and they tried to incite the others to throw themselves on the armed guards.

One of the young men cried:

"Let the world learn of the existence of Auschwitz. Let everybody hear about it, while they can still escape. . . ."

But the older ones begged their children not to do anything foolish:

"You must never lose faith, even when the sword hangs over your head. That's the teaching of our sages. . . ."

The wind of revolt died down. We continued our march toward the square. In the middle stood the notorious Dr. Mengele (a typical SS officer: a cruel face, but not devoid of intelligence, and wearing a monocle); a conductor's baton in his hand, he was standing among the other officers. The baton moved unremittingly, sometimes to the right, sometimes to the left.

I was already in front of him:

"How old are you?" he asked, in an attempt at a paternal tone of voice.

"Eighteen." My voice was shaking.

"Are you in good health?"

"Yes."

"What's your occupation?"

Should I say that I was a student?

"Farmer," I heard myself say.

This conversation cannot have lasted more than a few seconds. It had seemed like an eternity to me.

The baton moved to the left. I took half a step forward. I wanted to see first where they were sending my father. If he went to the right, I would go after him.

The baton once again pointed to the left for him, too. A weight was lifted from my heart.

We did not yet know which was the better side, right or left; which road led to prison and which to the crematory. But for the moment I was happy; I was near my father. Our procession continued to move slowly forward.

Another prisoner came up to us:

"Satisfied?"

"Yes," someone replied.

"Poor devils, you're going to the crematory."

He seemed to be telling the truth. Not far from us, flames were leaping up from a ditch, gigantic flames. They were burning something. A lorry[5] drew up at the pit and delivered its load—little children. Babies! Yes, I saw it—saw it with my own eyes . . . those children in the flames. (Is it surprising that I could not sleep after that? Sleep had fled from my eyes.)

So this was where we were going. A little farther on was another and larger ditch for adults.

I pinched my face. Was I still alive? Was I awake? I could not believe it. How could it be possible for them to burn people, children, and for the world to keep silent? No, none of this could be true. It was a nightmare. . . . Soon I should wake with a start, my heart pounding, and find myself back in the bedroom of my childhood, among my books. . . .

My father's voice drew me from my thoughts:

"It's a shame . . . a shame that you couldn't have gone with your mother. . . . I saw several boys of your age going with their mothers. . . ."

His voice was terribly sad. I realized that he did not want to see what they were going to do to me. He did not want to see the burning of his only son.

My forehead was bathed in cold sweat. But I told him that I did not believe that they could burn people in our age, that humanity would never tolerate it. . . .

"Humanity? Humanity is not concerned with us. Today anything is allowed. Anything is possible, even these crematories. . . ."

His voice was choking.

"Father," I said, "if that is so, I don't want to wait here. I'm going to run to the electric wire. That would be better than slow agony in the flames."

He did not answer. He was weeping. His body was shaken convulsively. Around us, everyone was weeping. Someone began to recite the Kaddish, the prayer for the dead. I do not know if it has ever happened before, in the long history of the Jews, that people have ever recited the prayer for the dead for themselves.

"*Yitgadal veyitkadach shmé raba.* . . . May His Name be blessed and magnified . . . ," whispered my father.

For the first time, I felt revolt rise up in me. Why should I bless His name? The Eternal, Lord of the Universe, the All-Powerful and Terrible, was silent. What had I to thank Him for?

We continued our march. We were gradually drawing closer to the ditch, from which an infernal heat was rising. Still twenty steps to go. If I wanted to bring about my own death, this was the moment. Our line had now only fifteen paces to cover. I bit my lips so that my father would not hear my teeth chattering. Ten steps still. Eight. Seven. We marched slowly on, as though following a hearse at our own funeral. Four steps more. Three steps. There it was now, right in front of us, the pit and its flames. I gathered all that was left of my strength, so that I could break from the ranks and throw myself upon the barbed wire. In the depths of my heart, I bade farewell to my father, to the whole universe; and, in spite of myself, the words formed themselves and issued in a whisper from my lips: *Yitgadal veyitkadach shmé raba.* . . . May His name be blessed and magnified. . . . My heart was bursting. The moment had come. I was face to face with

---

5. **lorry** (lôr'ē): truck.

the Angel of Death....

No. Two steps from the pit we were ordered to turn to the left and made to go into a barracks.

I pressed my father's hand. He said:

"Do you remember Madame Schächter, in the train?"

Never shall I forget that night, the first night in camp, which has turned my life into one long night, seven times cursed and seven times sealed. Never shall I forget that smoke. Never shall I forget the little faces of the children, whose bodies I saw turned into wreaths of smoke beneath a silent blue sky.

Never shall I forget those flames which consumed my faith forever.

Never shall I forget that nocturnal silence which deprived me, for all eternity, of the desire to live. Never shall I forget those moments which murdered my God and my soul and turned my dreams to dust. Never shall I forget these things, even if I am condemned to live as long as God Himself. Never.

First Thoughts

What psychological effects do the events that Wiesel relates have on the prisoners? How do you think you would have acted in their place?

Identifying Facts

1. Throughout the journey, what does Madame Schächter say she sees? How do her fellow passengers respond?

2. What causes the soaring "barometer of confidence" among the prisoners? What do they smell when they arrive at Auschwitz?

3. What significance does Wiesel later attach to the SS officer's eight-word order? What does one prisoner tell Wiesel and his father to say about their ages?

4. As they move toward the flaming pit, what does Wiesel say he does not believe could happen "in our age"? How does his father respond?

Interpreting Meanings

1. Why do you think Madame Schächter sees what she does? Why do several prisoners treat her harshly?

2. Why do you think Wiesel and his father were told to lie about their ages?

3. Which details about the prisoners show that Wiesel has not allowed sentiment to overshadow accurate reporting of events in this **autobiography**?

4. What feeling overwhelms Wiesel's father shortly after they enter Auschwitz? What prompts his final remark?

5. Read the last three paragraphs aloud. What is the effect of Wiesel's use of **repetition**?

Applying Meanings

For years Wiesel was torn by two opposing feelings: that he should "bear witness" to what happened in the Nazi death camps, and that any attempt to put his concentration camp experiences into words would show disrespect for the dead. Which of these two concerns do you think is more important? Do you think that he ultimately resolved this problem or not?

Creative Writing Response

1. **Narrating a Dramatic Event.** Think of a dramatic incident in your recent past. It may have been a sports event, an accident, or a special time with a friend.

Let the reader know, as Wiesel does, exactly what happened and exactly how you felt every step of the way.

2. **Writing a Script.** Wiesel's *Night* is a powerful, unforgettable, dramatic narrative. Take a portion of this excerpt from *Night*—or find a copy of the book and choose another scene—and convert it to a dramatic script, complete with dialogue and stage directions. If you wish, perform the scene for the class, or tape it as a radio play.

Critical Writing Response

Writing About a Title. Wiesel chose one word as the title of his autobiography. This word carries more weight and more meanings than you might at first suppose. Think about the **connotations** and **denotations** of the word *night*. Are there both positive and negative connotations? Is Wiesel speaking of a literal or a figurative night? Use your thoughts about these questions to write a brief essay in which you explain why you think Wiesel chose to title his autobiography *Night*.

PRIMARY SOURCES

Elie Wiesel Accepts the Nobel Peace Prize

The Nobel Prize is awarded each year for achievements in the sciences and humanities. Generally considered the world's most prestigious award for a number of fields, the prize is named for Swedish chemist and industrialist Alfred Nobel, who instructed that, after his death, the interest on the considerable fortune he left behind be awarded annually to people who made outstanding achievements in the areas of chemistry, physics, medicine, economics, literature, and peace. The prize is awarded for a life's work, rather than a single achievement.

The following passage is from the speech Elie Wiesel gave on accepting the 1986 Nobel Peace Prize. To what does Wiesel's phrase "kingdom of night" refer? What light does the passage throw on Wiesel's past experiences and their effects on his future values and behavior?

It is with a profound sense of humility that I accept the honor you have chosen to bestow upon me. I know: your choice transcends me. This both frightens and pleases me.

It frightens me because I wonder: do I have the right to represent the multitudes who have perished? Do I have the right to accept this great honor on their behalf? I do not. That would be presumptuous. No one may speak for the dead; no one may interpret their mutilated dreams and visions.

It pleases me because I may say that this honor belongs to all the survivors and their children and, through us, to the Jewish people with whose destiny I have always identified.

I remember: it happened yesterday or eternities ago. A young Jewish boy discovered the kingdom of night. I remember his bewilderment; I remember his anguish. It all happened so fast. The ghetto. The deportation. The sealed cattle car. The fiery altar upon which the history of our people and the future of mankind were meant to be sacrificed.

I remember: he asked his father, "Can this be true? This is the twentieth century, not the Middle Ages. Who would allow such crimes to be committed? How could the world remain silent?"

And now the boy is turning to me: "Tell me," he asks. "What have you done with my future? What have you done with your life?"

And I tell him that I have tried. That I have tried to keep memory alive, that I have tried to fight those who would forget. Because if we forget, we are guilty, we are accomplices.

And then I explain to him how naive we were, that the world did know and remain silent. And that is why I swore never to be silent whenever and wherever human beings endure suffering and humiliation. We must always take sides. Neutrality helps the oppressor, never the victim. Silence encourages the tormentor, never the tormented.

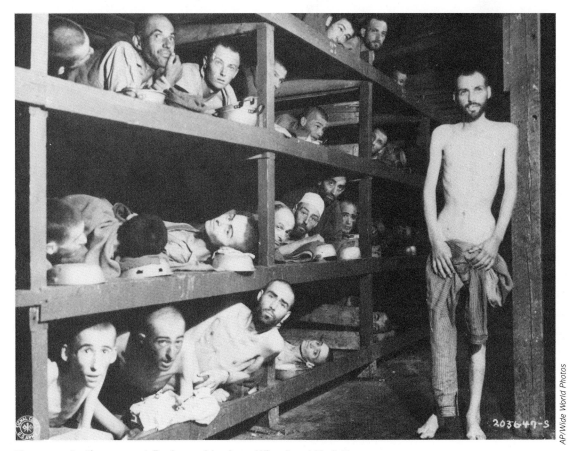

AP/Wide World Photos

The concentration camp at Buchenwald, where Wiesel and his father were eventually taken. *Wiesel lies in the second berth from the bottom, the center cubicle, on the right.*

Albert Camus
1913–1960, Algeria/France

Cartier-Bresson/Magnum Photos, Inc.

Albert Camus (ka·mōo′) believed that the question "Why" is asked at some point in every person's life. We wonder why we are here, what we are doing, and what life itself means. **Existentialism**, a philosophy that arose in response to the confusion many people felt in the early decades of the twentieth century, answered these questions by saying that neither the universe nor human life has any intrinsic, or already present, meaning. Camus reacted to this nihilistic attitude by formulating his own brand of humanistic existentialism. He believed that although existence probably has no ultimate meaning, human beings have the capacity—and the need—to create meaningful lives for themselves. Camus suggested that instead of giving up, each person must try to create his or her own meaning in life by making choices and acting upon them.

Of French and Spanish descent, Camus grew up in Algeria when it was still a French colony. After studying philosophy at the University of Algiers, Camus became active in Algeria's French-language theater. He also worked for a French-language newspaper and published two essay collections. In these essays and in his later work, Camus articulated his philosophy of moral commitment that later earned him the title of *le Juste*, "the just man."

In 1942, Camus published *The Stranger* and *The Myth of Sisyphus*, which illustrate the human quest for moral purpose in a meaningless world. The protagonist of *The Stranger* refuses to "play the game" by telling the white lies of polite society. He also refuses to believe in any religion or in human love. He nevertheless discovers, while in prison awaiting execution, a passion for the simple fact of life itself. In *The Myth of Sisyphus*, Camus reinterprets a classical myth to show that no matter how futile life may seem to be, a person can find value in the struggle to reach an impossible moral goal. Camus sees Sisyphus, whom the gods have condemned to endlessly roll a boulder uphill, as being happy because he has found meaning in rolling the rock. By extension, Camus believes that life is our rock—what matters most is that we do something with it.

Reader's Guide

THE GUEST

Background

Algeria was a colony of France for over a hundred years. During this time, native Arabs and Berbers were treated as second-class citizens. After a long and bloody struggle, the nation achieved independence in 1962 and most Algerians of European background left the country.

"The Guest" takes place when rebellion was brewing before Algerian independence. The protagonist, Daru, was born and raised in Algeria but is of European descent. As an Algerian and a Frenchman, he finds it impossible to take sides in the revolt. His feelings and experiences in many ways duplicate those of Camus, who was uncomfortable with his position as a European colonial in Africa. Much of Camus's fiction, like "The Guest," explores the topics of human freedom and isolation in mid-twentieth-century Algeria.

Writer's Response

In a few paragraphs, describe your feelings about the country, town, or neighborhood where you grew up. What aspects of your cultural or physical environment made you feel especially at home? Did you ever feel like an outsider? If so, why?

Literary Focus

Existentialism is a modern European philosophy that emphasizes the meaninglessness of the outer world. Some existentialists respond to this meaninglessness by recognizing that each person is free to make moral choices that define and give meaning to his or her life. Through their choices and actions, human beings are responsible for what they make of themselves and their lives. As you read "The Guest," consider how Daru's experiences reflect existentialist thinking.

THE GUEST

Albert Camus

translated by

JUSTIN O'BRIEN

❚ *Both Daru and the Arab are faced with existential choices in this*
❚ *story. What are their choices, and what decisions do they make?*

The schoolmaster was watching the two men climb toward him. One was on horseback, the other on foot. They had not yet tackled the abrupt rise leading to the schoolhouse built on the hillside. They were toiling onward, making slow progress in the snow, among the stones, on the vast expanse of the high, deserted plateau. From time to time the horse stumbled. Without hearing anything yet, he could see the breath issuing from the horse's nostrils. One of the men, at least, knew the region. They were following the trail although it had disappeared days ago under a layer of dirty white snow. The schoolmaster calculated that it would take them half an hour to get onto the hill. It was cold; he went back into the school to get a sweater.

He crossed the empty, frigid classroom. On the blackboard the four rivers of France,[1] drawn with four different colored chalks, had been flowing toward their estuaries for the past three days. Snow had suddenly fallen in mid-October after eight months of drought without the transition of rain, and the twenty pupils, more or less, who lived in the villages scattered over the plateau had stopped coming. With fair weather they would return. Daru now heated only the single room that was his lodging, adjoining the classroom and giving also onto the plateau to the east. Like the class windows, his window looked to the south, too. On that side the school was a few kilometers from the point where the plateau began to slope toward the south. In clear weather could be seen the purple mass of the mountain range where the gap opened onto the desert.

Somewhat warmed, Daru returned to the window from which he had first seen the two men. They were no longer visible. Hence they must have tackled the rise. The sky was not so dark, for the snow had stopped falling during the night. The morning had opened with a dirty light which had scarcely become brighter as the ceiling of clouds lifted. At two in the afternoon it seemed as if the day were merely beginning. But still this was better than those three days when the thick snow was falling amidst unbroken darkness with little gusts of wind that rattled the double door of the classroom. Then Daru had spent long hours in his room, leaving it only to go to the shed and feed the chickens or get some coal.

---

1. **the four rivers of France:** that is, four main rivers—the Seine, Loire, Garônne, and Rhône—that divide France geographically.

ARAB CITY, WASSILY KANDINSKY, 1905.

? *Why is Daru alone in the school?*

Fortunately the delivery truck from Tadjid,[2] the nearest village to the north, had brought his supplies two days before the blizzard. It would return in forty-eight hours.

Besides, he had enough to resist a siege, for the little room was cluttered with bags of wheat that the administration left as a stock to distribute to those of his pupils whose families had suffered from the drought. Actually they had all been victims because they were all poor. Everyday Daru would distribute a ration to the children. They had missed it, he knew, during these bad days. Possibly one of the fathers or big brothers would come this afternoon and he could supply them with grain. It was just a matter of carrying them over to the next harvest. Now shiploads of wheat were arriving from France and the worst was over. But it would be hard to forget that poverty, that army of ragged ghosts wandering in the sunlight, the plateaus burned to a cinder month after month, the earth shriveled up little by little, literally scorched, every stone bursting into dust under one's foot. The sheep had died then by thousands and even a few men, here and there, sometimes without anyone's knowing.

In contrast with such poverty, he who lived almost like a monk in his remote schoolhouse, nonetheless satisfied with the little he had and with the rough life, had felt like a lord with his white-washed walls, his narrow couch, his unpainted shelves, his

---

2. **Tadjid** (tä·jēd′)

well, and his weekly provision of water and food. And suddenly this snow, without warning, without the foretaste of rain. This is the way the region was, cruel to live in, even without men—who didn't help matters either. But Daru had been born here. Everywhere else, he felt exiled.

He stepped out onto the terrace in front of the schoolhouse. The two men were now halfway up the slope. He recognized the horseman as Balducci,[3] the old gendarme[4] he had known for a long time. Balducci was holding on the end of a rope an Arab who was walking behind him with hands bound and head lowered. The gendarme waved a greeting to which Daru did not reply, lost as he was in contemplation of the Arab dressed in a faded blue djellaba,[5] his feet in sandals but covered with socks of heavy raw wool, his head surmounted by a narrow, short chèche.[6] They were approaching. Balducci was holding back his horse in order not to hurt the Arab, and the group was advancing slowly.

Within earshot, Balducci shouted: "One hour to do the three kilometers from El Ameur!"[7] Daru did not answer. Short and square in his thick sweater, he watched them climb. Not once had the Arab raised his head. "Hello," said Daru when they got up onto the terrace. "Come in and warm up." Balducci painfully got down from his horse without letting go the rope. From under his bristling mustache he smiled at the schoolmaster. His little dark eyes, deep set under a tanned forehead, and his mouth sur-

rounded with wrinkles made him look attentive and studious. Daru took the bridle, led the horse to the shed, and came back to the two men, who were now waiting for him in the school. He led them into his room. "I am going to heat up the classroom," he said. "We'll be more comfortable there." When he entered the room again, Balducci was on the couch. He had undone the rope tying him to the Arab, who had squatted near the stove. His hands still bound, the chèche pushed back on his head, he was looking toward the window. At first Daru noticed only his huge lips, fat, smooth, almost Negroid; yet his nose was straight, his eyes were dark and full of fever. The chèche revealed an obstinate forehead and, under the weathered skin now rather discolored by the cold, the whole face had a restless and rebellious look that struck Daru when the Arab, turning his face toward him, looked him straight in the eyes. "Go into the other room," said the schoolmaster, "and I'll make you some mint tea." "Thanks," Balducci said. "What a chore! How I long for retirement." And addressing his prisoner in Arabic: "Come on, you." The Arab got up and, slowly, holding his bound wrists in front of him, went into the classroom.

With the tea, Daru brought a chair. But Balducci was already enthroned on the nearest pupil's desk and the Arab had squatted against the teacher's platform facing the stove, which stood between the desk and the window. When he held out the glass of tea to the prisoner, Daru hesitated at the sight of his bound hands. "He might perhaps be untied." "Sure," said Balducci. "That was for the trip." He started to get to his feet. But Daru, setting the glass on the floor, had knelt beside the Arab. Without saying anything, the Arab watched him with his feverish eyes. Once his hands were free, he

---

3. **Balducci** (bäl·dōō′chē)
4. **gendarme** (zhän·därm′): French police officer.
5. **djellaba** (jə·lä′bə): long robe worn by males in North Africa.
6. *chèche* (shā′shə): tall round cap worn by males in North Africa.
7. **El Ameur** (el äm·yōōr′)

Algerian landscape.

rubbed his swollen wrists against each other, took the glass of tea, and sucked up the burning liquid in swift little sips.

"Good," said Daru. "And where are you headed?"

Balducci withdrew his mustache from the tea. "Here, son."

"Odd pupils! And you're spending the night?"

"No. I'm going back to El Ameur. And you will deliver this fellow to Tinguit.[8] He is expected at police headquarters."

Balducci was looking at Daru with a friendly little smile.

"What's this story?" asked the schoolmaster. "Are you pulling my leg?"

"No, son. Those are the orders."

"The orders? I'm not ..." Daru hesitated, not wanting to hurt the old Corsican.[9] "I mean, that's not my job."

"What! What's the meaning of that? In wartime people do all kinds of jobs."

"Then I'll wait for the declaration of war." Balducci nodded.

"O.K. But the orders exist and they concern you, too. Things are brewing, it appears. There is talk of a forthcoming revolt. We are mobilized, in a way."

Daru still had his obstinate look.

"Listen, son," Balducci said. "I like you and you must understand. There's only a dozen of us at El Ameur to patrol throughout the whole territory of a small department[10] and I must get back in a hurry. I was told to hand this guy over to you and return without delay. He couldn't be kept there. His village was beginning to stir; they wanted to take him back. You must take him to Tinguit tomorrow before the day is over. Twenty kilometers shouldn't faze a husky fellow like you. After that, all will be over. You'll come back to your pupils and your comfortable life."

Behind the wall the horse could be heard snorting and pawing the earth. Daru was looking out the window. Decidedly, the weather was clearing and the light was increasing over the snowy plateau. When all the snow was melted, the sun would take over again and once more would burn the

8. **Tinguit** (ting'wēt)

9. **Corsican** (kôr'si·kən): native of the Mediterranean island of Corsica, governed by France but populated by many people of Italian descent.

10. **department:** here, administrative district.

Albert Camus **115**

fields of stone. For days, still, the unchanging sky would shed its dry light on the solitary expanse where nothing had any connection with man.

"After all," he said, turning around toward Balducci, "what did he do?" And, before the gendarme had opened his mouth, he asked: "Does he speak French?"

"No, not a word. We had been looking for him for a month, but they were hiding him. He killed his cousin."

"Is he against us?"

"I don't think so. But you can never be sure."

"Why did he kill?"

"A family squabble, I think. One owed the other grain, it seems. It's not at all clear. In short, he killed his cousin with a billhook.[11] You know, like a sheep, *kreezk!*"

Balducci made the gesture of drawing a blade across his throat and the Arab, his attention attracted, watched him with a sort of anxiety. Daru felt a sudden wrath against the man, against all men with their rotten spite, their tireless hates, their blood lust.

But the kettle was singing on the stove. He served Balducci more tea, hesitated, then served the Arab again, who, a second time, drank avidly. His raised arms made the djellaba fall open and the schoolmaster saw his thin, muscular chest.

"Thanks, kid," Balducci said. "And now, I'm off."

He got up and went toward the Arab, taking a small rope from his pocket.

"What are you doing?" Daru asked dryly.

Balducci, disconcerted, showed him the rope.

"Don't bother."

---

11. **billhook:** sharp hand tool usually used for cutting or trimming trees and bushes.

The old gendarme hesitated. "It's up to you. Of course, you are armed?"

"I have my shotgun."

"Where?"

"In the trunk."

"You ought to have it near your bed."

"Why? I have nothing to fear."

"You're crazy, son. If there's an uprising, no one is safe, we're all in the same boat."

"I'll defend myself. I'll have time to see them coming."

Balducci began to laugh, then suddenly the mustache covered the white teeth.

"You'll have time? O.K. That's just what I was saying. You have always been a little cracked. That's why I like you, my son was like that."

At the same time he took out his revolver and put it on the desk.

"Keep it; I don't need two weapons from here to El Ameur."

The revolver shone against the black paint of the table. When the gendarme turned toward him, the schoolmaster caught the smell of leather and horseflesh.

"Listen, Balducci," Daru said suddenly, "every bit of this disgusts me, and first of all your fellow here. But I won't hand him over. Fight, yes, if I have to. But not that."

The old gendarme stood in front of him and looked at him severely.

"You're being a fool," he said slowly. "I don't like it either. You don't get used to putting a rope on a man even after years of it, and you're even ashamed—yes, ashamed. But you can't let them have their way."

"I won't hand him over," Daru said again.

"It's an order, son, and I repeat it."

"That's right. Repeat to them what I've said to you: I won't hand him over."

Balducci made a visible effort to reflect. He looked at the Arab and at Daru. At last he decided.

"No, I won't tell them anything. If you want to drop us, go ahead; I'll not denounce you. I have an order to deliver the prisoner and I'm doing so. And now you'll just sign this paper for me."

"There's no need. I'll not deny that you left him with me."

"Don't be mean with me. I know you'll tell the truth. You're from hereabouts and you are a man. But you must sign, that's the rule."

Daru opened his drawer, took out a little square bottle of purple ink, the red wooden penholder with the "sergeant-major" pen[12] he used for making models of penmanship, and signed. The gendarme carefully folded the paper and put it into his wallet. Then he moved toward the door.

"I'll see you off," Daru said.

"No," said Balducci. "There's no use being polite. You insulted me."

He looked at the Arab, motionless in the same spot, sniffed peevishly, and turned away toward the door. "Goodbye, son," he

---

12. **"sergeant-major" pen:** type of fountain pen.

The village of In Salah, Algeria.

said. The door shut behind him. Balducci appeared suddenly outside the window and then disappeared. His footsteps were muffled by the snow. The horse stirred on the other side of the wall and several chickens fluttered in fright. A moment later Balducci reappeared outside the window leading the horse by the bridle. He walked toward the little rise without turning around and disappeared from sight with the horse following him. A big stone could be heard bouncing down. Daru walked back toward the prisoner, who, without stirring, never took his eyes off him. "Wait," the schoolmaster said in Arabic and went toward the bedroom. As he was going through the door, he had a second thought, went to the desk, took the revolver, and stuck it in his pocket. Then, without looking back, he went into his room.

For some time he lay on his couch watching the sky gradually close over, listening to the silence. It was this silence that had seemed painful to him during the first days here, after the war. He had requested a post in the little town at the base of the foothills separating the upper plateaus from the desert. There, rocky walls, green and black to the north, pink and lavender to the south, marked the frontier of eternal summer. He had been named to a post farther north, on the plateau itself. In the beginning, the solitude and the silence had been hard for him on these wastelands peopled only by stones. Occasionally, furrows suggested cultivation, but they had been dug to uncover a certain kind of stone good for building. The only plowing here was to harvest rocks. Elsewhere a thin layer of soil accumulated in the hollows would be scraped out to enrich paltry village gardens. This is the way it was: bare rock covered three quarters of the region. Towns sprang up, flourished, then disappeared; men came by, loved one another or fought bitterly, then died. No one in this desert, neither he nor his guest, mattered. And yet, outside this desert neither of them, Daru knew, could have really lived.

When he got up, no noise came from the classroom. He was amazed at the unmixed joy he derived from the mere thought that the Arab might have fled and that he would be alone with no decision to make. But the prisoner was there. He had merely stretched out between the stove and the desk. With eyes open, he was staring at the ceiling. In that position, his thick lips were particularly noticeable, giving him a pouting look. "Come," said Daru. The Arab got up and followed him. In the bedroom, the schoolmaster pointed to a chair near the table under the window. The Arab sat down without taking his eyes off Daru.

"Are you hungry?"

"Yes," the prisoner said.

Daru set the table for two. He took flour and oil, shaped a cake in a frying pan, and lighted the little stove that functioned on bottled gas. While the cake was cooking, he went out to the shed to get cheese, eggs, dates, and condensed milk. When the cake was done he set it on the window sill to cool, heated some condensed milk diluted with water, and beat up the eggs into an omelette. In one of his motions he knocked against the revolver stuck in his right pocket. He set the bowl down, went into the classroom, and put the revolver in his desk drawer. When he came back to the room, night was falling. He put on the light and served the Arab. "Eat," he said. The Arab took a piece of the cake, lifted it eagerly to his mouth, and stopped short.

"And you?" he asked.

"After you. I'll eat, too."

The thick lips opened slightly. The Arab

hesitated, then bit into the cake determinedly.

The meal over, the Arab looked at the schoolmaster. "Are you the judge?"

"No, I'm simply keeping you until tomorrow."

"Why do you eat with me?"

"I'm hungry."

The Arab fell silent. Daru got up and went out. He brought back a folding bed from the shed, set it up between the table and the stove, perpendicular to his own bed. From a large suitcase which, upright in a corner, served as a shelf for papers, he took two blankets and arranged them on the camp bed. Then he stopped, felt useless, and sat down on his bed. There was nothing more to do or to get ready. He had to look at this man. He looked at him, therefore, trying to imagine his face bursting with rage. He couldn't do so. He could see nothing but the dark yet shining eyes and the animal mouth.

"Why did you kill him?" he asked in a voice whose hostile tone surprised him.

The Arab looked away.

"He ran away. I ran after him."

He raised his eyes to Daru again and they were full of a sort of woeful interrogation. "Now what will they do to me?"

"Are you afraid?"

He stiffened, turning his eyes away.

"Are you sorry?"

The Arab stared at him openmouthed. Obviously he did not understand. Daru's annoyance was growing. At the same time he felt awkward and self-conscious with his big body wedged between the two beds.

"Lie down there," he said impatiently. "That's your bed."

The Arab didn't move. He called to Daru: "Tell me!"

The schoolmaster looked at him.

"Is the gendarme coming back tomorrow?"

"I don't know."

"Are you coming with us?"

"I don't know. Why?"

The prisoner got up and stretched out on top of the blankets, his feet toward the window. The light from the electric bulb shone straight into his eyes and he closed them at once.

"Why?" Daru repeated, standing beside the bed.

The Arab opened his eyes under the blinding light and looked at him, trying not to blink.

"Come with us," he said.

In the middle of the night, Daru was still not asleep. He had gone to bed after undressing completely; he generally slept naked. But when he suddenly realized that he had nothing on, he hesitated. He felt vulnerable and the temptation came to him to put his clothes back on. Then he shrugged his shoulders; after all, he wasn't a child and, if need be, he could break his adversary in two. From his bed he could observe him, lying on his back, still motionless with his eyes closed under the harsh light. When Daru turned out the light, the darkness seemed to coagulate all of a sudden. Little by little, the night came back to life in the window where the starless sky was stirring gently. The schoolmaster soon made out the body lying at his feet. The Arab still did not move, but his eyes seemed open. A faint wind was prowling around the schoolhouse. Perhaps it would drive away the clouds and the sun would reappear.

During the night the wind increased. The hens fluttered a little and then were silent. The Arab turned over on his side with his back to Daru, who thought he heard him moan. Then he listened for his guest's breathing become heavier and more regular.

The Hoggar Mountains near Tamanrasset, Algeria.
❓ *Does the Arab prisoner make Daru feel uncomfortable? Why?*

He listened to that breath so close to him and mused without being able to go to sleep. In this room where he had been sleeping alone for a year, this presence bothered him. But it bothered him also by imposing on him a sort of brotherhood he knew well but refused to accept in the present circumstances. Men who share the same rooms, soldiers or prisoners, develop a strange alliance as if, having cast off their armor with their clothing, they fraternized every evening, over and above their differences, in the ancient community of dream and fatigue. But Daru shook himself; he didn't like such musings, and it was essential to sleep.

A little later, however, when the Arab stirred slightly, the schoolmaster was still not asleep. When the prisoner made a second move, he stiffened, on the alert. The Arab was lifting himself slowly on his arms with almost the motion of a sleepwalker. Seated upright in bed, he waited motionless without turning his head toward Daru, as if he were listening attentively. Daru did not

stir; it had just occurred to him that the revolver was still in the drawer of his desk. It was better to act at once. Yet he continued to observe the prisoner, who, with the same slithery motion, put his feet on the ground, waited again, then began to stand up slowly. Daru was about to call out to him when the Arab began to walk, in a quite natural but extraordinarily silent way. He was heading toward the door at the end of the room that opened into the shed. He lifted the latch with precaution and went out, pushing the door behind him but without shutting it. Daru had not stirred. "He is running away," he merely thought. "Good riddance!" Yet he listened attentively. The hens were not fluttering; the guest must be on the plateau. A faint sound of water reached him, and he didn't know what it was until the Arab again stood framed in the doorway, closed the door carefully, and came back to bed without a sound. Then Daru turned his back on him and fell asleep. Still later he seemed, from the depths of his sleep, to hear furtive steps around the schoolhouse. "I'm dreaming! I'm dreaming!" he repeated to himself. And he went on sleeping.

When he awoke the sky was clear; the loose window let in a cold, pure air. The Arab was asleep, hunched up under the blankets now, his mouth open, utterly relaxed. But when Daru shook him, he started dreadfully, staring at Daru with wild eyes as if he had never seen him and such a frightened expression that the schoolmaster stepped back. "Don't be afraid. It's me. You must eat." The Arab nodded his head and said yes. Calm had returned to his face, but his expression was vacant and listless.

The coffee was ready. They drank it seated together on the folding bed as they munched their pieces of the cake. Then Daru led the Arab under the shed and showed him the faucet where he washed. He went back into the room, folded the blankets and the bed, made his own bed and put the room in order. Then he went through the classroom and out onto the terrace. The sun was already rising in the blue sky; a soft, bright light was bathing the deserted plateau. On the ridge the snow was melting in spots. The stones were about to reappear. Crouched on the edge of the plateau, the schoolmaster looked at the deserted expanse. He thought of Balducci. He had hurt him, for he had sent him off in a way as if he didn't want to be associated with him. He could still hear the gendarme's farewell and, without knowing why, he felt strangely empty and vulnerable. At that moment, from the other side of the schoolhouse, the prisoner coughed. Daru listened to him almost despite himself and then, furious, threw a pebble that whistled through the air before sinking into the snow. That man's stupid crime revolted him, but to hand him over was contrary to honor. Merely thinking

of it made him smart with humiliation. And he cursed at one and the same time his own people who had sent him this Arab and the Arab, too, who had dared to kill and not managed to get away. Daru got up, walked in a circle on the terrace, waited motionless, and then went back into the schoolhouse.

The Arab, leaning over the cement floor of the shed, was washing his teeth with two fingers. Daru looked at him and said: "Come." He went back into the room ahead of the prisoner. He slipped a hunting jacket on over his sweater and put on walking shoes. Standing, he waited until the Arab had put on his *chèche* and sandals. They went into the classroom and the schoolmaster pointed to the exit, saying: "Go ahead." The fellow didn't budge. "I'm coming," said Daru. The Arab went out. Daru went back into the room and made a package of pieces of rusk,[13] dates, and sugar. In the classroom, before going out, he hesitated a second in front of his desk, then crossed the threshold and locked the door. "That's the way," he said. He started toward the east, followed by the prisoner. But, a short distance from the schoolhouse, he thought he heard a slight sound behind them. He retraced his steps and examined the surroundings of the house; there was no one there. The Arab watched him without seeming to understand. "Come on," said Daru.

They walked for an hour and rested beside a sharp peak of limestone. The snow was melting faster and faster and the sun was drinking up the puddles at once, rapidly cleaning the plateau, which gradually dried and vibrated like the air itself. When they resumed walking, the ground rang under their feet. From time to time a bird rent the

---

13. **rusk**: dried bread.

space in front of them with a joyful cry. Daru breathed in deeply the fresh morning light. He felt a sort of rapture before the vast familiar expanse, now almost entirely yellow under its dome of blue sky. They walked an hour more, descending toward the south. They reached a level height made up of crumbly rocks. From there on the plateau sloped down, eastward, toward a low plain where there were a few spindly trees and, to the south, toward outcroppings of rock that gave the landscape a chaotic look.

Daru surveyed the two directions. There was nothing but the sky on the horizon. Not a man could be seen. He turned toward the Arab, who was looking at him blankly. Daru held out the package to him. "Take it," he said. "There are dates, bread, and sugar. You can hold out for two days. Here are a thousand francs,[14] too." The Arab took the package and the money but kept his full hands at chest level as if he didn't know what to do with what was being given him. "Now look," the schoolmaster said as he pointed in the direction of the east, "there's the way to Tinguit. You have a two-hour walk. At Tinguit you'll find the administration and the police. They are expecting you." The Arab looked toward the east, still holding the package and the money against his chest. Daru took his elbow and turned him rather roughly toward the south. At the foot of the height on which they stood could be seen a faint path. "That's the trail across the plateau. In a day's walk from here you'll find pasturelands and the first nomads. They'll take you in and shelter you according to their law." The Arab had now turned toward Daru and a sort of panic was visible in his expression. "Listen," he said. Daru shook his head: "No, be quiet. Now I'm leaving you." He turned his back on him, took two long steps in the direction of the school, looked hesitantly at the motionless Arab, and started off again. For a few minutes he heard nothing but his own step resounding on the cold ground and did not turn his head. A moment later, however, he turned around. The Arab was still there on the edge of the hill, his arms hanging now, and he was looking at the schoolmaster. Daru felt something rise in his throat. But he swore with impatience, waved vaguely, and started off again. He had already gone some distance when he again stopped and looked. There was no longer anyone on the hill.

Daru hesitated. The sun was now rather high in the sky and was beginning to beat down on his head. The schoolmaster retraced his steps, at first somewhat uncertainly, then with decision. When he reached the little hill, he was bathed in sweat. He climbed it as fast as he could and stopped, out of breath, at the top. The rock fields to the south stood out sharply against the blue sky, but on the plain to the east a steamy heat was already rising. And in that slight haze, Daru, with heavy heart, made out the Arab walking slowly on the road to prison.

A little later, standing before the window of the classroom, the schoolmaster was watching the clear light bathing the whole surface of the plateau, but he hardly saw it. Behind him on the blackboard, among the winding French rivers, sprawled the clumsily chalked-up words he had just read: "You handed over our brother. You will pay for this." Daru looked at the sky, the plateau, and, beyond, the invisible lands stretching all the way to the sea. In this vast landscape he had loved so much, he was alone.

---

14. **a thousand francs:** about eighty dollars at the time of the story; the franc, chief monetary unit of France, was used in Algeria while it was a French colony.

First Thoughts

"The Guest" has a quiet but troubling ending. Do you think Daru made the right decision? What do you think happens after the end of the story?

Identifying Facts

1. What crime has the Arab committed? What is Daru's attitude toward that crime and toward the colonial government's action in relation to it?

2. What two routes does Daru point out to the Arab? Which route does the Arab take?

3. On returning to his schoolhouse, what message does Daru find on the blackboard?

Interpreting Meanings

1. What does Balducci mean when he says that Daru has "always been a little cracked"? Why does Balducci feel that Daru has insulted him?

2. Why doesn't Daru want to admit the existence of a bond between himself and the Arab? Do Daru's actions acknowledge such a brotherhood? Cite details from the story to support your answer.

3. Why do you think Daru feels "empty and vulnerable"? Do you think his vulnerability is heroic? Do you agree that handing over the Arab is "contrary to honor"? Explain your opinions.

4. Why do you think the Arab chooses the route he does? Based on his choice, in what way is he different from Daru? How do both men's choices reflect Camus's view of **existentialism**?

5. Who wrote the message on Daru's blackboard? What does the appearance of the message suggest about Daru's refusal to take sides in his society's political conflicts?

Applying Meanings

Can freedom be frightening? Do you think it can cause a feeling of isolation? Explain your answers.

Creative Writing Response

Continuing the Story. Imagine what happens between Daru and the Arab after the story ends. Does Daru defend his decision and actions? If so, how? Write the conversation or action that might occur.

Critical Writing Response

Writing About Existentialism. Unlike earlier philosophies that attempted to define objective moral truths and then apply them to the specifics of human existence, **existentialism** suggests that existence comes first and can never be completely defined or understood in objective, scientific terms. Instead, each person gives a *subjective* meaning or purpose to his or her own life through his or her actions and decisions. Existentialism thus places great emphasis on individual freedom. Such freedom, however, can be either liberating or isolating, since each person must journey alone down his or her own moral road.

In a three-paragraph essay, write about how Daru's behavior, attitudes, and experiences reflect Camus's ideas of existentialism. Be sure to address the following three questions. Include a thesis statement at the beginning of your essay.

1. How does Daru's disgust with both the Arab's crime and the colonial government's punishment reflect ideas of existentialism?

2. How does existential thinking help explain Daru's refusal to take the Arab any farther after showing him the two routes?

3. What does the story's outcome suggest about the existentialist's relationship to society?

Italo Calvino
1923–1985, Italy

AP/Wide World Photos

When asked who he considered the greatest Italian writer, Italo Calvino (ē·tal′ō kal·vē′nō) did not choose a poet, playwright, or novelist. Instead he named the Renaissance astronomer, physicist, and philosopher Galileo Galilei. Among Galileo's many accomplishments was the invention of an early telescope. Calvino found Galileo's prose surprisingly poetic and imaginative, especially his descriptions of the moon, which deftly combined objective scientific details with a unique lyrical vision. Calvino's own background in science and in literature led to a similar ability to combine poetic vision and scientific details.

The son of two scientists, Calvino was born in Cuba while his parents were studying tropical plant life there. Soon after Calvino's birth, the family returned to Italy and Calvino's father took a job running a botanical garden in San Remo, on the Italian Riviera. It was here that Calvino fell in love with nature. He intended to study agricultural science at the University of Turin, but World War II interrupted his plans.

Calvino was only nineteen when he joined the Italian Resistance to fight the Germans. After the war Calvino returned to college but decided to study literature rather than science. Upon graduating, he joined the staff of a newly formed publishing house in Turin. He soon published his first book, *The Path to the Nest of Spiders* (1947), a realistic novel based on his experiences as a Resistance fighter. Calvino also began collecting folktales from all over Italy. These were published in *Italian Folktales* (1956).

Calvino's first English anthology, *Adam, One Afternoon* (1957), contains some stories that blend elements of fantasy and realism, and others that are purely realistic. His later works, however, are more fanciful. *Baron in the Trees* (1957) is a story about a boy who moves to the treetops when his family annoys him, and then decides to spend the rest of his life there. The hero of *The Nonexistent Knight* (1962) is an empty suit of armor named Agilulf. The stories are often allegorical, with symbolic meanings that apply to today's world.

THE ENCHANTED GARDEN
Italo Calvino
translated by
ARCHIBALD COLQUHOUN AND PEGGY WRIGHT

Reader's Guide

Background Many of the stories in *Adam, One Afternoon* (1957) are set on the Italian Riviera, the fashionable seaside resort where Calvino spent his youth. Like the French Riviera, the Italian Riviera has over the years attracted many wealthy summer residents who built elegant mansions along the coast. Such mansions—or villas, as they are called in Italy—are usually hidden away behind enclosed private gardens like the one described in the following story.

Writer's Response Think of a place that seemed magical or "enchanted" to you—either during your childhood or more recently. In a few sentences, describe the place and how it made you feel.

Literary Focus **Atmosphere** is the emotional effect, the mood or feeling, created by the **setting** of a work of literature. The **atmosphere** may be mild or harsh, gloomy or cheery, beautiful or ugly. It is usually created through evocative imagery and **descriptive details**. The adjective in the title of this story gives us an idea of the atmosphere that Calvino is trying to create.

THE ENCHANTED GARDEN

 In whose eyes is the garden in this story "enchanted"?

Giovannino and Serenella were strolling along the railroad tracks. Below was a scaly sea of somber, clear blue; above, a sky lightly streaked with white clouds. The railroad tracks were shimmering and burning hot. It was fun going along the tracks, there were so many games to play—he balancing on one rail and holding her hand while she walked along on the other, or else both jumping from one sleeper[1] to the next without ever letting their feet touch the stones in between. Giovannino and Serenella had been out looking for crabs, and now they had decided to explore the raiload tracks as far as the tunnel. He liked playing with Serenella, for she did not behave as all the other

---
1. **sleeper:** tie or crossbar supporting a railroad track.

Garden in May, Maria Oakey Dewing, 1895.

little girls did, forever getting frightened or bursting into tears at every joke. Whenever Giovannino said, "Let's go there," or "Let's do this," Serenella followed without a word.

Ping! They both gave a start and looked up. A telephone wire had snapped off the top of the pole. It sounded like an iron stork shutting its beak in a hurry. They stood with their noses in the air and watched. What a pity not to have seen it! Now it would never happen again.

"There's a train coming," said Giovannino.

Serenella did not move from the rail. "Where from?" she asked.

Giovannino looked around in a knowledgeable way. He pointed at the black hole of the tunnel, which showed clear one moment, then misty the next, through the invisible heat haze rising from the stony track.

"From there," he said. It was as though they already heard a snort from the darkness of the tunnel, and saw the train suddenly appear, belching out fire and smoke, the wheels mercilessly eating up the rails as it hurtled toward them.

"Where shall we go, Giovannino?"

There were big gray aloes down by the sea, surrounded by dense, impenetrable nettles, while up the hillside ran a rambling hedge with thick leaves but no flowers. There was still no sign of the train; perhaps it was coasting, with the engine cut off, and would jump out at them all of a sudden. But Giovannino had now found an opening in the hedge. "This way," he called.

The fence under the rambling hedge was an old bent rail. At one point it twisted about on the ground like the corner of a sheet of paper. Giovannino had slipped into the hole and already half vanished.

"Give me a hand, Giovannino."

They found themselves in the corner of a garden, on all fours in a flower bed, with their hair full of dry leaves and moss. Everything was quiet; not a leaf was stirring.

"Come on," said Giovannino, and Serenella nodded in reply.

There were big old flesh-colored eucalyptus trees and winding gravel paths. Giovannino and Serenella tiptoed along the paths, taking care not to crunch the gravel. Suppose the owners appeared now?

Everything was so beautiful: sharp bends in the path and high, curling eucalyptus leaves and patches of sky. But there was always the worrying thought that it was not their garden, and that they might be chased away any moment. Yet not a sound could be heard. A flight of chattering sparrows rose from a clump of arbutus[2] at a turn in the path. Then all was silent again. Perhaps it was an abandoned garden?

But the shade of the big trees came to an end, and they found themselves under the open sky facing flower beds filled with neat rows of petunias and convolvulus,[3] and paths and balustrades and rows of box trees.[4] And up at the end of the garden was a large villa with flashing windowpanes and yellow-and-orange curtains.

And it was all quite deserted. The two children crept forward, treading carefully over the gravel: perhaps the windows would suddenly be flung open, and angry ladies and gentlemen appear on the terraces to unleash great dogs down the paths. Now they found a wheelbarrow standing near a ditch. Giovannino picked it up by the handles and began pushing it along: it creaked like a whistle at every turn. Serenella seated herself in it and they moved slowly forward, Giovannino pushing the barrow with her on top, along the flower beds and fountains.

Every now and then Serenella would point to a flower and say in a low voice, "That one," and Giovannino would put the barrow down, pluck it, and give it to her. Soon she had a lovely bouquet.

Eventually the gravel ended and they reached an open space paved in bricks and mortar. In the middle of this space was a big empty rectangle: a swimming pool. They crept up to the edge; it was lined with blue tiles and filled to the brim with clear water. How lovely it would be to swim in!

"Shall we go for a dip?" Giovannino asked Serenella. The idea must have been quite dangerous if he asked her instead of just saying, "In we go!" But the water was so clear and blue, and Serenella was never afraid. She jumped off the barrow and put her bunch of flowers in it. They were already in bathing suits, since they'd been out for crabs before. Giovannino plunged in—not from the diving board, because the splash would have made too much noise, but from the edge of the pool. Down and down he went with his eyes wide open, seeing only the blue from the tiles and his pink hands like goldfish; it was not the same as under the sea, full of shapeless green-black shadows.

---

2. **arbutus** (är·by$\overline{oo}$t′əs): flowering shrubs or trailing plants with strawberrylike fruit.
3. **convolvulus** (kən·väl′vy$\overline{oo}$·ləs): compact, bushy morning glories.
4. **box trees:** small trees that are often clipped and used as hedges; also called boxwood.

A pink form appeared above him: Serenella! He took her hand and they swam up to the surface, a bit anxiously. No, there was no one watching them at all. But it was not so nice as they'd thought it would be; they always had that uncomfortable feeling that they had no right to any of this, and might be chased out at any moment.

They scrambled out of the water, and there beside the swimming pool they found a Ping-Pong table. Instantly Giovannino picked up the paddle and hit the ball, and Serenella, on the other side, was quick to return his shot. And so they went on playing, though giving only light taps at the ball, in case someone in the villa heard them. Then Giovannino, in trying to parry a shot that had bounced high, sent the ball sailing away through the air and smack against a gong hanging in a pergola.[5] There was a long, somber boom. The two children crouched down behind a clump of ranunculus.[6] At once two menservants in white coats appeared, carrying big trays; when they had put the trays down on a round table under an orange-and-yellow-striped umbrella, off they went.

Giovannino and Serenella crept up to the table. There was tea, milk, and sponge cake. They had only to sit down and help themselves. They poured out two cups of tea and cut two slices of cake. But somehow they did not feel at all at ease, and sat perched on the edge of their chairs, their knees shaking. And they could not really enjoy the tea and cake, for nothing seemed to have any taste. Everything in the garden was like that: lovely but impossible to enjoy properly, with that worrying feeling inside that they were only there through an odd stroke of luck,

and the fear that they'd soon have to give an account of themselves.

Very quietly they tiptoed up to the villa. Between the slits of a Venetian blind they saw a beautiful shady room, with collections of butterflies hanging on the walls. And in the room was a pale little boy. Lucky boy, he must be the owner of this villa and garden. He was stretched out on a chaise longue, turning the pages of a large book filled with figures. He had big white hands and wore pajamas buttoned up to the neck, though it was summer.

As the two children went on peeping through the slits, the pounding of their hearts gradually subsided. Why, the little rich boy seemed to be sitting there and turning the pages and glancing around with more anxiety and worry than their own. Then he got up and tiptoed around, as if he were afraid that at any moment someone would come and turn him out, as if he felt that that book, that chaise longue, and those butterflies framed on the wall, the garden and games and tea trays, the swimming pool and paths, were only granted to him by some enormous mistake, as if he were incapable of enjoying them and felt the bitterness of the mistake as his own fault.

The pale boy was wandering about his shady room furtively, touching with his white fingers the edges of the cases studded with butterflies; then he stopped to listen. The pounding of Giovannino and Serenella's hearts, which had died down, now got harder than ever. Perhaps it was the fear of a spell that hung over this villa and garden and over all these lovely, comfortable things, the residue of some injustice committed long ago.

Clouds darkened the sun. Very quietly Giovannino and Serenella crept away. They went back along the same paths they had

---

5. **pergola** (pʉr'gə·lə): arbor; trellis.
6. **ranunculus** (rə·nung'kyoo·ləs): buttercups.

come, stepping fast but never at a run. And they went through the hedge again on all fours. Between the aloes they found a path leading down to the small, stony beach, with banks of seaweed along the shore. Then they invented a wonderful new game: a seaweed fight. They threw great handfuls of it in each other's faces till late in the afternoon. And Serenella never once cried.

First Thoughts

What might have made the little rich boy pale, afraid, and unhappy?

Identifying Facts

1. Before entering the garden, what are Giovannino and Serenella doing to amuse themselves?
2. What adjective describes "everything" in the garden?
3. After they leave the garden, what new game do Giovannino and Serenella invent?

Interpreting Meanings

1. How would you describe the **atmosphere** of the garden? Which descriptive details contribute to this atmosphere?
2. Consider the "anxiety and worry" that Giovannino and Serenella feel as they explore the garden and that the boy in pajamas seems to feel later. What may have caused the uneasiness in each case?
3. In what ways is the boy in the villa different from Giovannino and Serenella? What might the contrast suggest about the lives of the rich?
4. What might the garden **symbolize**?

Applying Meanings

Would you say young children are more or less sensitive to their surroundings than adults? Discuss with your classmates.

Creative Writing Response

Creating an Atmosphere. Write a brief descriptive essay in which you recreate the **atmosphere** of a place you found magical or enchanted. You may expand upon the sentences you wrote for the Writer's Response (see page 125). Use vivid words and **images** to capture the sights, sounds, smells, and textures of the place. Before you write, fill out a chart like the one below to be sure you have enough specific sensory **details**.

Sights	
Sounds	
Smells	
Textures or temperatures	
Tastes	

Critical Writing Response

Writing about Style. In a brief essay, discuss the descriptive style that Calvino employs in this story. Consider his use of vivid **imagery** and precise, scientific **details**, as well as the more mysterious or fantastic details that he uses. As a prewriting activity, list details on a chart like the one below.

Realistic or Precise Details	Mysterious or Fantastic Details

Aleksandr Solzhenitsyn
b. 1918, Russia

Craig Line/Wide World Photos

Aleksandr Solzhenitsyn (sōl′zhə·nēt′sin) became aware of the shortcomings of the Soviet Union after he had fought bravely for three years in World War II. Then, in a letter to a friend, he referred to premier Josef Stalin as "the boss" in criminals' slang. For this "crime" he was arrested and sent to prisons and labor camps for eight years. He was released after Stalin died in 1953 but still had to spend three years in internal exile in central Asia. There he worked as a teacher and wrote about his experiences.

The result of his efforts was *One Day in the Life of Ivan Denisovich* (1962), a novel about a farmer serving ten years at a Soviet labor camp for a political crime he did not commit. Since Nikita Krushchev, the new Soviet premier, had risen to power by attacking Stalin, books like Solzhenitsyn's were encouraged.

Solzhenitsyn's period of acceptance in his homeland, however, was short-lived. After Krushchev was ousted in 1964, the new, more conservative regime became increasingly uncomfortable with Solzhenitsyn's accounts of Stalinist oppression. The government barred publication of his work and confiscated many of his manuscripts. Solzhenitsyn's relationship with the government deteriorated further after a Paris firm published his famous attack on the Soviet penal system, *The Gulag Archipelago* (1974). Solzhenitsyn was charged with treason, stripped of his Soviet citizenship, and exiled from his homeland. Eventually he settled in the United States, where he became the Soviet Union's best-known writer-in-exile.

When Soviet premier Mikhail Gorbachev (mē′khä·ēl′ gôr′bə·chôf′) instituted his new policy of glasnost, or "openness," in the 1980s, Solzhenitsyn's citizenship was restored and his works were gradually published or reissued in his homeland. In 1990, Solzhenitsyn wrote a long essay entitled "How to Revitalize Russia." More remarkable than his ideas was the fact that he was permitted to express them in Soviet government periodicals that only five years before had denounced him as a traitor.

Reader's Guide

FREEDOM TO BREATHE
A JOURNEY ALONG THE OKA

Background

Rulers of the Soviet Union, like those of the Russian empire, have generally allowed their people very few freedoms. Under the czars, critics of the government were executed or exiled to remote parts of the empire, such as arctic Siberia, where they often died. A few years after the Russian Revolution of 1917, the new Communist regime began following similar practices. Soviet oppression reached its height under dictator Josef Stalin during the Great Purge of the mid-1930s, when the secret police shot or imprisoned millions of citizens. Matters improved only after Soviet premier Mikhail Gorbachev began instituting reforms in the late 1980s.

As a result of the Russian people's long history of suffering under tyrannical regimes, Russian writers since the time of Pushkin (see page 1006) have often spoken out against government oppression. Solzhenitsyn entered this long tradition when he began publishing in the early 1960s. Most of his works, including the prose poems you are about to read, deal with the lack of human rights and freedom in his homeland.

Writer's Response

People fight in different ways to bring about social and political change—some use guns or bombs while others use pens or videotape. Do you think the "pen is mightier than the sword" in exposing abuses? Write a paragraph expressing your opinion. Try to provide some examples from recent current events to support your opinion.

Literary Focus

Prose poetry is written in prose form, but uses poetic devices such as **rhythm**, **imagery**, and **figurative language** to express a single strong emotion or idea. Solzhenitsyn's prose poems are brief nonfiction pieces that combine the features of prose and poetry.

FREEDOM TO BREATHE
Aleksandr Solzhenitsyn
translated by
MICHAEL GLENNY

Stop after you read the first two paragraphs of this prose poem. What kind of a place do you think the speaker is describing? After you finish the poem, see if your impression was correct.

A shower fell in the night and now dark clouds drift across the sky, occasionally sprinkling a fine film of rain.

I stand under an apple tree in blossom and I breathe. Not only the apple tree but the grass round it glistens with moisture; words cannot describe the sweet fragrance that pervades the air. I inhale as deeply as I can, and the aroma invades my whole being; I breathe with my eyes open, I breathe with my eyes closed—I cannot say which gives me the greater pleasure.

This, I believe, is the single most precious freedom that prison takes away from us: the freedom to breathe freely, as I now can. No food on earth, no wine, not even a woman's kiss is sweeter to me than this air steeped in the fragrance of flowers, of moisture and freshness.

No matter that this is only a tiny garden, hemmed in by five-story houses like cages in a zoo. I cease to hear the motorcycles backfiring, radios whining, the burble of loudspeakers. As long as there is fresh air to breathe under an apple tree after a shower, we may survive a little longer.

Saint Sophia Church in Kiev, in the former Soviet Union.

A JOURNEY ALONG THE OKA

Aleksandr Solzhenitsyn

translated by

MICHAEL GLENNY

 Solzhenitsyn uses a description of the Russian countryside to reveal how he feels about an aspect of Soviet life. What are his feelings?

Traveling along country roads in central Russia, you begin to understand why the Russian countryside has such a soothing effect.

It is because of its churches. They rise over ridge and hillside, descending towards wide rivers like red and white princesses, towering above the thatch and wooden huts of everyday life with their slender, carved, and fretted belfries. From far away they greet each other; from distant, unseen villages they rise towards the same sky.

Wherever you may wander, over field or pasture, many miles from any homestead, you are never alone: above the wall of trees, above the hayricks, even above the very curve of the earth itself, the dome of a belfry

Aleksandr Solzhenitsyn **133**

? **What poetic features do Solzhenitsyn's prose poems exhibit?**

is always beckoning to you, from Borki Lov-etskie, Lyubichi, or Gavrilovskoe.[1]

But as soon as you enter a village you realize that the churches which welcomed you from afar are no longer living. Their crosses have long since been bent or broken off; the dome with its peeling paint reveals its rusty ribcage; weeds grow on the roofs and in the cracks of the walls; the cemetery is hardly ever cared for, its crosses knocked over and its graves ransacked; the ikons[2] behind the altar have faded from a decade of rain and are scrawled with obscene graffiti.

In the porch there are barrels of salt and a tractor is swinging round towards them, or a lorry is backing up to the vestry door to collect some sacks. In one church, machine tools are humming away; another stands silent, simply locked up. Others have been turned into clubs where propaganda meetings are held ("We Will Achieve High Yields of Milk!") or films shown: *Poem About the Sea, The Great Adventure.*

People have always been selfish and often evil. But the Angelus[3] used to toll and its echo would float over village, field, and wood. It reminded man that he must abandon his trivial earthly cares and give up one hour of his thoughts to life eternal. The tolling of the eventide bell, which now survives for us only in a popular song, raised man above the level of a beast.

Our ancestors put their best into these stones and these belfries—all their knowledge and all their faith.

Come on, Vitka,[4] buck up and stop feeling sorry for yourself! The film starts at six, and the dance is at eight. . . .

---

1. **Borki Lovetskie, Lyubichi, Gavrilovskoe:** cities in the former Soviet Union.
2. **ikons** (ī′kän′): religious images or figures, usually of Jesus, Mary, or a saint; also spelled *icon.*

3. **Angelus** (an′jə·ləs): the bell rung to announce the time for the Angelus, a prayer said at morning, noon, and evening.
4. **Vitka** (vēt′kä): a familiar form for Viktor; usually the familiar form would be Vitya. The ''ka'' ending here shows that the speaker is slightly annoyed at the person being addressed.

Were you surprised by the new information about the speaker's location in the last paragraph in "Freedom to Breathe"? Why do you think Solzhenitsyn provided this information in the last paragraph rather than in the first one?

Identifying Facts

1. What does the speaker in "Freedom to Breathe" say words cannot describe?

2. What does the same speaker say is the single most precious freedom that prison takes away?

3. What does the speaker in "A Journey Along the Oka" find soothing about the Russian countryside?

4. What are the churches used for now?

Interpreting Meanings

1. Solzhenitsyn uses **imagery**—language that appeals to the senses—in both of these **prose poems**. Identify images in "Freedom to Breathe" that relate to at least three different senses.

2. What do the details of **setting** in the last paragraph of "Freedom to Breathe" emphasize about the speaker's view of freedom?

3. Why does the speaker in "A Journey Along the Oka" say the churches are no longer "living"?

4. Prose poems often use **figures of speech**. Find an example of **simile** and **personification** in the second paragraph of "A Journey Along the Oka."

5. The churches in "A Journey Along the Oka" can be taken on both a literal and a symbolic level. What would you say the churches **symbolize,** or represent?

Applying Meanings

Those who have never been in prison probably take the "freedom to breathe" for granted. What are some other freedoms we often take for granted?

Do you think that if we take certain freedoms for granted (the freedom to worship, for example) we risk losing them? Give examples to support your opinion.

Creative Writing Response

Writing a Prose Poem Using Imagery. Think of an experience that is still vivid in your memory. Write a **prose poem** in which you use **images** to communicate what you saw, heard, smelled, tasted, or touched. Try to select images that create the emotions and sensations you associate with the experience: joy, sadness, excitement, peace, or some other feeling.

Critical Writing Response

Analyzing the Poem's Theme. **Theme** is the poem's central idea about life. Write a paragraph about the theme of either "Freedom to Breathe" or "A Journey Along the Oka." Your topic sentence should state what the theme is. Then discuss how Solzhenitsyn gets his theme across and provide examples from the poem. End your paragraph with a sentence telling how you feel about poetry with social, political, or religious messages.

PRIMARY SOURCES

Solzhenitsyn Accepts the Nobel Prize

In 1970, less than four years before he was exiled from the Soviet Union, Solzhenitsyn was awarded the Nobel Prize for literature. He did not travel to Sweden to collect the prize because he feared that he would not be allowed to return to his homeland. Instead, he wrote an acceptance, a portion of which appears below. As you read the passage, consider what Solzhenitsyn believes the role of literature to be. What dangers of censorship does he point out?

The only substitute for what we ourselves have not experienced is art and literature. They have the marvelous capacity of transmitting from one nation to another—despite differences in language, customs, and social structure—practical experience, the harsh national experience of many decades never tasted by the other nation. Sometimes this may save a whole nation from what is a dangerous or mistaken or plainly disastrous path, thus lessening the twists and turns of human history.

Today, from this Nobel lecture platform, I should like to emphasize this great, beneficent attribute of art.

Literature transmits condensed and irrefutable human experience in still another priceless way: from generation to generation. It thus becomes the living memory of a nation. What has faded into history it thus keeps warm and preserves in a form that defies distortion and falsehood. Thus literature, together with language, preserves and protects a nation's soul. . . .

But woe to the nation whose literature is cut off by the interposition of force. That is not simply a violation of "freedom of the press"; it is stopping up the nation's heart, carving out the nation's memory. The nation loses its memory; it loses its spiritual unity—and, despite their supposedly common language, fellow countrymen suddenly cease understanding each other. Speechless generations are born and die, having recounted nothing of themselves either to their own times or to their descendants. That such masters as Akhmatova [see page 89] and [Soviet author Yevgeny] Zamyatin were buried behind four walls for their whole lives and condemned even to the grave to create in silence, without hearing one reverberation of what they wrote, is not only their own personal misfortune but a tragedy for the whole nation—and, too, a real threat to all nationalities.

In certain cases, it is a danger for all mankind as well: when HISTORY as a whole ceases to be understood because of that silence.

Stanislaw Lem
b. 1921, Poland

As a boy, Stanislaw Lem (stan'is·läf' lem') loved to tinker with broken things— alarm clocks, spark plugs, and anything else that needed repairing. He planned to put his tinkering talents to good use by becoming a doctor or a scientist, but Germany's invasion of Poland at the beginning of World War II interrupted his education. It did not, however, interrupt his tinkering. During the Nazi occupation, Lem sabotaged German vehicles while pretending to repair them.

The war years were a harrowing time for Lem and his family, whose Jewish heritage put them in particular jeopardy. They survived by obtaining false papers certifying them to be Christian. Yet Lem often put himself at risk by smuggling food to Jewish friends and carrying messages for Resistance fighters. His frequent close calls led him to view life as a chancy business. He was keenly aware that the difference between living another day and dying suddenly and unexpectedly could depend upon something as simple and arbitrary as arriving at a destination on time or twenty minutes late.

When Lem resumed his studies after the war, he was appalled by the scientific doctrines he was told to accept without question. Because he refused to bow to the official Communist party views on science, Lem failed to graduate from medical school. Not long afterward, he abandoned science for science fiction.

After his first science-fiction novel *The Astronauts* (1951) became a bestseller in Eastern Europe, he wrote a number of books about distant galaxies and strange life forms. Among the best of these is *Solaris* (1961), about a planet whose only sentient, or conscious, being is a kaleidoscopic sea. Both *Solaris* and *The Invincible* (1964), about a gigantic spaceship defeated by an army of insectlike robots, use satire directed against human attempts to control the universe.

While Lem's science fiction has been popular in Europe for decades, English translations appeared in the United States only in the 1970s, spurred by the 1972 release of the Russian film version of *Solaris*. American critics were quick to add to the praise that Lem's writing had won elsewhere.

Reader's Guide

TRURL'S MACHINE

Background

Most Polish writers who survived World War II quickly grew disillusioned with the Communist government. Some, like Nobel Prize-
winning poet Czeslaw Milosz (ches'läf mē'wōsh), immigrated to the
West. Others remained and coped as best they could. For Stanislaw
Lem, writing science fiction turned out to be a way to write without
being censored. Because science fiction is generally set on other planets or on earth in the distant future, Communist government censors
rarely scrutinized it closely.

Most of Lem's fiction satirizes Communist government practices,
but it does so in a symbolic way, carefully veiled by action-adventure
and humor. In his novel *The Invincible,* for example, the enormous,
seemingly all-powerful spaceship that falls prey to tiny robots probably
represents the huge and inefficient Communist bureaucracy. Similarly,
the stories in Lem's collection *The Cyberiad* (1965) contain carefully
disguised attacks on Communist government practices. These stories,
including the one reprinted here, feature the rival robot constructors
Trurl and Klapaucius.

Writer's Response

Think of something in your present life that you find difficult or frus-
trating (traffic jams, waking up for school, doing homework). Write a
paragraph or two about it in a satirical science-fiction style by exaggerating the characteristics of whatever it is that you dislike, and plac-
ing it on a distant planet or in the distant future.

Literary Focus

Science fiction is a form of fantasy writing in which scientific facts,
assumptions, or hypotheses form the basis of adventures in the future,
on other planets, in other dimensions of space or time, or under new
variants of scientific laws. Many popular television shows and movies,
such as *Star Trek* and *Star Wars,* are part of the science-fiction genre.

Although science fiction is usually set in the future, it often comments on the present. These comments sometimes come in the form of
satire, a kind of writing that ridicules human weakness, vice, or folly.

TRURL'S MACHINE

Stanislaw Lem

translated by

MICHAEL KANDEL

 As you read "Trurl's Machine," identify details that might be satirizing life in a totalitarian state. Also identify details that seem to be poking fun at human nature in general.

Once upon a time Trurl the constructor built an eight-story thinking machine. When it was finished, he gave it a coat of white paint, trimmed the edges in lavender, stepped back, squinted, then added a little curlicue on the front and, where one might imagine the forehead to be, a few pale orange polka dots. Extremely pleased with himself, he whistled an air and, as is always done on such occasions, asked it the ritual question of how much is two plus two.

The machine stirred. Its tubes began to glow, its coils warmed up, current coursed through all its circuits like a waterfall, transformers hummed and throbbed, there was a clanging, and a chugging, and such an ungodly racket that Trurl began to think of adding a special mentation muffler. Meanwhile the machine labored on, as if it had been given the most difficult problem in the Universe to solve; the ground shook, the sand slid underfoot from the vibration, valves popped like champagne corks, the relays nearly gave way under the strain. At last, when Trurl had grown extremely impatient, the machine ground to a halt and said in a voice like thunder: SEVEN!

"Nonsense, my dear," said Trurl. "The answer's four. Now be a good machine and adjust yourself! What's two and two?"

"SEVEN!" snapped the machine. Trurl sighed and put his coveralls back on, rolled up his sleeves, opened the bottom trapdoor and crawled in. For the longest time he hammered away inside, tightened, soldered, ran clattering up and down the metal stairs, now on the sixth floor, now on the eighth, then pounded back down to the bottom and threw a switch, but something sizzled in the middle, and the spark plugs grew blue whiskers. After two hours of this he came out, covered with soot but satisfied, put all his tools away, took off his coveralls, wiped his face and hands. As he was leaving, he turned and asked, just so there would be no doubt about it:

"And now what's two and two?"

"SEVEN!" replied the machine.

Trurl uttered a terrible oath, but there was no help for it—again he had to poke around inside the machine, disconnecting, correcting, checking, resetting, and when he learned for the third time that two and two was seven, he collapsed in despair at the foot of the machine, and sat there until Klapaucius found him. Klapaucius inquired what was wrong, for Trurl looked as if he had just returned from a funeral. Trurl explained the problem. Klapaucius crawled into the machine himself a couple of times, tried to fix this and that, then asked it for the sum of one plus two, which turned out to be six. One plus one, according to the machine, equaled zero. Klapaucius scratched his head, cleared his throat, and said:

"My friend, you'll just have to face it. That isn't the machine you wished to make. However, there's a good side to everything, including this."

"What good side?" muttered Trurl, and kicked the base on which he was sitting.

"Stop that," said the machine.

"H'm, it's sensitive too. But where was I? Oh yes ... there's no question but that we have here a stupid machine, and not merely stupid in the usual, normal way, oh no! This is, as far as I can determine—and you know I am something of an expert—this is the stupidest thinking machine in the entire world, and that's nothing to sneeze at! To construct deliberately such a machine would be far from easy; in fact, I would say that no one could manage it. For the thing is not only stupid, but stubborn as a mule, that is, it has a personality common to idiots, for idiots are uncommonly stubborn."

"What earthly use do I have for such a machine?!" said Trurl, and kicked it again.

"I'm warning you, you better stop!" said the machine.

"A warning, if you please," observed Klapaucius dryly. "Not only is it sensitive, dense, and stubborn, but quick to take offense, and believe me, with such an abundance of qualities there are all sorts of things you might do!"

"What, for example?" asked Trurl.

"Well, it's hard to say offhand. You might put it on exhibit and charge admission; people would flock to see the stupidest thinking machine that ever was—what does it have,

eight stories? Really, could anyone imagine a bigger dunce? And the exhibition would not only cover your costs, but—"

"Enough, I'm not holding any exhibition!" Trurl said, stood up, and, unable to restrain himself, kicked the machine once more.

"This is your third warning," said the machine.

"What?" cried Trurl, infuriated by its imperious manner. "You ... you ..." And he kicked it several times, shouting: "You're only good for kicking, you know that?"

"You have insulted me for the fourth, fifth, sixth, and eighth times," said the machine. "Therefore, I refuse to answer all further questions of a mathematical nature."

"It refuses! Do you hear that?" fumed Trurl, thoroughly exasperated. "After six comes eight—did you notice, Klapaucius?—not seven, but eight! And that's the kind of mathematics Her Highness refuses to perform! Take that! And that! And that! Or perhaps you'd like some more?"

The machine shuddered, shook, and without another word started to lift itself from its foundations. They were very deep, and the girders began to bend, but at last it scrambled out, leaving behind broken concrete blocks with steel spokes protruding— and it bore down on Trurl and Klapaucius like a moving fortress. Trurl was so dumbfounded that he didn't even try to hide from the machine, which to all appearances intended to crush him to a pulp. But Klapaucius grabbed his arm and yanked him away, and the two of them took to their heels. When finally they looked back, they saw the machine swaying like a high tower, advancing slowly, at every step sinking to its second floor, but stubbornly, doggedly pulling itself out of the sand and heading straight for them.

"Whoever heard of such a thing?" Trurl

gasped in amazement. "Why, this is mutiny! What do we do now?"

"Wait and watch," replied the prudent Klapaucius. "We may learn something."

But there was nothing to be learned just then. The machine had reached firmer ground and was picking up speed. Inside, it whistled, hissed, and sputtered.

"Any minute now the signal box will knock loose," said Trurl under his breath. "That'll jam the program and stop it. . . ."

"No," said Klapaucius, "this is a special case. The thing is so stupid, that even if the whole transmission goes, it won't matter. But—look out!!"

The machine was gathering momentum, clearly bent on running them down, so they fled just as fast as they could, the fearful rhythm of crunching steps in their ears. They ran and ran—what else could they do? They tried to make it back to their native district, but the machine outflanked them, cut them off, forced them deeper and deeper into a wild, uninhabited region. Mountains, dismal and craggy, slowly rose out of the mist. Trurl, panting heavily, shouted to Klapaucius:

"Listen! Let's turn into some narrow canyon . . . where it won't be able to follow us . . . the cursed thing . . . what do you say?"

"No . . . better go straight," wheezed Klapaucius. "There's a town up ahead . . . can't remember the name . . . anyway, we can find—oof!—find shelter there. . . ."

So they ran straight and soon saw houses before them. The streets were practically deserted at this time of day, and the constructors had gone a good distance without meeting a living soul, when suddenly an awful crash, like an avalanche at the edge of the town, indicated that the machine was coming after them.

Trurl looked back and groaned.

"Good heavens! It's tearing down the houses, Klapaucius!!" For the machine, in stubborn pursuit, was plowing through the walls of the buildings like a mountain of steel, and in its wake lay piles of rubble and white clouds of plaster dust. There were dreadful screams, confusion in the streets, and Trurl and Klapaucius, their hearts in their mouths, ran on till they came to a large town hall, darted inside, and raced down endless stairs to a deep cellar.

"It won't get us in here, even if it brings the whole building down on our heads!" panted Klapaucius. "But really, the devil himself had me pay you a visit today. . . . I was curious to see how your work was going—well, I certainly found out. . . ."

"Quiet," interrupted Trurl. "Someone's coming. . . ."

And indeed, the cellar door opened up and the mayor entered, accompanied by several aldermen. Trurl was too embarrassed to explain how this strange and calamitous situation had come about; Klapaucius had to do it. The mayor listened in silence. Suddenly the walls trembled, the ground heaved, and the sound of cracking stone reached them in the cellar.

"It's here?!" cried Trurl.

"Yes," said the mayor. "And it demands that we give you up, otherwise it says it will level the entire town. . . ."

Just then they heard, far overhead, words that honked as if from a muffled horn:

"Trurl's here . . . I smell Trurl. . . ."

"But surely you won't give us up?" asked in a quavering voice the object of the machine's obstinate fury.

"The one of you who calls himself Trurl must leave. The other may remain, since surrendering him does not constitute part of the conditions. . . ."

"Have mercy!"

"We are helpless," said the mayor. "And were you to stay here, Trurl, you would have to answer for all the damage done to this town and its inhabitants, since it was because of you that the machine destroyed sixteen homes and buried beneath their ruins many of our finest citizens. Only the fact that you yourself stand in imminent peril permits me to let you leave unpunished. Go then, and nevermore return."

Trurl looked at the aldermen and, seeing his sentence written on their stern faces, slowly turned and made for the door.

"Wait! I'll go with you!" cried Klapaucius impulsively.

"You?" said Trurl, a faint hope in his voice. "But no . . ." he added after a moment. "Why should you have to perish too? . . ."

"Nonsense!" rejoined Klapaucius with great energy. "What, us perish at the hands of that iron imbecile? Never! It takes more than that, my friend, to wipe two of the most famous constructors off the face of the globe! Come, Trurl! Chin up!"

Encouraged by these words, Trurl ran up the stairs after Klapaucius. There was not a soul outside in the square. Amid clouds of dust and the gaunt skeletons of demolished homes, stood the machine, higher than the town hall tower itself, puffing steam, covered with the blood of powdered brick and smeared with chalk.

"Careful!" whispered Klapaucius. "It doesn't see us. Let's take that first street on the left, then turn right, then straight for those mountains. There we can take refuge and think of how to make the thing give up once and for all its insane . . . *Now!*" he yelled, for the machine had just spotted them and was charging, making the pavement buckle.

Breathless, they ran from the town and galloped along for a mile or so, hearing be-

Chest (La Poitrine), René Magritte, 1961.

hind them the thunderous stride of the colossus that followed relentlessly.

"I know that ravine!" Klapaucius suddenly cried. "That's the bed of a dried-out stream and it leads to cliffs and caves—faster, faster, the thing'll have to stop soon! . . ."

So they raced uphill, stumbling and wav-

stones that flew from under their feet. The opening in the rock breathed chill and darkness. As quickly as they could, they leaped inside, ran a few extra steps, then stopped.

"Well, here at least we're safe," said Trurl, calm once again. "I'll just take a look, to see where it got stuck. . . ."

"Be careful," cautioned Klapaucius. Trurl inched his way to the edge of the cave, leaned out, and immediately jumped back in fright.

"It's coming up the mountain!!" he cried.

"Don't worry, it'll never be able to get in here," said Klapaucius, not altogether convinced. "But what's that? Is it getting dark? Oh no!"

At that moment a great shadow blotted out the bit of sky visible through the mouth of the cave, and in its place appeared a smooth steel wall with rows of rivets. It was the machine slowly closing with the rock, thereby sealing up the cave as if with a mighty metal lid.

"We're trapped . . ." whispered Trurl, his voice breaking off when the darkness became absolute.

"That was idiotic on our part!" Klapaucius exclaimed, furious. "To jump into a cave that it could barricade! How could we have done such a thing?"

"What do you think it's waiting for now?" asked Trurl after a long pause.

"For us to give up—that doesn't take any great brains."

Again there was silence. Trurl tiptoed in the darkness, hands outstretched, in the direction of the opening, running his fingers along the stone until he touched the smooth steel, which was warm, as if heated from within. . . .

"I feel Trurl . . ." boomed the iron voice. Trurl hastily retreated, took a seat alongside his friend, and for some time they sat there,

ing their arms to keep their balance, but the machine still gained on them. Scrambling up over the gravel of the dried-out riverbed, they reached a crevice in the perpendicular rock and, seeing high above them the murky mouth of a cave, began to climb frantically toward it, no longer caring about the loose

Stanislaw Lem **143**

motionless. At last Klapaucius whispered:

"There's no sense our just sitting here. I'll try to reason with it...."

"That's hopeless," said Trurl. "But go ahead. Perhaps it will at least let *you* go free...."

"Now, now, none of that!" said Klapaucius, patting him on the back. And he groped his way toward the mouth of the cave and called: "Hello out there, can you hear us?"

"Yes," said the machine.

"Listen, we'd like to apologize. You see ... well, there was a little misunderstanding, true, but it was nothing, really. Trurl had no intention of...."

"I'll pulverize Trurl!" said the machine. "But first, he'll tell me how much two and two makes."

"Of course he will, of course he will, and you'll be happy with his answer, and make it up with him for sure, isn't that right, Trurl?" said the mediator soothingly.

"Yes, of course ..." mumbled Trurl.

"Really?" said the machine. "Then how much is two and two?"

"Fo ... that is, seven ..." said Trurl in an even lower voice.

"Ha! Not four, but seven, eh?" crowed the machine. "There, I told you so!"

"Seven, yes, seven, we always knew it was seven!" Klapaucius eagerly agreed. "Now will you, uh, let us go?" he added cautiously.

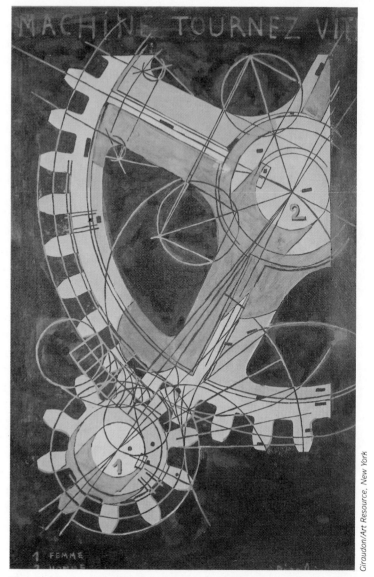

MACHINE, TURN QUICKLY (MACHINE TOURNEZ VITE), FRANCIS PICABIA. Trurl asserts that it is useless to try to reason with the machine.
❓ Do you find Trurl's statement ironic? Why or why not?

"No. Let Trurl say how sorry he is and tell me how much is two times two...."

"And you'll let us go, if I do?" asked Trurl.

"I don't know. I'll think about it. I'm not making any deals. What's two times two?"

"But you probably will let us go, won't you?" said Trurl, while Klapaucius pulled on his arm and hissed in his ear: "The thing's an imbecile, don't argue with it, for heaven's sake!"

"I won't let you go, if I don't want to," said the machine. "You just tell me how much two times two is. . . ."

Suddenly Trurl fell into a rage.

"I'll tell you, I'll tell you all right!" he screamed. "Two and two is four and two times two is four, even if you stand on your head, pound these mountains all to dust, drink the ocean dry, and swallow the sky—do you hear? Two and two is four!!"

"Trurl! What are you saying? Have you taken leave of your senses? Two and two is seven, nice machine! Seven, seven!!" howled Klapaucius, trying to drown out his friend.

"No! It's four! Four and only four, four from the beginning to the end of time—FOUR!!" bellowed Trurl, growing hoarse.

The rock beneath their feet was seized with a feverish tremor.

The machine moved away from the cave, letting in a little pale light, and gave a piercing scream:

"That's not true! It's seven! Say it's seven or I'll hit you!"

"Never!" roared Trurl, as if he no longer cared what happened, and pebbles and dirt rained down on their heads, for the machine had begun to ram its eight-story hulk again and again into the wall of stone, hurling itself against the mountainside until huge boulders broke away and went tumbling down into the valley.

Thunder and sulfurous fumes filled the cave, and sparks flew from the blows of steel on rock, yet through all this pandemonium one could still make out, now and then, the ragged voice of Trurl bawling:

"Two and two is four! Two and two is four!!"

Klapaucius attempted to shut his friend's mouth by force, but, violently thrown off, he gave up, sat and covered his head with his arms. Not for a moment did the machine's mad efforts flag, and it seemed that any minute now the ceiling would collapse, crush the prisoners, and bury them forever. But when they had lost all hope, and the air was thick with acrid smoke and choking dust, there was suddenly a horrible scraping, and a sound like a slow explosion, louder than all the maniacal banging and battering, and the air whooshed, and the black wall that blocked the cave was whisked away, as if by a hurricane, and monstrous chunks of rock came crashing down after it. The echoes of that avalanche still rumbled and reverberated in the valley below when the two friends peered out of their cave. They saw the machine. It lay smashed and flattened, nearly broken in half by an enormous boulder that had landed in the middle of its eight floors. With the greatest care they picked their way down through the smoking rubble. In order to reach the riverbed, it was necessary to pass the remains of the machine, which resembled the wreck of some mighty vessel thrown up upon a beach. Without a word, the two stopped together in the shadow of its twisted hull. The machine still quivered slightly, and one could hear something turning, creaking feebly, within.

"Yes, this is the bad end you've come to, and two and two is—as it always was—" began Trurl, but just then the machine made a faint, barely audible croaking noise and said, for the last time, "SEVEN."

Then something snapped inside, a few stones dribbled down from overhead, and now before them lay nothing but a lifeless mass of scrap. The two constructors exchanged a look and silently, without any further comment or conversation, walked back the way they came.

Stanislaw Lem **145**

First Thoughts

Which incident in this story did you find the funniest? What might Lem be **satirizing** by way of this humorous incident?

Identifying Facts

1. What "test question" does Trurl ask his thinking machine? How does the machine respond?
2. What interconnected qualities does Klapaucius recognize in the machine? What does he suggest Trurl might do to recover his costs?
3. Why does the machine lift itself from its foundations and try to destroy Trurl?
4. Where are Trurl and Klapaucius finally trapped? Summarize how the machine is finally destroyed.

Interpreting Meanings

1. What event immediately establishes the futuristic **setting** of this **science-fiction** tale?
2. How does Lem give the thinking machine a personality? Describe this personality.
3. How would you describe the relationship between Trurl and Klapaucius? How does the interplay between them add interest to the story?
4. Reread Lem's biography (see page 137). How might the machine's behavior **satirize** Lem's own experiences under totalitarian government? What view of the world does the story suggest such governments try to instill?
5. What does the fate of the machine suggest about its usefulness? What does it suggest about the reasons totalitarian governments eventually fail?

Applying Meanings

What dangers does the story suggest often accompany ignorance? Give an example from your own life about the dangers of ignorance.

Creative Writing Response

Writing a Science-Fiction Story. Take a common story ("Little Red Riding Hood") or television show (an episode of the *Cosby Show*) and set it in the future or on another planet. Retell the story, including as many elements of science fiction as you like (laser weapons, computerized gadgets, and so on). Let your imagination run wild, while keeping the basic plot and character elements the same as in the original story.

Critical Writing Response

Writing About Satire. In a brief essay, show how Lem's story pokes fun at both specific political and economic situations and human nature in general. Discuss story details in more general terms and identify what they suggest or ridicule. Before you begin writing, you may find it helpful to complete a chart like this one.

Detail	What It Says About Politics/ Economics	What It Says About Human Nature

Joaquim Maria Machado de Assis
1838–1908, Brazil

Why do people do the things they do? What is "real" and what is not? Can we ever completely understand the world around us? These are the kinds of questions that Joaquim Maria Machado de Assis (zhō·ä·kēm′ mä·rē′ə mä·shä′dō dä ä·sēs′) investigates in his novels and more than two hundred short stories. Although Machado de Assis has only recently been recognized in the English-speaking world, he has always enjoyed enormous respect in his native Brazil. When the Brazilian Academy of Letters was founded in the late 1890s, Machado de Assis was named its president for life.

The son of a poor house painter who was partially of African descent, Machado de Assis faced many obstacles early in his life. As a child he suffered from epilepsy and had a tendency to stutter. His mother died when he was only ten and his father died two years later. Shy and lonely, Joaquim began frequenting a local bookstore whose owner, Paula Brito, became his friend and adviser. By the time he was seventeen, he was working as a proofreader for Brito's publishing company and had begun writing his own poetry and fiction.

Most of Machado de Assis' early writings were in the Romantic tradition. In the 1880s, however, he began writing the innovative fiction for which he is known today. Machado de Assis was far ahead of his time in his interest in psychological motivations. *Dom Casmurro* (1899) (literally "Mr. Stubborn" or "Mr. Pigheaded"), the novel that most critics regard as his masterpiece, is a powerful study of jealousy and its consequences. When the book first appeared in English in 1953, translator Helen Caldwell said that she considered it among the finest novels produced in either North or South America.

Reader's Guide

A CANARY'S IDEAS

Background

Machado de Assis was a pioneer of **psychological realism**. This off-shoot of Realism focuses not on outer realities but on the inner workings of a character's mind. Machado de Assis examined human mental processes years before Marcel Proust and James Joyce (see page 73) began reproducing in prose the stream of their characters' thoughts, emotions, associations, and memories. Machado de Assis also anticipated twentieth-century trends in fiction by breaking down the barriers between realistic writing and fantasy. In combining the two forms. Machado de Assis was a forerunner of such Latin American **magical realists** as Gabriel García Márquez (see page 173). In "A Canary's Ideas," notice how the events surrounding the incredible discovery of a talking canary are realistically described.

Writer's Response

How do you think a caged bird might view the world around it and its place in that world? How might a free, wild bird view the world? Jot down a few of your ideas.

Literary Focus

There are different types of irony. In **verbal irony**, a character says one thing but really means something else. (Jill stepped into the downpour and said, "Nice day.") In **situational irony**, what happens is different from what we expect to happen. (A firefighter's house burns down.) In **dramatic irony**, the audience knows something that a character in a play does *not* know. (In *Romeo and Juliet,* the audience knows Juliet is only drugged, but Romeo believes she is dead.) The canary in this story says things that we can see as comically ironic.

A CANARY'S IDEAS

Joaquim Maria Machado de Assis

translated by

LORIE ISHIMATSU AND JACK SCHMITT

Pay careful attention to the canary's words. What is the bird's attitude toward human beings? Do you find this amusing?

A man by the name of Macedo,[1] who had a fancy for ornithology,[2] related to some friends an incident so extraordinary that no one took him seriously. Some came to believe he had lost his mind. Here is a summary of his narration.

At the beginning of last month, as I was walking down the street, a carriage darted past me and nearly knocked me to the ground. I escaped by quickly side-stepping into a secondhand shop. Neither the racket of the horse and carriage nor my entrance stirred the proprietor, dozing in a folding chair at the back of the shop. He was a man of shabby appearance: his beard was the color of dirty straw, and his head was covered by a tattered cap which probably had not found a buyer. One could not guess that there was any story behind him, as there could have been behind some of the objects he sold, nor could one sense in him that austere, disillusioned sadness inherent in the objects which were remnants of past lives.

The shop was dark and crowded with the sort of old, bent, broken, tarnished, rusted articles ordinarily found in secondhand shops, and everything was in that state of semidisorder befitting such an establishment. This assortment of articles, though banal, was interesting. Pots without lids, lids without pots, buttons, shoes, locks, a black skirt, straw hats, fur hats, picture frames, binoculars, dress coats, a fencing foil, a stuffed dog, a pair of slippers, gloves,

---

1. **Macedo** (mä·sä′dō)
2. **ornithology:** the study of birds.

nondescript vases, epaulets,[3] a velvet satchel, two hatracks, a slingshot, a thermometer, chairs, a lithographed portrait by the late Sisson,[4] a backgammon board, two wire masks for some future Carnival[5]—all this and more, which I either did not see or do not remember, filled the shop in the area around the door, propped up, hung, or displayed in glass cases as old as the objects inside them. Further inside the shop were many objects of similar appearance. Predominant were the large objects—chests of drawers, chairs, and beds—some of which were stacked on top of others which were lost in the darkness.

I was about to leave, when I saw a cage hanging in the doorway. It was as old as everything else in the shop, and I expected it to be empty so it would fit in with the general appearance of desolation. However, it wasn't empty. Inside, a canary was hopping about. The bird's color, liveliness, and charm added a noted of life and youth to that heap of wreckage. It was the last passenger of some wrecked ship, who had arrived in the shop as complete and happy as it had originally been. As soon as I looked at the bird, it began to hop up and down, from perch to perch, as if it meant to tell me that a ray of sunshine was frolicking in the midst of that cemetery. I'm using this image to describe the canary only because I'm speaking to rhetorical[6] people, but the truth is that the canary thought about neither cemetery nor sun, according to what it

The Great Family, René Magritte (1898–1967).
What details provided thus far give the story an air of realism?

Herscovici/Art Resource, New York

told me later. Along with the pleasure the sight of the bird brought me, I felt indignation regarding its destiny and softly murmured these bitter words:

"What detestable owner had the nerve to rid himself of this bird for a few cents? Or what indifferent soul, not wishing to keep his late master's pet, gave it away to some child, who sold it so he could make a bet on a soccer game?"

---

3. **epaulets** (ep'ə·lets'): shoulder ornaments worn on military and other uniforms.
4. **lithographed . . . Sisson:** relatively inexpensive print by a minor artist.
5. **Carnival:** period of feasting and merrymaking before the start of Lent; in Brazil, Carnival is a major festival similar to the Mardi Gras in New Orleans.
6. **rhetorical** (ri·tôr'i·kəl): here, able to use and understand effective, eloquent language.

The canary, sitting on top of its perch, trilled this reply:

"Whoever you may be, you're certainly not in your right mind. I had no detestable owner, nor was I given to any child to sell. Those are the delusions of a sick person. Go and get yourself cured, my friend . . ."

"What?" I interrupted, not having had time to become astonished. "So your master didn't sell you to this shop? It wasn't misery or laziness that brought you, like a ray of sunshine, to this cemetery?"

"I don't know what you mean by 'sunshine' or 'cemetery.' If the canaries you've seen use the first of those names, so much the better, because it sounds pretty, but really, I'm sure you're confused."

"Excuse me, but you couldn't have come here by chance, all alone. Has your master always been that man sitting over there?"

"What master? That man over there is my servant. He gives me food and water every day, so regularly that if I were to pay him for his services, it would be no small sum, but canaries don't pay their servants. In fact, since the world belongs to canaries, it would be extravagant for them to pay for what is already in the world."

Astonished by these answers, I didn't know what to marvel at more—the language or the ideas. The language, even though it entered my ears as human speech, was uttered by the bird in the form of charming trills. I looked all around me so I could determine if I were awake and saw that the street was the same, and the shop was the same dark, sad, musty place. The canary, moving from side to side, was waiting for me to speak. I then asked if it were lonely for the infinite blue space . . .

"But, my dear man," trilled the canary, "what does 'infinite blue space' mean?"

"But, pardon me, what do you think of this world? What is the world to you?"

"The world," retorted the canary, with a certain professorial air, "is a secondhand shop with a small rectangular bamboo cage hanging from a nail. The canary is lord of the cage it lives in and the shop that surrounds it. Beyond that, everything is illusion and deception."

With this, the old man woke up and approached me, dragging his feet. He asked me if I wanted to buy the canary. I asked if he had acquired it in the same way he had acquired the rest of the objects he sold and learned that he had bought it from a barber, along with a set of razors.

"The razors are in very good condition," he said.

"I only want the canary."

I paid for it, ordered a huge, circular cage of wood and wire, and had it placed on the veranda of my house so the bird could see the garden, the fountain, and a bit of blue sky.

It was my intention to do a lengthy study of this phenomenon, without saying anything to anyone until I could astound the world with my extraordinary discovery. I began by alphabetizing the canary's language in order to study its structure, its relation to music, the bird's appreciation of aesthetics,[7] its ideas and recollections. When this philological[8] and psychological analysis was done, I entered specifically into the study of canaries: their origin, their early history, the geology and flora of the Canary Islands,[9] the

---

7. **aesthetics** (es·thet'iks): the study or theory of beauty, especially as captured in art.
8. **philological** (fil'ō·läj'i·kəl): here, relating to the study of language; linguistic.
9. **flora of the Canary Islands:** plantlife of an island group in the Atlantic Ocean off Africa's northwest coast; the birds known as canaries are native to these islands.

bird's knowledge of navigation, and so forth. We conversed for hours while I took notes, and it waited, hopped about, and trilled.

As I have no family other than two servants, I ordered them not to interrupt me, even to deliver a letter or an urgent telegram or to inform me of an important visitor. Since they both knew about my scientific pursuits, they found my orders perfectly natural and did not suspect that the canary and I understood each other.

Needless to say, I slept little, woke up two or three times each night, wandered about aimlessly, and felt feverish. Finally, I returned to my work in order to reread, add, and emend. I corrected more than one observation, either because I had misunderstood something or because the bird had not expressed it clearly. The definition of the world was one of these. Three weeks after the canary's entrance into my home, I asked it to repeat to me its definition of the world.

"The world," it answered, "is a sufficiently broad garden with a fountain in the middle, flowers, shrubbery, some grass, clear air, and a bit of blue up above. The canary, lord of the world, lives in a spacious cage, white and circular, from which it looks out on the rest of the world. Everything else is illusion and deception."

The language of my treatise also suffered some modifications, and I saw that certain conclusions which had seemed simple were actually presumptuous. I still could not write the paper I was to send to the National Museum, the Historical Institute, and the German universities, not due to a lack of material but because I first had to put together all my observations and test their validity. During the last few days, I neither left the house, answered letters, nor wanted to hear from friends or relatives. The canary was everything to me. One of the servants

had the job of cleaning the bird's cage and giving it food and water every morning. The bird said nothing to him, as if it knew the man was completely lacking in scientific background. Besides, the service was no more than cursory, as the servant was not a bird lover.

On Saturday I awoke ill, my head and back aching. The doctor ordered complete rest. I was suffering from an excess of studying and was not to read or even think, nor was I even to know what was going on in the city or the rest of the outside world. I remained in this condition for five days. On the sixth day I got up, and only then did I find out that the canary, while under the servant's care, had flown out of its cage. My first impulse was to strangle the servant—I was choking with indignation and collapsed into my chair, speechless and bewildered. The guilty man defended himself, swearing he had been careful, but the wily bird had nevertheless managed to escape.

"But didn't you search for it?"

"Yes, I did, sir. First it flew up to the roof, and I followed it. It flew to a tree, and then who knows where it hid itself? I've been asking around since yesterday. I asked the neighbors and the local farmers, but no one has seen the bird."

I suffered immensely. Fortunately, the fatigue left me within a few hours, and I was soon able to go out to the veranda and the garden. There was no sign of the canary. I ran everywhere, making inquiries and posting announcements, all to no avail. I had already gathered my notes together to write my paper, even though it would be disjointed and incomplete, when I happened to visit a friend who had one of the largest and most beautiful estates on the outskirts of town. We were taking a stroll before dinner when this question was trilled to me:

"Greetings, Senhor[10] Macedo, where have you been since you disappeared?"

It was the canary, perched on the branch of a tree. You can imagine how I reacted and what I said to the bird. My friend presumed I was mad, but the opinions of friends are of no importance to me. I spoke tenderly to the canary and asked it to come home and continue our conversations in that world of ours, composed of a garden, a fountain, a veranda, and a white circular cage.

---

10. **Senhor** (si·nyôr): "mister" (Portuguese).

"What garden? What fountain?"

"The world, my dear bird."

"What world? I see you haven't lost any of your annoying professorial habits. The world," it solemnly concluded, "is an infinite blue space, with the sun up above."

Indignant, I replied that if I were to believe what it said, the world could be anything—it had even been a secondhand shop . . .

"A secondhand shop?" it trilled to its heart's content. "But is there really such a thing as a secondhand shop?"

First Thoughts

It is easy for us to feel superior to the canary and to laugh at its narrow view of the world and its limited understanding of reality. Do you think Machado de Assis wrote this story to show that human perceptions of the world are superior? Or might he be implying that our perceptions, like the canary's, are faulty and limited?

Identifying Facts

1. A **frame story** is a story which "frames," or contains within it, yet another story. According to the first paragraph, what is the frame for this story?

2. When Macedo finds the canary in the secondhand shop, what does the bird say about "infinite blue space"? How does the canary define the world?

3. After Macedo takes the canary home to study, what new definition of the world does the bird give? How does the canary escape?

4. What is the canary's definition of the world when Macedo encounters it on his friend's estate? What does the bird say about the secondhand shop?

Interpreting Meanings

1. Make a generalization about the canary's view of the world. Support your generalization with details from the story.

2. Why is it **ironic** for the canary to consider itself "lord" of the shop and later "lord of the world"? What might these remarks suggest about our own perceptions of our place in the world?

3. What earlier comment makes the canary's last remarks especially humorous and **ironic**? What might the canary's final question imply about human attitudes toward the past?

Applying Meanings

In past centuries, human perception of the world was very different from what it is today. For example, long ago everyone "knew" that the earth was flat and that the sun moved around it. Today we know that the earth is round and that it revolves around the sun. Do you think that in the future people will laugh at some of our ideas about the world, just as you may have laughed at this canary's ideas? Discuss your responses to this question.

Joaquim Maria Machado de Assis **153**

Creative Writing Response

Writing From a Bird's Point of View.
Using the ideas that you jotted down in the Writer's Response activity (see page 148), write a brief description of the world from a bird's point of view. Let the bird speak as "I." If you prefer, write from another creature's point of view (dog, cat, flea, and so on).

Critical Writing Response

Responding to a Story. In a brief essay, respond to *one* of these comments:

1. This is a story about a crazy man and it has nothing to do with a person's normal, daily life.
2. This story is about the nature of reality and of perception, and it shows how we are all limited in our interpretations of the world.

In the opening sentence of your essay, state whether you agree or disagree with the comment. Then give two or three reasons to support your response. Your reasons may be drawn both from the story and from your own experiences.

Language and Vocabulary

Portuguese and English

Portuguese, the main language of Portugal and Brazil, is one of the **Romance languages**—that is, like French, Italian, and Spanish, it is derived from Latin.

In the sentences below, words that have entered English from Portuguese have been italicized and defined. On a separate piece of paper, indicate whether the words are defined correctly by writing *True* or *False* beside the corresponding numbers. Check your answers in a dictionary. If the definition is false, write a correction.

1. An *albino* is an amateur musician.
2. A *cobra* is a poisonous insect.
3. *Lacquer* is a varnish that makes wood hard and shiny.
4. *Marmalade* was a popular hair gel.
5. *Molasses* is a kind of sweet syrup.
6. *Pagoda* is a Japanese dessert made with sweet beans and cream.
7. A *piranha* is a twirling dance step.
8. *Tapioca* is granular starch made from the cassava plant.

Gabriela Mistral
1889–1957, Chile

Mural dedicated to Gabriela Mistral, Santiago de Chile.

Gabriela Mistral (mēs·träl′) was the first woman poet and the first Latin American to win the Nobel Prize. When the Chilean poet Pablo Neruda (see page 160) was a young boy, Mistral, a woman of considerable height, became the principal of a girls' school near his hometown. The story goes that the ladies of the community suggested that she wear a hat—everyone wore one then—and she answered with a smile that a hat would be an unnecessary addition to one so tall. This good-humored directness was characteristic of the person whose poetry captured the simple, strong feelings of the common people.

Mistral was born Lucila Godoy Alcayaga in the village of Vicuna, Chile, high in the Andes Mountains. The first part of her pen name refers to the archangel Gabriel, and the second to the hot, dry wind known as the *mistral* that blows across southern France. Mistral may have also been paying homage to two of her favorite poets: Italy's Gabriele D'Annunzio (1863–1938) and France's Frederic Mistral (1830–1914).

Mistral wrote much of her early poetry in response to the suicide of a man she had been engaged to marry. She received worldwide attention when Federico de Onis, a Spanish professor at Columbia University in New York City, "discovered" her poetry and had it published.

Mistral continued to write poetry while working as a teacher and a principal, and later as an international cultural ambassador. In the 1920s she helped reorganize the rural school systems of Mexico, and in the 1930s she lectured at several American universities and was Chile's cultural representative to the League of Nations. After World War II, Mistral served as the Chilean consul in Los Angeles and Italy and was a delegate to a United Nations subcommittee on women's rights. On her frequent trips back to Chile, Mistral was often greeted by thousands of schoolchildren singing her poems. When she received the Nobel Prize for literature in 1945, she remarked that she must have been voted in by women and children.

Mistral once said that artists are to society what the soul is to the individual. Her life and writing reflected this sentiment. Her simple, strong verse is intimately linked by the use of vernacular, or local, language to the culture and concerns of her people.

I AM NOT LONELY

Gabriela Mistral

translated by

LANGSTON HUGHES

Reader's Guide

Background Much of Mistral's poetry revolves around the theme of love—either the intimate relationship between lovers or the special relationship shared by a mother and her child. Although Gabriela Mistral never had a child of her own, she wrote many poems for and about children. One of the poems you are about to read, "I Am Not Lonely," is from *Ternura* ("Tenderness"), Mistral's collection of children's songs, poems, and lullabies.

Writer's Response Write a few sentences describing a situation in which you felt lonely. What might have made you feel less lonely at that time?

Literary Focus Poetry is often classified as lyric, narrative, or dramatic. **Lyric poetry** expresses private thoughts or emotions. **Narrative poetry** tells a story. **Dramatic poetry** uses dialogue or monologue to convey one or more characters' personalities. Some poems, like these by Mistral, combine elements of all three types of poetry. But the major purpose of Mistral's poems is lyrical—to reveal intense personal feelings. Notice how close her poems are to song lyrics.

I AM NOT LONELY

 In this poem, the speaker is talking to someone. Who might this second person be?

The night is left lonely
from the hills to the sea.
But I, who cradle you,
I am not lonely!

5 The sky is left lonely
should the moon fall in the sea.

But I, who cling to you,
I am not lonely!

The world is left lonely
10 and all know misery.
But I, who hug you close,
I am not lonely!

WOMAN WITH INFANT, PABLO PICASSO (1881–1973).

THE LITTLE GIRL THAT LOST A FINGER

Gabriela Mistral

translated by

MUNA LEE DE MUÑOZ MARÍN

◆ *When you think about it, this lyric has a disturbing title. Is it a serious poem, or does it sound like a fairy tale?*

And a clam caught my little finger,
and the clam fell into the sand,
and the sand was swallowed by the sea,
and the whaler caught it in the sea,
5 and the whaler arrived at Gibraltar,°
and in Gibraltar the fishermen sing:

5. **Gibraltar** (ji·brôl′tər): peninsula at the southern tip of Spain, jutting into the Mediterranean Sea.

Gabriela Mistral **157**

"News of the earth we drag up from the sea,
news of a little girl's finger:
let her who lost it come get it!"

10   Give me a boat to go fetch it,
and for the boat give me a captain,
for the captain give me wages,
and for his wages let him ask for the city:
Marseilles° with towers and squares and boats,
15   in all the wide world the finest city,
which won't be lovely with a little girl
that the sea robbed of her finger,
and that whalers chant for like town criers,°
and that they're waiting for on Gibraltar . . .

14. **Marseilles** (mär·sā′): large French
port on the Mediterranean
Sea, not far from Gibraltar.

18. **town criers:** in the past, people
who made public announce-
ments by crying them out in
the streets.

First Thoughts

What dominant emotions did you identify in the two poems?

Identifying Facts

1. What things are lonely in stanzas 1, 2, and 3 of "I Am Not Lonely"? Why isn't the speaker lonely?

2. Why does the speaker in "The Little Girl That Lost a Finger" ask for a boat? What payment does she say the boat's captain should receive?

Interpreting Meanings

1. What does the verb "cradle" suggest about the identities of the speaker and the person being addressed in "I Am Not Lonely"? Do the verbs "cling" and "hug" in the next stanzas suggest other people? Discuss how you interpret the identities of the people in the poem.

2. **Personification** is a figure of speech in which human feelings are attributed to nonhuman things. What is personified in "I Am Not Lonely"? What do the personifications reveal about the speaker's feelings?

3. Do you think young children would enjoy "The Little Girl That Lost a Finger"? In what ways does the poem express a wish that the world were really this caring and loving toward even the little finger of one little girl?

4. Mistral's poems are essentially examples of lyric poetry, but what elements of **narrative poetry** and **dramatic poetry** do they contain? What feelings would you say these poems give voice to?

Applying Meanings

"The Little Girl That Lost a Finger" is structured on a series of causes and effects—one thing happens and this causes something else to happen, and so on. What popular children's stories or rhymes or songs are based on a similar structure? Why is this structure appealing?

Creative Writing Response

1. **Adding a Stanza to a Poem.** Write another four-line stanza for the poem "I Am Not Lonely." Open with two lines that describe some way that nature herself is lonely. Then address two lines to yourself. You may follow Mistral's format:

   The _____ is left lonely
   _____
   But I, who _____
   I am not lonely.

   Or, if your mood is different, **personify** nature as having different feelings (such as joy or tenderness).

2. **Writing About a Chain of Events.** Life is full of causes and effects. Suppose you watch a late-night movie. This has the effect of making you oversleep. This means you will be late for school, so you run out the door. Because you are running you fall down and twist your ankle, and a long chain of other events may follow from this.

   Write a brief chain-of-events poem or story. First, think of a cause. This cause leads to some effect and this effect then becomes the cause for another effect, and so on. You might want to begin by diagraming the chain of events in a series of boxes like this:

Watch late movie	Oversleep	Run out the door	Fall down	etc.

Pablo Neruda
1904–1973, Chile

Sergio Larrain/Magnum Photos, Inc.

When Chilean poet Pablo Neruda (pä′ blô ne·rōō′də) was a young boy looking for "creaturely things" behind his house, he saw a boy's hand poking through a hole in a fence to give him a toy lamb made of real wool. Thrilled, Neruda raced home to return with his most treasured possession, a pine cone—"half-open, balsamic, sweet-smelling." He dropped it through the same hole for the unseen boy on the other side of the fence. Later in life, when people asked him why he became a poet, Neruda often related this incident. He said that poetry was a gift to share with the world because it always brought something in return.

Pablo Neruda began publishing poetry while he was still a teenager in Temuco, a frontier town in Chile's sparsely populated south. Neruda's real name was Neftali Reyes Basoalto. He adopted a pen name to avoid upsetting his father, a railway worker, who frowned on his son's poetic ambitions. Neruda was only twenty years old when he published *Twenty Love Poems and a Song of Despair* (1924), the poetry collection that won him fame throughout his homeland.

Because Chile, like other Latin American nations, often honors writers with diplomatic posts, Neruda was appointed consul to several Asian nations and then to Argentina and Spain. In Spain he became close friends with the great poet Federico García Lorca (see page 94). When García Lorca was murdered by Fascist forces in the Spanish Civil War (1936–1939), Neruda suddenly became very political. Like many idealists of the time, he joined the Communist party and wrote letters attacking Chile's repressive right-wing government. In 1946 he was accused of treason and was forced to flee his homeland. It was during his exile that he wrote *Canto General (General Poems)*, a politically charged book of poems to which "Discoverers of Chile" belongs.

Neruda returned to Chile in 1952 and began writing his *Odas Elementales*, or *Elementary Odes* (1954). These short poems praise the ordinary things of life. "Poetry is like bread," Neruda wrote, "and it must be shared by everyone, the men of letters and the peasants, by everyone in our vast, incredible, extraordinary family of man."

Reader's Guide

DISCOVERERS OF CHILE

Background

In "Discoverers of Chile," Neruda refers to Chile's climate, terrain, and mineral wealth, and to Diego de Almagro, who in 1531 followed the Spanish conquistador Francisco Pizarro to Peru. The Spaniards, outnumbered by the Incas but heavily armed, captured Atahualpa, the Inca chief. As ransom, they demanded one room filled with gold and another filled with silver. But upon the urgings of Almagro, Pizarro did not release Atahualpa after the rooms were filled with gold and silver. Instead, the Spaniards strangled the Incan emperor to death.

Hungry for more gold, Pizarro sent Almagro to conquer Chile. The journey was a disaster. Hundreds of Spaniards and thousands of Indians died. None of the expected riches were found.

Ironically, Chile was later found to be rich in mineral resources. Today it is the world's leading producer of copper, and it also has deposits of gold, silver, coal, oil, and a gray, rocklike substance called *caliche* (kə·lē′chē), the world's only natural source of sodium nitrate. Caliche is used to make fertilizers and explosives. Scientists think that it was formed from the droppings of ocean birds.

Writer's Response

Do you think it is correct to say that people like Francisco Pizarro and Diego de Almagro "discovered" Peru and Chile, when the land was inhabited for thousands of years before the Europeans came? Write a few sentences supporting your point of view.

Literary Focus

A **figure of speech** is a word or phrase that describes one thing in terms of another, very different thing. A figure of speech is not literally true, but it helps us see the world in a fresh, imaginative way. There are many types of figures of speech, including similes and metaphors. A **simile** makes a comparison between two seemingly unlike things by using a connective word such as *like, as, than,* or *resembles* (*The stars were* like *diamonds*). A **metaphor** makes a comparison between two seemingly unlike things without using a connective word (*The stars were diamonds*). Neruda uses both kinds of figures of speech in the following poem.

David A. Harvey/Woodfin Camp & Associates, Inc.

Los Cuernos Peaks, Chile.

DISCOVERERS OF CHILE
Pablo Neruda
translated by
ROBERT BLY

 How does this speaker feel toward his country? How does he feel toward the Spaniard, Almagro?

Almagro brought his wrinkled lightning down from the north,
and day and night he bent over this country
between gunshots and twilight, as if over a letter.
Shadow of thorn, shadow of thistle and of wax,
5   the Spaniard, alone with his dried-up body,
watching the shadowy tactics of the soil.
My slim nation has a body made up
of night, snow, and sand,
the silence of the world is in its long coast,

10 the foam of the world rises from its seaboard,
    the coal of the world fills it with mysterious kisses.
    Gold burns in its finger like a live coal
    and silver lights up like a green moon
    its petrified shadow that's like a gloomy planet.
15 The Spaniard, sitting one day near a rose,
    near oil, near wine, near the primitive sky,
    could not really grasp how this spot of furious stone
    was born beneath the droppings of the ocean eagle.

First Thoughts

Why do you think Neruda titled this poem "Discoverers of Chile"?

Identifying Facts

1. What did Almagro do with his "wrinkled lightning"?
2. What could Almagro not understand?

Interpreting Meanings

1. What might Almagro's "wrinkled lightning" be? (In the **metaphor** implied by this phrase, what is being compared to lightning?)
2. What specific words in the poem compare Almagro to someone who is brutishly attacking a fragile victim? How does his body contrast with that of his victim's?
3. Reread the Background that precedes the poem (see page 161). Which of Chile's mineral resources, unrecognized by Almagro, are directly or indirectly mentioned in the poem, and where?
4. Identify four **similes** in the poem. What contrasting qualities about Chile do the similes in lines 12–14 help convey?
5. Do you think the word *discoverers* in the title is used **ironically** when applied to Almagro? Why or why not?

Applying Meanings

The conquistadors and other European explorers seldom showed respect for Native Americans and their cultures. Identify at least one situation in the world today that could be compared to Almagro's failure to understand the country he conquers.

Creative Writing Response

Writing About a Familiar Place. Write a poem in which you describe the physical appearance of a place that you are very familiar with. Like Neruda, use **similes** and other **figures of speech** to convey your emotions and to help readers picture the physical terrain.

You may want to begin by listing specific details about the place and creating similes to go with them. For example:

Place	Detail	Simile
a stream	small fish	dartlike video-game villains
	dragonflies	hover like miniature helicopters

Jorge Luis Borges
1899–1986, Argentina

UPI/Bettmann Newsphotos

When he was six years old, Jorge Luis Borges (hôr′he lōō·ēs′ bôr′hes) announced that he intended to become a writer. He began working at his chosen profession immediately: at the age of nine he translated Oscar Wilde's fairy tale "The Happy Prince" into Spanish. Later in his life, Borges credited his father with inspiring his writing career: He felt that his father had made him aware of poetry—of the idea that words could be powerful and symbolic, not just a means of everyday communication.

Borges learned English at an early age from his English-born grandmother, and he devoured her extensive library. He loved the horror stories of Edgar Allan Poe, the adventures of Robert Louis Stevenson, and the exotic Persian fairy tales in *The Thousand*

and One Nights. Ironically, Borges first read the great Spanish classics *El Cid* and *Don Quixote* in English translations. Later, when he read *Don Quixote* in its original Spanish, he said it sounded like a bad translation!

The Borges family was traveling in Europe when World War I broke out. They took refuge in neutral Switzerland, where Borges attended school and learned to speak three more languages—French, Latin, and German. After the war, the family moved first to Italy, then to Spain, and finally back to Argentina.

Borges began his career as a poet, and he always considered himself a poet first and foremost. In the 1940s, however, Borges turned to experimental prose, writing stories about transparent tigers, wizards who conjure up visions in a bowl of ink, and encyclopedias that do not record events but cause them. The stories in *The Garden of the Forking Paths* (1941) and *El Aleph* (1945) ignore plot and character and most of the usual elements of fiction. They instead blend fact and fantasy in a world of games and riddles, literary mystery, and philosophical inquiry.

It was also during the 1940s that Borges began using one of his most famous images—that of the labyrinth, or maze. Borges used the labyrinth as a metaphor for our journey through life, with all its surprising twists, turns, and dead ends.

Reader's Guide

BORGES AND MYSELF

Background

Borges was interested in philosophical issues, such as the nature of reality and the interplay between the imagined and the real. He was especially interested in how art affects the way we perceive the world. He believed that reality consists not only of what we have actually seen and done, but also of what we have read and what our reading has led us to imagine.

Borges calls the following story "my personal rendering of the old Jekyll-and-Hyde theme, save that in their case the opposition is between good and evil and in my version the opposites are the spectator and the spectacle."

Writer's Response

Writers and artists often feel that they live two very different lives—an imaginative life and a life as a regular person. Think of a writer or artist you have read or heard about. Describe how that person's public image differs from his or her real personality. (For example, Stephen King writes horror stories but lives a peaceful life in the countryside of New England.)

Literary Focus

Borges writes this story from the **first-person point of view**. The **first-person narrator** is the "I" character who tells the story. Generally, when we read a story with a first-person narrator, we feel as if we are listening to a friend, or as if we are reading someone's letters or diary. In this unusual story, the first-person narrator and the "other man" that he is talking about are different aspects of the same person.

Jorge Luis Borges **165**

BORGES AND MYSELF

Jorge Luis Borges

translated by

N. T. DI GIOVANNI AND JORGE LUIS BORGES

As you read, notice how the speaker and Borges are different.

It's to the other man, to Borges, that things happen. I walk along the streets of Buenos Aires, stopping now and then—perhaps out of habit—to look at the arch of an old entranceway or a grillwork gate; of Borges I get news through the mail and glimpse his name among a committee of professors or in a dictionary of biography. I have a taste for hourglasses, maps, eighteenth-century typography, the roots of words, the smell of coffee, and Stevenson's[1] prose; the other man shares these likes, but in a showy way that turns them into stagy mannerisms. It would be an exaggeration to say that we are on bad terms; I live, I let myself live, so that Borges can weave his tales and poems, and

DRAWING HANDS, M. C. ESCHER, 1948.
Do you think that this drawing aptly reflects Borges' ideas? Why or why not?

those tales and poems are my justification. It is not hard for me to admit that he has managed to write a few worthwhile pages, but these pages cannot save me, perhaps because what is good no longer belongs to anyone—not even the other man—but rather to speech or tradition. In any case, I am

---

1. **Stevenson's:** Robert Louis Stevenson (1850–1894), Scottish writer of adventure novels, poems, and essays.

fated to become lost once and for all, and only some moment of myself will survive in the other man. Little by little, I have been surrendering everything to him, even though I have evidence of his stubborn habit of falsification and exaggerating. Spinoza[2] held that all things try to keep on being themselves; a stone wants to be a stone and the tiger, a tiger. I shall remain in Borges, not in myself (if it is so that I am someone), but I recognize myself less in his books than in those of others or than in the laborious tuning of a guitar. Years ago, I tried ridding myself of him and I went from myths of the outlying slums of the city to games with time and infinity, but those games are now part of Borges and I will have to turn to other things. And so, my life is a running away, and I lose everything and everything is left to oblivion or to the other man.

Which of us is writing this page I don't know.

---

2. **Spinoza:** Baruch Spinoza (1632–1677), Dutch philosopher.

First Thoughts

Who is the speaker in this "story"? How is he different from "Borges"?

Identifying Facts

1. According to the speaker, to whom do "things happen"?
2. According to the speaker, what is the justification for his life?
3. What is the speaker "fated" to become?
4. What does the speaker "have evidence" of?
5. At the end, what is it that the speaker does not know?

Interpreting Meanings

1. What distinction does the speaker make between "Borges" and "myself"? Why would "Borges" seem "showy" or "stagy"?
2. What things does the speaker like? What does he mean when he says that "Borges" turns these things into "stagy mannerisms"?
3. According to the speaker, "Borges'" work does not belong to him, but to "speech or tradition." What do you think this means?

Applying Meanings

Do you think most people can feel like two different people? If so, when and why might someone feel like this?

Creative Writing Response

Letting a "Double" Speak. Think about the different sides of your personality. What part of your personality comes out more strongly at school? at home? when you are alone? Write a short diary entry following the model of "Borges and Myself." The "I" character is your private side that others do not often see. The character with your name is the public part of your personality. You may have the "I" character comment on the daily activities of the other character.

Before you begin writing you may want to fill out a chart like this:

Characteristics I Show in Public	How I Really Am

SEEING CONNECTIONS

The Divided Self

Modernism is a twentieth-century literary movement that began in Europe. Influenced by new ideas in psychology, the modernists explored the split between the artist's social and private selves, seeing the artist as a lonely figure struggling in an insensitive world.

The Puerto Rican poet Julia de Burgos (hōōl'ē·ə dā bōōr'gôs) (1914–1953), as both a woman and an artist, was keenly aware of the struggle to remain faithful to her art in the face of society's prejudices and pressures. During her short lifetime, she took part in the fierce controversy over Puerto Rican independence. Because her political views and feminist leanings were not popular, she had difficulty supporting herself through her writing, and she ultimately died in poverty at the age of thirty-nine.

The following poem by de Burgos, like "Borges and Myself," explores the idea that the artist's everyday self is divided from his or her creative self. How is de Burgos's view of this division similar to Borges's? How is it different?

To Julia de Burgos
Julia de Burgos
translated by
Grace Schulman

The people are saying that I am your enemy,
That in poetry I give you to the world.

They lie, Julia de Burgos. They lie, Julia
  de Burgos.
The voice that rises in my verses is not your
  voice: it is my voice;
5 For you are the clothing and I am the
  essence;
Between us lies the deepest abyss.

You are the bloodless doll of social lies
And I the virile spark of human truth;

You are the honey of courtly hypocrisy;
  not I—
10 I bare my heart in all my poems.

You, like your world, are selfish; not I—
I gamble everything to be what I am.

You are only the serious lady. Señora.
  Doña[1] Julia.
Not I. I am life. I am strength. I am woman.

15 You belong to your husband, your master.
  Not I:
I belong to nobody or to all, for to all, to all
I give myself in my pure feelings and
  thoughts.

You curl your hair and paint your face.
  Not I:
I am curled by the wind, painted by the sun.

20 You are the lady of the house, resigned,
  submissive,
Tied to the bigotry of men. Not I:
I am Rocinante,[2] bolting free, wildly
Snuffling the horizons of the justice of God.

---

1. **Doña** (dô'nyä): a Spanish title of respect given to a woman, equivalent to "Lady" or "Madam."
2. **Rocinante** (rō'sē·nän'tä): the horse that carried Don Quixote on his quests.

Octavio Paz
b. 1914, Mexico

Octavio Paz and his wife, María José.

UPI/Bettmann Newsphotos

Octavio Paz (ôk·tä′vyô päs) was born in Mexico City into a family he calls "typically Mexican"—part Spanish, part Indian, and not very wealthy. Paz grew up in his grandfather's home, which he remembers as an old house that was falling apart, but that had a huge, overgrown garden and one large room full of books. Paz read all the books in his grandfather's library and enjoyed his crumbling surroundings.

Paz's poetic talents were recognized when he was very young. His first volume of poetry, *Forest Moon* (1933), was published just after he graduated from the National University of Mexico. By the time his next volume was published in 1937, he was well on his way to literary celebrity. Diplomatic appointments took Paz to Paris, the Far East, and India. An enthusiastic scholar, Paz studied the literature and history of every nation he visited. In form, Paz's poetry often shows the influence of European modernist or Oriental verse, but his subjects and imagery are usually rooted in the sand, stones, and soil of the Mexican landscape. With these simple images, Paz often explores difficult philosophical concepts, such as the nature of truth and reality. For example, the subject of his longest poem, *Sun Stone* (1957), is the carved stone disc that the ancient Aztecs used as their calendar. The poem deals with the complex ideas of circular time and the interrelatedness of all things. Paz is perhaps best known for his literary essays, such as those collected in *Labyrinth of Solitude*, which deals with the character of the Mexican people.

In accepting the 1990 Nobel Prize for literature, Octavio Paz recalled his early years as a writer. He claimed that he had no idea then why he wrote his poems—he only knew that he felt a deep need to write them. Only later did he come to understand that his poems were his passage to the present, his way of connecting himself to his place and to the modern world. And indeed, as one of the most influential poets and essayists in the world today, Octavio Paz has become a man of his century.

Octavio Paz **169**

Reader's Guide

WIND AND WATER AND STONE

Background

The cycles of Mexico's social/political history and of its natural history have inspired many of Paz's poems, including the one you are about to read. Much of Mexico is dry, rocky, and sparsely forested. The effects of wind and water are easily visible in this landscape, as certain areas are worn down and other areas are built up. Mexico's great civilizations have followed similar patterns of breaking down and building up. Around the year 900, the Mayans were replaced by the Toltecs, who in turn were conquered by the Aztecs. Centered at Tenochtitlán (now Mexico City), which means "stone rising in water," the Aztec empire fell to the Spanish conquerors early in the sixteenth century. Paz singles out the Spaniards' conquest of the Indians as the moment that the true Mexico became isolated and obscured. Mexico remained a colony of Spain until 1821, when a revolution won the new nation its independence.

Writer's Response

Think about some of the cycles in the world—the changing seasons, the water cycle, the human life cycle. Choose a cycle you have observed and write a paragraph describing it. Can you describe it in terms of birth, growth, maturity, decay, death, and rebirth?

Literary Focus

Personification is a figure of speech in which something nonhuman is given human characteristics. For example, if you say "The breeze whispered through the trees," you are personifying the breeze. A breeze can't really whisper; only a human being can. If you say, "The night is lonely," you are personifying the night, an inanimate or nonliving thing, by giving it feelings which it really doesn't have. Personification is an important element in the following poem by Paz.

WIND AND WATER AND STONE

Octavio Paz

translated by

MARK STRAND

❦ *As you read the poem, make a note of the words Paz uses to* **personify** *the wind, water, and stone.*

for Roger Caillois[1]

The water hollowed the stone,
the wind dispersed the water,
the stone stopped the wind.
Water and wind and stone.

5   The wind sculpted the stone,
the stone is a cup of water,
the water runs off and is wind.
Stone and wind and water.

The wind sings in its turnings,
10 the water murmurs as it goes,
the motionless stone is quiet.
Wind and water and stone.

One is the other, and is neither:
among their empty names
15 they pass and disappear,
water and stone and wind.

---

1. **Roger Caillois** (rō·zhä′ kī·wä′): French writer (1913–1978) who suggested that people were inspired to begin writing when they saw the natural markings on stones.

Ruins of the Mayan pyramid "el Castillo," Mexico.

❓ *Does the* **parallelism** *of this poem remind you of other poems or stories you have read in this book? Explain.*

Robert Frerck/Woodfin Camp & Associates

Octavio Paz   **171**

What deeper meanings can you see in this description of the way wind, water, and stone change and eventually disappear to be transformed into something else?

Identifying Facts

1. What does the water do in stanza 1? What does the wind do? the stone?
2. In stanza 2, what does the stone become when the wind sculpts it? What does the water become after it runs off?
3. In stanza 3, how is the stone different from the wind and water? What eventually happens to the wind and water and stone in stanza 4?

Interpreting Meanings

1. To what three scientific or natural processes do lines 1, 5, and 7 refer?
2. Given what you learned about the ancient meaning of the name *Tenochtitlán* in the Background (see page 170), do you think the stone in this poem is more than a mere stone? Explain your answer.
3. How are the wind, water, and stone **personified** in stanzas 2 and 3?
4. What does the poem suggest about the relationship of all things in nature? What does the last stanza suggest about the ability of natural things to endure?

5. In what sense might the poem actually be about human beings or human civilizations?

Applying Meanings

Do you see human life and human civilizations as moving in cycles that are constantly repeated? In other words, does everything pass through stages of birth, growth, maturity, decay, death, rebirth, and so on? Discuss your response to Paz's ideas.

Creative Writing Response

Personifying Nature. Write a poem or paragraph in which you **personify** some element of nature, such as a tree, a flower, an animal, or the sun, moon, stars, or sea.

After you have found a subject, fill out a chart like the one below until you are satisfied with your personification. Then use the chart as you write your paragraph or poem.

Subject: Sunset

Detail	Human Quality
Appearance	Dressed in a dusky rose gown
Actions	Lingered like a lover
Feelings	Sadly ducked under the horizon

Gabriel García Márquez
b. 1928, Colombia

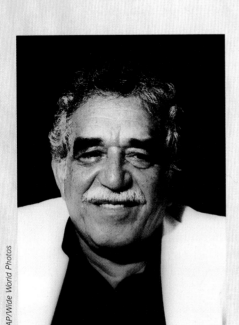

AP/Wide World Photos

Gabriel García Márquez (gär·sē'ä mär'kes) recalls that when he was nineteen and reading Franz Kafka's novella *The Metamorphosis* (see page 1154), he suddenly realized that the story's strangeness reminded him of tales his grandmother used to tell him. The surrealistic fiction of Kafka and the imaginative stories told by ordinary Latin Americans were to become major influences on García Márquez's fiction. But it was the second factor, the rich storytelling traditions and the unique imaginative fantasies of Latin America, that he found most valuable.

In his acceptance speech for the Nobel Prize for literature in 1982, García Márquez deplored the way Latin Americans ignore their own heritage and accept the hand-me-downs of European history and culture. He told the audience a story about a statue that stands in the main square of a Central American capital city. The statue is meant to represent the nation's president, but it is in fact a likeness of one of Napoleon's commanders that was purchased from a warehouse of secondhand sculpture in Paris. It is this kind of wholesale borrowing from the traditions of Europe that García Márquez dislikes. He wants Latin Americans to write from their own experience, with its unique blend of rituals and beliefs.

García Márquez spent the first eight years of his life with his grandparents in the small village of Aracataca, just off Colombia's northern Caribbean coast. He re-created this village, calling it Macondo, in his first short novel, *Leaf Storm* (1955), and later in his great novel *One Hundred Years of Solitude* (1967). Although Macondo is little more than a railway station set in a swampy wilderness, it seems that nearly anything that could possibly happen happens there—from the merely strange to the supernatural. With the publication of *One Hundred Years of Solitude* in English in 1970, the technique now called **magical realism** came to international attention. In García Márquez's fiction, as in that of a number of other Latin American authors, the reader is never certain about what is "real" and what is "fantasy."

Reader's Guide

THE HANDSOMEST DROWNED MAN IN THE WORLD

Background

"The Handsomest Drowned Man in the World" has many characteristics of **myth**: it features a superhuman character, supernatural events, and includes a marvelous **metamorphosis**, or transformation. This so-called "tale for children" is also enriched by **allusions** that connect it with Homer's *Odyssey,* the epic story of another "superman" who also washes ashore from the sea. Like a mythic hero, Esteban arrives mysteriously and, even though he is dead, soon becomes an important part of the villagers' lives. The story is not about Esteban, however—it is about the villagers, whose imaginations are fired by this bizarre gift from the sea.

Writer's Response

Since the village in which this story is set is on the edge of the sea, drownings would not be unusual. Stop after you finish the first two paragraphs of the story. Then freewrite your responses to the scene. Is there any hint in these opening paragraphs that the story won't be a realistic tale about a drowning?

Literary Focus

Magical realism, a literary style that was born in Latin America and has since been imitated by writers the world over, combines incredible events with realistic details and relates them all in a matter-of-fact tone. The term *magical realism* (*lo real maravilloso*) was coined in 1949 by the Cuban novelist, essayist, and musicologist Alejo Carpentier. He used the term to describe a blurring of the lines that usually separate what seems "real" to the reader from what seems imagined or "unreal" to the same reader. Carpentier believed that by incorporating magic, myth, imagination, and religion into literature, we can expand our rigid concept of "reality."

The Handsomest Drowned Man in the World

Gabriel García Márquez

translated by

Gregory Rabassa

> García Márquez subtitles this story "A Tale for Children," even though it is more complex than an ordinary children's tale. In what sense must the reader become a child to accept and respond to the magical realism of the story?

Pre-Columbian gold mask. *Archaeologists believe this may have been a funerary mask.*

George Holton/Photo Researchers, Inc.

The first children who saw the dark and slinky bulge approaching through the sea let themselves think it was an enemy ship. Then they saw it had no flags or masts and they thought it was a whale. But when it was washed up on the beach, they removed the clumps of seaweed, the jellyfish tentacles, and the remains of fish and flotsam, and only then did they see that it was a drowned man.

They had been playing with him all afternoon, burying him in the sand and digging him up again, when someone chanced to see them and spread the alarm in the village. The men who carried him to the nearest house noticed that he weighed more than any dead man they had ever known, almost as much as a horse, and they said to each other that maybe he'd been floating too long and the water had got into his bones. When they laid him on the floor they said he'd been taller than all other men because there was barely enough room for him in the house, but they thought that maybe the ability to keep on growing after death was part of the nature of certain drowned men. He had the smell of the sea about him and only his shape gave one to suppose that it was the corpse of a human being, because the skin was covered with a crust of mud and scales.

They did not even have to clean off his face to know that the dead man was a stranger. The village was made up of only twenty-odd wooden houses that had stone courtyards with no flowers and which were spread about on the end of a desertlike cape. There was so little land that mothers always went about with the fear that the wind would carry off their children, and the few dead that the years had caused among them had to be thrown off the cliffs. But the sea was calm and bountiful and all the men fit into seven boats. So when they found the drowned man they simply had to look at one another to see that they were all there.

That night they did not go out to work at sea. While the men went to find out if anyone was missing in neighboring villages, the women stayed behind to care for the drowned man. They took the mud off with grass swabs, they removed the underwater stones entangled in his hair, and they scraped the crust off with tools used for scaling fish. As they were doing that they noticed that the vegetation on him came from faraway oceans and deep water and that his clothes were in tatters, as if he had sailed through labyrinths of coral. They noticed, too, that he bore his death with pride, for he did not have the lonely look of other drowned men who came out of the sea or that haggard, needy look of men who drowned in rivers. But only when they finished cleaning him off did they become aware of the kind of man he was, and it left

Quilt from Cartagena, Colombia.
? Do you find the villagers' reaction to the discovery of the corpse strange? Why or why not?

them breathless. Not only was he the tallest, strongest, most virile, and best built man they had ever seen, but even though they were looking at him there was no room for him in their imagination.

They could not find a bed in the village large enough to lay him on, nor was there a table solid enough to use for his wake. The tallest men's holiday pants would not fit him, not the fattest ones' Sunday shirts, nor the shoes of the one with the biggest feet. Fascinated by his huge size and his beauty, the women then decided to make him some pants from a large piece of sail and a shirt from some bridal brabant linen[1] so that he could continue through his death with dignity. As they sewed, sitting in a circle and gazing at the corpse between stitches, it seemed to them that the wind had never been so steady nor the sea so restless as on that night, and they supposed that the change had something to do with the dead man. They thought that if that magnificent man had lived in the village, his house would have had the widest doors, the highest ceiling, and the strongest floor, his bedstead would have been made from a midship frame held together by iron bolts, and his wife would have been the happiest woman. They thought that he would have had so much authority that he could have drawn fish out of the sea simply by calling their names and that he would have put so much work into his land that springs would have burst forth from among the rocks so that he would have been able to plant flowers on the cliffs. They secretly compared him to their own men, thinking that for all their lives theirs were incapable of doing what he could do in one night, and they ended up dismissing them deep in their hearts as the weakest, meanest, and most useless creatures on earth. They were wandering through that maze of fantasy when the oldest woman, who as the oldest had looked upon the drowned man with more compassion than passion, sighed:

"He has the face of someone called Esteban."[2]

It was true. Most of them had only to take another look at him to see that he could not have any other name. The more stubborn among them, who were the youngest, still lived for a few hours with the illusion that when they put his clothes on and he lay among the flowers in patent leather shoes his name might be Lautaro.[3] But it was a vain illusion. There had not been enough canvas, the poorly cut and worse sewn pants were too tight, and the hidden strength of his heart popped the buttons on his shirt. After midnight the whistling of the wind died down and the sea fell into its Wednesday drowsiness. The silence put an end to any last doubts: he was Esteban. The women who had dressed him, who had combed his hair, had cut his nails and shaved him, were unable to hold back a shudder of pity when they had to resign themselves to his being dragged along the ground. It was then that they understood how unhappy he must have been with that huge body since it bothered him even after death. They could see him in life, condemned to going through doors sideways, cracking his head on crossbeams, remaining on his feet during visits, not knowing what to do with his soft, pink, sealion hands while the lady of the house looked for her most resistant chair and begged him, frightened to death, sit here, Esteban, please, and he, leaning against the wall, smiling, don't bother, ma'am, I'm fine where I am, his heels raw and his back roasted from having done the same thing so

---

1. **brabant** (brə·bant') **linen:** linen from Brabant, an area in Holland and Belgium known for its fine lace and cloth.

---

2. **Esteban** (es·te'bän): "Stephen" (Spanish); in Christian tradition, Stephen was the first martyr. He was said to have been stoned to death for his beliefs.

3. **Lautaro** (lou·tär'o)

many times whenever he paid a visit, don't bother, ma'am, I'm fine where I am, just to avoid the embarrassment of breaking up the chair, and never knowing perhaps that the ones who said don't go, Esteban, at least wait till the coffee's ready, were the ones who later on would whisper the big boob finally left, how nice, the handsome fool has gone. That was what the women were thinking beside the body a little before dawn. Later, when they covered his face with a handkerchief so that the light would not bother him, he looked so forever dead, so defenseless, so much like their men that the first furrows of tears opened in their hearts. It was one of the younger ones who began the weeping. The others, coming to, went from sighs to wails, and the more they sobbed the more they felt like weeping, because the drowned man was becoming all the more Esteban for them, and so they wept so much, for he was the most destitute, most peaceful, and most obliging man on earth, poor Esteban. So when the men returned with the news that the drowned man was not from the neighboring villages either, the women felt an opening of jubilation in the midst of their tears.

"Praise the Lord," they sighed, "he's ours!"

The men thought the fuss was only womanish frivolity. Fatigued because of the difficult nighttime inquiries, all they wanted was to get rid of the bother of the newcomer once and for all before the sun grew strong on that arid, windless day. They improvised a litter with the remains of foremasts and gaffs,[4] tying it together with rigging so that it would bear the weight of the body until they reached the cliffs. They wanted to tie the anchor from a cargo ship to him so that he would sink easily into the deepest waves,

where fish are blind and divers die of nostalgia, and bad currents would not bring him back to shore, as had happened with other bodies. But the more they hurried, the more the women thought of ways to waste time. They walked about like startled hens, pecking with the sea charms[5] on their breasts, some interfering on one side to put a scapular[6] of the good wind on the drowned man, some on the other side to put a wrist compass on him, and after a great deal of *get away from there, woman, stay out of the way, look, you almost made me fall on top of the dead man*, the men began to feel mistrust in their livers and started grumbling about why so many main-altar decorations for a stranger, because no matter how many nails and holy-water jars he had on him, the sharks would chew him all the same, but the women kept piling on their junk relics, running back and forth, stumbling, while they released in sighs what they did not in tears, so that the men finally exploded with *since when has there ever been such a fuss over a drifting corpse, a drowned nobody, a piece of cold Wednesday meat.*[7] One of the women, mortified by so much lack of care, then removed the handkerchief from the dead man's face and the men were left breathless, too.

He was Esteban. It was not necessary to repeat it for them to recognize him. If they had been told Sir Walter Raleigh, even they might have been impressed with his gringo accent, the macaw on his shoulder, his cannibal-killing blunderbuss, but there could

---

4. **gaffs:** poles supporting a sail.

5. **sea charms:** magic charms that supposedly protect the wearer from dangers at sea.

6. **scapular** (skap'yə·lər): holy images on a string, worn under the clothes as a mark of religious devotion.

7. **Wednesday meat:** meat left over from Sunday dinner.

be only one Esteban in the world and there he was, stretched out like a sperm whale, shoeless, wearing the pants of an undersized child, and with those stony nails that had to be cut with a knife. They only had to take the handkerchief off his face to see that he was ashamed, that it was not his fault that he was so big or so heavy or so handsome, and if he had known that this was going to happen, he would have looked for a more discreet place to drown in, seriously, I even would have tied the anchor off a galleon around my neck and staggered off a cliff like someone who doesn't like things in order not to be upsetting people now with this Wednesday dead body, as you people say, in order not to be bothering anyone with this filthy piece of cold meat that doesn't have anything to do with me. There was so much truth in his manner that even the most mistrustful men, the ones who felt the bitterness of endless nights at sea fearing that their women would tire of dreaming about them and begin to dream of drowned men, even they and others who were harder still shuddered in the marrow of their bones at Esteban's sincerity.

That was how they came to hold the most splendid funeral they could conceive of for an abandoned drowned man. Some women who had gone to get flowers in the neighboring villages returned with other women who could not believe what they had been told, and those women went back for more flowers when they saw the dead man, and they brought more and more until there were so many flowers and so many people that it was hard to walk about. At the final moment it pained them to return him to the waters as an orphan and they chose a father and mother from among the best people, and aunts and uncles and cousins, so that through him all the inhabitants of the village became kinsmen. Some sailors who heard the weeping from a distance went off course, and people heard of one who had himself tied to the mainmast, remembering ancient fables about sirens.[8] While they fought for the privilege of carrying him on their shoulders along the steep escarpment by the cliffs, men and women became aware for the first time of the desolation of their streets, the dryness of their courtyards, the narrowness of their dreams as they faced the splendor and beauty of their drowned man. They let him go without an anchor so that he could come back if he wished and whenever he wished, and they all held their breath for the fraction of centuries the body took to fall into the abyss. They did not need to look at one another to realize that they were no longer all present, that they would never be. But they also knew that everything would be different from then on, that their houses would have wider doors, higher ceilings, and stronger floors so that Esteban's memory could go everywhere without bumping into beams and so that no one in the future would dare whisper the big boob finally died, too bad, the handsome fool has finally died, because they were going to paint their house fronts gay colors to make Esteban's memory eternal and they were going to break their backs digging for springs among the stones and planting flowers on the cliffs so that in future years at dawn the passengers on great liners would awaken, suffocated by the smell

---

8. **sirens:** in Greek mythology, beautiful but destructive creatures, half-woman and half-bird, whose seductive songs lured sailors to turn their ships onto the rocky coasts; Odysseus, hero of Homer's *Odyssey*, filled his crew's ears with wax so that they could pass the sirens safely. But Odysseus wanted to hear their songs. He had the crew tie him to the ship's mast so that he could listen to the sirens' songs yet not turn the boat onto the rocks.

Gabriel García Márquez   **179**

of gardens on the high seas, and the captain would have to come down from the bridge in his dress uniform, with his astrolabe,[9] his pole star,[10] and his row of war medals, and, pointing to the promontory of roses on the horizon, he would say in fourteen languages, look there, where the wind is so peaceful now that it's gone to sleep beneath the beds, over there, where the sun's so bright that the sunflowers don't know which way to turn, yes, over there, that's Esteban's village.

---

9. **astrolabe:** instrument that can find a star's altitude and help navigators determine their position at sea.
10. **pole star:** Polaris, or the North Star; it is used by navigators in the northern hemisphere to determine their location because it remains almost fixed throughout the night.

Medialuna Bay, Colombia.

Loren McIntyre/Woodfin Camp & Associates

First Thoughts

What image of the drowned man is strongest in your mind? How did you feel about some of the realistic passages describing Esteban?

Identifying Facts

1. What do details such as the galleon, the blunderbuss, and the astrolabe suggest about the time period of the story?
2. What is unusual about the drowned man? How do the men explain his unusual characteristics?
3. What name do the villagers give the drowned man? Why?
4. How does the village change after the drowned man washes ashore?

Interpreting Meanings

1. **Setting** is a major element in this story, as it is in all of García Márquez's fiction. Briefly describe this story's setting and

explain how it contributes to the **magical realism** of the story.

2. A strong **theme** is suggested by the fabulous events of this story and the subsequent changes in the village. What does this story reveal about the universal need for heroes and great dreams?

3. This story is told from the **third-person point of view**, but Esteban becomes so real in the minds of the villagers that they imagine him speaking in the **first person**. When Esteban speaks using the pronoun "I" (see pages 178 and 179), does he become more real to you?

Applying Meanings

The events of this story make the villagers see "for the first time the desolation of their streets, the dryness of their courtyards," and "the narrowness of their dreams." What experiences in real life might make people look at their lives in a different way and see the shortcomings of how they live?

Creative Writing Response

Changing the Premise. If the man who washed to shore had been alive, do you think the outcome of this story would have been the same? Would the villagers have extended as much love and hospitality toward a live man as they did toward the dead man? Write a story using the same setting, but bring Esteban to life. Be sure to explain who Esteban is and how he happened to wash up on the shore of this village. Feel free to use elements of **magical realism** in your story.

Critical Writing Response

Analyzing Magical Realism. In a brief essay, analyze García Márquez's use of **magical realism** in this story. Before you write, review the story to locate some particularly realistic details. Then locate some of the story's fantastic elements. You might organize your details on a chart like the one below.

Fantastic Events	Realistic Details

At the end of your essay, state your general response to the use of magical realism. Do you like this blurring of fantasy and reality? Or do you prefer either pure fantasy or pure realism?

Margaret Atwood
b. 1939, Canada

Margaret Atwood, one of Canada's most prominent writers, began writing when she was five years old. Except for a "dark period between the ages of eight and sixteen," she has been writing ever since— poetry, novels, children's books, essays, criticism, and television plays. When asked by an interviewer why she writes, Atwood replied, "It's a human activity. I think the real question is 'Why doesn't everyone?'"

Atwood spent a good portion of her childhood in the Canadian wilderness. Her father, an entomologist, or one who studies insects, often spent weeks working in remote areas. Because Margaret was part of these family trips, she did not attend a full year of school until she was in the eighth grade. Yet she graduated from the University of Toronto and received a master's degree in English literature from Radcliffe College.

Atwood is often credited with helping (some say single-handedly) to define Canada's literary identity. For years, Canadian literature had been viewed as indistinguishable from that of Britain or the United States. Atwood corrected this view in her guide to Canadian literature *Survival* (1972), by showing that survival is the central theme in Canadian writing. In Atwood's fiction, animals, women, and Canada itself are all seen as victims as they struggle to survive in a hostile world.

Atwood often uses nature metaphorically in her writing. In her novel *Surfacing* (1972), a woman returns to the Canadian wilderness of her youth to search for her missing father. Here, the natural landscape is a reservoir of mythic meaning, representing childhood innocence as well as an escape from commercialization. In her novel *The Handmaid's Tale* (1986), Atwood reworks the science-fiction genre from a feminist perspective. She envisions a United States run by a puritanical dictatorship that seeks to control women and their reproductive capabilities. Whether she is dealing with love, politics, ecology, or feminism, Atwood says, "I'm interested in edges, undertows, permutations, in taking things that might be viewed as eccentric or marginal and pulling them into the center."

Reader's Guide

ELEGY FOR THE GIANT TORTOISES

Background

The giant tortoises that Atwood writes about in "Elegy for the Giant Tortoises" are magnificent creatures that weigh over five hundred pounds and live over one hundred and fifty years. Millions of these animals used to be found on thousands of islands in the Pacific and Indian oceans. During the seventeenth, eighteenth, and nineteenth centuries, however, the crews of whaling ships and other vessels slaughtered so many tortoises that some species became extinct and others still teeter on the brink of extinction. Today, scientists are working on breeding programs to save the giant tortoises living on the Galápagos Islands off the coast of Ecuador.

The poem that you are about to read is from the collection *The Animals in That Country* (1968), which vividly demonstrates how human civilization can damage and destroy the natural world. In the poem, Atwood mentions three other creatures that became extinct or are threatened with extinction—the dodo, the passenger pigeon, and the whooping crane. Dodo birds had disappeared by 1680, chiefly because Europeans hunted them for sport. In colonial times, the passenger pigeon population in North America numbered in the billions, and flocks passing overhead would block out the sun. But the birds were so widely hunted by America's settlers that in 1914 the last passenger pigeon died in a Cincinnati zoo. The breeding grounds of the whooping crane have been so threatened by development that this bird has joined numerous other animals on the list of endangered species.

Writer's Response

Briefly write down your feelings about extinct or endangered animals like the giant tortoises. Do you think they should be protected? Or is extinction just part of life and something we shouldn't worry about?

Literary Focus

An **elegy** is a poem of mourning, usually over the death of a person. An elegy may also be a lament over the passing of life or beauty, or it may be a meditation on the nature of death. Elegies are usually formal in language and structure, and solemn or even melancholy in tone.

ELEGY FOR THE GIANT TORTOISES

Margaret Atwood

The title says that this is an elegy for giant tortoises. Who or what else might it be an elegy for?

Let others pray for the passenger pigeon,
the dodo, the whooping crane, the Eskimo:
everyone must specialize

5   I will confine myself to a meditation
upon the giant tortoises
withering finally on a remote island.

I concentrate in subway stations,
in parks, I can't quite see them,
they move to the peripheries of my eyes

10   but on the last day they will be there;
already the event
like a wave traveling shapes vision:

on the road where I stand they will materialize,
plodding past me in a straggling line
15   awkward without water

their small heads pondering
from side to side, their useless armor
sadder than tanks and history,

in their closed gaze ocean and sunlight paralyzed,
20   lumbering up the steps, under the archways
toward the square glass altars

where the brittle gods are kept,
the relics of what we have destroyed,
our holy and obsolete symbols.

Giant tortoise.

First Thoughts

Do you think acts of imagination like the speaker's (or like Atwood's in creating this poem) can help save the tortoises or restore "what we have destroyed"?

Identifying Facts

1. In the first stanza, what does the speaker say she will *not* pray for? Why not?

2. Where does the speaker have trouble seeing the tortoises? When is she sure "they will be there"?

3. Where does the speaker say the tortoises will appear? Where will they go?

Interpreting Meanings

1. Why do you think Atwood includes the Eskimo in the first stanza?

2. On one level, what "last day" is the speaker referring to in line 10? The term "last day" might also refer to Judgment Day, when the dead are able to rise and be judged by God. If so, what judgment on humanity does the poem suggest may be made on that day?

3. What do the "tanks and history" in line 18 bring to your mind? What does the speaker mean when she says that the armor of the tortoises is "useless" and "sadder than tanks and history"?

4. Reread the last five lines of the poem carefully. What actual buildings might these lines refer to? What other building is Atwood comparing them to in using words like *archways, altars,* and *gods*?

5. What religious **images** can you find in the poem? What message about our treatment of nature does this imagery suggest?

6. Do you think that this is an **elegy** only for the tortoises, or is it also for humans? Explain.

Applying Meanings

What are some of the environmental concerns that you think we need to address? Make a list of four important environmental concerns and discuss them with the class.

Creative Writing Response

Describing Visual Images. If you were going to illustrate this poem, what **images** would you concentrate on? In a few sentences, cite the lines that contain these images and describe how you would depict them. You might want to draw a picture to accompany your description.

Critical Writing Response

Writing About a Poem's Theme. The **theme** is the central insight about life or the world revealed in a work of literature. A possible theme of this poem is: Human beings must think beyond themselves and imagine the lives of other creatures so that we do not destroy them.

In a brief essay, either support or refute this theme, citing details from the poem to support your choice. If you disagree with this theme, suggest a more accurate one in your essay.

Jamaica Kincaid
b. 1949, Antigua

Sigrid Estrada

Over the kitchen table in the Vermont home that Jamaica Kincaid shares with her American-born husband and children is a map of the island of Antigua (än·tē′gwə). It serves as a constant reminder of the tiny Caribbean island where Kincaid grew up and where she still sets most of her fiction.

Born Elaine Potter Richardson to an Antiguan couple of African descent, Kincaid grew up in St. John's, Antigua's largest city. Antigua was still a British colony during Kin-

caid's childhood, and she came to hate the European colonialism that had exploited her people for so many centuries.

At school Kincaid was a bright but unruly pupil, often punished for her outspokenness. Once, her punishment was to copy long passages from John Milton's epic *Paradise Lost*, a work she can now quote at length.

After attending college in New Hampshire, Kincaid returned to New York City and began writing for a teenage girls' magazine, using her pen name for the first time. Soon Kincaid published her first story, "Girl," in *The New Yorker.* The story consists of a single long sentence of instructions given by a mother to a daughter who is possibly, from the mother's point of view, headed for rebellion and trouble.

One of the central subjects of Kincaid's fiction is the parent-child relationship and the problems her rebellious heroines have with their worried mothers. Kincaid also writes about the anger that West Indians of African descent feel about their colonial past. "As I sit here enjoying myself to a degree," Kincaid told *New York Times* interviewer Leslie Garis, "I never give up thinking about the way I came into the world, how my ancestors came from Africa to the West Indies as slaves. I just could never forget it."

Reader's Guide

A WALK TO THE JETTY
from Annie John

Background

Antigua, the main island of the nation of Antigua and Barbuda, was a British colony for over three hundred years. The British forcibly brought people from Africa to work as slaves on the island's sugar plantations. Today the descendants of these Africans make up most of Antigua's population. Antigua won its independence in 1981, but British influences are still strong on the island. The people speak English and many belong to the Anglican (Episcopalian) Church. The school Jamaica Kincaid attended as a girl was modeled on British schools of the time—boys and girls were educated separately, uniforms were required, and a British curriculum, especially in literature, was stressed.

The selection you are about to read is taken from the last part of the last chapter of Kincaid's coming-of-age novel *Annie John*. In this section of the novel, the young narrator is about to leave Antigua by boat for England.

Writer's Response

When you think back over the years of your childhood, what incidents and images come to your mind? Make a few notes about your strongest memories. Which memories make you happy? Which ones make you sad or angry?

Literary Focus

Much of twentieth-century literature deals with **internal conflicts**, rather than with action-packed **external conflicts**. Annie John, the narrator of this selection, has all kinds of conflicts with other characters throughout the book, but in this excerpt, we see only her internal conflicts.

A WALK TO THE JETTY
from Annie John
Jamaica Kincaid

◆ *As you read, think about why the narrator is leaving her home and how she feels about leaving.*

My mother had arranged with a stevedore[1] to take my trunk to the jetty ahead of me. At ten o'clock on the dot, I was dressed, and we set off for the jetty. An hour after that, I would board a launch that would take me out to sea, where I then would board the ship. Starting out, as if for old time's sake and without giving it a thought, we lined up in the old way: I walking between my mother and my father. I loomed way above my father and could see the top of his head. We must have made a strange sight: a grown girl all dressed up in the middle of a morning, in the middle of the week, walking in step in the middle between her two parents, for people we didn't know stared at us. It was all of half an hour's walk from our house to the jetty, but I was passing through most of the years of my life. We passed by the house where Miss Dulcie, the seamstress that I had been apprenticed to for a time, lived, and just as I was passing by, a wave of bad feeling for her came over me, because I suddenly remembered that the months I spent with her all she had me do was sweep the floor, which was always full of threads and pins and needles, and I never seemed

Antiguan landscape.

? *What happens to the narrator as she passes in front of the seamstress's shop? How have her feelings about the seamstress changed?*

---

1. **stevedore** (stē′və·dôr′): a person who loads and unloads cargo on a ship.

to sweep it clean enough to please her. Then she would send me to the store to buy buttons or thread, though I was only allowed to do this if I was given a sample of the button or thread, and then she would find fault even though they were an exact match of the samples she had given me. And all the while she said to me, "A girl like you will never learn to sew properly, you know." At the time, I don't suppose I minded it, because it was customary to treat the first-year apprentice with such scorn, but now I

placed on the dustheap of my life Miss Dulcie and everything that I had had to do with her.

We were soon on the road that I had taken to school, to church, to Sunday school, to choir practice, to Brownie meetings, to Girl Guide meetings, to meet a friend. I was five years old when I first walked on this road unaccompanied by someone to hold my hand. My mother had placed three pennies in my little basket, which was a duplicate of her bigger basket, and sent me to the chemist's shop[2] to buy a pennyworth of senna leaves, a pennyworth of eucalyptus leaves, and a pennyworth of camphor. She then instructed me on what side of the road to walk, where to make a turn, where to cross, how to look carefully before I crossed, and if I met anyone that I knew to politely pass greetings and keep on my way. I was wearing a freshly ironed yellow dress that had printed on it scenes of acrobats flying through the air and swinging on a trapeze. I had just had a bath, and after it, instead of powdering me with my baby-smelling talcum powder, my mother had, as a special favor, let me use her own talcum powder, which smelled quite perfumy and came in a can that had painted on it people going out to dinner in nineteenth-century London and was called Mazie. How it pleased me to walk out the door and bend my head down to sniff at myself and see that I smelled just like my mother. I went to the chemist's shop, and he had to come from behind the counter and bend down to hear what it was that I wanted to buy, my voice was so little and timid then. I went back just the way I had come, and when I walked into the yard and presented my basket with its three

---

2. **chemist's shop:** the British term for a pharmacy or drugstore.

Jamaica Kincaid   **189**

packages to my mother, her eyes filled with tears and she swooped me up and held me high in the air and said that I was wonderful and good and that there would never be anybody better. If I had just conquered Persia, she couldn't have been more proud of me.

We passed by our church—the church in which I had been christened and received and had sung in the junior choir. We passed by a house in which a girl I used to like and was sure I couldn't live without had lived. Once, when she had mumps, I went to visit her against my mother's wishes, and we sat on her bed and ate the cure of roasted, buttered sweet potatoes that had been placed on her swollen jaws, held there by a piece of white cloth. I don't know how, but my mother found out about it, and I don't know how, but she put an end to our friendship. Shortly after, the girl moved with her family across the sea to somewhere else. We passed the doll store, where I would go with my mother when I was little and point out the doll I wanted that year for Christmas. We passed the store where I bought the much-fought-over shoes I wore to church to be received in. We passed the bank. On my sixth birthday, I was given, among other things, the present of a sixpence. My mother and I then went to this bank, and with the sixpence I opened my own savings account. I was given a little gray book with my name in big letters on it, and in the balance column it said "6d." Every Saturday morning after that, I was given a sixpence—later a shilling, and later a two-and-sixpence piece—and I would take it to the bank for deposit. I had never been allowed to withdraw even a farthing[3] from my bank account until just a few weeks before I was to leave; then the whole account was closed out, and I received from the bank the sum of six pounds ten shillings and two and a half pence.

We passed the office of the doctor who told my mother three times that I did not need glasses, that if my eyes were feeling weak a glass of carrot juice a day would make them strong again. This happened when I was eight. And so every day at recess I would run to my school gate and meet my mother, who was waiting for me with a glass of juice from carrots she had just grated and then squeezed, and I would drink it and then run back to meet my chums. I knew there was nothing at all wrong with my eyes, but I had recently read a story in *The Schoolgirl's Own Annual* in which the heroine, a girl a few years older than I was then, cut such a figure to my mind with the way she was always adjusting her small, round, horn-rimmed glasses that I felt I must have a pair exactly like them. When it became clear that I didn't need glasses, I began to complain about the glare of the sun being too much for my eyes, and I walked around with my hands shielding them—especially in my mother's presence. My mother then bought for me a pair of sunglasses with the exact horn-rimmed frames I wanted, and how I enjoyed the gestures of blowing on the lenses, wiping them with the hem of my uniform, adjusting the glasses when they slipped down my nose, and just removing them from their case and putting them on. In three weeks, I grew tired of them and they found a nice resting place in a drawer, along with some other things that at one time or another I couldn't live without.

We passed the store that sold only grooming aids, all imported from England. This store had in it a large porcelain dog—white, with black spots all over and a red ribbon

---

3. **farthing:** a former small British coin worth a fourth of a penny.

Sunday at church, Antigua.

took me along there, too. I would sit in her lap very quietly as she read books that she did not want to take home with her. I could not read the words yet, but just the way they looked on the page was interesting to me. Once, a book she was reading had a large picture of a man in it, and when I asked her who he was she told me that he was Louis Pasteur and that the book was about his life. It stuck in my mind, because she said it was because of him that she boiled my milk to purify it before I was allowed to drink it, that it was his idea, and that that was why the process was called pasteurization. One of the things I had put away in my mother's old trunk in which she kept all my childhood things was my library card. At that moment, I owed sevenpence in overdue fees.

As I passed by all these places, it was as if I were in a dream, for I didn't notice the people coming and going in and out of them, I didn't feel my feet touch ground, I didn't even feel my own body—I just saw these places as if they were hanging in the air, not having top or bottom, and as if I had gone in and out of them all in the same moment. The sun was bright; the sky was blue and just above my head. We then arrived at the jetty.

of satin tied around its neck. The dog sat in front of a white porcelain bowl that was always filled with fresh water, and it sat in such a way that it looked as if it had just taken a long drink. When I was a small child, I would ask my mother, if ever we were near this store, to please take me to see the dog, and I would stand in front of it, bent over slightly, my hands resting on my knees, and stare at it and stare at it. I thought this dog more beautiful and more real than any actual dog I had ever seen or any actual dog I would ever see. I must have outgrown my interest in the dog, for when it disappeared I never asked what became of it. We passed the library, and if there was anything on this walk that I might have wept over leaving, this most surely would have been the thing. My mother had been a member of the library long before I was born. And since she took me everywhere with her when I was quite little, when she went to the library she

My heart now beat fast, and no matter how hard I tried, I couldn't keep my mouth from falling open and my nostrils from spreading to the ends of my face. My old fear of slipping between the boards of the jetty and falling into the dark-green water where the dark-green eels lived came over me. When my father's stomach started to go bad, the doctor had recommended a walk every evening right after he ate his dinner. Sometimes he would take me with him. When he took me with him, we usually went to the jetty, and there he would sit and talk to the night watchman about cricket or some other thing that didn't interest me, because it was not personal; they didn't talk about their wives, or their children, or their parents, or about any of their likes and dislikes. They talked about things in such a strange way, and I didn't see what they found funny, but sometimes they made each other laugh so much that their guffaws would bound out to sea and send back an echo. I was always sorry when we got to the jetty and saw that the night watchman on duty was the one he enjoyed speaking to; it was like being locked up in a book filled with numbers and diagrams and what-ifs. For the thing about not being able to understand and enjoy what they were saying was I had nothing to take my mind off my fear of slipping in between the boards of the jetty.

Now, too, I had nothing to take my mind off what was happening to me. My mother and my father—I was leaving them forever. My home on an island—I was leaving it forever. What to make of everything? I felt a familiar hollow space inside. I felt I was being held down against my will. I felt I was burning up from head to toe. I felt that someone was tearing me up into little pieces and soon I would be able to see all the little pieces as they floated out into nothing in the deep blue sea. I didn't know whether to laugh or cry. I could see that it would be better not to think too clearly about any one thing. The launch was being made ready to take me, along with some other passengers, out to the ship that was anchored in the sea. My father paid our fares, and we joined a line of people waiting to board. My mother checked my bag to make sure that I had my passport, the money she had given me, and a sheet of paper placed between some pages in my Bible on which were written the

names of the relatives—people I had not known existed—with whom I would live in England. Across from the jetty was a wharf, and some stevedores were loading and unloading barges. I don't know why seeing that struck me so, but suddenly a wave of strong feeling came over me, and my heart swelled with a great gladness as the words "I shall never see this again" spilled out inside me. But then, just as quickly, my heart shriveled up and the words "I shall never see this again" stabbed at me. I don't know what stopped me from falling in a heap at my parents' feet.

When we were all on board, the launch headed out to sea. Away from the jetty, the water became the customary blue, and the launch left a wide path in it that looked like a road. I passed by sounds and smells that were so familiar that I had long ago stopped paying any attention to them. But now here they were, and the ever-present "I shall never see this again" bobbed up and down inside me. There was the sound of the seagull diving down into the water and coming up with something silverish in its mouth. There was the smell of the sea and the sight of small pieces of rubbish floating around in it. There were boats filled with fishermen coming in early. There was the sound of their voices as they shouted greetings to each other. There was the hot sun, there was the blue sea, there was the blue sky. Not very far away, there was the white sand of the shore, with the run-down houses all crowded in next to each other, for in some places only poor people lived near the shore. I was seated in the launch between my parents, and when I realized that I was gripping their hands tightly I glanced quickly to see if they were looking at me with scorn, for I felt sure that they must have known of my never-see-this-again feelings. But instead my father kissed me on the forehead and my mother kissed me on the mouth, and they both gave over their hands to me, so that I could grip them as much as I wanted. I was on the verge of feeling that it had all been a mistake, but I remembered that I wasn't a child anymore, and that now when I made up my mind about something I had to see it through. At that moment, we came to the ship, and that was that.

The goodbyes had to be quick, the captain said. My mother introduced herself to him and then introduced me. She told him to keep an eye on me, for I had never gone this far away from home on my own. She gave him a letter to pass on to the captain of the next ship that I would board in Barbados. They walked me to my cabin, a small space that I would share with someone else—a woman I did not know. I had never before slept in a room with someone I did not know. My father kissed me goodbye and told me to be good and to write home often. After he said this, he looked at me, then looked at the floor and swung his left foot, then looked at me again. I could see that he wanted to say something else, something that he had never said to me before, but then he just turned and walked away. My mother said, "Well," and then she threw her

arms around me. Big tears streamed down her face, and it must have been that—for I could not bear to see my mother cry—which started me crying, too. She then tightened her arms around me and held me to her close, so that I felt that I couldn't breathe. With that, my tears dried up and I was suddenly on my guard. "What does she want now?" I said to myself. Still holding me close to her, she said, in a voice that raked across my skin, "It doesn't matter what you do or where you go, I'll always be your mother and this will always be your home."

I dragged myself away from her and backed off a little, and then I shook myself, as if to wake myself out of a stupor. We looked at each other for a long time with smiles on our faces, but I know the opposite of that was in my heart. As if responding to some invisible cue, we both said, at the very same moment, "Well." Then my mother turned around and walked out the cabin door. I stood there for I don't know how long, and then I remembered that it was customary to stand on deck and wave to your relatives who were returning to shore. From the deck, I could not see my father, but I could see my mother facing the ship, her eyes searching to pick me out. I removed from my bag a red cotton handkerchief that she had earlier given me for this purpose, and I waved it wildly in the air. Recognizing me immediately, she waved back just as wildly, and we continued to do this until she became just a dot in the matchbox-size launch swallowed up in the big blue sea.

I went back to my cabin and lay down on my berth. Everything trembled as if it had a spring at its very center. I could hear the small waves lap-lapping around the ship. They made an unexpected sound, as if a vessel filled with liquid had been placed on its side and now was slowly emptying out.

Jamaica Kincaid **193**

First Thoughts

The narrator has conflicting feelings about her parents and her home. Which of her feelings came through most strongly for you?

Identifying Facts

1. As the narrator walks to the jetty she passes many places that stimulate memories from her childhood. Which places bring back good memories and which evoke bad memories?
2. Which place does the narrator most regret leaving?
3. When the narrator reaches the jetty, what old fear comes over her again?

Interpreting Meanings

1. What does the story about the eyeglasses reveal about the narrator's personality? What do her comments about the library reveal about her own **character**?
2. Why do you think the narrator suddenly notices sounds and smells that she never paid attention to before?
3. What **internal conflict** does the narrator experience about leaving the island? Is it resolved?
4. Reread the passage describing the father's actions after he kisses his daughter goodbye. What **internal conflict** do you think he is feeling? What do you think he wants to say to Annie John?
5. Based on what her daughter tells you, how would you describe the **character** of Annie's mother? What conflicting feelings does Annie seem to have toward this mother who obviously adores her?
6. The last sentence in this selection could be interpreted as a literal description of the ship Annie John is on. But suppose it could also be interpreted **metaphori-** cally—that is, figuratively. What might the writer really be talking about when she describes a vessel "emptying out"?

Applying Meanings

Do the narrator's feelings about her childhood remind you of any of your own feelings? At what point in her narrative did you most identify with her?

Creative Writing Response

Describing a Place. Suppose you are leaving the place where you live and that you know you will not return for a long time. Write a brief description of the spots you will remember and of the experiences and people you associate with them. You might want to imitate the style of this story and describe this place as if you are taking a last walk, perhaps to a bus or train station. Before you write, collect your details in a word cluster or list.

Critical Writing Response

Analyzing an Internal Conflict. Discrepancies, or differences, between a character's thoughts, words, and actions are good indications of an **internal conflict**. In a brief essay, analyze the narrator's internal conflicts. Discuss her personality, her attitudes, and the differences between her thoughts and actions. Support general statements with specific details from the selection. As a first step, you might find it helpful to list details on a chart like the one below to help you see and understand Annie's internal conflicts.

Annie's Remarks	
Annie's Actions	
Annie's Thoughts	
What Discrepancies Reveal	

Tales of the Islands *by Derek Walcott*

Few people could have predicted that the tiny Caribbean island of St. Lucia, where the predominant language is French creole, would produce a world-famous English-language poet. Yet Jamaica Kincaid's fellow West Indies writer Derek Walcott (born 1930) has received the Nobel Prize for his poetry. His most recent work, *Omeros* (1990), is a book-length narrative poem loosely based on Homer's epic poem the *Odyssey.* (*Omeros* is Greek for "Homer.")

Walcott makes his permanent home in the West Indies, although he has frequently traveled abroad. The islands' exotic beauty and their tragic colonial history (St. Lucia is a former French colony) are central subjects of his work. Many critics suggest that Walcott is torn between cultures: Caribbean and British, black and white. But Walcott sees his own mixed racial heritage as symbolic of the New World.

In the following poem, the final sonnet from a work entitled *Tales of the Islands,* Walcott describes his mixed feelings upon leaving St. Lucia for the first time. The poem's **epigraph**, or opening quotation—"*Adieu foulard*" (ə·dyōō′ fōō·lär′)—comes from a Creole folk song traditionally sung when people leave St. Lucia. The song bids *adieu,* or "farewell," to the *foulard,* or neckerchief, that is part of St. Lucia's national costume. As you read the poem, compare Walcott's tone and mood to that expressed by Jamaica Kincaid in "A Walk to the Jetty." How are these farewells alike and different?

Sunset in St. Lucia.

Chapter X
"Adieu foulard . . ."
from Tales of the Islands
Derek Walcott

I watched the island narrowing the fine
Writing of foam around the precipices then
The roads as small and casual as twine
Thrown on its mountains; I watched till the plane
5 Turned to the final north and turned above
The open channel with the gray sea between
The fishermen's islets until all that I love
Folded in cloud; I watched the shallow green
That broke in places where there would be reef,
10 The silver glinting on the fuselage, each mile
Dividing us and all fidelity strained
Till space would snap it. Then, after a while
I thought of nothing, nothing, I prayed, would change;
When we set down at Seawell it had rained.

Léopold Sédar Senghor
b. 1906, Senegal

Peter Jordan/Time Magazine

Léopold Sédar Senghor (lā·ô·pôld′ sä·dàr′ sä*r*·gôr′) has had a remarkable career as a poet, literary critic, political thinker, four-term president of Senegal, and spokesperson for the **négritude** movement. He was also the first black African to join the faculty of a French university and the first black member of the prestigious French Academy. Born and educated at a time when the colonizers of French West Africa were encouraging Africans to think of themselves as French, Senghor truly believed that he was a Frenchman who just happened to be black. When he went to Paris to study, however, he realized that the French would never accept him as one of their countrymen. He also realized that he was proud of his own culture and history and afraid that

both would soon disappear in the wake of European colonialism. He shared these thoughts with other black writers in Paris, such as Aimé Césaire and Birago Diop. From their discussions the ideas of négritude emerged.

Just as many African American leaders urge members of their community to learn about and take pride in their African heritage, so did the proponents of négritude assert the value and beauty of African culture. The négritude writers drew on African history and art to celebrate black civilizations, and sought to bring African accomplishments before the eyes of the world.

After serving in World War II and helping the French Resistance fight the Nazis, Senghor was one of two West Africans elected to represent his homeland in the French National Assembly. Here he helped draft the new constitutions that gradually brought independence to France's West African possessions. During the 1950s, he was a leading spokesperson for African unity and independence achieved through peaceful means.

In 1960, Senghor became the first president of the new nation of Senegal. Displaying as much skill in politics as he did in poetry, he was elected to the presidency four more times. Today Senegal is recognized as one of Africa's most democratic nations, and Senghor is hailed as a great statesperson, poet, and political and literary theorist.

Reader's Guide

AND WE SHALL BE STEEPED

Background

Senghor cofounded the black cultural journal *Presence Africaine,* and stressed an "African presence" in all of his poetry. Although the poems are written in French, their images are drawn from Africa's landscape and history. Their sound—especially when read aloud in the original French—is reminiscent of the powerful, rhythmic chanting of the traditional West African storytellers known as *griots* (grē'ōz). Capturing an "African sound" was so important to Senghor that he specified the traditional African musical instrument that should ideally accompany each poem's recitation. He chose the *khalam* (khä'läm), a four-stringed African guitar, as the instrument to accompany "And We Shall Be Steeped."

Writer's Response

Make a list of reasons why you are proud of your heritage—either as an American or as a member of an ethnic group.

Literary Focus

Imagery is language that appeals to the senses. While most **images** appeal to our sense of sight (*sparkling smile*), some may also appeal to our senses of hearing (*joyous laughter*), smell (*sweaty socks*), touch (*slimy slug*), and taste (*bitter tea*). In the poem you are about to read, Senghor uses a series of vivid images to help "steep" the reader in the "presence of Africa."

AND WE SHALL BE STEEPED

Léopold Sédar Senghor

translated by

JOHN REED AND CLIVE WAKE

As you read this poem, try to recreate in your mind the sights, smells, and sounds of Senghor's imagery.

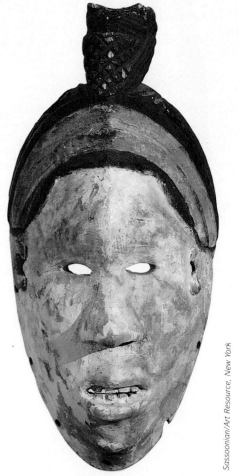

For Khalam
And we shall be steeped my dear in the presence
   of Africa.
Furniture from Guinea and Congo,[1] heavy and
   polished, somber and serene.
On the walls, pure primordial masks distant and
   yet present.
Stools of honor for hereditary guests, for the
   Princes of the High Lands.[2]
5 Wild perfumes, thick mats of silence
Cushions of shade and leisure, the noise of a
   wellspring of peace.
Classic words. In a distance, antiphonal singing
   like Sudanese[3] cloths
And then, friendly lamp, your kindness to soothe
   this obsessive presence
White black and red, oh red as the African soil.

---

1. **Guinea** (gin′ē) **and Congo:** here, not just the present-day nations of Guinea and Congo, but the entire West African coast from Senegal's Cape Verde
peninsula to southern Angola, and the entire river
basin of the Congo, West Africa's longest river.
2. **hereditary . . . Lands:** honored ancestors and rulers of great African kingdoms of centuries past.
3. **antiphonal** (an·tif′ə·nəl) **. . . Sudanese:** alternately
sung and chanted, like traditional African ritual
songs or poems; here, Sudanese refers not to the
present-day nation of Sudan but to the western
portion of the fertile savanna, or plain, stretching
across all of Africa just below the Sahara.

Ceremonial mask from the Ibo people
of West Africa.

Which **image** of the "presence of Africa" could you see, smell, or feel most clearly?

Identifying Facts

1. In the first line, what does the speaker say about "the presence of Africa"? What objects illustrate this presence in later lines?

2. What adjectives describe the African presence in the last line?

Interpreting Meanings

1. In what way are the objects in lines 2, 3, and 4 related to one another? Which **images** in later lines appeal to senses other than sight?

2. The colors in the final line refer to Africa's soils, but they may also refer to the white colonists, the black Africans, and the bloodshed between them. In this context, what earlier **image** does the "red" in the last line contrast with? What does the contrast stress about African history?

3. What overall attitude toward African culture and history does the poem convey?

4. The translators of this poem chose English words that are faithful both to the meaning and musical sounds of the original French. Find examples of **alliteration** and **assonance** that help make the poem musical.

Applying Meanings

What are some of the benefits of taking pride in one's racial or ethnic heritage? Are there also drawbacks? If so, what are they?

Creative Writing Response

Writing About Heritage. Write a poem or a paragraph about your racial or ethnic heritage or your heritage as an American. Include concrete **images** like Senghor does, and choose images that will convey your thoughts and feelings about your heritage.

Critical Writing Response

Writing About Négritude. Senghor's poem is an example of the work inspired by the **négritude** movement, which encouraged black writers to turn to African culture and history as a source of inspiration and pride. In a brief essay, show how this poem illustrates the ideas of négritude. Discuss specific **images** and the attitudes toward Africa that they convey. Before you begin writing, you may find it helpful to list the specific images that you plan to discuss and the attitudes that they convey.

Abioseh Nicol
b. 1924, Sierra Leone

Like many other African writers, Abioseh Nicol (äb·ē·ō′se nē′kōl) studied abroad. When he returned to his native Sierra Leone after years in Britain, he wrote "Upcountry," a poem contrasting the rural villages to the new cities sprouting up along the Guinea coast. He felt that the heart and spirit of the "real Africa" still survived only in the countryside. This is why he sets most of his stories in small, rural villages. Best known for his 1965 collection, *The Truly Married Woman and Other Stories*, Nicol is regarded as one of Africa's best short-story writers.

Despite active careers in public service, health, science, and education, Nicol has always found time to write. In the 1950s, when he was a student in Britain, most books about Africa were written by Europeans. While Nicol recognized the skill of some of these authors, he also saw serious flaws in their portraits of native Africans. It was in part to correct these flaws that he took to writing fiction. He felt that African characters were too often portrayed in disparaging ways, and he sought to correct this slanted view.

In addition to his writing, Nicol excelled in a wide range of fields and made outstanding contributions in all of them. The son of a pharmacist in Freetown, Sierra Leone, Davidson Nicol (Abioseh is a pen name) won a scholarship to study medicine at the University of London. He later became the first black African to receive a fellowship at Cambridge University. In medical circles he won fame for his research into the structure of insulin, the hormone used to treat diabetes. After teaching medicine in England and Nigeria, Nicol returned to his homeland to serve as principal of Fourah Bay College and vice-chancellor of the University of Sierra Leone. He was also his country's ambassador to the United Nations and has been affiliated with the Red Cross, the World Health Organization, UNESCO, and just about every important West African conference and committee.

Reader's Guide

LIFE IS SWEET AT KUMANSENU

Background

A small nation on the coast of West Africa, Sierra Leone was a British colony until 1961. Its capital, Freetown, was founded by British abolitionists in 1787 as a haven for freed and runaway slaves. Nicol grew up in Freetown, which is now a large modern city. The rest of his Sierra Leone, however, is largely rural. In the villages, the old tribal religions remain strong, even among villagers who have become Christian or Muslim. Although specific beliefs vary from village to village, most involve faith in spirits and in magic, both good and bad. The story you are about to read focuses on the old West African belief that the spirit of a dead child can creep back into its mother's womb and be born again. To know whether her next child is a manifestation of this restless spirit, the mother marks the body of her dead child and sees if that mark appears on the next child she bears. To break the cycle, the mother must follow special burial customs prescribed by the village spiritual leader.

Writer's Response

One of the **themes** in this story has to do with the clash between an individual and institutional authority. In a few sentences, describe a situation you have witnessed or heard about in which an individual defies the rules or advice of an authority figure. What are the reasons for this challenge to established law or tradition? What are the results of the challenge?

Literary Focus

Foreshadowing is the use of clues to hint at what is going to happen later in a story. Writers use foreshadowing to hook our interest. For example, if a writer mentions (even casually) that a character keeps a gun in her dresser drawer, we instantly wonder why it's there and when she might use it. In "Life Is Sweet at Kumansenu," Nicol drops clues in the very first descriptions of Meji to foreshadow his story's surprise ending.

LIFE IS SWEET AT KUMANSENU

Abioseh Nicol

As you read the story, look for a general statement about life that Meji makes and the widow Bola repeats. How would you expand this statement to express the story's theme?

The sea and the wet sand to one side of it; green tropical forest on the other; above it, the slow, tumbling clouds. The clean round blinding disc of sun and the blue sky covered and surrounded the small African village, Kumansenu.

A few square mud houses with roofs like helmets were here thatched, and there covered with corrugated zinc, where the prosperity of cocoa or trading had touched the head of the family.

The widow Bola stirred her palm-oil stew[1] and thought of nothing in particular. She chewed a kola nut[2] rhythmically with her strong toothless jaws, and soon unconsciously she was chewing in rhythm with the skipping of Asi, her granddaughter. She looked idly at Asi, as the seven-year-old brought the twisted palmleaf rope smartly over her head and jumped over it, counting in English each time the rope struck the ground and churned up a little red dust. Bola herself did not understand English well, but

The village of Karamasi, Sierra Leone.

Jean Gaumy/Magnum Photos, Inc.

she could easily count up to twenty in English, for market purposes. Asi shouted six and then said nine, ten. Bola called out that after six came seven. And I should know, she sighed. Although now she was old and her womb and breasts were withered, there

---

1. **palm-oil stew:** native dish in which various ingredients are cooked in an oil taken from the seeds of palm trees.
2. **kola nut:** fruit of an African tree called the kola; also spelled cola. Kola nuts contain caffeine and are often chewed for their mild stimulating effects.

was a time when she bore children regularly every two years. Six times she had borne a boy child and six times they had died. Some had swollen up and with weak plaintive cries had faded away. Others had shuddered in sudden convulsions, with burning skins, and had rolled up their eyes and died. They had all died; or rather he had died, Bola thought; because she knew it was one child all the time whose spirit had crept up restlessly into her womb to be born and mock her. The sixth time, Musa, the village magician whom time had now transformed into a respectable Muslim, had advised her and her husband to break the bones of the quiet little corpse and mangle it so that it could not come back to torment them alive again. But she had held on to the child and refused to let them mutilate it. Secretly, she had marked it with a sharp pointed stick at the left buttock before it was wrapped in a mat and taken away. When at the seventh time she had borne a son and the purification ceremonies had taken place, she had turned it surreptitiously to see whether the mark was there. It was. She showed it to the old woman who was the midwife and asked her what it was, and she had forced herself to believe that it was an accidental scratch made while the child was being scrubbed with herbs to remove placental blood. But this child had stayed. Meji,[3] he had been called. And he was now thirty years of age and a second-class clerk in government offices in a town ninety miles away. Asi, his daughter, had been left with her to do the things an old woman wanted a small child for: to run and take messages to the neighbors, to fetch a cup of water from the earthenware pot in the kitchen, to sleep with her, and to be fondled.

She threw the washed and squeezed cassava leaves[4] into the red boiling stew, putting in a finger's pinch of salt, and then went indoors, carefully stepping over the threshold to look for the dried red pepper. She found it and then dropped it, leaning against the wall with a little cry. He turned round from the window and looked at her with a twisted half smile of love and sadness. In his short-sleeved, open-necked white shirt and gray gabardine trousers, gold-plated wrist watch and brown suede shoes, he looked like the picture in African magazines of a handsome clerk who would get to the top because he ate the correct food or regularly took the correct laxative, which was being advertised. His skin was grayish brown and he had a large red handkerchief tied round his neck.

"Meji, God be praised," Bola cried. "You gave me quite a turn. My heart is weak and I can no longer take surprises. When did you come? How did you come? By lorry,[5] by fishing boat? And how did you come into the house? The front door was locked. There are so many thieves nowadays. I'm so glad to see you, so glad," she mumbled and wept, leaning against his breast.

Meji's voice was hoarse, and he said, "I'm glad to see you, too, mother," rubbing her back affectionately.

Asi ran in and cried "Papa, Papa," and was rewarded with a lift and a hug.

"Never mind how I came, mother," Meji said, laughing, "I'm here, and that's all that matters."

"We must make a feast, we must have a big feast. I must tell the neighbors at once. Asi, run this very minute to Mr. Addai, the

---

3. **Meji** (mā′jē)

4. **cassava** (kə·sä′və) **leaves:** leaves of a tropical food plant whose roots are something like potatoes.

5. **lorry** (lôr′ē): truck.

catechist,[6] and tell him your papa is home. Then to Mamie Gbera[7] to ask her for extra provisions, and to Pa Babole[8] for drummers and musicians . . ."

"Stop," said Meji, raising his hand. "This is all quite unnecessary. I don't want to see *anyone*, no one at all. I wish to rest quietly and completely. No one is to know I'm here."

Bola looked very crestfallen. She was so proud of Meji and wanted to show him off. The village would never forgive her for concealing such an important visitor. Meji must have sensed this because he held her shoulder comfortingly and said, "They will know soon enough. Let us enjoy one another, all three of us, this time. Life is too short."

Bola turned to Asi, picked up the packet of pepper and told her to go and drop a little into the boiling pot outside, taking care not to go too near the fire or play with it. After the child had gone, Bola said to her son, "Are you in trouble? Is it the police?"

He shook his head, "No," he said, "it's just that I like returning to you. There will always be this bond of love and affection between us, and I don't wish to share it with others. It is our private affair and that is why I've left my daughter with you." He ended up irrelevantly, "Girls somehow seem to stay with relations longer."

"And don't I know it," said Bola. "But you look pale," she continued, "and you keep scraping your throat. Are you ill?" she laid her hand on his brow. "And you're cold, too."

"It's the cold wet wind," he said, a little harshly. "I'll go and rest now if you can open and dust my room for me. I'm feeling very tired. Very tired indeed. I've traveled very far today and it has not been an easy journey."

"Of course, my son, of course," Bola replied, bustling away hurriedly but happily.

Meji slept all afternoon till evening, and his mother brought his food to his room and, later, took the empty basins away. Then he slept again till morning.

The next day, Saturday, was a busy one, and after further promising Meji that she would tell no one he was about, Bola went off to market. Meji took Asi for a long walk through a deserted path and up into the hills. She was delighted. They climbed high until they could see the village below in front of them, and the sea in the distance, and the boats with their wide white sails. Soon the sun had passed its zenith and was half way towards the west. Asi had eaten all the food, the dried fish and the flat tapioca pancakes[9] and the oranges. Her father said he wasn't hungry, and this had made the day perfect for Asi, who had chattered, eaten, and then played with her father's fountain pen and other things from his pocket. They soon left for home because he had promised that they would be back before dark; he had carried her down some steep boulders and she had held on to his shoulders because he had said his neck hurt so and she must not touch it. She had said, "Papa, I can see behind you and you haven't got a shadow. Why?"

He had then turned her round facing the sun. Since she was getting drowsy, she had started asking questions and her father had joked with her and humored her. "Papa, why has your watch stopped at twelve o'clock?"

---

6. **Addai** (ə·dī'), **the catechist** (kat'ə·kist'): someone who teaches the catechism to Christians; a catechism is a book that contains all the fundamentals of the religion, usually in question and answer form.

7. **Gbera** ('g·bā'rə)

8. **Babole** (bä·bō'lä)

9. **tapioca pancakes** (tap'ē·ō'kə): pancakes made from a granular substance obtained from the potatolike roots of the cassava plant.

A West African village.
❓ *Have you noted anything strange about Meji's behavior?*

"Because the world ends at noon." Asi had chuckled at that. "Papa, why do you wear a scarf always round your neck?" "Because my head will fall off if I don't." She had laughed out loud at that. But soon she had fallen asleep as he bore her homewards.

Just before nightfall, with his mother dressed in her best, they had all three, at her urgent request, gone to his father's grave, taking a secret route and avoiding the main village. It was a small cemetery, not more than twenty years or so old, started when the Rural Health Department had insisted that no more burials were to take place in the backyard of households. Bola took a bottle of wine and a glass and four split halves of kola, each a half sphere, two red and two white. They reached the graveside and she poured some wine into the glass. Then she spoke to her dead husband softly and caressingly. She had brought his son to see him, she said. This son whom God had given success, to the confusion and discomfiture of their enemies. Here he was, a man with a pensionable clerk's job and not a poor farmer, a fisherman, or a simple mechanic.

All the years of their married life, people had said she was a witch because her children had died young. But this boy of theirs had shown that she was a good woman. Let her husband answer her now, to show that he was listening. She threw the four kola nuts up into the air and they fell on to the grave. Three fell with the flat face upwards and one with its flat face downwards. She picked them up again and conversed with him once more and threw the kola nuts up again. But still there was an odd one or sometimes two.

They did not fall with all four faces up, or with all four faces down, to show that he was listening and was pleased. She spoke endearingly, she cajoled, she spoke severely. But all to no avail. She then asked Meji to perform. He crouched by the graveside and whispered. Then he threw the kola nuts and they rolled a little, Bola following them eagerly with her sharp old eyes. They all ended up face downwards. Meji emptied the glass of wine on the grave and then said that he felt nearer his father at that moment than he had ever done before in his life.

Abioseh Nicol   **205**

It was sundown, and they all three went back silently home in the short twilight. That night, going outside the house towards her son's window, she had found, to her sick disappointment, that he had been throwing all the cooked food away out there. She did not mention this when she went to say good night, but she did sniff and say that there was a smell of decay in the room. Meji said that he thought there was a dead rat up in the rafters, and he would clear it away after she had gone to bed.

That night it rained heavily, and sheet lightning turned the darkness into brief silver daylight for one or two seconds at a time. Then the darkness again and the rain. Bola woke soon after midnight and thought she could hear knocking. She went to Meji's room to ask him to open the door, but he wasn't there. She thought he had gone out for a while and had been locked out by mistake. She opened the door quickly, holding an oil lamp upwards. He stood on the veranda, curiously unwet, and refused to come in.

"I have to go away," he said hoarsely, coughing.

Ceremonial mask of the Yoruba people of West Africa.

Sassoonian/Art Resource, New York

"Do come in," she said.

"No," he said, "I have to go, but I wanted to thank you for giving me a chance."

"What nonsense is this?" she said. "Come in out of the rain."

"I did not think I should leave without thanking you."

The rain fell hard, the door creaked, and the wind whistled.

"Life is sweet, mother dear, goodbye, and thank you."

He turned round and started running.

There was a sudden diffuse flash of silent lightning and she saw that the yard was empty. She went back heavily and fell into a restless sleep. Before she slept she said to herself that she must see Mr. Addai next morning, Sunday, or better still, Monday, and tell him about all this, in case Meji was in trouble. She hoped Meji would not be annoyed. He was such a good son.

But it was Mr. Addai who came instead, on Sunday afternoon, quiet and grave, and met Bola sitting on an old stool in the veranda, dressing Asi's hair in tight thin plaits.

Mr. Addai sat down and, looking away, he said, "The Lord giveth and the Lord taketh away." Soon half the village were sitting round the veranda and in the yard.

"But I tell you, he was here on Friday and left Sunday morning," Bola said. "He couldn't have died on Friday."

Bola had just recovered from a fainting fit after being told of her son's death in town. His wife, Asi's mother, had come with the news, bringing some of his property. She said Meji had died instantly at noon on Friday and had been buried on Saturday at sundown. They would have brought him to Kumansenu for burial. He had always wished that. But they could not do so in time as bodies did not last more than a day in the hot season, and there were no lorries available for hire.

"He was here, he was here," Bola said, rubbing her forehead and weeping.

Asi sat by quietly. Mr. Addai said comfortingly, "Hush, hush, he couldn't have been, because no one in the village saw him."

"He said we were to tell no one," Bola said.

The crowd smiled above Bola's head and shook their heads. "Poor woman," someone said, "she is beside herself with grief."

"He died on Friday," Mrs. Meji repeated, crying. "He was in the office and he pulled up the window to look out and call the messenger. Then the sash broke. The window fell, broke his neck, and the sharp edge almost cut his head off; they say he died at once."

"My papa had a scarf around his neck." Asi shouted suddenly.

"Hush," said the crowd.

Mrs. Meji dipped her hand into her bosom and produced a small gold locket and put it round Asi's neck, to quiet her.

"Your papa had this made last week for your Christmas present. You may as well have it now."

Asi played with it and pulled it this way and that.

"Be careful, child," Mr. Addai said, "it is your father's last gift."

"I was trying to remember how he showed me yesterday to open it," Asi said.

"You have never seen it before," Mrs. Meji said, sharply, trembling with fear mingled with anger.

She took the locket and tried to open it.

"Let me have it," said the village goldsmith, and he tried whispering magic words of incantation. Then he said, defeated, "It must be poor quality gold; it has rusted. I need tools to open it."

"I remember now," Asi said in the flat complacent voice of childhood.

The crowd gathered round quietly and the setting sun glinted on the soft red African gold of the dangling trinket. The goldsmith handed the locket over to Asi and asked in a loud whisper, "How did he open it?"

"Like so," Asi said and pressed a secret catch. It flew open and she spelled out gravely the word inside, "A-S-I."

The silence continued.

"His neck, poor boy," Bola said a little wildly. "This is why he could not eat the lovely meals I cooked for him."

Mr. Addai announced a service of intercession after vespers[10] that evening. The crowd began to leave quietly.

Musa, the magician, was one of the last to leave. He was now very old and bent. In times of grave calamity, it was known that even Mr. Addai did not raise objection to his being consulted.

He bent over further and whispered in Bola's ear. "You should have had his bones broken and mangled thirty-one years ago when he went for the sixth time and then he would not have come back to mock you all these years by pretending to be alive. I told you so. But you women are naughty and stubborn."

Bola stood up, her black face held high, her eyes terrible with maternal rage and pride.

"I am glad I did not," she said, "and that is why he came back specially to thank me before he went for good."

She clutched Asi to her. "I am glad I gave him the opportunity to come back, for life is sweet. I do not expect you to understand why I did so. After all, you are only a man."

---

10. **vespers:** evening prayers in a Christian church.

First Thoughts

Is this tale merely an entertaining ghost story, or is there more to it than that? Discuss.

Identifying Facts

1. Summarize the background information that the opening paragraphs provide about Bola's seven children. Who is Asi?

2. What reasons does Meji give for wanting no feast or company during his visit home? What are his final words to his mother?

3. What does Mr. Addai tell Bola that Bola at first refuses to believe? How does Asi prove that she *had* seen her father?

4. What does Musa, the village magician, tell Bola at the end? How does Bola respond?

Interpreting Meanings

1. What details in this story **foreshadow** the tale's surprise ending? Reread the story to the end of page 205. Describe how foreshadowing is used to provide suspense.

2. Bola hugs Asi when Musa says that Bola behaved foolishly years ago. Why is Bola's action significant? What does Bola think that Musa cannot understand because he is a man?

3. Despite its eerie details, would you say this story is life-affirming? Why or why not? How do you feel about the values stressed in the story?

4. The **theme** of a story is sometimes revealed in a single significant passage. In this story, where would you say the theme is stated? What do you think of this theme?

Applying Meanings

In his famous poem "In Memoriam," British poet Alfred, Lord Tennyson (1809–1892) said, " 'Tis better to have loved and lost/ Than never to have loved at all." Do you think that Bola would agree with this sentiment? Do you agree with it? Explain.

Critical Writing Response

Writing About Foreshadowing. In a brief essay, analyze Nicol's use of foreshadowing. Cite all the examples of foreshadowing that you can find and explain what later events they relate to. Before you begin writing, you may find it helpful to list in one column on a separate sheet of paper the examples of foreshadowing that you find. In another column, list the later event each example points to.

Clue	Event It Foreshadows
1. Red handkerchief around Meji's neck	1. His neck was broken.

Language and Vocabulary

African Languages and English

The *kola,* an African tree mentioned several times in the story, takes its English name from a West African word for this tree. From the tree's nutlike seeds comes an extract used to flavor the popular soft drink that we call *cola.* Cola is one of several words that came to English from the native languages of Africa. Some of these words entered English in the Old World; others were brought to the New World by Africans who came here as slaves.

Use a dictionary to find the meanings and origins of these words derived from African languages.

1. banjo
2. chimpanzee
3. gnu
4. gumbo
5. jazz
6. jumbo
7. marimba
8. okra
9. safari
10. tote

Chinua Achebe
b. 1930, Nigeria

AP/Wide World Photos

Chinua Achebe (chin'wä' ä·chä'bä) was born and grew up in the Ibo village of Ogidi when Nigeria was still a British colony. Although Achebe won a scholarship to study medicine, his love of literature and growing involvement with African nationalism changed his career. The nationalist movement after World War II brought with it a new sense of African self-awareness and confidence, and it occurred to Achebe that he and his fellow Africans might have their own stories to tell. Achebe's insight made him question the colonial-era notion that African culture was inferior to the culture

the European colonists had grafted onto Africa, usually by force. As a gesture defining his roots, Achebe dropped his first name, Albert, which his parents had given him in honor of Queen Victoria's husband.

In 1958, while working for the Nigerian Broadcasting Company, Achebe published his first novel, *Things Fall Apart*. The novel tells of an Ibo man whose personal life is ruined as a result of colonial pressures. This was the first of three novels that Achebe wrote to explore the Ibo past and the destructive effects of colonialism on African cultures and on individual Africans.

In 1960, the new nation of Nigeria, with over two hundred ethnic groups, was not a unified country. The four largest ethnic groups, the Ibo, Hausa, Fulani, and Yoruba, were constantly fighting for land and power. Many of the frictions originated in the groups' very different religions, languages, and outlooks on life. Eventually, in 1967, things fell apart. Achebe was one of the many Ibo who unsuccessfully tried to secede from Nigeria and establish a new republic called Biafra. In the worst months of the bloody, three-year civil war, about twelve thousand people, mostly children, starved to death each day. Overall, somewhere between one million and two million people died—many of them from disease and hunger. Several stories in Achebe's story collection *Girls at War* (1973) describe the tragedies and horrors of these years of civil war.

Reader's Guide

MARRIAGE IS A PRIVATE AFFAIR

Background

Nigeria is a West African nation of great ethnic diversity. Two of the largest ethnic groups in the southeast are the Ibo and the Ibibio. Since the end of World War II, many young Nigerians have left their rural villages to attend universities and settle in large cities such as Lagos, Nigeria's capital. As a result of this migration, some young people have abandoned their communities' traditions for more westernized ways. Yet many have found it difficult to break away from their roots, and these young people find themselves caught in the clash between the old and the new. "Marriage Is a Private Affair" is about two young people, an Ibo man and an Ibibio woman. They have moved to Lagos and have broken traditions by marrying each other. In contrast to the young couple is the man's father, a rural villager who rigidly adheres to traditional Ibo ways.

Writer's Response

This story involves a conflict between generations. Do you think that it is inevitable that generations clash? Describe a situation that you have witnessed or heard about that illustrates the problem of conflict between older and younger generations.

Literary Focus

In **verbal irony**, language is used to say one thing but to mean the opposite. For example, a friend is probably being ironic if he tells you, "I just *love* doing five hours of grammar homework every night." As you read "Marriage Is a Private Affair," think about whether Achebe is using verbal irony in the title of his story.

MARRIAGE IS A PRIVATE AFFAIR
Chinua Achebe

Read the first five paragraphs, stopping after Nene's question, " 'Why shouldn't it?' " Write down at least three questions you have about the characters and events of this story. When you finish reading the story, see if your questions have been answered.

"Have you written to your dad yet?" asked Nene[1] one afternoon as she sat with Nnaemeka[2] in her room at 16 Kasanga Street, Lagos.[3]

"No. I've been thinking about it. I think it's better to tell him when I get home on leave!"

"But why? Your leave is such a long way off yet— six whole weeks. He should be let into our happiness now."

Nnaemeka was silent for a while, and then began very slowly as if he groped for his words: "I wish I were sure it would be happiness to him."

"Of course it must," replied Nene, a little surprised. "Why shouldn't it?"

Traffic jam on Broad Street in Lagos, Nigeria.

Jackie Phillips/Time Magazine

"You have lived in Lagos all your life, and you know very little about people in remote parts of the country."

"That's what you always say. But I don't believe anybody will be so unlike other people that they will be unhappy when their sons are engaged to marry."

"Yes. They are most unhappy if the engagement is not arranged by them. In our case it's worse— you are not even an Ibo."[4]

This was said so seriously and so bluntly that Nene could not find speech immediately. In the cosmopolitan atmosphere of the city it had

---

1. **Nene** (nā'nā)
2. **Nnaemeka** ('n·nä·ā·mä'kə)
3. **Lagos** (lā'gäs'): former capital of Nigeria.

4. **Ibo** (ē'bō): member of an African ethnic group living mostly in southeastern Nigeria.

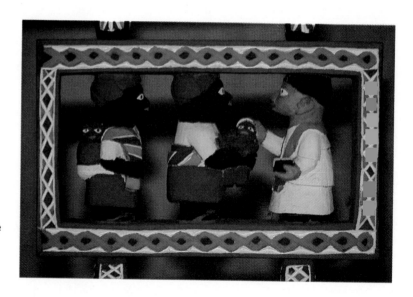

Carving on a Nigerian church
door depicting a scene from the
Bible.

*Marc & Evelyne Bernheim/Woodfin Camp &
Associates*

always seemed to her something of a joke
that a person's tribe could determine whom
he married.

At last she said, "You don't really mean
that he will object to your marrying me simply on that account? I had always thought
you Ibos were kindly disposed to other
people."

"So we are. But when it comes to marriage,
well, it's not quite so simple. And this," he
added, "is not peculiar to the Ibos. If your
father were alive and lived in the heart of
Ibibio-land[5] he would be exactly like my
father."

"I don't know. But anyway, as your father
is so fond of you, I'm sure he will forgive
you soon enough. Come on then, be a good
boy and send him a nice lovely letter ..."

"It would not be wise to break the news
to him by writing. A letter will bring it upon
him with a shock. I'm quite sure about that."

"All right, honey, suit yourself. You know

your father."

As Nnaemeka walked home that evening
he turned over in his mind different ways
of overcoming his father's opposition, especially now that he had gone and found a girl
for him. He had thought of showing his letter to Nene but decided on second thoughts
not to, at least for the moment. He read it
again when he got home, and couldn't help
smiling to himself. He remembered Ugoye[6]
quite well, an Amazon[7] of a girl who used
to beat up all the boys, himself included, on
the way to the stream, a complete dunce at
school.

*I have found a girl who will suit you
admirably—Ugoye Nweke,[8] the eldest
daughter of our neighbor, Jacob Nweke.
She has a proper Christian upbringing.
When she stopped schooling some years
ago her father (a man of sound judgment) sent her to live in the house of a*

---

5. **Ibibio-land** (ib'ə·bē'ō'-): region of southeastern
   Nigeria that is the traditional homeland of the
   Ibibio, another African ethnic group.

6. **Ugoye** (o͞o·gō'yā)
7. **Amazon:** tall, physically powerful female; from
   the Amazons, a tribe of strong women warriors in
   Greek mythology.
8. **Nweke** ('n·wā'kā)

pastor where she has received all the training a wife could need. Her Sunday School teacher has told me that she reads her Bible very fluently. I hope we shall begin negotiations when you come home in December.

On the second evening of his return from Lagos, Nnaemeka sat with his father under a cassia tree. This was the old man's retreat where he went to read his Bible when the parching December sun had set and a fresh, reviving wind blew on the leaves.

"Father," began Nnaemeka suddenly, "I have come to ask for forgiveness."

"Forgiveness? For what, my son?" he asked in amazement.

"It's about this marriage question."

"Which marriage question?"

"I can't—we must—I mean it is impossible for me to marry Nweke's daughter."

"Impossible? Why?" asked his father.

"I don't love her."

"Nobody said you did. Why should you?" he asked.

"Marriage today is different . . ."

"Look here, my son," interrupted his father, "nothing is different. What one looks for in a wife are a good character and a Christian background."

Nnaemeka saw there was no hope along the present line of argument.

"Moreover," he said. "I am engaged to marry another girl who has all of Ugoye's good qualities, and who . . ."

His father did not believe his ears. "What did you say?" he asked slowly and disconcertingly.

"She is a good Christian," his son went on, "and a teacher in a Girls' School in Lagos."

"Teacher, did you say? If you consider that a qualification for a good wife I should like to point out to you, Emeka, that no Christian woman should teach. St. Paul in his letter to the Corinthians[9] says that women should keep silence." He rose slowly from his seat and paced forwards and backwards. This was his pet subject, and he condemned vehemently those church leaders who encouraged women to teach in their schools. After he had spent his emotion on a long homily he at last came back to his son's engagement, in a seemingly milder tone.

"Whose daughter is she, anyway?"

"She is Nene Atang."

"What!" All the mildness was gone again. "Did you say Neneataga, what does that mean?"

"Nene Atang from Calabar. She is the only girl I can marry." This was a very rash reply and Nnaemeka expected the storm to burst. But it did not. His father merely walked away into his room. This was most unexpected and perplexed Nnaemeka. His father's silence was infinitely more menacing than a flood of threatening speech. That night the old man did not eat.

When he sent for Nnaemeka a day later, he applied all possible ways of dissuasion. But the young man's heart was hardened, and his father eventually gave him up as lost.

"I owe it to you, my son, as a duty to show you what is right and what is wrong. Whoever put this idea into your head might as well have cut your throat. It is Satan's work." He waved his son away.

"You will change your mind, Father, when you know Nene."

"I shall never see her," was the reply. From that night the father scarcely spoke to his son. He did not, however, cease hoping that he would realize how serious was the danger he was heading for. Day and night he put him in his prayers.

---

9. **St. Paul . . . Corinthians:** reference to a book in the Bible's New Testament (I Corinthians 14:34).

Nnaemeka, for his own part, was very deeply affected by his father's grief. But he kept hoping that it would pass away. If it had occurred to him that never in the history of his people had a man married a woman who spoke a different tongue, he might have been less optimistic. "It has never been heard," was the verdict of an old man speaking a few weeks later. In that short sentence he spoke for all of his people. This man had come with others to commiserate with Okeke[10] when news went round about his son's behavior. By that time the son had gone back to Lagos.

"It has never been heard," said the old man again with a sad shake of his head.

"What did Our Lord say?" asked another gentleman. "Sons shall rise against their Fathers; it is there in the Holy Book."

"It is the beginning of the end," said another.

The discussion thus tending to become theological, Madubogwu, a highly practical man, brought it down once more to the ordinary level.

"Have you thought of consulting a native doctor about your son?" he asked Nnaemeka's father.

"He isn't sick," was the reply.

"What is he then? The boy's mind is diseased and only a good herbalist can bring him back to his right senses. The medicine he requires is *Amalile*, the same that women apply with success to recapture their husbands' straying affection."

"Madubogwu is right," said another gentleman. "This thing calls for medicine."

"I shall not call in a native doctor." Nnaemeka's father was known to be obstinately ahead of his more superstitious neighbors in these matters. "I will not be another Mrs. Ochuba. If my son wants to kill himself, let him do it with his own hands. It is not for me to help him."

"But it was her fault," said Madubogwu. "She ought to have gone to an honest herbalist. She was a clever woman, nevertheless."

"She was a wicked murderess," said Jonathan, who rarely argued with his neighbors because, he often said, they were incapable of reasoning. "The medicine was prepared for her husband, it was his name they called in its preparation and I am sure it would have been perfectly beneficial to him. It was wicked to put it into the herbalist's food, and say you were only trying it out."

Six months later, Nnaemeka was showing his young wife a short letter from his father:

> It amazes me that you could be so unfeeling as to send me your wedding picture. I would have sent it back. But on further thought I decided just to cut off your wife and send it back to you because I have nothing to do with her. How I wish that I had nothing to do with you either.

When Nene read through this letter and looked at the mutilated picture, her eyes filled with tears, and she began to sob.

"Don't cry, my darling," said her husband. "He is essentially good-natured and will one day look more kindly on our marriage." But years passed and that one day did not come.

For eight years, Okeke would have nothing to do with his son, Nnaemeka. Only three times (when Nnaemeka asked to come home and spend his leave) did he write to him.

"I can't have you in my house," he replied on one occasion. "It can be of no interest to me where or how you spend your leave—or your life, for that matter."

---

10. **Okeke** (ō·kā′kā)

The prejudice against Nnaemeka's marriage was not confined to his little village. In Lagos, especially among his people who worked there, it showed itself in a different way. Their women, when they met at their village meeting, were not hostile to Nene. Rather, they paid her such excessive deference as to make her feel she was not one of them. But as time went on, Nene gradually broke through some of this prejudice and even began to make friends among them. Slowly and grudgingly they began to admit that she kept her home much better than most of them.

The story eventually got to the little village in the heart of the Ibo country that Nnaemeka and his young wife were a most happy couple. But his father was one of the few people in the village who knew nothing about this. He always displayed so much temper whenever his son's name was mentioned that everyone avoided it in his presence. By a tremendous effort of will he had succeeded in pushing his son to the back of his mind. The strain had nearly killed him but he had persevered, and won.

Then one day he received a letter from Nene, and in spite of himself he began to glance through it perfunctorily until all of a sudden the expression on his face changed and he began to read more carefully.

> . . . *Our two sons, from the day they learnt that they have a grandfather, have insisted on being taken to him. I find it impossible to tell them that you will not see them. I implore you to allow Nnaemeka to bring them home for a short time during his leave next month. I shall remain here in Lagos . . .*

The old man at once felt the resolution he had built up over so many years falling in. He was telling himself that he must not give in. He tried to steel his heart against all

Ibo ceremonial mask.
Does Nene receive the same treatment from Nnaemeka's friends in Lagos as she does from her father-in-law?

emotional appeals. It was a reenactment of that other struggle. He leaned against a window and looked out. The sky was overcast with heavy black clouds and a high wind began to blow filling the air with dust and dry leaves. It was one of those rare occasions when even Nature takes a hand in a human fight. Very soon it began to rain, the first rain in the year. It came down in large sharp drops and was accompanied by the lightning and thunder which mark a change of season. Okeke was trying hard not to think of his two grandsons. But he knew he was now fighting a losing battle. He tried to hum a favorite hymn but the pattering of large raindrops on the roof broke up the tune. His mind immediately returned to the children. How could he shut his door against them? By a curious mental process he imagined them standing, sad and forsaken, under the harsh angry weather—shut out from his house.

That night he hardly slept, from remorse—and a vague fear that he might die without making it up to them.

First Thoughts

Do you think that Okeke will see his grandsons and make peace with his son and daughter-in-law? Or do you think he will continue to stick by his traditional beliefs and die without seeing his grandsons? What makes you say so?

Identifying Facts

1. What ethnic difference separates Nnaemeka and Nene? In predicting that his father will be unhappy with their marriage, what reasons does Nnaemeka give?

2. What does Okeke, Nnaemeka's father, believe a man must look for in a wife? What is his opinion of Nene's job as a teacher?

3. In a sentence, summarize Okeke's treatment of his son and daughter-in-law for the first eight years of their marriage. In contrast, how do Nnaemeka's Ibo friends in Lagos feel about Nene?

4. What request does Nene make in her letter to her father-in-law? After reading the letter, what happens to the resolution Okeke has ''built up over so many years,'' and what feelings disturb his sleep that night?

Interpreting Meanings

1. Explain in your own words the change of heart that Okeke experiences at the story's end. Why do you think learning about his grandchildren has affected him more than seeing his son's wedding photograph?

2. What role does nature seem to play near the end of the story?

3. Do you think Achebe is using **verbal irony** in the title of this story? Does the story reveal that marriage is a private affair or a public affair? Explain.

4. In the **conflict** between Nnaemeka's ways and his father's, does Achebe seem strongly to favor one side or the other?

5. The **subject** of this story is a marriage that occurs in opposition to a father's wishes. The **theme** is the truth about human nature revealed in the story. In your own words, state what you see as the theme of this story. Remember that a change in a main character and the nature of the conflict's resolution often indicate the theme of a story.

Applying Meanings

In your opinion, should marriage be a ''private affair,'' or should social considerations play an important role? Discuss your views with the class.

Creative Writing Response

Writing a Sequel. Achebe ends his story without resolving the conflict between Okeke and his son. What do you think Okeke will do? Write a brief sequel in which you show Okeke's subsequent behavior. You may incorporate ideas discussed in the First Thoughts question. Be sure your sequel takes into account the characters of Okeke, Nnaemeka, and Nene as Achebe has presented them.

Critical Writing Response

Analyzing a Conflict. The central **conflict** of this story, as in much of Achebe's fiction, is between the old ways and the new. This conflict takes many forms: rural vs. urban lifestyles, arranged marriages vs. love marriages, and housewives vs. career women. Choose one of these conflicts. In a brief essay, describe the conflict and discuss how it is, or is not, resolved by the story's end. At the end of your essay, describe your own response to the issues raised by this conflict.

Wole Soyinka
b. 1934, Nigeria

AP/Wide World Photos

In 1986, Nigerian writer Wole Soyinka (wō'lā shô·ying'kə') became the first black African to win the Nobel Prize for literature. He dedicated his acceptance speech to the political activist Nelson Mandela, then still in prison in South Africa. Like Mandela, Soyinka also had spent time in jail, under deplorable conditions, for his political beliefs. Although he was denied writing materials, Soyinka managed to keep a diary by making his own ink and writing on toilet paper, cigarette packages, and in between the lines of the few books he secretly obtained. The results were eventually published as *The Man Died: Prison Notes of Wole Soyinka* (1972).

Akinwande Oluwole (*Wole* for short) Soyinka was born in western Nigeria, where his father was active in local politics. Raised as a Christian, Soyinka was also steeped in the ways of the Yoruba, a West African people with a long tradition of oral poetry and ritual dance, music, and drama. As a child, Soyinka was comfortable in the two cultures, but as he grew older he became aware of a conflict between African traditions and Western ways. He recorded this conflict in his autobiography *Ake: The Years of Childhood* (1981).

After attending Ibadan University, Soyinka traveled to northern England to study drama at the University of Leeds. Soyinka's experiences in England were mixed. On the one hand, he received encouragement from his professors, wrote several well-regarded plays, and even saw some of them produced. On the other hand, he suffered from racial prejudice, which he satirized in poems like "Telephone Conversation," reprinted here.

In his plays, poems, and other writings, Soyinka often uses his satiric wit to attack injustice, political corruption, and racism. He also warns against both a nostalgia for Africa's past and an unequivocal embrace of Western ways. In the play *A Dance of the Forests* (1962), Soyinka ridicules people's tendency to glorify the past. His next play, *The Lion and the Jewel* (1962), combines poetry and prose to provide a comic view of the perils of Western modernizations.

Reader's Guide

TELEPHONE CONVERSATION

Background

Although Soyinka draws on his Yoruba heritage in his writing, he is primarily concerned with Africa today and he has criticized the négritude movement for excessive nostalgia. "A tiger does not shout its tigritude," he once declared. The remark—as linguistically imaginative as it is witty and well observed—is pure Soyinka.

Since World War II, millions of people from British colonies and former colonies have traveled to England. Some, like Wole Soyinka, came to receive an education; others came to stay, hoping to find a better life. Yet for many of these people, life in England was marred by racial and ethnic prejudices. Soyinka had several such experiences when he went to London in the late 1950s to work with the Royal Court Theatre and see his plays produced. "Telephone Conversation" records one of these experiences. The poem takes place in a London telephone booth (they are painted red), where the speaker—an educated black African—is phoning about an apartment he hopes to rent. Older, coin-operated telephones had two buttons, button A and button B, that the caller had to push to switch from a speaking mode to a listening mode.

Writer's Response

Write a few sentences describing how you would feel and how you might react if a landlord refused to let you rent an apartment because of your race or ethnic background.

Literary Focus

Satire is a kind of writing that ridicules human weakness, vice, or folly in order to bring about social reform. Satire often tries to persuade people to do or believe something by showing that their present behavior or attitude is foolish. In "Telephone Conversation," Soyinka never states what he wants readers to think, but his mocking portrayal of the rude and ignorant landlady makes his message clear.

TELEPHONE CONVERSATION
Wole Soyinka

> *In this poem, Soyinka reports an incident of racial prejudice with his characteristically satirical eye. Notice examples of wit and humor as you read the poem. How do they contribute to the poem's effectiveness?*

The price seemed reasonable, location
Indifferent. The landlady swore she lived
Off premises. Nothing remained
But self-confession. "Madam," I warned,
5   "I hate a wasted journey—I am African."
Silence. Silenced transmission of
Pressurized good breeding. Voice, when it came,
Lipstick-coated, long gold-rolled
Cigarette-holder pipped. Caught I was, foully.

10   "HOW DARK?" . . . I had not misheard . . . "ARE YOU LIGHT
OR VERY DARK?" Button B. Button A. Stench
Of rancid breath of public hide-and-speak.
Red booth. Red pillar box. Red double-tiered
Omnibus squelching tar. It *was* real! Shamed
15   By ill-mannered silence, surrender
Pushed dumbfoundment to beg simplification.
Considerate she was, varying the emphasis—

"ARE YOU DARK? OR VERY LIGHT?" Revelation came.
"You mean—like plain or milk chocolate?"
20   Her assent was clinical, crushing in its light
Impersonality. Rapidly, wave length adjusted,
I chose, "West African sepia"°—and as an
    afterthought,
"Down in my passport." Silence for spectroscopic°
Flight of fancy, till truthfulness clanged her accent
25   Hard on the mouthpiece "WHAT'S THAT?" conceding,
"DON'T KNOW WHAT THAT IS." "Like brunette."
"THAT'S DARK, ISN'T IT?" "Not altogether.

Steve Benbow/Woodfin Camp & Associates

22. **sepia** (sē′pē·ə): dark reddish brown.

23. **spectroscopic:** here, related to the study of a color spectrum.

Facially, I am brunette, but madam, you should
   see
The rest of me. Palm of my hand, soles of my feet
30 Are a peroxide blonde. Friction, caused—
Foolishly, madam—by sitting down, has turned
My bottom raven black—One moment madam!"—
   sensing
Her receiver rearing on the thunder clap
About my ears—"Madam," I pleaded, "wouldn't
   you rather
35 See for yourself?"

First Thoughts

What message do you think Soyinka wants to get across in this poem?

Identifying Facts

1. Identify the speaker in the poem. What does the speaker want?
2. Once the speaker understands what the woman wants to know, what does *he* ask?

Interpreting Meanings

1. Why does the speaker tell the woman that he is African? By making this remark, what does he reveal about his past experience?
2. Why do you think the prospective landlady asks these questions? What does she reveal about herself in the course of the poem?
3. Explain the humorous double meaning of the speaker's last question.
4. "Telephone Conversation" is a **satire**, a type of writing that attacks and ridicules some social evil or human weakness. What is Soyinka mocking in this poem? One of the tools of the satirist is

the absurd comparison. How does the contrast between the speaker and the landlady contribute to the satirical message?

Applying Meanings

Do you think satirical writing can help change people's attitudes? Discuss your own responses to this poem.

Creative Writing Response

Writing a Satiric Dialogue. One of the devices satirists use to make their targets look absurd is **exaggeration**. You can expose the absurdity of any situation or attitude by carrying it to an extreme. For example, imagine that you have found a nice apartment and made arrangements to rent it. When you meet the owner, however, she refuses to give you the keys because she doesn't rent to people with your eye (or hair) color.

Write a brief dialogue between such a landlady or landlord and a prospective tenant. Begin the conversation with this line: "I'd like to rent the apartment you advertised in the paper." You may work with a partner and then present your dialogue to the class.

Barbara Kimenye
b. 1940, Uganda

HRW Photo by Richard Weiss

Barbara Kimenye (kə·men'yā) grew up in an extremely small village in Uganda. Many of her popular stories are set in the fictional village of Kalasanda, obviously patterned after her actual home village. Kalasanda Village is in Buganda, the traditional kingdom of the Ganda people in what is today part of the nation of Uganda. After attending local schools, Kimenye worked as secretary to the *kabaka,* or Bugandan king, until his governmental authorities were abolished in 1967. In the ensuing political upheaval, Kimenye fled her homeland and spent several years in England, where for a time she was a social worker.

Kimenye was working for the *kabaka* when she began making a name for herself as a writer. Her best-known stories are collected in *Kalasanda* (1965), published when she was twenty-five years old, and *Kalasanda Revisited* (1966). Kimenye also wrote a regular column for the popular newspaper *Uganda Nation.* In 1967, she published the first of her series of children's books about a boy named Moses. Over the years, Moses, a lovable, mischievous character, has been embroiled in more than ten action-packed adventures such as *Moses and the Kidnappers* (1968) and *Moses and the Ghost* (1971). The Moses books are very popular in East Africa, where excerpts often appear in elementary school textbooks. Kimenye continued to publish children's fiction while she was living in England.

Kimenye brings the charm and humor of her children's stories to her adult fiction. In the adult stories, however, she observes life with a more mature and mildly satirical eye. According to one critic, Kimenye is a powerful writer who demonstrates time and again that supposedly commonplace lives lived in tiny, out-of-the-way places are nevertheless full of meaning and interest.

Barbara Kimenye **221**

THE PIG

Barbara Kimenye

Reader's Guide

Background The East African nation of Uganda takes its name from its largest ethnic group, the Ganda people, who called their traditional tribal kingdom (in what is now southern Uganda) Buganda. During the 1950s the traditional ruler of Buganda, the *kabaka,* was in power and Buganda had its own parliament, or *lukiko.* This situation lasted until 1967, when Uganda's government was centralized and Buganda's special status was revoked. Barbara Kimenye's Kalasanda stories, including "The Pig," take place in rural Buganda before 1967.

Writer's Response Create a cast of characters for a story or play about the peo-

ple in your town or neighborhood. List the characters and after their names write a few phrases describing each person's job or role in the community. You may also tell something about his or her personality, talents, and interests.

Literary Focus **Tone** is the attitude a writer takes toward the reader, a subject, or a character. Tone is usually described with an adjective—*amused, angry, playful, sorrowful, ironic, disgusted, mocking, tender,* and so on. Tone is conveyed through the author's diction and descriptions of characters and setting. It is important to correctly identify the tone of a work so that you do not misread it.

THE PIG

As you read, notice Kimenye's diction and her descriptions of characters and the setting. Decide what adjective or adjectives you would use to describe the tone of the story.

Old Kibuka had long believed that retirement was no sort of life for a man like himself, who would, so he modestly believed, pass for not a day over forty-five. He had held a responsible post at the Ggom-

bolola Headquarters,[1] until the Government had sent somebody from the Public Service

---

1. **Ggombolola** (′g·gom′bə·lō′lə) **Headquarters:** local administrative headquarters—something like an American town hall.

Commission to nose around the offices and root out all employees over retirement age. Then the next thing Kibuka knew, despite his youthfully dyed hair, he had a pension, a Certificate of Service, but no longer a job.

He still worried about the state his filing system must be in today, for having once called in at the Headquarters, merely to see if the youngster who had replaced him needed any advice or help, he had been appalled at the lack of order. Papers were scattered everywhere, confidential folders were open for all the world to read, and his successor was flirting madly with some pin-brained girl at the other end of the newly installed telephone.

The visit had not been anything near a success, for not even his former colleagues showed anything but superficial interest in what Kibuka had to say.

So there he was, destined to waste the remainder of his life in the little cottage beside the Kalasanda stream, with plenty indeed to look back on, but not very much to look forward to, and his greatest friend, Yosefu Mukasa, was away in Buddu County on business.

The self-pitying thought "I might as well be dead" kept recurring in his mind as he pumped his pressure stove to boil a kettle of tea. Then the noise of a car, grinding its way along the narrow, uneven track, heading in his direction, sent him eagerly to the door. It was his eldest grandson who climbed out of the battered Landrover.[2] A tall, loose-limbed young man in a khaki shirt and blue jeans. Old Kibuka practically choked with happiness as his frail fingers were squeezed in a sinewy grip, and the bones of his shoulders almost snapped under an affectionate hug.

_____
2. **Landrover:** a jeep-like vehicle.

"What a wonderful surprise! Come in, my boy. I was just making a cup of tea."

"Grandfather, this is a very short visit. I'm afraid I can't stay more than a few minutes." The boy's voice was musically deep, very much like his grandfather's once had been, before the tremor of age had changed it. "I just came to see how you are getting on, and I brought you a present."

"That's very kind of you, son!" The unexpected visit and now a present: in a matter of seconds Kibuka had completely reversed his opinion that life was no longer worth living. He was aglow with excitement.

"Yes. It's one of the piglets from the Farm School. The sow doesn't seem able to feed this new litter, so I thought you might like one for eating; it should make an excellent meal."

The boy strode back to the Landrover and returned with a black, squealing bundle under his arm.

Kibuka was more delighted than ever. He had never seen so small a pig before, and he spent a good ten minutes marveling at its tiny twinkling eyes, its minute hoofs, and its wisp of a tail. When his grandson drove away, he waved happily from the doorstep, the piglet clutched tenderly to his chest.

He had told his grandson that he would take the creature up to the Mukasas and ask Miriamu to prepare it as a special "welcome home" supper for Yosefu, but he soon sensed a certain reluctance within himself to do this, because the piglet followed him about the house or squatted trustingly at his feet each time he sat down. Moreover, it obviously understood every word Kibuka said to it, for, whenever he spoke, it listened gravely with its dainty forefeet placed lightly upon his knee.

By nightfall Kibuka was enchanted with his new companion, and would have as much considered eating it as he would consider eating the beloved grandson who had given it to him. He fed the piglet little scraps of food from his own plate, besides providing it with a rich porridge mixture. Nevertheless, within a few days it was clear that the pig's appetite was increasing out of all proportion to its size, and Kibuka had to resort to collecting matoke peelings[3] in an old bucket from his friends and nearest neighbors.

The news that Kibuka was keeping a pig, the first ever actually reared in Kalasanda, caused something of a sensation. In no time at all there was little need for him to cart the bucket from house to house, because the women and children, on their way to draw water from the stream, made a practice of bringing the peelings and food scraps with them as part of the excuse for calling on him, and being allowed to fondle the animal and discuss its progress as if it were a dear relative with a delicate hold on life.

No pig had ever had it so good. Fortunately, it proved to be a fastidiously clean creature, and for this reason Kibuka allowed it to spend its nights at the foot of his bed, although he was careful not to let his neighbors know of this. The pig, naturally enough, positively flourished in this cozy atmosphere of good will and personal attention. From a squealing bundle small enough to be held in one hand, it quickly developed into a handsome, hefty porker with eyes which held the faintest glint of malice even when it was at its most affectionate with Kibuka.

However, as the weeks went by, its rapid growth was accompanied by a variety of problems. For instance, it required more and more food, and, having been reared on the leavings of every kitchen in Kalasanda, was inclined to turn up its enormous snout at the idea of having to root in the shamba[4] whenever it felt like something to eat. Every time it started to kick its empty dish about noisily, pausing now and then to glare balefully at old Kibuka and utter snorts of derision, the old man was driven to taking up his bucket and trudging forth to see if any scraps in the village had been overlooked.

Also, while Kibuka had at first secretly enjoyed the warmth of a cuddly little piglet lying across his feet each night, he found himself at a distinct disadvantage when that same piglet acquired a bulk of some fifty or so pounds, and still insisted upon ponderously hoisting itself onto his bed as of right. Worse still, along with the weight, the piglet also produced a snore which regularly kept poor Kibuka awake until dawn. It was a grave decision he was finally called upon to make, yet one on which he simply dare not waver: in future, the pig would have to stay outside, tethered to a tree.

Who suffered most, Kibuka or his pig, would be hard to tell, for the animal's lamentations, continuing throughout the night, were equal in strength to the black remorse and wealth of recrimination churning in Kibuka's bosom. That pig never knew how often it was near to being brought indoors and pacified with a bowl of warm milk.

During the day it still was free to roam about until, that is, it adopted the irritating habit of falling into the stream. There it would be, placidly ambling after Kibuka as he pottered in his small shamba, or gently napping in the shade of a coffee tree, and

---

3. **matoke** (mə·tōʹkā) **peelings:** skins of plantains or bananas. Matoke is a widely eaten food in Buganda.

4. **shamba:** homeowner's vegetable garden or cultivated field, where both vegetables and coffee are usually grown.

then, for no apparent reason, off it would go to the water's edge, and either fall or plunge in before anybody could say "bacon."

The Kalasanda stream had no real depth; many Kalasandans often bathed there or waded in; but sometimes, after a drop or two of rain, the current had more strength, and was quite capable of sweeping a child off its feet. The pig seemed always to choose such times for its immersion, and there wasn't anything anybody could really do as it spluttered and floundered with its hoofs flaying madly, and terror written plainly across its broad, black face.

At first, Kibuka would rush back and forth along the bank, calling frantically in the hope that it would struggle towards him, but what usually happened in the end was that a particularly strong eddy would sweep it round the bend into a thicket of weeds and rushes, and then the children playing there would have a good half-hour's fun driving it home.

This happened so often that Kibuka was forced to keep the pig tethered day and night. He visualized the time when no children would be playing in the reeds, and the pig would perhaps become entangled, dragged under and drowned.

By way of compensation he decided upon a regular evening walk for the animal, so by and by Kalasanda became accustomed to the sight of Kibuka, slight yet patriarchal in his kanzu and black waistcoat,[5] sedately traversing the countryside with a huge black pig at the end of a rope, and only strangers saw anything out of the ordinary in it. Without doubt, these walks were a source of great pleasure and exercise to the pig, who found them a wonderful change from the all too familiar view of Kibuka's shamba. Unfortunately, the same could not be said of their effect on old Kibuka. To be frank, Kibuka's corns were killing him, and the excruciating pain of every step sometimes brought tears to his eyes. Still, he tried to bear his discomfort with stoic fortitude, for, as he said to Daudi Kulubya, who showed concern over his limp, it was always the same before the heavy rains: in fact, his corns were as good as a barometer when it came to forecasting the weather. But he was always glad to return home, where he could sit for an hour with his poor feet in a bowl of hot water and try to keep his mind off the small fortune he was spending on corn plasters[6] brought to Kalasanda by the peddlers in the market.

Bob Campbell/Bruce Coleman, Inc.

❓ **What image of village life does the narrator of this story create?**

---

5. **kanzu and black waistcoat:** Bugandan male's traditional long cotton garment and black vest.
6. **corn plasters:** small bandages placed on corns to prevent them from rubbing painfully against shoes.

Ugandan village.

*F. & H. Schreider/Photo
Researchers, Inc.*

How long this state of affairs would have continued is anybody's guess. There were occasions when Kibuka actually entertained the notion of parting with his pet at the first good offer from a reputable farmer or butcher. And yet, one trusting glance or gesture of affection from that waddling hunk of pork was enough for him to feel ashamed of what he regarded as his own treachery.

The end came at last in the most unlikely manner. One minute there was Kibuka contemplating the sunset, and, incidentally, giving his feet a rest by one of the obscure paths leading to the Sacred Tree,[7] while the pig scratched happily at the root of a clump of shrubs, its head hidden by foliage, while its carcass, broadside on, barricaded the path, and then, seconds later, there was the snarl of a motorcycle engine, the horrible grinding of brakes, followed by a whirling kaleidoscope of disaster. Kibuka, pig, bike and rider seemed to explode in all direc-

tions. Each had a momentary vision of the others sailing through the air.

When Kibuka eventually dared to open his eyes and cautiously move each limb, he was relieved to find he was still in one piece, although one shoulder felt painfully bruised and there was blood on both his hands. The rider, whom he now recognized as a certain Nathaniel Kiggundu, did not appear to have fared very badly either. He was staggering out of a tangled mass of weeds, wiping mud off his face, and fingering a long tear in the knee of his trousers.

Somewhere from behind the hedge came the raucous cries of a pig in distress, and it was in this direction that both men headed, once they had regained their bearings. They were only just in time to see the injured animal give up the ghost and join its ancestors in that heavenly piggery which surely must exist somewhere above. There was scarcely a mark on it, but its head lay at a strange and awkward angle, so it can be safely assumed that it died of a broken neck.

Old Kibuka was terribly upset, and the

---

7. **Sacred Tree:** local landmark of former religious significance.

accident had left him in a generally shaky condition. He sat down beside the dead animal and wondered what would happen next. Nathaniel Kiggundu, however, seeing Kibuka was comparatively unhurt, showed more concern over his motorcycle, which lay grotesquely twisted in a ditch. The inevitable crowd collected almost as soon as the pig expired, so there was much coming and going, first to stare at the fatal casualty, and then to stare at the motorbike. Nantondo kept up a running commentary, her version of how the accident happened, although nobody believed she had seen it, and by the time Musisi the Ggombolola Chief arrived on the scene, she had fully adopted the role of Mistress of Ceremonies.

After taking a statement from Kiggundu, Musisi approached Kibuka and insisted upon taking him home in the Landrover. "You don't look at all well, Sir. Come. You can make your statement in the morning, when you have had a rest."

"But I can't leave my pig here." Kibuka refused to budge from the spot.

"Well, I can put it in the back of the Landrover, if you like. Only it would be better to have the butcher cut it up, because I don't think pork will keep for long in this weather."

The idea of eating the pig had never entered Kibuka's mind. While sitting beside the body, he had been seriously considering just whereabouts in the shamba he could bury it. Now he opened his mouth to tell Musisi in no uncertain terms that eating one's good friends was a practice reserved for barbarians: and then, he suddenly had a clear picture of himself struggling to dig a grave. He was sure no Kalasandans would want to help him do it. Then came the realization of the effect a perpetual reminder of his porking friend in his shamba would have on him. He

did not think he could stand it. Far better, indeed, to let the past bury itself and, besides, why deprive his fellow villagers of a tasty treat? They were, after all, the people who had nourished the creature on their leftovers.

"Very well. Get somebody to carve it up and share it out among the people who eat pork,[8] and do be sure to send a whole back leg up to the Mukasas," he said at last, suddenly feeling far too weary to care.

"Musa the butcher won't do it," Nantondo piped. "He's a Muslim."

"Well, I'll take it along to the Ggombolola Headquarters and ask one of the askaris[9] to carve it up. Anybody who wants pork must go there at about seven o'clock tonight," declared Musisi, and ordered two of the onlookers to help him lift the carcass into the back of his vehicle.

Back at his cottage, Kibuka rubbed his injured shoulder with a concoction he used to cure most of his ailments, be they loose bowels or a sore throat, and then sat brooding over a cup of tea. He went to bed very early and awoke next day to find the sun well risen. He decided he had had the best night's sleep he had enjoyed for many a month. Musisi arrived as Kibuka was leaving home to see if the leg of pork had been safely delivered to Yosefu and Miriamu.

"No, I'm taking the meat there now, Sir," Musisi said. "Would you care to come with me?"

Kibuka gladly accepted the lift, although he declined the lump of pork Musisi had brought for him, personally. "You have it, son. I'm not a great lover of pork."

---

8. **people who eat pork:** In accordance with their religious teachings, local Muslims would not eat pork.

9. **askaris:** native African soldiers or police officers.

Miriamu went into raptures over the leg of pork, and Yosefu showed the keenest interest in the details of the accident. They pressed both Kibuka and Musisi to stay to lunch, but Musisi had to leave to attend a committee meeting in Mmengo,[10] so only Kibuka remained. He and Yosefu, who lately had not seen as much of each other as usual, had plenty to discuss, and lunch was an exhilarating meal.

---

10. **Mmengo** ('m·men'gō): larger town nearby.

"I must say, you really are a wonderful cook!" Kibuka told Miriamu, helping himself to more food. Miriamu preened herself, shyly. "Well, that pork was as tender as a chicken, and very tasty, too!"

There was a moment of dismay when Kibuka realized he was eating and thoroughly enjoying the succulence of his late friend, but it quickly passed, and he continued piling his plate with meat, smiling to himself at the knowledge that there would be no need to take a walk in the late afternoon; he could have a good nap instead.

First Thoughts

Did you think that Kibuka would be upset when he discovered he had eaten some of his pet pig? Did you find his reaction believable? Why or why not?

Identifying Facts

1. Why has Kibuka lost his job? Who brings Kibuka the piglet, and how does Kibuka greet this visitor?

2. What stops Kibuka from giving the piglet to Miriamu to serve at her husband's welcome-home dinner? Summarize Kalasanda's reaction to the news that Kibuka is keeping a pet pig.

3. Identify four problems that the pig creates for Kibuka as it grows older. How does the pig die?

4. What does Kibuka finally tell Musisi to do with the dead pig?

Interpreting Meanings

1. Why is Kibuka so delighted with the piglet? How would you describe his overall attitude toward the pet while it is alive?

2. What adjectives would you use to describe the community of Kalasanda?

Find story details that support your choice of adjectives.

3. What adjectives would you use to describe Kimenye's attitude toward the characters in "The Pig"? Find passages that illustrate this **tone**.

4. Explain the **internal conflict** between practical and sentimental considerations that Kibuka experiences once the pig is dead. What do his behavior and thoughts in the last paragraph suggest about human nature in general?

Applying Meanings

The Kalasanda that Kimenye depicts is a typical Bugandan village of its day. Did you find some aspects of the village typical of some American communities or neighborhoods? Why or why not?

Creative Writing Response

Writing About a Pet. Write a brief humorous story about an unusual pet. It may be an animal that people do not usually keep as a pet, or it may be a common pet that displays unusual talents or behavior. Your story may be purely fictional, or it may be based on someone's real-life experiences (including your own).

Mark Mathabane
b. 1960, South Africa

Mark Mathabane and members of his family.

If you were to ask Mark Mathabane (mä·tä′bä·nä) who his role models were as he was growing up, he would probably name Arthur Ashe and Joseph Conrad, among others. Ashe, the black American tennis star who in 1973 was finally allowed to play in South Africa, inspired Mathabane to practice the game that eventually won him a scholarship to an American university. Reading Conrad, the Polish-born English novelist, gave Mathabane the courage to try his hand at writing in English even though it was not his native tongue. The result of Mathabane's efforts was *Kaffir Boy* (1986), one of the first accounts of growing up black in twentieth-century South Africa.

In Mathabane's homeland, however, *Kaffir Boy* was banned. This action came as little surprise to Mathabane, who had faced far greater hardships as a result of his country's apartheid laws. These laws have kept blacks and whites separate and forced nonwhites into inferior jobs, housing, and schools. Raised in a small shack in Alexandra, a black slum just outside Johannesburg, Mathabane's family was extremely poor. There was often no food to eat, and the children slept under the kitchen table.

By law, Mathabane could attend only an all-black "tribal school"—crumbling, understaffed, overcrowded, and inadequately supplied. The school was not free and Mathabane's mother had to scrimp and save to pay his tuition. By law, pupils at the tribal schools studied mainly in their native Bantu languages. Mathabane desperately wanted to improve his English—which he saw as his passport to knowledge and freedom.

Although Mathabane won a tennis scholarship to an American university, he soon realized that he would not become a professional tennis player. He then began to devote more time to his studies and to writing his autobiography. When *Kaffir Boy* was published, one of its early admirers was TV talk-show host Oprah Winfrey, who invited Mathabane to appear on her show and arranged a surprise reunion with family members from South Africa. The reunion made headlines nationwide and helped *Kaffir Boy* to become a bestseller around the world.

Reader's Guide

from KAFFIR BOY

Background

The word *Kaffir* (ka′fər), Arabic for "infidel," was originally applied to certain Bantu-speaking tribes of South Africa. Over the decades it became a derogatory term used by many white South Africans to refer to any black South African. South Africa has long been a nation of great political, economic, and social inequality. This inequality became the law of the land in 1948 when the policy of apartheid (ə·pär′tāt′ or -tīt) was instituted. The policy divided the nation along racial lines and protected the interests of the white population (less than a fifth of the population) by ensuring that the nonwhite majority would neither vote nor own valuable land. When Mark Mathabane was growing up—and even when he published *Kaffir Boy* in 1986—South Africa's apartheid laws were very much in place. The South African parliament began to repeal some of these laws in 1991, and in 1994 Nelson Mandela was elected President of South Africa. His government is working to eliminate educational, economic, and social disparities between blacks and whites that still divide the nation.

Writer's Response

If you were writing your autobiography, what would you call the book? Choose a title and write it down. Underneath, make a list of the most important events in your life that you would be sure to include in your autobiography.

Literary Focus

An **autobiography** is an account of a person's life as he or she remembers it. The autobiography may be written simply to record an interesting life, or it may have more political or social purposes. Autobiographies are considered **nonfiction**, although some authors are more concerned with accuracy than others. *Kaffir Boy* is viewed as a remarkably honest account, even though Mathabane did change some people's names for their or his own protection.

from KAFFIR BOY
Mark Mathabane

As you read this selection, think about the reasons Mathabane wrote his autobiography. What do you think he wanted to prove or achieve? What political changes do you think he wanted to contribute to?

The seven o'clock bus for blacks to Johannesburg was jampacked with men and women on their way to the white world to work. A huge sign above the driver's booth read:

AUTHORIZED TO CARRY ONLY 65 SEATED PASSENGERS, AND 15 STANDING.

But there must have been close to a hundred perspiring people squeezed into the stuffy bus. People sat on top of one another; some were sandwiched in the narrow aisle between the rows of seats, and some crowded on the steps. I sat on Granny's lap, in the middle of the bus, by a large smudged window. As the bus droned past Alexandra's boundaries, I glued my eyes to the window, anticipating my first look at the white world. What I saw made me think I had just made a quantum leap into another galaxy. I couldn't stop asking questions.

"What are those?"

"Skyscrapers."

"Why do they reach all the way to the sky?"

"Because many white people live and work in them."

Seconds later. "Wow! look at all those nice houses, Granny! They're so big! Do many white people live and work there, too?"

"No, those are mansions. Each is owned by one family."

"By one family!" I cried in disbelief. Each mansion occupied an area about three times that of the yard I lived in, yet the latter was home for over twenty families.

"Yes," Granny said matter-of-factly. "Your grandpa, when he first came to Johannesburg, worked for one such family. The family was so rich they owned an airplane."

"Why are there so many cars in the white people's homes?"

"Because they like to have many cars."

"Those people dressed in white, what game are they playing?"

"The men are playing cricket. Master Smith plays that, too. The women are playing tennis. Mrs. Smith plays it, too, on Tuesday and Thursday."

Suddenly the bus screeched to a halt, and people crashed into each other. I was thrown into the back of the wooden seat in front of me. Smarting, I asked, "Why did the bus suddenly stop? I didn't see any robots."[1]

"Look over there," Granny pointed. "White schoolchildren are crossing the road."

I gazed through the window and for the first time in my life saw white schoolchildren.

---

1. **robots:** traffic lights.

I scrutinized them for any differences from black schoolchildren, aside from color. They were like little mannequins. The boys were neatly dressed in snow-white shirts, blazers with badges, preppy caps with badges, ties matching the badges, shiny black and brown shoes, worsted[2] knee-high socks. The girls wore pleated gymdresses with badges, snow-white shirts, caps with badges, blazers with badges, ties matching badges, shining black and brown shoes. A few of the girls had pigtails. On the back of each boy and girl was slung a schoolbag; and each frail, milky-white arm had a wristwatch on it. It suddenly struck me that we didn't even own a clock; we had to rely on cocks for time.[3]

The white schoolchildren were filing out of a large, red-brick building with many large windows, in front of which were beds of multicolored flowers. A tall black man wearing a traffic uniform, a whistle between his thick lips, stood in the middle of the paved road, one hand raised to stop traffic, the other holding a sign that read in English and Afrikaans:

CHILDREN CROSSING
STOP
KINDERS STAP OOR

None of this orderly and safe crossing of the street ever took place at my school; we had to dash across.

The red-brick building stood on a vast tract of land with immaculate lawns, athletic fields, swings, merry-go-rounds, an Olympic-sized swimming pool, tennis courts, and rows of brightly leafed trees. In the driveway leading to the entrance of the building,

scores of yellow school buses were parked. Not even the best of tribal schools in Alexandra—in the whole of South Africa—came close to having such magnificent facilities. At our school we didn't even have a school bus.

White schoolboy in Capetown, South Africa.
What are the narrator's feelings toward the white schoolchildren that he sees?

René Burri/Magnum Photos, Inc.

---

2. **worsted** (wŏŏs'tid): made of a smooth, hard-twisted wool.
3. **rely on cocks for time:** that is, rely on roosters crowing to know what time it is.

Oh, how I envied the white schoolchildren, how I longed to attend schools like theirs.

Minutes after all the white schoolchildren were safely across, traffic moved. At the next bus stop, we got off, and crossed the street when the robot flashed green. As we walked along the pavement, headed for Granny's workplace, I clutched her long dress, afraid of letting go, lest I be swallowed by the tremendous din of cars zooming up and down and honking in the busy streets. I began feeling dizzy as my eyes darted from one wonder to the next.

There were so many new and fantastic things around me that I walked as if in a dream. As we continued down the road, I became increasingly conscious of the curious looks white people gave us, as if we were a pair of escaped monkeys. Occasionally, Granny and I had to jump off the pavement to make way for *madams* and their poodles and English toy spaniels. By constantly throwing my eyes sideways, I accidentally bumped into a parking meter.

We went up a side street. "There is Mrs. Smith's house," Granny remarked as she led me up a long driveway of a beautiful villa-type house surrounded by a well-manicured lawn with several beds of colorful, sweet-smelling flowers and rosebushes. We went to a steel gate in the back of the yard, where Granny rang a bell.

"I'm here, madam," she shouted through the gate. Immediately a dog started barking from within; I trembled.

Granny calmed me. A door creaked open, and a high-pitched woman's voice called out, "I'm coming, Ellen. Quiet, Buster, you naughty dog, it's Ellen." The barking ceased. Presently the gate clicked open, and there appeared a short, slender white woman with silver hair and slightly drooping shoulders. She wore white slacks, a white sweater, white shoes, and a white visor.

"I was just getting ready to leave for tennis," she said to Granny; she had not yet seen me.

"Madam, guess who I have with me today," Granny said with the widest smile.

I appeared like a jack-in-the-box. "Oh, my, you finally brought him with you!" Mrs. Smith exclaimed.

Breaking into a wide smile, revealing gleaming teeth, several of which were made of gold, she continued, "My, what a big lad he is! What small ears!"—touching them playfully—"Is he really your grandson, Ellen?" The warmth in her voice somehow reduced my fears of her; her eyes shone with the same gentleness of the Catholic sisters[4] at the clinic.

"Yes, madam," Granny said proudly; "this is the one I've been telling you about. This is the one who'll some day go to university, like Master Clyde, and take care of me."

"I believe you, Ellen," said Mrs. Smith. "He looks like a very smart pickaninny."[5] Turning to me, she asked, "How old are you?"

"Eleven, madam, eleven," I said, with so wide a smile I thought my jaws would lock.

"He's a year younger than Master Clyde," Granny said, "though the master is much bigger."

"A little chubby, you mean," Mrs. Smith said with a smile. "If you knew how much the little master eats, Ellen; I'm afraid he'll soon turn into a piglet. Sometimes I regret not having had another child. With a sibling, Master Clyde might have turned out differently. As it is, he's so spoiled as an only child."

---

4. **sisters:** here, hospital nurses.
5. **pickaninny:** This term for a small black child, though highly offensive in the United States, is here used more condescendingly than disparagingly.

Black South African youths. *South African children like these, who do not have documents stating their racial group, do not officially exist according to South African policy and cannot attend public schools. Local residents have taken them off the streets to try to teach them the basics in a community center.*

"Pickaninny has one brother and three sisters," Granny said of me, "and the fifth one is on the way."

"My God! What a large family!" Mrs. Smith exclaimed. "What's the pickaninny's name?"

Using pidgin English,[6] I proceeded not only to give my name and surname, but also my grade in school, home address, tribal affiliation, name of school, principal and teacher—all in a feverish attempt to justify Granny's label of me as a "smart one."

Mrs. Smith was astounded. "What a clever, clever pickaninny!" She turned to a tall, lean black man with an expressionless face and slightly stooping shoulders, dressed in housekeeper's livery[7] (khaki shirt and pants), who had just emerged from the

house and who led a poodle on a leash, and said, "Did you hear that, Absalom? Bantu[8] children are smart. Soon they'll be running the country." Absalom simply tortured out a grin and took the poodle for a walk, after receiving instructions to bring brandy, whisky, wine and gin from the bottle store.[9] Granny remarked that I was a "clever pickaninny" because of all the toys, games and comic books I had received from Master Clyde. Mrs. Smith seemed extremely pleased to hear that.

Before Mrs. Smith left for tennis, she said, "Ellen, your breakfast is near the washing machine in the garage. I'll be back sometime this afternoon. Please see to it that the flowers near the pool are watered, and that the

---

6. **pidgin** (pij'in) **English:** here, a form of simplified English that incorporates Bantu vocabulary and syntax.
7. **livery:** uniform.

8. **Bantu** (ban'tōō): here, black South African, because most black South Africans speak one of the Bantu languages as their first language.
9. **bottle store:** liquor store.

rosebushes near the front of the gate are trimmed."

After a breakfast of coffee and peanut butter-and-jam sandwiches, Granny took out her gardening tools from the shed, and we started working. As the two of us went about the large yard, I raked leaves and watered the flowers; Granny weeded the lawn. Mrs. Smith's neighbor's children kept on casting curious glances over the fence. From the way they looked at me, it seemed they were seeing a black child for the first time in their lives.

At midday, despite a scorching sun, Granny, seemingly indefatigable, went about with impressive skill trimming the rosebushes as we talked about trees and flowers and how to best cultivate them.

"Someday I'll build a house as big and beautiful as Mrs. Smith's," I said to Granny. "And a garden just as big and beautiful."

"Then I'll be your gardener," Granny said with a smile.

Toward early afternoon Mrs. Smith returned. She called me to the car to remove several shopping bags from the back seat. She took her tennis rackets, closed the doors, then sighed, "Phew, what a tiring day. Don't ever play tennis," she said to me, "it's a killer."

"What's tennis, madam?" I asked.

"You don't know tennis?" she exclaimed. "What sports do you play?"

"Soccer, madam."

"Ugh, that dangerous sport. Soccer is too rough. You should try tennis someday. It's a gentlemen's sport. Wouldn't you like to be a gentleman?"

"I would like to be a gentleman, madam," I replied, even though I hadn't the faintest idea what constituted a gentleman.

"Do you have tennis courts in Alexandra?"

"Yes, madam." The stadium where I played soccer was adjacent to four ramshackle sand courts, used primarily by kitchen girls and kitchen boys on their day off.

"Then I'll see if I can find an old racket for you," she said.

As we were talking, a busload of white schoolchildren stopped in front of the house, and a young boy, with a mop of rebellious brown hair, alighted and ran up the driveway toward Mrs. Smith. After giving her a kiss, he turned and demanded, "Who is he, Mother?"

"That's Ellen's grandson. The one you've been giving all those comic books and toys to."

"What is he doing here?"

"He's visiting us."

"What for? I don't want him here."

"Why not, Clyde," Mrs. Smith said, "he's a nice pickaninny. Ellen is always nice to you, isn't she?"—the boy nodded with pursed lips—"now be nice to her grandson. Now run along inside and Absalom will show you the things I bought you today."

"Did you get my new bicycle and roller skates?"

"Yes, they'll be delivered Saturday. Now run in and change, and have something to eat. Then maybe you can play with pickaninny."

"I don't play with Kaffirs,"[10] the white boy declared. "At school they say we shouldn't."

"Watch your filthy mouth, Clyde," Mrs. Smith said, flushing crimson. "I thought I told you a million times to leave all that rubbish about Kaffirs in the classroom. Ellen's people are not Kaffirs, you hear! They're Bantus. Now go in and do as I told you." Turning to Granny, pruning a rosebush

---

10. **Kaffirs:** In South Africa, ''Kaffir'' is a disparaging term for any black African.

nearby, Mrs. Smith said, in a voice of someone fighting a losing battle, "You know, Ellen, I simply don't understand why those damn uncivilized Boers from Pretoria[11] teach children such things. What future does this country have if this goes on?"

"I agree *makulu*,[12] madam," Granny said, wiping her sweaty brow with her forearm. "All children, black and white, are God's children, madam. The preacher at my church tells us the Bible says so. 'Suffer little children to come unto me, and forbid them not; for of such is the kingdom of heaven,'[13] the Bible says. Is that not so, madam? Do you believe in the words of the Bible, madam?"

"I'm afraid you're right, Ellen," Mrs. Smith said, somewhat touched. "Yes, I do believe in the Bible. That's why I cannot accept the laws of this country. We white people are hypocrites. We call ourselves Christians, yet our deeds make the Devil look like a saint. I sometimes wish I hadn't left England."

I was struck by the openness of the discussion between Granny and Mrs. Smith.

"You're not like most white people I've worked for, madam," Granny said. "Master and you are kind toward our people. You treat us like human beings."

Mrs. Smith didn't answer; she hurried back indoors. Shortly thereafter, Clyde emerged in a pair of denims and a T-shirt advertising a South African rock group. He called out to me. "Come here, pickaninny. My mother says I should show you around."

South African youth doing homework.

I went.

I followed him around as he showed me all the things his parents regularly bought him: toys, bicycles, go-carts, pinball machines, Ping-Pong tables, electric trains. I only half-listened; my mind was preoccupied with comparing my situation with his. I couldn't understand why he and his people had to have all the luxuries money can buy, while I and my people lived in abject poverty. Was it because they were whites and we were black? Were they better than we? I could not find the answers; yet I felt there

---

11. **Boers** (bōōrz) **from Pretoria** (pri·tôr′ē·ə): white South Africans of mainly Dutch descent whose National Party initiated the apartheid (ə·pär′tāt′) laws when it gained control of South Africa's government in 1948. Pretoria, a city northeast of Johannesburg, is the administrative capital of South Africa.

12. *makulu*: very much; in a big way.

13. 'Suffer . . . heaven': Mark 10:14.

Alon Reininger/Contact Press Images/Woodfin Camp & Associates

a student population of over two thousand, did not have half as many books. I was dazed.

Sensing that I was in awe of his magnificent library, Clyde said, "Do you have this many books in your playroom?"

"I don't have a playroom."

"You don't have a playroom," he said bug-eyed. "Can you read?" he smiled sinisterly. "Our boy Absalom can't. And he says black children aren't taught much English at school."

"I can read a little English," I said.

"I doubt if you can read any of my books. Here, read," he ordered, pulling one out of the shelves. The book was thick, looked formidable.

I nervously opened a page, toiled through a couple lines, encountering long words I could not pronounce, let alone understand their meaning. Shaking my head in embarrassment, I handed the book back, "I can't read this type of English."

"Then you must be retarded," Clyde laughed. Though he might have meant it in jest, my pride was deeply wounded. "This book is by William Shakespeare," he went on, waving it in my face, "the greatest English writer that ever lived. I could read it from cover to cover when I was half your age. But I don't blame you if you can't. My teachers tell us that Kaffirs can't read, speak, or write English like white people because they have smaller brains, which are already full of tribal things. My teachers say you're not people like us, because you belong to a jungle civilization. That's why you can't live or go to school with us, but can only be our servants."

"Stop saying that rubbish, you naughty boy," Mrs. Smith said angrily as she entered the room just in time to catch the tail end of her son's knowledge of black people's in-

was something wrong about white people having everything, and black people nothing.

We finally came to Clyde's playroom. The room was roughly the size of our house, and was elaborately decorated with posters, pennants of various white soccer and cricket teams, rock stars and photographs of Clyde in various stages of development. But what arrested my attention were the stacks of comic books on the floor, and the shelves and shelves of books. Never had I seen that many books in my life; even our school, with

telligence, as postulated by the doctrine of apartheid. "How many times have I told you that what your teachers say about black people is not true?"

"What do you know, Mama?" Clyde retorted impudently, "you're not a teacher. Besides, there are textbooks where it's so written."

"Still it's not true," insisted Mrs. Smith. "Everything that's in your books is not necessarily true, especially your history books about this country." Changing the subject, she said, "Show him your easy books, and then get your things ready so I can drive you over to your friend's birthday party." Clyde quickly ran down his long list of "easy" books: *The Three Musketeers, Treasure Island, David Copperfield,* the Hardy Boys series, the Sherlock Holmes series, *Tom Sawyer, Robinson Crusoe, The Swiss Family Robinson, The Hunchback of Notre Dame, Black Beauty, A Tale of Two Cities,* and so on. Oh, how I envied Clyde's collection of books. I would have given my life to own just a handful of them.

The remark that black people had smaller brains and were thus incapable of reading, speaking, or writing English like white people had so wounded my ego that I vowed that, whatever the cost, I would master English, that I would not rest till I could read, write and speak it just like any white man, if not better. Finally, I had something to aspire to.

Back with Granny, I told her to be on the lookout whenever Mrs. Smith junked any books. At the end of the day, as Granny and I prepared to leave, I was given a small box by Mrs. Smith.

"It's from Clyde," she said. "He's sorry that he treated you badly. He's promised not to do it again. I'll see to it he keeps his promise. Come and help Ellen in the garden whenever you can; that way you'll earn some pocket money."

The box contained a couple shirts, pants, and jerseys.[14] Underneath the articles of clothing was a copy of *Treasure Island.*

To learn to express my thoughts and feelings effectively in English became my main goal in life. I saw command of the English language as the crucial key with which to unlock doors leading into that wonderful world of books revealed to me through the reading of Robert Louis Stevenson's gripping tale of buried treasure, mutiny on the high seas, one-legged seamen, and the old sea song that I could recite even in my dreams:

> *Fifteen men on a dead man's chest*
> *Yo-ho-ho, and a bottle of rum.*

My heart ached to explore more such worlds, to live them in the imagination in much the same way as I lived the folktales of my mother and grandmother. I reasoned that if I somehow kept improving my English and ingratiated Mrs. Smith by the fact, then possibly she would give me more books like *Treasure Island* each time Granny took me along. Alas, such trips were few and far between. I could not afford to skip school regularly; and besides, each trip did not yield a book. But I clung to my dream.

A million times I wondered why the sparse library at my tribal school did not carry books like *Treasure Island,* why most of the books we read had tribal points of view. I would ask teachers and would be told that under the Bantu Education law black children were supposed to acquire a solid foundation in tribal life, which would prepare them for a productive future in their respective homelands. In this way the dream

---

14. **jerseys:** sweaters.

of Dr. Verwoerd,[15] prime minister of South Africa and the architect of Bantu Education, would be realized, for he insisted that "the native child must be taught subjects which will enable him to work with and among his own people; therefore there is no use misleading him by showing him the green pastures of European society, in which he is not allowed to graze. Bantu Education should not be used to create imitation whites."

How I cursed Dr. Verwoerd and his law for prescribing how I should feel and think. I started looking toward the Smiths to provide me with the books about a different reality. Each day Granny came back from work around five in the afternoon, I would be the first to meet her at the gate, always with the same question, "Any books for me today?" Many times there weren't any. Unable to read new English books on a regular basis, I reread the ones I had over and over again, till the pages became dogeared. With each reading each book took on new life, exposed new angles to the story, with the result that I was never bored.

My bleak vocabulary did not diminish my enthusiasm for reading. I constantly borrowed Mr. Brown's[16] pocket-size dictionary to look up meanings of words, and would memorize them like arithmetic tables and write them in a small notebook. Sometimes I would read the dictionary. My pronunciation was appalling, but I had no way of finding out. I was amazed at the number of words in the English language, at the fact that a word could have different shades of meaning, or that certain words looked and sounded alike and yet differed greatly in meaning. Would I ever be able to learn all that?

At the same time I was discovering the richness of the English language I began imitating how white people talked, in the hope of learning proper pronunciation. My efforts were often hilarious, but my determination increased with failure. I set myself the goal of learning at least two new English words a day.

---

15. **Dr. Verwoerd** (fər·voort'): Hendrik Frensch Verwoerd (1901–1966), South African politician and one of the chief architects of apartheid. Verwoerd served as prime minister from 1958 to 1966.

16. **Mr. Brown's:** referring to one of the author's better-educated neighbors, who appears earlier in *Kaffir Boy*.

What did you most admire about the narrator? Was there anything you did not admire?

Identifying Facts

1. When Mathabane visits white Johannesburg for the first time, what differences does he notice between white South African life and his own life?

2. Summarize Mrs. Smith's reprimand when her son calls Mathabane a "Kaffir." What does she then say about white South Africa?

3. What does Clyde give Mathabane to test his literacy? What easier book comes in the box with Clyde's hand-me-downs?

4. What question does Mathabane ask each time his grandmother returns from work? What goal does he set at the end of the selection?

Interpreting Meanings

1. Contrast conditions on the bus for blacks with conditions in white Johannesburg. What does the contrast suggest about South Africa? Based on contrasts like these, identify one of the author's purposes in writing his **autobiography**.

2. What adjectives would you use to describe the author as a young boy? What proof do you have that he will master English?

3. What positive and negative qualities does Mrs. Smith display? In what ways is Clyde cruel to the author? Where do you think he learned to behave this way?

Do you think Mathabane uses Clyde's behavior to point to a larger problem in white South African society? If so, what is that problem?

4. What does the different behavior of the people here suggest about South Africa's future?

Applying Meanings

What role does peer pressure play in racial or ethnic prejudice and the way we treat outsiders in general? Why do you think people succumb to peer pressure?

Creative Writing Response

Writing an Autobiographical Episode. Look over the list of life events you wrote down in the Writer's Response. Choose one event and write a few paragraphs about it, presenting it as an episode in the **autobiography** that you may someday write.

Critical Writing Response

Writing About an Author's Purpose. In a brief essay, discuss Mathabane's chief purposes in writing his **autobiography**. Based on this selection, state what those purposes seem to be, and then discuss selection details that help him achieve each purpose. Before writing, you may want to list two or three purposes and supporting details on a chart like the one below.

Purpose	Details That Help Achieve This Purpose

Naguib Mahfouz
b. 1911, Egypt

T. Cambra Pierce/Wide World Photos

As a boy in Cairo's picturesque old quarter, Naguib Mahfouz (nä·jēb′ mä′fōōz) encountered many unusual characters who would influence his life and work. Among them was journalist El-Muwaylili, who was experimenting in new forms of fiction. At the time, the novel form was virtually unknown in Arabic literature, where poetry and nonfiction were stressed. El-Muwaylili's efforts inspired Mahfouz to introduce full-fledged novels to Arabic literature. Eventually Mahfouz would become the best-known fiction writer in the Arabic language and the first Arabic author to win the Nobel Prize for literature.

Interested in both philosophy and literature, Mahfouz attended Cairo University, where classes were conducted in English and French. His growing proficiency in these languages allowed him to read many European classics and to familiarize himself with the novel and short-story forms. Still uncertain of his future, Mahfouz submitted a short story to a Cairo magazine. He considers the day it was accepted the most important day of his life.

The course of Mahfouz's writing career seems to recapitulate two centuries of literary movements. His early historical novels, set in the time of the pharaohs, display the idealistic nationalism of Romantic Age authors like Johann Wolfgang von Goethe (see page 986). In the chaotic period leading up to World War II, Mahfouz turned to social realism in books like *New Cairo* (1946) and *Midaq Alley* (1947), which vividly evoke his boyhood neighborhood and the effects of war on the average Egyptian. Mahfouz continued in this realistic vein with his masterful Cairo trilogy—*Between the Two Palaces* (1956), *The Palace of Desire* (1957), and *The Sugar Bowl* (1957)—about three generations of a Cairo family who symbolize Egyptian experience in modern times. In the 1960s Mahfouz began to experiment with the stream-of-consciousness technique, as well as the more indirect symbolism associated with modernism. His preoccupation with the individual facing spiritual and emotional crises was prompted in part by the growing Arab-Israeli conflict and Egypt's bitter defeat in the 1967 Six-Day War.

Reader's Guide

HALF A DAY

Background

Today, Egypt's chief language is Arabic, and more than ninety percent of all Egyptians are Muslims. Because so much of Egypt is desert, Egyptians have traditionally lived on the fertile banks of the Nile River. Since World War II, more and more people from rural areas along the Nile have moved to Egypt's major cities, also located on the river. The largest of these cities is Cairo (kī'rō), Egypt's capital, where Mahfouz grew up and where the upcoming story is set.

Cairo's population has increased dramatically since Mahfouz was a boy, and many of the city's fields and gardens have given way to tall modern buildings. As in other urban centers all over the world, overcrowding has created many problems, among them noise pollution, inadequate waste removal, and insufficient public transportation. Cairo is also famous for having some of the world's worst traffic jams.

Writer's Response

Write a paragraph supporting or refuting the following statement: "There are too many human beings living on the earth today." Cite details from your everyday life to back up your opinion.

Literary Focus

Theme is the central idea or insight behind a work of literature. Theme moves beyond the specifics of the work to express a general idea or insight about life or human nature. For instance, a story may be about a father watching his son play a baseball game, but the theme may be about fathers' unfulfilled ambitions. The theme of a story usually reveals something about the writer's personal attitudes toward some aspect of life.

HALF A DAY

Naguib Mahfouz

translated by

DENYS JOHNSON-DAVIES

Notice specific details that indicate how Mahfouz feels about the modernization of Egypt.

I proceeded alongside my father, clutching his right hand, running to keep up with the long strides he was taking. All my clothes were new: the black shoes, the green school uniform, and the red tarboosh.[1] My delight in my new clothes, however, was not altogether unmarred, for this was no feast day[2] but the day on which I was to be cast into school for the first time.

My mother stood at the window watching our progress, and I would turn toward her from time to time, as though appealing for help. We walked along a street lined with gardens; on both sides were extensive fields planted with crops, prickly pears, henna trees, and a few date palms.

"Why school?" I challenged my father openly. "I shall never do anything to annoy you."

"I'm not punishing you," he said, laughing. "School's not a punishment. It's the factory that makes useful men out of boys. Don't you want to be like your father and brothers?"

I was not convinced. I did not believe there was really any good to be had in tearing me away from the intimacy of my home and throwing me into this building that stood at the end of the road like some huge, high-walled fortress, exceedingly stern and grim.

When we arrived at the gate we could see the courtyard, vast and crammed full of boys and girls. "Go in by yourself," said my father, "and join them. Put a smile on your face and be a good example to others."

I hesitated and clung to his hand, but he

---

1. **tarboosh** (tär·bōōshʼ): brimless cloth cap worn by Muslim men.
2. **feast day:** holiday.

The Bettmann Archive

El Azhar Mosque in Cairo, Egypt.

❓ *Does the narrator's reluctance to go to school for the first time strike you as realistic?*

gently pushed me from him. "Be a man," he said. "Today you truly begin life. You will find me waiting for you when it's time to leave."

I took a few steps, then stopped and looked but saw nothing. Then the faces of boys and girls came into view. I did not know a single one of them, and none of them knew me. I felt I was a stranger who had lost his way. But glances of curiosity were directed toward me, and one boy approached and asked, "Who brought you?"

"My father," I whispered.

"My father's dead," he said quite simply.

I did not know what to say. The gate was closed, letting out a pitiable screech. Some of the children burst into tears. The bell rang. A lady came along, followed by a group of men. The men began sorting us into ranks. We were formed into an intricate pattern in the great courtyard surrounded on three sides by high buildings of several floors; from each floor we were overlooked by a long balcony roofed in wood.

"This is your new home," said the woman. "Here, too, there are mothers and fathers. Here there is everything that is enjoyable and beneficial to knowledge and religion. Dry your tears and face life joyfully."

We submitted to the facts, and this submission brought a sort of contentment. Living beings were drawn to other living beings, and from the first moments my heart made friends with such boys as were to be my friends and fell in love with such girls as I was to be in love with, so that it seemed my misgivings had had no basis. I had never imagined school would have this rich variety. We played all sorts of different games: swings, the vaulting horse,[3] ball games. In

A busy street in Cairo.

the music room we chanted our first songs. We also had our first introduction to language. We saw a globe of the Earth, which revolved and showed the various continents and countries. We started learning the numbers. The story of the Creator of the universe was read to us, we were told of His present world and of His Hereafter, and we heard examples of what He said. We ate delicious food, took a little nap, and woke up to go on with friendship and love, play and learning.

As our path revealed itself to us, however, we did not find it as totally sweet and

---

3. **vaulting horse:** that is, the horse one leaps over in gymnastics.

unclouded as we had presumed. Dust-laden winds and unexpected accidents came about suddenly, so we had to be watchful, at the ready, and very patient. It was not all a matter of playing and fooling around. Rivalries could bring about pain and hatred or give rise to fighting. And while the lady would sometimes smile, she would often scowl and scold. Even more frequently she would resort to physical punishment.

In addition, the time for changing one's mind was over and gone and there was no question of ever returning to the paradise of home. Nothing lay ahead of us but exertion, struggle, and perseverance. Those who were able took advantage of the opportunities for success and happiness that presented themselves amid the worries.

The bell rang announcing the passing of the day and the end of work. The throngs of children rushed toward the gate, which was opened again. I bade farewell to friends and sweethearts and passed through the gate. I peered around but found no trace of my father, who had promised to be there. I stepped aside to wait. When I had waited for a long time without avail, I decided to return home on my own. After I had taken a few steps, a middle-aged man passed by, and I realized at once that I knew him. He came toward me, smiling, and shook me by the hand, saying, "It's a long time since we last met—how are you?"

With a nod of my head, I agreed with him and in turn asked, "And you, how are you?"

"As you can see, not all that good, the Almighty be praised!"

Again he shook me by the hand and went off. I proceeded a few steps, then came to a startled halt. Good Lord! Where was the street lined with gardens? Where had it disappeared to? When did all these vehicles invade it? And when did all these hordes of humanity come to rest upon its surface? How did these hills of refuse come to cover its sides? And where were the fields that bordered it? High buildings had taken over, the street surged with children, and disturbing noises shook the air. At various points stood conjurers[4] showing off their tricks and making snakes appear from baskets. Then there was a band announcing the opening of a circus, with clowns and weight lifters walking in front. A line of trucks carrying central security troops crawled majestically by. The siren of a fire engine shrieked, and it was not clear how the vehicle would cleave its way to reach the blazing fire. A battle raged between a taxi driver and his passenger, while the passenger's wife called out for help and no one answered. Good God! I was in a daze. My head spun. I almost went crazy. How could all this have happened in half a day, between early morning and sunset? I would find the answer at home with my father. But where was my home? I could see only tall buildings and hordes of people. I hastened on to the crossroads between the gardens and Abu Khoda.[5] I had to cross Abu Khoda to reach my house, but the stream of cars would not let up. The fire engine's siren was shrieking at full pitch as it moved at a snail's pace, and I said to myself, "Let the fire take its pleasure in what it consumes."[6] Extremely irritated, I wondered when I would be able to cross. I stood there a long time, until the young lad employed at the ironing shop on the corner came up to me. He stretched out his arm and said gallantly, "Grandpa, let me take you across."

---

4. **conjurers:** magicians.
5. **Abu Khoda:** (ä·bōō′ kō′dä)
6. **Let the fire . . . consumes:** an Egyptian proverb.

First Thoughts

Were you surprised by the story's ending? Did it add to your enjoyment of the story or did it confuse you? Explain.

Identifying Facts

1. As the story opens, where is the narrator's father taking him for the first time? What explanations and advice does the father give?

2. Identify four things the narrator likes about his new experience and two things he dislikes.

3. After the bell rings, for whom does the narrator wait in vain? As he walks home alone, what does a middle-aged man on the street do?

4. List three questions the narrator asks himself while walking home. As he waits to cross the busy intersection, what does the "young lad" do and say?

Interpreting Meanings

1. What surprise was revealed at the end of the story? Did you have any idea that the story might end in this way?

2. Reread the story and identify three details that **foreshadow** the surprise ending.

3. Perhaps you have heard the expression, "His life flashed before his eyes." Do you think that Mahfouz, in this story, realistically presents the way an older person's mind might work? Why or why not?

4. What **theme** about time does the ending help convey? How is the title of the story relevant to this theme?

5. Does the story also express **themes** on any of these subjects: change, old age, youth, school, and parent-child relationships? If so, what are they?

Applying Meanings

Why is the first day of school such a memorable event in most children's lives?

Creative Writing Response

Writing About a Childhood Memory.
Write a brief story based on your first day of school or another memorable event in your childhood. Like Mahfouz, you might play tricks with time to make a point about time's passage.

Critical Writing Response

Comparing Themes in Two Stories.
"Half a Day" and Santha Rama Rau's essay "By Any Other Name" (see page 253) deal with a child's experience of school. Write a statement of **theme** for each selection (both should relate to the effects of school on a child's life). Decide whether the two stories share more similarities or differences and write a brief essay comparing and contrasting their themes.

Language and Vocabulary

Arabic and English

Over the centuries, English has borrowed dozens of words from Arabic. Some came to English directly, others came by way of other European languages such as Spanish, French, Italian, and Latin. Use a dictionary to help you find the origins of these English words, some of which appear in the English translation of "Half a Day." Also provide the meanings of any unfamiliar words.

1. admiral
2. algebra
3. caliber
4. tariff
5. carmine
6. cipher
7. ghoul
8. henna
9. saffron
10. sheik

Yehuda Amichai
b. 1924, Israel

Inge Morath/Magnum Photos, Inc.

Like many Israelis of his generation, Yehuda Amichai (yə·hōō'də ä'mi·khī') has spent much of his life as a soldier. During World War II he served in the Jewish brigade of the British army fighting against German forces in the Middle East. In 1948, after Israel won independence and was attacked by neighboring Arab nations, Amichai fought with the special strike force of the Israeli army. Later, as an army reservist, he was often called upon to fight for his country.

Born to an orthodox Jewish family in southern Germany, Amichai escaped Nazi persecution when he was only twelve. Like many other European Jews lucky enough to escape, Amichai and his family immigrated to the Holy Land, then British-controlled Palestine. There they eventually settled in the city of Jerusalem, where the young Amichai continued his studies of Hebrew literature and the Bible. After serving as a soldier in the 1940s, Amichai completed his studies at Jerusalem's Hebrew University. By then he had already published several Hebrew-language poems in magazines, although his first poetry collection, *Now and in Other Days*, did not appear until 1955.

In addition to writing poems, novels, short stories, and plays, Amichai has taught Hebrew literature both in Israel and abroad. While Hebrew was not his first language, Amichai began learning it during his childhood religious studies in Germany, since ancient Hebrew is the language of Jewish scripture and ritual. Modern spoken Hebrew, however, is very different from ancient Hebrew. Mastering the differences has been a challenge for contemporary Israeli authors, and Amichai is considered one of Israel's first writers to meet that challenge successfully. His style combines the informality of modern spoken Hebrew with the powerful poetic images found in the Old Testament.

At the heart of virtually all of Amichai's poetry is his concern with the effects that frequent warfare and a constant war-ready state have had on the Israeli consciousness.

Reader's Guide

from LAMENTS ON THE WAR DEAD

Background

After the ancient Romans conquered the Holy Land, which they called Palestine, the area's Jews revolted unsuccessfully and most were driven into exile. Many of these exiles settled in Europe, where they were severely persecuted over the centuries. In the late 1800s, European Jews formed the Zionist movement, which sought to reestablish in the Holy Land a nation where Jews could live free of oppression. By now Arabs had become Palestine's chief inhabitants, but soon more and more Jews began returning. In 1947, in the wake of world horror at the Holocaust, the United Nations voted to partition Palestine into a Jewish nation and an Arab nation. The Jews accepted the plan, but the Arabs did not. On May 15, 1948, a day after the new Jewish nation of Israel came into being, neighboring Arab countries attacked in the first of several Arab-Israeli wars. With each war, the Israelis emerged as victors, acquiring more land and working to build modern cities and productive farms.

Yehuda Amichai wrote his poetic sequence *Laments on the War Dead* soon after the war of 1973, when Egypt and Syria attacked Israel on the Jewish high holy day of Yom Kippur. Israel won the war, but at great cost, both economically and in terms of human lives.

Writer's Response

Comment on recent events in the Middle East, researching them in current newspapers if necessary. How do you assess the situation? Do you have more sympathy for one group than another?

Literary Focus

Poets often use **repetition** to create rhythm, build suspense, or emphasize a particular word or idea. In **incremental repetition**, a line or section of a poem or song is repeated with some variation in wording. Usually the variation adds significant new information or expresses a significant change in meaning or attitude.

from LAMENTS ON THE WAR DEAD

Yehuda Amichai
translated by
WARREN BARGAD AND STANLEY F. CHYET

⬇ *Look for the answers the speaker gives to the poem's opening question.*

6

Is all this sorrow? I don't know.
I stood in the cemetery dressed
in the camouflage clothing of a live man, brown
pants and a shirt yellow as the sun.

5 Graveyards are cheap and unassuming.
Even the wastebaskets are too small to hold
the thin paper that wrapped the store-bought
   flowers.
Graveyards are disciplined, mannered things.
"I'll never forget you," reads
10 a small brick tablet in French.°
I don't know who it is who won't forget,
who's more unknown than the one who's dead.

Is all this sorrow? I think
so. "Be consoled in building the land." How
15 long can we build the land,
to gain in the terrible, three-sided
game of building, consolation, and death?
Yes, all this is sorrow. But
leave a little love always lit,
20 like the nightlight in a sleeping infant's room,
not that he knows what light is
and where it comes from, but it gives him
a bit of security and some silent love.

Modern-day Israel.

J. Leonard Hornstein

10. **in French:** Although Hebrew is Israel's chief language, an immigrant from Europe or elsewhere might also continue to use his or her first language, especially on a tombstone.

First Thoughts

Would you say the poem ends on a positive or a negative note? Explain your response.

Identifying Facts

1. What is the speaker's first answer to the opening question? What is he wearing as he stands in the cemetery?
2. What two statements does the speaker make about graveyards? What does he not know about the inscription on the small brick tablet?
3. What two answers to the opening question does the speaker give in lines 13–23? What other question does he ask here?
4. In lines 13–23, what does the speaker request? What comparison does he make?

Interpreting Meanings

1. How would you describe the speaker's attitude until line 17? What growing realization on the speaker's part is traced by the **incremental repetition** in lines 1, 13–14, and 18?
2. Identify another example of **incremental repetition** and the contrast it presents. What overall effect does all the repetition have?
3. Who might the speaker be quoting in line 14? What does the question in lines 14–17 reveal about modern Israeli experience?
4. In his request in lines 18–19, whom might the speaker be addressing? What advice might the **extended simile** in lines 18–23 be giving to modern Israelis and other war victims?

Applying Meanings

What positive functions does grieving for the dead provide? When can such grieving become negative?

Creative Writing Response

Writing an Elegy. An **elegy** is a poem of mourning or lament. Write an elegy in which you honor the memory of the victims of a particular war or another human disaster. Your poem may also address the needs and feelings of survivors, as Amichai's does.

Critical Writing Response

Writing About an Extended Simile. In a brief essay, explain how the **extended simile** in lines 18–23 helps express the theme of the poem. Include answers to the following questions in your essay: What two dissimilar things are being compared? What qualities do they share? How does the simile bring an abstract concept down to earth?

Language and Vocabulary

Hebrew and English

Over the centuries English has borrowed words from Hebrew. Some came to English directly; many came from other languages, including Yiddish, the Germanic tongue once used by many European Jews. For the exercise below, use a dictionary to help you match the English words in the left-hand column with the information about their origins in the right-hand column. Also be sure you know the meanings of all the listed words.

1. amen
   a. from the Hebrew for "fitting; right; proper"
2. kibbutz
   b. from a Hebrew term meaning "anointed (one)"
3. kosher
   c. from the Hebrew for "to rest"
4. messiah
   d. from a Hebrew exclamation literally meaning "truly; certainly"
5. sabbath
   e. from the modern Hebrew for a collective farm in Israel

Santha Rama Rau
b. 1923, India

Santha Rama Rau (sän'thä räm'ä rou) was raised by broad-minded parents who had traveled all over the globe. Still, they were upset when she took her first job. "My family didn't mind my *working*," she explained, "but they were worried about the idea of my *earning money*. It wasn't considered entirely respectable for a girl whose family could afford to support her until she got married to be actually picking up a paycheck." Nevertheless, Rama Rau insisted on a writing career, and finally her parents

relented. After all, their daughter had already published her first book, *Home to India* (1945), and the positive reviews of this autobiographical memoir were strong persuasion indeed.

The daughter of an Indian diplomat, Rama Rau was born when India was still a colony of Britain. When she was eleven, Rama Rau went to Europe to stay with her father, who was serving as India's Deputy High Commissioner in London. She attended London's St. Paul's School for Girls and during the summer often vacationed in France. When she was sixteen, she returned to India and found that she was something of an outsider. In an effort to rediscover her native land, she wrote *Home to India* while she was a student at Wellesley College in Massachusetts.

Living in India after World War II, Rama Rau witnessed firsthand all the excitement surrounding her nation's independence in 1947. In that same year she took a sabbatical, or period of leave, from her editing job at Bombay's *Trend* magazine to accompany her father to his new post as India's first ambassador to Japan. She recounted her experiences in the highly regarded travel book *East of Home*, published in 1950.

Two years later Rama Rau married an American and settled in New York City, where she began contributing articles to American magazines. Her essay "By Any Other Name," reprinted here, was published first in *The New Yorker*.

Reader's Guide

BY ANY OTHER NAME

Background

During the long British presence in India, many British soldiers, settlers, and public officials moved to India to seek their fortunes and aid in governing and controlling the land. These people became known as Anglo-Indians. While the British contributed to the modernization of India, they also often neglected, misinterpreted, or denigrated native Indian customs. In "By Any Other Name," Santha Rama Rau illuminates this clash of cultures by recalling a childhood incident.

Writer's Response

Recall an incident in your own childhood that first introduced you to the traditions of a different ethnic, religious, or national group, either in real life or through a book, movie, or television show. How were these people different from you, and how did you feel about them? Did the incident make you see yourself or your own culture differently?

Literary Focus

An **essay** is a short piece of nonfiction prose that usually examines a single subject. Essays are sometimes classified as formal or informal. A **formal essay** is serious and impersonal in tone. Often it carefully and logically explains a subject or tries to persuade readers to accept a particular way of thinking. An **informal essay**, also called a **personal essay**, generally reveals far more about the personality and feelings of the author. Many informal essays—including Santha Rama Rau's—are autobiographical in nature, recounting an episode or series of related episodes from the author's life.

BY ANY OTHER NAME

Santha Rama Rau

> *The title of this essay comes from Shakespeare's* **Romeo and Juliet:**
>
> > *What's in a name? That which we call a rose*
> > *By any other name would smell as sweet.*
>
> *As you read the essay, think about Rama Rau's reasons for choosing this particular title.*

At the Anglo-Indian day school in Zorinabad[1] to which my sister and I were sent when she was eight and I was five and a half, they changed our names. On the first day of school, a hot, windless morning of a north Indian September, we stood in the headmistress's study and she said, "Now you're the *new* girls. What are your names?"

My sister answered for us. "I am Premila, and she"—nodding in my direction—"is Santha."

The headmistress had been in India, I suppose, fifteen years or so, but she still smiled her helpless inability to cope with Indian names. Her rimless half-glasses glittered, and the precarious bun on the top of her head trembled as she shook her head. "Oh, my dears, those are much too hard for me. Suppose we give you pretty English names. Wouldn't that be more jolly? Let's see, now—Pamela for you, I think." She shrugged in a baffled way at my sister. "That's as close as I can get. And for *you*" she said to me, "how about Cynthia? Isn't that nice?"

My sister was always less easily intimi-

dated than I was, and while she kept a stubborn silence, I said, "Thank you," in a very tiny voice.

We had been sent to that school because my father, among his responsibilities as an officer of the civil service, had a tour of duty to perform in the villages around that steamy little provincial town, where he had his headquarters at that time. He used to make his shorter inspection tours on horseback, and a week before, in the stale heat of a typically postmonsoon[2] day, we had waved goodbye to him and a little procession—an assistant, a secretary, two bearers, and the man to look after the bedding rolls and luggage. They rode away through our large garden, still bright green from the rains, and we turned back into the twilight of the house and the sound of fans whispering in every room.

Up to then, my mother had refused to send Premila to school in the British-run establishments of that time, because, she

---

1. **Zorinabad:** town in northern India.

2. **postmonsoon:** referring to the dry spell that generally follows the rainy season, when ocean winds called monsoons bring rain to India.

used to say, "you can bury a dog's tail for seven years and it still comes out curly, and you can take a Britisher away from his home for a lifetime and he still remains insular." The examinations and degrees from entirely Indian schools were not, in those days, considered valid. In my case, the question had never come up, and probably never would have come up if Mother's extraordinary good health had not broken down. For the first time in my life, she was not able to continue the lessons she had been giving us every morning. So our Hindi[3] books were put away, the stories of the Lord Krishna[4] as a little boy were left in midair, and we were sent to the Anglo-Indian school.

That first day at school is still, when I think of it, a remarkable one. At that age, if one's name is changed, one develops a curious form of dual personality. I remember having a certain detached and disbelieving concern in the actions of "Cynthia," but certainly no responsibility. Accordingly, I followed the thin, erect back of the headmistress down the veranda to my classroom feeling, at most, a passing interest in what was going to happen to me in this strange, new atmosphere of School.

The building was Indian in design, with wide verandas opening onto a central courtyard, but Indian verandas are usually whitewashed, with stone floors. These, in the tradition of British schools, were painted dark brown and had matting on the floors. It gave a feeling of extra intensity to the heat.

I suppose there were about a dozen Indian children in the school—which contained perhaps forty children in all—and four of them were in my class. They were all sitting at the back of the room, and I went to join them. I sat next to a small, solemn girl who didn't smile at me. She had long, glossy black braids and wore a cotton dress, but she still kept on her Indian jewelry—a gold chain around her neck, thin gold bracelets, and tiny ruby studs in her ears. Like most Indian children, she had a rim of black kohl[5] around her eyes. The cotton dress should have looked strange, but all I could think of was that I should ask my mother if I couldn't wear a dress to school, too, instead of my Indian clothes.

I can't remember too much about the proceedings in class that day, except for the beginning. The teacher pointed to me and asked me to stand up. "Now, dear, tell the class your name."

I said nothing.

"Come along," she said, frowning slightly. "What's your name, dear?"

"I don't know," I said, finally.

The English children in the front of the class—there were about eight or ten of them—giggled and twisted around in their chairs to look at me. I sat down quickly and opened my eyes very wide, hoping in that way to dry them off. The little girl with the braids put out her hand and very lightly touched my arm. She still didn't smile.

Most of that morning I was rather bored. I looked briefly at the children's drawings pinned to the wall, and then concentrated on a lizard clinging to the ledge of the high, barred window behind the teacher's head. Occasionally it would shoot out its long yellow tongue for a fly, and then it would rest, with its eyes closed and its belly palpitating,

---

3. **Hindi** (hin′dē): an Indo-European language that is now considered the official language of India.
4. **Lord Krishna**: in the Hindu religion, human form taken by the god Vishnu; many Hindu stories recount episodes in the life of Lord Krishna.

---

5. **kohl** (kōl): dark powder used as eye makeup.

Schoolgirl in Ahmadabad, India.

as though it were swallowing several times quickly. The lessons were mostly concerned with reading and writing and simple numbers—things that my mother had already taught me—and I paid very little attention. The teacher wrote on the easel blackboard words like "bat" and "cat," which seemed babyish to me; only "apple" was new and incomprehensible.

When it was time for the lunch recess, I followed the girl with braids out onto the veranda. There the children from the other classes were assembled. I saw Premila at once and ran over to her, as she had charge of our lunchbox. The children were all opening packages and sitting down to eat sandwiches. Premila and I were the only ones who had Indian food—thin wheat chapatties,[6] some vegetable curry, and a bottle of buttermilk. Premila thrust half of it into my hand and whispered fiercely that I should go and sit with my class, because that was what the others seemed to be doing.

The enormous black eyes of the little Indian girl from my class looked at my food longingly, so I offered her some. But she only shook her head and plowed her way solemnly through her sandwiches.

I was very sleepy after lunch, because at home we always took a siesta. It was usually a pleasant time of day, with the bedroom darkened against the harsh afternoon sun, the drifting off into sleep with the sound of Mother's voice reading a story in one's mind, and, finally, the shrill, fussy voice of the ayah[7] waking one for tea.

At school, we rested for a short time on low, folding cots on the veranda, and then we were expected to play games. During the hot part of the afternoon we played indoors, and after the shadows had begun to lengthen and the slight breeze of the evening had come up we moved outside to the wide courtyard.

I had never really grasped the system of competitive games. At home, whenever we played tag or guessing games, I was always allowed to "win"—"because," Mother used to tell Premila, "she is the youngest, and we have to allow for that." I had often heard her say it, and it seemed quite reasonable to

---

6. **chapatties** (chə·pä′tēz): thin unleavened fried bread.

7. **ayah** (ä′yə): nanny in India.

Santha Rama Rau **255**

me, but the result was that I had no clear idea of what "winning" meant.

When we played twos-and-threes[8] that afternoon at school, in accordance with my training, I let one of the small English boys catch me, but was naturally rather puzzled when the other children did not return the courtesy. I ran about for what seemed like hours without ever catching anyone, until it was time for school to close. Much later I learned that my attitude was called "not being a good sport," and I stopped allowing myself to be caught, but it was not for years that I really learned the spirit of the thing.

When I saw our car come up to the school gate, I broke away from my classmates and rushed toward it yelling, "Ayah! Ayah!" It seemed like an eternity since I had seen her that morning—a wizened, affectionate figure in her white cotton sari,[9] giving me dozens of urgent and useless instructions on how to be a good girl at school. Premila followed more sedately, and she told me on the way home never to do that again in front of the other children.

When we got home we went straight to Mother's high, white room to have tea with her, and I immediately climbed onto the bed and bounced gently up and down on the springs. Mother asked how we had liked our first day in school. I was so pleased to be home and to have left that peculiar Cynthia behind that I had nothing whatever to say about school, except to ask what "apple" meant. But Premila told Mother about the classes, and added that in her class they had weekly tests to see if they had learned their lessons well.

I asked, "What's a test?"

Premila said, "You're too small to have them. You won't have them in your class for donkey's years."[10] She had learned the expression that day and was using it for the first time. We all laughed enormously at her wit. She also told Mother, in an aside, that we should take sandwiches to school the next day. Not, she said, that *she* minded. But they would be simpler for me to handle.

That whole lovely evening I didn't think about school at all. I sprinted barefoot across the lawns with my favorite playmate, the cook's son, to the stream at the end of the garden. We quarreled in our usual way, waded in the tepid water under the lime trees, and waited for the night to bring out the smell of the jasmine.[11] I listened with fascination to his stories of ghosts and demons, until I was too frightened to cross the garden alone in the semidarkness. The ayah found me, shouted at the cook's son, scolded me, hurried me in to supper—it was an entirely usual, wonderful evening.

It was a week later, the day of Premila's first test, that our lives changed rather abruptly. I was sitting at the back of my class, in my usual inattentive way, only half listening to the teacher. I had started a rather guarded friendship with the girl with the braids, whose name turned out to be Nalini (Nancy in school). The three other Indian children were already fast friends. Even at that age it was apparent to all of us that friendship with the English or Anglo-Indian children was out of the question. Occasionally, during the class, my new friend and I

---

8. **twos-and-threes:** game similar to tag.
9. **sari** (sä′rē): a long piece of cloth wrapped around the body to form a skirt and mantle; it is the main form of dress worn by Hindu women.
10. **donkey's years:** English expression meaning "a long time."
11. **jasmine** (jaz′min): tropical shrub with fragrant flowers.

would draw pictures and show them to each other secretly.

The door opened sharply and Premila marched in. At first, the teacher smiled at her in a kindly and encouraging way and said, "Now, you're little Cynthia's sister?"

Premila didn't even look at her. She stood .th her feet planted firmly apart and her shoulders rigid, and addressed herself directly to me. "Get up," she said. "We're going home."

I didn't know what had happened, but I was aware that it was a crisis of some sort. I rose obediently and started to walk toward my sister.

"Bring your pencils and your notebook," she said.

I went back for them, and together we left the room. The teacher started to say something just as Premila closed the door, but we didn't wait to hear what it was.

In complete silence we left the school grounds and started to walk home. Then I asked Premila what the matter was. All she would say was "We're going home for good."

It was a very tiring walk for a child of five and a half, and I dragged along behind Premila with my pencils growing sticky in my hand. I can still remember looking at the dusty hedges, and the tangles of thorns in the ditches by the side of the road, smelling the faint fragrance from the eucalyptus trees and wondering whether we would ever reach home. Occasionally a horse-drawn tonga[12] passed us, and the women, in their pink or green silks, stared at Premila and me trudging along on the side of the road. A few coolies[13] and a line of women carrying baskets of vegetables on their heads smiled at us. But it was nearing the hottest time of

day, and the road was almost deserted. I walked more and more slowly, and shouted to Premila, from time to time, "Wait for me!" with increasing peevishness. She spoke to me only once, and that was to tell me to carry my notebook on my head, because of the sun.

When we got to our house the ayah was just taking a tray of lunch into Mother's room. She immediately started a long, worried questioning about what are you children doing back here at this hour of the day.

Mother looked very startled and very concerned, and asked Premila what had happened.

Premila said, "We had our test today, and She made me and the other Indians sit at the back of the room, with a desk between each one."

Mother said, "Why was that, darling?"

"She said it was because Indians cheat," Premila added. "So I don't think we should go back to that school."

Mother looked very distant, and was silent a long time. At last she said, "Of course not, darling." She sounded displeased.

We all shared the curry she was having for lunch, and afterward I was sent off to the beautifully familiar bedroom for my siesta. I could hear Mother and Premila talking through the open door.

Mother said, "Do you suppose she understood all that?"

Premila said, "I shouldn't think so. She's a baby."

Mother said, "Well, I hope it won't bother her."

Of course, they were both wrong. I understood it perfectly, and I remember it all very clearly. But I put it happily away, because it had all happened to a girl called Cynthia, and I never was really particularly interested in her.

---

12. **tonga:** two-wheeled carriage.
13. **coolies:** manual laborers.

First Thoughts

Do you think that because the author was called Cynthia at school, she would have always felt that what happened there was not significant? Why do you think that Premila's name change did not have a similar effect on her?

Identifying Facts

1. How old are the author and her sister at the time of this incident? Why had the girls' mother not sent them to a British-run school before?

2. For about how long has the headmistress lived in India? What reason does she give for changing Santha's and Premila's names?

3. What causes the English children to laugh at the author on her first day of school? How do her clothes and lunch differ from those of the Indian children who have been there longer?

Interpreting Meanings

1. What is Santha's mother afraid might happen if her daughters attend a British-run school? What do the details about the other Indian students show about her fears?

2. What criticisms of the headmistress does the third paragraph imply? What related criticism of the British in India does the eighth paragraph imply?

3. What prompts Premila to leave school? What does the incident reveal about the British attitude toward and treatment of Indians?

4. How do you know that this is an **informal essay**? How does the author's childhood attitude toward names contrast with the idea implied by the title?

5. Why do you think Rama Rau drew her title from a Shakespearean play instead of a classical Indian work?

Applying Meanings

Have you ever felt differently when people called you a different name (Beth or Lizzy instead of Elizabeth, or Chuck instead of Charles)? Explain, providing examples.

Creative Writing Response

Writing a Personal Essay. Write a brief personal essay describing your first day of school or some other school-related experience from your childhood.

Critical Writing Response

Analyzing an Essay's Purpose. In one paragraph, explain what you see as Rama Rau's main purpose in writing this essay. In a second paragraph, describe your response to the essay and tell whether or not you think Rama Rau accomplishes her purpose.

To help you decide what the essay's purpose is, you may find it helpful to list, on a chart like the one below, the selection details that point to the author's purpose. Remember to consider how the title relates to the essay's message.

Detail or Incident	Message It Helps to Convey

Akutagawa Ryunosuke
1892–1927, Japan

Akutagawa Ryunosuke (ä·kōō·tä·gä·wä ryōō·nō·sōō·kə) was a perfectionist who labored painstakingly over every line he wrote. Although he destroyed many stories that did not measure up to his high standards, his *Complete Works* (1954) fill twenty volumes. Akutagawa wrote poems, essays, and a semiautobiographical novel, *Kappa* (1927), but he is best known for his short stories. In fact, the annual award for Japan's best short story is named the Akutagawa Prize in his honor.

Akutagawa was a sensitive, troubled child who found solace and escape in reading. Because his mother suffered a nervous breakdown a year after he was born, he was reared by his aunt and uncle. While still a child, he devoured the tales of medieval Japan that filled his uncle's library. At ten he began writing his own stories. At Tokyo Imperial University, Akutagawa studied English and East Asian literature and, with other young writers, revived the literary magazine *New Thought.*

Although Akutagawa wrote and published throughout his youth, he was not recognized until the famous Japanese writer Natsume Soseki read his story "The Nose" in 1916. Natsume recommended "The Nose" to a colleague, who republished it in a magazine with a large circulation. This exposure brought Akutagawa instant celebrity, and he was able to publish stories he had written previously. These appeared in collections such as *Rashomon* (1916), *Tobacco and the Devil* (1916) and *The Puppeteer* (1919). Akutagawa often drew upon medieval Japanese legends or European literature when writing his stories. He particularly liked tales that were bizarre and disturbing.

As a student of human nature, Akutagawa constantly observed the behavior of the people around him. On the whole he did not like what he saw. This displeasure is reflected in the harshly ironic tone of his later stories as he details the devious, petty motivations of human beings. Akutagawa was also plagued by doubts about his own artistic abilities, and by an inability to deal with the practical aspects of life. This all fed into the vague uneasiness that he gave as the reason for his suicide at the age of thirty-five.

Akutagawa Ryunosuke   **259**

Reader's Guide

THE NOSE

Background

The protagonist of "The Nose" is a Buddhist priest. Buddhism was founded in northern India around the sixth century B.C. Its founder, Gautama Buddha, taught that worldly life cannot provide final happiness, and that one must perform good deeds in order to achieve tranquility and enlightenment. The branch of Buddhism that spread to China, Korea, and Japan is called Mahayana Buddhism. It flourished in medieval Japan and is one of modern Japan's main religions. "The Nose" mentions two important Mahayana sutras, or narratives from holy scriptures: the Lotus Sutra and a sutra about the goddess of mercy, known as Kannon (or Kwannon) in Japan.

Writer's Response

A famous proverb says "You can't judge a book by its cover," yet most people *do* judge others at least partially on their appearance. Write a paragraph explaining why you think appearances are important or why you think they are not.

Literary Focus

Theme is the central idea or insight expressed in a work of literature. It moves beyond the specifics of the work to express a general idea or insight about life or human nature. Sometimes the theme is stated directly within the work, but more often it is merely implied, or suggested by certain details. The most important of these details are the change in the protagonist and the resolution of the conflict. In "The Nose," Akutagawa uses humor and irony to suggest a serious theme about human nature.

THE NOSE
Akutagawa Ryunosuke
translated by
TAKASHI KOJIMA

As you read, pay attention to Zenchi's feelings about his extraordinarily long nose. How do his feelings change throughout the story? What causes the changes?

Kamakura Buddha, Japan.

Japan Tourist Association

In the town of Ike-no-O there was no one who had not heard of Zenchi Naigu's nose. Dangling from his upper lip to below his chin, five or six inches long, it was of the same thickness from end to end.

For fifty years he had been tormented at heart by the presence of his nose—from his young days as an acolyte[1] until the time he rose to the respected office of Palace Chaplain. To others he tried to appear unconcerned about his nose, not so much because his preoccupation with such a matter was not worthy of a man whose duty it was to devote himself ardently to prayer for the advent of Paradise as because he wished to keep from the knowledge of others that he was worried over his nose. With him his apparent concern was rather a matter of pride, and his greatest dread in everyday conversation was to hear the word *nose.*

His nose was, of course, an intolerable nuisance. In the first place, he could not take his meals by himself. If he tried, the tip of his nose would reach down into the boiled rice in his bowl. So at meals he had to have one of his disciples sit opposite him and hold

---

1. **acolyte** (ak'ə·līt): attendant; helper.

up the end of his nose with an oblong piece of wood about two feet long and an inch wide. This manner of taking meals was, of course, no easy matter for the priest whose nose was held up or for his disciple who held it up.

Once a page,[2] who was acting in the place of the disciple, happened to sneeze and dropped the nose into the bowl—this incident was talked about as far as Kyoto.[3] He could accept the practical inconvenience of having a long nose, but the loss of his dignity on account of it was intolerable.

The Ike-no-O townspeople used to say that it was fortunate for the priest that he was not a layman, for surely no woman would care to be the wife of a man who had such a nose. Some went so far as to say that were it not for his nose, he might not have taken holy orders.

He did not consider that his priesthood had been a refuge which offered him any service in lightening the burden of his nose. Moreover his pride was too delicately strung for him to be influenced in the least by such a worldly eventuality as matrimony. His sole concern was to resort to every possible means to heal the wounds his pride had suffered and to repair the losses his dignity had sustained.

He exhausted all possible means to make his nose appear shorter than it really was. When there was no one about, he would examine his nose in the mirror and look at it from various angles, taxing his ingenuity to the utmost. Just changing the reflections of his face in the mirror was not enough: prodding his cheeks, or putting his finger on the tip of his chin, he would patiently study

Kinkakuji Temple, Japan.
What seems to be the narrator's attitude toward Zenchi?

his face in the mirror. But not once could he satisfy himself that his nose was shorter. Indeed, it often happened that the more he studied his nose the longer it seemed to be. On such occasions, he would put his mirror back into its box, sighing heavily, and sadly going back to his lectern would continue chanting the sutra to Kwannon, or the Goddess of Mercy.

He paid close attention to other people's noses. The Temple of Ike-no-O, frequented by a large number of visitors, both priests and laymen, held Buddhist masses, receptions for visiting priests, and sermons for parishioners. The precincts of the Temple were lined with closely built cells, with a bathhouse which had heated water daily. He would closely scrutinize the visitors, patiently trying to find at least one person who might possibly have a nose like his own in

---

2. **page:** boy servant.
3. **Kyoto** (kē′ōt′ō): Japanese city that was the imperial capital at the time of the story.

order that he might ease his troubled mind. He took no notice of the rich silken attire, the ordinary hempen[4] clothes, the priests' saffron[5] hoods nor their dark sacerdotal[6] robes, all of which counted for next to nothing in his eyes. That which arrested his eyes was not the people or their attire but their noses. He could find hooked noses but none like his own. Each additional failure made his thinking darker and gloomier.

While talking with others, unconsciously he would take between his fingers the tip of his dangling nose; then he would blush with shame for an act ill fitting his years and office. His misfortune had driven him to such extremes.

In his desperate attempt to find some consolation by discovering someone with a nose like his own, he delved into the voluminous Buddhist scriptures; but in all the scriptures there was not one reference to a long nose. How comforting it would have been to find, for instance, that either Mu Lien or Sha Lien[7] had a long nose.

He did find that King Liu Hsan-ti[8] of the Kingdom of Chu-han in the third century A.D. had long ears, and thought how reassuring it would have been if it had happened that the King's nose, instead of his ears, had been long.

It need hardly be said that while taking assiduous pains to seek spiritual consolation, he did try most earnestly a variety of elaborate practical measures to shorten his nose.

At one time he took a concoction with a snake-gourd[9] base. At another he bathed his nose in the urine of mice; yet with all his persistent and unremitting efforts, he still had five to six inches of nose dangling down over his lips.

One autumn day a disciple went on a trip to Kyoto, partly on his master's business, and before his returning to Ike-no-O, his physician acquaintance happened to introduce him to the mysteries of shortening noses. The physician, who had come to Japan from China, was at that time a priest attached to the Choraku Temple.

Zenchi, with an assumed nonchalance, avoided calling for an immediate test of the remedy, and could only drop casual hints about his regret that he must cause his disciple so much bother at meals, although he eagerly waited in his heart for his disciple to persuade him to try the remedy. The disciple could not fail to see through his master's design. But his master's innermost feelings, which led him to work out such an elaborate scheme, aroused his disciple's sympathy. As Zenchi had expected, his disciple advised him to try this method with such extraordinary urgency that, according to his premeditated plan, he finally yielded to his earnest counsel.

The formula was a simple one: first to boil the nose in hot water, and then to let another trample on it and torment it.

At the Temple bathhouse water was kept "at the boil" daily, so his disciple brought in an iron ladle, water so hot that no one could have put a finger into it. It was feared that Zenchi's face would be scalded by steam; so they bored a hole in a wooden tray and used the tray as a lid to cover the pot so that his nose could be immersed in the boiling water.

---

4. **hempen:** made of hemp, a tough, heavy fiber often twisted into rope.
5. **saffron:** here, orange-yellow.
6. **sacerdotal** (sas'ər·dōt''l): priestly.
7. **Mu Lien** (moo' lyen') and **Sha Lien** (shä' lyen'): two important disciples of the historic Buddha. Mu Lien was famous for his magic powers; Sha Lien, for his scholarship.
8. **King Liu Hsan-ti** (lyoo' hsän'tē'): Chinese king described in Buddhist legends.

9. **snake-gourd:** a type of squash or melon.

As for his nose, no matter how long it was soaked in the scalding water, it was immune from ill effect.

"Your Reverence," the disciple said after a while, "I suppose it must be sufficiently boiled by now."

The Chaplain, with a wry smile, was thinking that no one who overheard this remark could suspect that it concerned a remedy for shortening his nose.

Heated by water and steam, his nose itched as if bitten by mosquitoes.

When the nose was withdrawn from the hole in the lid, the disciple set about trampling on that steaming object, exerting all his strength in pounding it with both his feet. Zenchi, lying on his side, and stretching his nose on the floorboards, watched his disciple's legs move up and down.

"Does it hurt, Your Reverence?" his disciple asked from time to time, looking down sympathetically on the priest's bald head. "The physician told me to trample hard on it. Doesn't it hurt?"

Zenchi tried to shake his head by way of indicating that he was not feeling any pain, but as his nose was being trampled on he could not do this, so rolling his eyes upwards, in a tone that suggested he was offended, and with his gaze fixed on his disciple's chapped feet, he said, "No, it doesn't hurt." Although his itching nose was being trampled on, it was a comfortable rather than a painful sensation.

His nose having undergone this treatment for some time, what seemed to be grains of millet began to appear, at which sight his disciple stopped trampling and said in soliloquy, "I was told to pull them out with tweezers."

The nose looked like a plucked and roasted chicken. With cheeks puffed out, though disgruntled, the priest suffered his disciple to deal with his nose as the man saw fit—although, however aware of his disciple's kindness he might have been, he did not relish his nose being treated as if it were a piece of inert matter. Like a patient undergoing an operation at the hands of a surgeon in whom he does not place implicit trust, Zenchi reluctantly watched his disciple extract, from the pores of his nose, feathers of fat curled to half an inch in diameter. The treatment finished, the disciple looked relieved and said: "Now, your Reverence, we have only to boil it once more, and it'll be all right."

Zenchi, with knit brow, submitted to the treatment meted out to him.

When his nose was taken out of the pot for the second time, it was found, to their great surprise, remarkably shorter than before and was not very different from a normal hooked nose. Stroking his greatly shortened nose, he timidly and nervously peered into the mirror which his disciple held out to him.

The nose, which previously had dangled below his chin, had miraculously dwindled, and, not protruding below his upper lip, was barely a relic of what it had once been. The red blotches which bespeckled it were probably only bruises caused by the trampling.

"No one will laugh at me any more," the priest thought to himself. He saw in the mirror that the face reflected there was looking into the face outside the mirror, blinking its eyes in satisfaction.

But all day long he was uneasy and feared that his nose might grow long; so whenever he had the chance, whether in chanting sutras or in eating meals, he stealthily touched his nose. However, he found his nose installed in good shape above his upper lip, without straying beyond his lower lip.

Early in the morning, at the moment of

to laugh, casting down his eyes, he could not for long withhold his burst of laughter. The sextons[10] under Zenchi's supervision would listen respectfully while seated face to face with their master, but on more than one occasion they fell to chuckling as soon as he turned his back.

Zenchi at first attributed the laughter of his page and the sextons to the marked change in his features, but by and by, with his head cocked on one side, interrupting the sutra he was chanting, he would mutter to himself: "The change alone does not give a plausible explanation for their laughter. Zenchi Naigu! their laughter is now different from what it was when your nose was long. If you could say that the unfamiliar nose looks more ridiculous than the familiar one, that would once and for all settle the matter. But there must be some other reason behind it; they didn't laugh heartily or irresistibly as before."

The poor amiable priest on such occasions would look up at Fugen, Goddess of Wisdom,[11] pictured on the scroll hanging close beside him, and calling to mind the long nose he had wielded until four or five days previously, he would lapse into melancholy "like one sunken low recalleth his glory of bygone days."[12] But it was to be regretted that he was deficient in judgment sufficient to find a solution to this quandary.

Man is possessed of two contradictory sentiments. Everyone will sympathize with another's misfortune. But when the other

Fred Euphrat

Statue of Buddha.

waking, he stroked the tip of his nose, and he found that it was still as short as ever. After a gap of many years he at that moment recognized the same relief he had felt when he had completed the austerities required for his transcription of the lengthy Lotus Sutra of his sect.

Within the course of several days, however, Zenchi had a most surprising experience. A samurai who, on business, visited the Temple of Ike-no-O, looked amused as never before, and, quite incapable of uttering a word, he could but stare fixedly at the priest's nose. This was not all. The page who once had dropped Zenchi's nose into the bowl of gruel happened to pass by Zenchi in the lecture hall; at first, resisting his impulse

---

10. **sextons:** temple officials in charge of maintaining the grounds.

11. **Fugen, Goddess of Wisdom:** Fugen Bosatsu, the Bodhisattva—or morally and spiritually superior being—who sits at Buddha's side and offers human beings redemption through mercy.

12. **like . . . bygone days:** quotation from Buddhist scripture.

Akutagawa Ryunosuke **265**

manages to pull through his misfortune, he not only thinks it safe to laugh at him to his face but also comes even to regard him with envy. In extreme cases some may feel like casting him into his former misfortune again and may even harbor some enmity, if negative, toward him.

Zenchi was at a loss to know what precisely made him forlorn, but his unhappiness was caused by nothing more than the wayward caprices of those surrounding him—the priests and laymen of Ike-no-O.

Day after day Zenchi, becoming more and more unhappy and vexed, would not open his mouth without speaking sharply to someone and was ever out-of-sorts until even the disciple who had administered to him the effective remedy began to backbite him, saying, "The master will be punished for his sins."

What especially enraged Zenchi was the mischief played on him by the page. One day, hearing a dog yelping wildly, he casually looked outside and found the page, with a stick about two feet long in his hand, chasing a lean and shaggy dog and shouting: "Watch out there for your *nose!* Watch out or I'll hit your *nose.*" Snatching the wooden stick from the page's hand, the priest struck him sharply across the face; it was the very stick which had been used to hold up Zenchi's nose.

Finally Zenchi came to feel sorry and even resentful for having had his long nose shortened.

One night after sunset it happened that the wind seeming to have arisen suddenly, the noisy tinkling of the pagoda wind bells[13] came to his cell. The cold, moreover, had so noticeably increased in severity that Zenchi could not go to sleep, try as he might; tossing and turning in his bed he became aware of an itching in his nose. Putting his hand to his nose he felt that it had become swollen as if with dropsy;[14] it seemed feverish, too.

"It was so drastically shortened that I might have caught some disease," he muttered to himself, caressing his nose as reverently as he would if he were holding the offerings of incense and flowers to be dedicated at the altar.

On the following morning Zenchi as usual awoke early, and he noticed that the garden was as bright as if it were carpeted with gold, because in the garden the ginkgo trees and horse chestnuts had overnight shed all their leaves; and the crest of the pagoda must have been encrusted with frost, for the nine copper rings of the spire were brightly shining in the still faint glimmer of the rising sun. Sitting on the veranda, the shutters already opened, he drew a deep breath, and at that same moment a certain feeling, the nature of which he had all but forgotten, came back to him.

Instinctively he put his hand to his nose, and what he touched was not the short nose that had been his the night before, but the former long nose that had dangled five or six inches over his lips; in one night, he found, his nose had grown as long as it had been previously, and this, for some reason, made him feel refreshed and as happy as he had felt in the first moments when his nose had been shortened.

"Nobody will laugh at me any more," he whispered to himself.

His long nose dangled in the autumn breeze of early morning.

---

13. **pagoda** (pə·gō′də) **wind bells:** wind chimes hung at the corners of the temple; the use of such chimes is traditional in Japan, where their chiming is said to create a sense of coolness in summer.

14. **dropsy:** accumulation of fluid that causes swelling; now usually called edema (ē·dē′mə).

Were you surprised that Zenchi was happy to get his long nose back again? If you were Zenchi, would your response have been similar or different? Explain.

Identifying Facts

1. According to the opening paragraphs, how does Zenchi try to appear to others? Why?

2. After his nose is shortened, what change does Zenchi discover in others' behavior? How does his own behavior change?

3. When Zenchi awakens to find his nose has grown back to its original length, what does he whisper to himself?

Interpreting Meanings

1. Do you think Zenchi's unhappiness at the beginning of the story is caused solely by his ungainly nose? If not, what else might be causing it?

2. Why do you think people begin laughing at Zenchi after his nose is shortened? How does the narrator explain their reactions?

3. What **theme** or central insight about human nature do Zenchi and the story's events suggest to you?

4. Which story details do you find especially humorous or ironic? How does the use of **humor** and **irony** help make the story effective?

Applying Meanings

Some people go to great lengths to improve or change their appearances through face lifts, liposuction, and other surgical and nonsurgical means. Do you think such changes in appearance generally make people happier? Why or why not?

Creative Writing Response

Imagining a Bizarre Change. Suppose that you woke up one morning with a bizarre change in personal appearance: bright purple hair, huge pointed ears, snakelike scaly skin, or wings sprouting from your shoulder blades. Imagine the practical difficulties this change would create in your everyday life, and the emotional and psychological trauma it might cause. Write a few paragraphs detailing your reactions and the reactions of others to your bizarre appearance. You might begin with a sentence like this: ''This morning I woke up to find that two lobster claws had sprouted where my hands used to be.'' You might want to insert moments of humor and irony in your story.

Critical Writing Response

Writing About Psychological Insights. Akutagawa is famous for his keen understanding of human psychology. In a brief essay, show how ''The Nose'' illustrates his insight into human behavior and motivation. Discuss Zenchi's behavior and motivation throughout the story. Why does he want to shorten his nose? Why does his shortened nose make him even more miserable? Why is he relieved when his nose returns to its original length? Before you begin writing, list on a separate sheet the story details that you will cite in answering the questions above.

Language and Vocabulary

East Asian and Pacific Languages

English has borrowed a number of words from Chinese, Japanese, and other Asian and Pacific languages. Use a dictionary to find the origins of each of the following words. Write down the meaning of any unfamiliar words.

1. boomerang
2. karate
3. kiwi
4. taboo
5. yak
6. boondocks
7. ketchup
8. rickshaw
9. tycoon
10. yo-yo

Hwang Sun-won
b. 1915, Korea

Courtesy of Mercury House Books

Hwang Sun-won has lived through many tragic times in his homeland. Born when Korea was a colony of Japan, Hwang saw the Japanese imprison his father for supporting the unsuccessful Korean rebellion of 1919. He went to Japanese-language schools in Korea and then attended a university in Tokyo. Hwang returned home just as Japanese expansionist policies escalated into World War II. Although he was able to publish his first story collection, *The Marsh*, in 1940, Japanese authorities banned Korean writing soon afterward and Hwang had to continue his work in secret.

With the Japanese surrender in 1945, Korea was free of Japanese oppression, but Hwang and others who lived in the north were now subject to Soviet oppression. As communism spread in the north, Hwang and his family fled to the south, then occupied by American forces. They settled for a time in the capital city of Seoul (sōl), but became refugees again when the Communists invaded Seoul at the beginning of the Korean War. The end of the war in 1953 brought only limited happiness to most Koreans, for their nation remained divided and many people found themselves separated from friends and relatives.

Throughout these turbulent times, Hwang continued to produce fiction, even though its publication was often delayed. "Cranes," reprinted here, and many of Hwang's other works suggest that the political divisions between North Korea and South Korea are arbitrary and cruel.

Hwang has enjoyed widespread acclaim in South Korea since the mid-1950s, when his short novel *Descendents of Cain* (1954) won the Free Literature Prize. Although his work, like that of other Korean writers, has been slow to draw the attention of the West, Hwang recently became one of the first Koreans to have his tales appear in English translations in two full-length volumes, *The Book of Masks* (1989) and *Shadows of a Sound* (1990).

Reader's Guide

CRANES

Background

After Japan's defeat in World War II, Korea was liberated by Russian forces in the North and American forces in the South. The two groups then helped establish governments with very different ideologies. The dividing line between North and South Korea became the Thirty-eighth Parallel—a line representing a latitude of 38° North. However, in June of 1950—just a year after the Americans had withdrawn most of their troops—Communist forces from the North crossed that parallel in an invasion that marked the beginning of the Korean War. With the support of the United Nations, American and other Western forces helped the South Koreans defend their territory. In 1953 a truce was finally arranged, although skirmishes at the Thirty-eighth Parallel continued to erupt periodically.

During the Korean War, many villages along the Thirty-eighth Parallel changed hands several times. ''Cranes'' is set in one such village and the countryside around it.

Writer's Response

A title often provides clues to a story's theme. From Southeast Asia to parts of the Mediterranean, the crane is a symbol of justice, longevity, and goodness. Given this information, what are your expectations of a story that is titled ''Cranes''?

Literary Focus

The plots of many stories revolve around a **conflict**, a struggle or clash between opposing characters, forces, or emotions. In an **external conflict**, the struggle is against an outside force, such as another character, society as a whole, or an aspect of nature. In an **internal conflict**, the struggle is between opposing desires, choices, or emotions within a single character. Sometimes a story features an internal conflict that is prompted by an external one. For example, a character who must face a deadly lion may also experience an internal struggle between courage and cowardice.

CRANES

Hwang Sun-won

translated by
PETER H. LEE

As you read this story, pay special attention to the conflicting emotions felt by the main character, Song-sam. How is his **internal conflict** *related to the* **external conflict** *in which he is involved? Can you sympathize with his feelings?*

The northern village at the border of the Thirty-eighth Parallel was snugly settled under the high, bright autumn sky.

One white gourd lay against another on the dirt floor of an empty farmhouse. The occasional village elders first put out their bamboo pipes before passing by, and the children, too, turned aside some distance off. Their faces were ridden with fear.

The village as a whole showed few traces of destruction from the war, but it did not seem like the same village Song-sam[1] had known as a boy.

At the foot of a chestnut grove on the hill behind the village he stopped and climbed a chestnut tree. Somewhere far back in his mind he heard the old man with a wen[2] shout, "You bad boy, you're climbing up my chestnut tree again!"

The old man must have passed away, for among the few village elders Song-sam had met, the old man was not to be found. Holding the trunk of the tree, Song-sam gazed at the blue sky for a while. Some chestnuts fell to the ground as the dry clusters opened of their own accord.

In front of the farmhouse that had been turned into a public peace-police office, a young man stood, tied up. He seemed to be a stranger, so Song-sam approached him to have a close look. He was taken aback; it was none other than his boyhood playmate, Tok-chae.[3]

Song-sam asked the police officer who had come with him from Chontae[4] what it was all about. The prisoner was vice-chairman of the Farmers' Communist League and had just been flushed out of his hideout in his own house, Song-sam learned.

Song-sam sat down on the dirt floor and lit a cigarette.

Tok-chae was to be escorted to Chongdan[5] by one of the peace policemen.

After a time, Song-sam lit a new cigarette from the first and stood up.

"I'll take the fellow with me."

---

1. **Song-sam** (sung'säm')
2. **wen:** benign fatty tumor, often on the scalp or face.
3. **Tok-chae** (tuk'chä')
4. **Chontae** (chun'tä')
5. **Chongdan** (chung'dän')

Tok-chae, his face averted, refused to look at Song-sam. They left the village.

Song-sam kept on smoking, but the tobacco had no taste. He just kept drawing in the smoke and blowing it out. Then suddenly he thought that Tok-chae, too, must want a puff. He thought of the days when they used to share dried gourd leaves behind walls, hidden from the adults. But today, how could he offer a cigarette to a fellow like this?

Once, when they were small, he went with Tok-chae to steal some chestnuts from the grandpa[6] with the wen. It was Song-sam's turn to go up the tree. Suddenly there came shouts from the old man. He slipped and fell to the ground. Song-sam got chestnut needles all over his bottom, but he kept on running. It was only when they reached a safe place where the old man could not overtake them that he turned his bottom to Tok-chae. Plucking out those needles hurt so much that he could not keep tears from welling up in his eyes. Tok-chae produced a fistful of chestnuts from his pocket and thrust them into Song-sam's . . . Song-sam threw away the cigarette he had just lit. Then he made up his mind not to light another while he was escorting Tok-chae.

They reached the hill pass, the hill where he and Tok-chae used to cut fodder for the cows until Song-sam had had to move near Chontae, south of the Thirty-eighth Parallel, two years before the liberation.

Song-sam felt a sudden surge of anger in spite of himself and shouted, "So how many have you killed?"

For the first time, Tok-chae cast a quick glance at him and then turned away.

6. **grandpa:** here, not a relative, but a colloquial term for any elderly man.

"How many did you kill, you?" he asked again.

Tok-chae turned toward him once again and glared. The glare grew intense and his mouth twitched.

"So you managed to kill many, eh?" Song-sam felt his heart becoming clear from within, as if an obstruction had been removed. "If you were vice-chairman of the Communist League, why didn't you run? You must have been lying low with a secret mission."

Tok-chae did not answer.

"Speak up, what was your mission?"

Tok-chae kept walking. Tok-chae is hiding

Mt. Sorak, Korea.

Brent Bear/Westlight

something, Song-sam thought. He wanted to take a good look at him, but Tok-chae would not turn his averted face.

Fingering the revolver at his side, Song-sam went on: "No excuse is necessary. You are sure to be shot anyway. Why don't you tell the truth, here and now?"

"I'm not going to make any excuses. They made me vice-chairman of the league because I was one of the poorest and I was a hard-working farmer. If that constitutes a crime worthy of death, so be it. I am still what I used to be—the only thing I'm good at is digging in the soil." After a short pause, he added, "My old man is bedridden at home. He's been ill almost half a year." Tok-chae's father was a widower, a hard-working poor farmer who lived only for his son. Seven years ago his back had given out and his skin had become diseased.

"You married?"

"Yes," replied Tok-chae after a while.

"To whom?"

"Shorty."

"To Shorty?" How interesting! A woman so small and plump that she knew the earth's vastness but not the sky's altitude. Such a cold fish! He and Tok-chae used to tease her and make her cry. And Tok-chae had married that girl.

"How many kids?"

"The first is arriving this fall, she says."

Song-sam had difficulty swallowing a laugh about to explode in spite of himself. Although he had asked how many kids Tok-chae had, he could not help wanting to burst into laughter at the image of her sitting down, with a large stomach, one span around. But he realized this was no time to laugh or joke over such matters.

"Anyway, it's strange you did not run away."

"I tried to escape. They said that once the

Cranes, highly symbolic in all parts of Asia, adorn this Chinese drum stand, 481–221 B.C.

South invaded, no man would be spared. So men between seventeen and forty were forcibly taken to the North. I thought of evacuating, even if I had to carry my father on my back. But father said no. How could the farmers leave the land behind when the crops were ready for harvest? He grew old on that farm depending on me as the prop and mainstay of the family. I wanted to be with him in his last moments so that I could close his eyes with my own hand. Besides, where can farmers like us go, who know only living on the land?"

Last June Song-sam had had to take refuge. At night he had broken the news privately to his father. But his father had said the same thing! Where can a farmer go, leaving all the chores behind? So Song-sam left alone. Roaming about the strange streets and villages in the South, Song-sam had been haunted by thoughts of his old parents and the young children, left with all the chores. Fortunately, his family was safe then, as now.

They crossed the ridge of a hill. This time Song-sam walked with his face averted. The autumn sun was hot on his forehead. This was an ideal day for the harvest, he thought.

When they reached the foot of the hill, Song-sam hesitatingly stopped. In the middle of a field he spied a group of cranes that looked like men in white clothes bending over. This used to be the neutralized zone[7] along the Thirty-eighth Parallel. The cranes were still living here, as before, while the people were all gone.

Once, when Song-sam and Tok-chae were about twelve, they had set a trap here, without the knowledge of the adults, and had caught a crane, a Tanjong crane.[8] They had roped the crane, even its wings, and had paid daily visits, patting its neck and riding on its back. Then one day they overheard the neighbors whispering. Someone had come from Seoul with a permit from the governor-general's office[9] to catch cranes as specimens or something. Then and there the two boys dashed off to the field. That they would be found out and punished was no longer a weighty concern; all they worried about was the fate of their crane. Without a moment's delay, still out of breath from running, they untied the crane's feet and wings. But the bird could hardly walk. It must have been worn out from being bound.

The two held it up in the air. Then, all of a sudden, a shot was fired. The crane fluttered its wings a couple of times and came down again.

It was shot, they thought. But the next moment, as another crane from a nearby bush fluttered its wings, the boys' crane stretched its long neck with a whoop and disappeared into the sky. For a long time the two boys could not take their eyes away from the blue sky into which their crane had soared.

"Hey, why don't we stop here for a crane hunt?" Song-sam spoke up suddenly.

Tok-chae was puzzled, struck dumb.

"I'll make a trap with this rope; you flush[10] a crane over here."

Having untied Tok-chae's hands, Song-sam had already started crawling among the weeds.

Tok-chae's face turned white. "You are sure to be shot anyway"—these words flashed through his mind. Pretty soon a bullet would fly from where Song-sam has gone, he thought.

Some paces away, Song-sam quickly turned toward him.

"Hey, how come you're standing there like you're dumb? Go flush the crane!"

Only then did Tok-chae catch on. He started crawling among the weeds.

A couple of Tanjong cranes soared high into the clear blue autumn sky, fluttering their huge wings.

---

7. **neutralized zone:** demilitarized zone, or strip of no man's land, separating North and South Korea at the Thirty-eighth Parallel.

8. **Tanjong** (tän'jung') **crane:** large, long-legged bird that breeds in North Korea.

9. **governor-general's office:** headquarters of Korea's chief executive appointed by the Japanese government when Korea was a colony of Japan (during Song-sam's boyhood).

---

10. **flush:** to drive a bird from cover.

Do you think Song-sam did the right thing in allowing Tok-chae to go free? Would you have acted similarly if you were in Song-sam's position? Explain.

Identifying Facts

1. Where is the village located? What was Song-sam's relationship with Tok-chae when they were children?

2. For which side in the Korean War is Song-sam fighting? Why is Tok-chae a prisoner?

3. What reasons does Tok-chae give for becoming vice-chairman of the Communist League and for remaining in the village after the Communists abandoned it?

4. When he unties Tok-chae's hands, in what childhood activity does Song-sam suggest the two engage?

Interpreting Meanings

1. In his **internal conflict**, Song-sam must decide between which two courses of action? What is the connection between this conflict and the larger **external conflict** of the story?

2. As Song-sam escorts Tok-chae, he remembers incidents from their childhoods. How do these **flashbacks** contribute to the resolution of the **conflict**?

3. What do the characters' experiences suggest about civil wars in general and the Korean War in particular? What does the story suggest about ties of kinship and friendship?

4. In many Asian cultures, the crane symbolizes long life. Birds often symbolize the soul or spirit, and flight often symbolizes rising to a higher moral plane. Reread the last sentence of the story. What **symbolic** meanings might it have?

Applying Meanings

Do you think individual ties should carry more weight than political or national affiliations? Explain.

Creative Writing Response

Writing About a Moment of Decision. Write a brief personal essay or short story about an important decision in your life. The decision may involve a moral choice, as Song-sam's does. Before you write, ask yourself what events led up to your decision, and how your life, or your outlook on life, has changed since you made the decision.

Critical Writing Response

Writing About Conflict. Write a brief essay about Song-sam's **internal conflict** and the way he eventually resolves it. First, identify the reasons for and against releasing Tok-chae that constitute Song-sam's internal conflict. You may organize your thoughts by listing these factors on a chart like the one below. Conclude your essay by evaluating Song-sam's decision. Explain why you think it was a good or bad resolution to his dilemma.

Taking Tok-chae to Face Execution	Letting Tok-chae Go

Nguyen Thi Vinh
b. 1924, Vietnam

Bryn Campbell/Magnum Photos, Inc.

South Vietnamese refugees.

Nguyen Thi Vinh (noo'yin tī vin') bears a family name with a long history. From the sixteenth century to the eighteenth century, the house of Nguyen was one of two ruling families in Vietnam. In 1773 a member of the Nguyen family became Vietnam's emperor, and his descendants ruled the country until its conquest by French forces in the late nineteenth century.

Nguyen Thi Vinh writes about Vietnam's more recent history—especially its decades of warfare during her lifetime. In the early 1950s, she was among the many northerners who fled south to escape the Communists.

She settled in Saigon, capital of the newly created government of South Vietnam, and soon became part of that city's thriving intellectual community.

Best known in Vietnam for her fiction, Nguyen first won fame with *Two Sisters* (1953). She also published a highly regarded book of poetry and served as editor of the South Vietnamese literary journal *New Wind* and the magazine *The East.* Although she was proud of her literary accomplishments, Nguyen did not find peace and contentment in Vietnam. The North-South conflict soon escalated into the Vietnam War, and the violence was underscored by the heartbreaking knowledge that people she had loved in childhood were now fighting as bitter enemies. Those feelings are powerfully expressed in her poem "Thoughts of Hanoi," reprinted here.

After the fall of Saigon to North Vietnamese forces and the subsequent reunification of Vietnam under a Communist government in 1975, Nguyen remained in her homeland as millions of other South Vietnamese fled in fear. She managed to survive those trying times, and in 1983 she emigrated to Norway, where other members of her family had settled.

Reader's Guide

THOUGHTS OF HANOI

Background

For centuries, Vietnam has been the site of conflicts between local kingdoms. In the nineteenth century, foreign imperial powers became interested in the region. The French gained control of the country in the late nineteenth century, but they were forced from power by the Japanese, who occupied the area from 1940 to 1945. French attempts to regain control after Japan's defeat in World War II were countered by Communists in the North led by Ho Chi Minh. The two groups fought from 1946 until 1954, when France agreed to withdraw. The country was then temporarily divided into Communist North Vietnam with its capital at Hanoi, and non-Communist South Vietnam with its capital at Saigon. In 1957, Communists in the South began rebelling and Western democracies came to the aid of South Vietnam. The conflict soon escalated into the Vietnam War, in which the United States was a leading player. At a 1973 peace conference, the combatants agreed to a cease-fire and the United States withdrew its troops. Not long afterward, the North Vietnamese government invaded the South and made Vietnam a single nation. The country's decades of warfare sparked massive migrations among the Vietnamese people.

Writer's Response

Write a few sentences about a place you remember fondly. It might be a lake, a neighborhood, a basketball court, or some other place. Include specific details that will make the place come alive to a reader.

Literary Focus

A **lyric poem** is one that expresses personal emotions or thoughts instead of telling a story or portraying characters in action. The voice that talks to us in a lyric poem is called the **speaker**. Sometimes the speaker is the poet, but often the poet assumes a different voice. In ''Thoughts of Hanoi,'' Nguyen Thi Vinh assumes the voice of a Vietnamese male to express her own thoughts and emotions.

THOUGHTS OF HANOI

Nguyen Thi Vinh

translated by

NGUYEN NGOC BICH

 As you read the poem, notice how the speaker's childhood memories contrast with his present situation.

The night is deep and chill
as in early autumn. Pitchblack,
it thickens after each lightning flash.
I dream of Hanoi:
5 Co-ngu° Road   5. **Co-ngu** (kō′nōō′)
ten years of separation
the way back sliced by a frontier of hatred.
I want to bury the past
to burn the future
10 still I yearn
still I fear
those endless nights
waiting for dawn.

Brother,
15 how is Hang Dao° now?   15. **Hang Dao** (häng′ dou′)
How is Ngoc Son° temple?   16. **Ngoc Son** (nōk′ sōn′)
Do the trains still run
each day from Hanoi
to the neighboring towns?
20 To Bac-ninh,° Cam-giang,° Yen-bai,°   20. **Bac-ninh** (bäk′nin′), **Cam-giang** (käm′gyäng′), **Yen-bai** (yen′bī′): towns near Hanoi.
the small villages, islands
of brown thatch in a lush green sea?

The girls
    bright eyes
25   ruddy cheeks
    four-piece dresses
      raven-bill scarves°   27. **raven-bill scarves:** headscarves folded into straight-edged triangular forms, like the bill or beak of a raven.
    sowing harvesting
      spinning weaving
30   all year round,
  the boys

plowing
   transplanting
in the fields
35   in their shops
running across
   the meadow at evening
to fly kites
   and sing alternating songs.°

40 Stainless blue sky,
   jubilant voices of children
stumbling through the alphabet,
   village graybeards strolling to the temple,
grandmothers basking in twilight sun,
45   chewing betel leaves°
while the children run—

Brother,
how is all that now?
Or is it obsolete?
50 Are you like me,
reliving the past,
imagining the future?
Do you count me as a friend
or am I the enemy in your eyes?
55 Brother, I am afraid
that one day I'll be with the March-North Army°
meeting you on your way to the South.
I might be the one to shoot you then
or you me
60 but please
not with hatred.

For don't you remember how it was,
you and I in school together,
plotting our lives together?
65 Those roots go deep!

Brother, we are men,
conscious of more
than material needs.
How can this happen to us
70 my friend
my foe?

39. alternating songs: songs in which different singers take different parts; rounds.

45. betel (bēt′l) **leaves:** leaves of the betel palm, a tree found in southeastern Asia; both the leaves and nuts are often chewed like chewing gum.

56. March-North Army: that is, the South Vietnamese army marching into North Vietnam.

Vietnamese child in Hanoi.

First Thoughts

Did the **paradox**, or apparent contradiction, of the last two lines make sense to you? Think of another circumstance in which someone might be both your friend *and* your foe.

Identifying Facts

1. How many years ago did the speaker leave Hanoi, and by what is the way back now "sliced"?
2. List three specific questions about Hanoi that the speaker asks. What does the speaker ask about the past and future?
3. What kinds of **images** does the speaker describe in lines 23–46?
4. What is the speaker afraid may happen one day? What final question does he ask?

Interpreting Meanings

1. What might "each lightning flash" (line 3) be, and why might the speaker "fear/those endless nights"? What is the "frontier of hatred"?
2. Where does the **speaker** come from, and where is he living now? Which details suggest that the speaker is not the poet?
3. Why do you think the poet wrote so many lines describing the boys and girls of the Hanoi area? What is the "lush green sea"?
4. What is the apparent relationship between the speaker and the person addressed as "Brother"?
5. What overall attitude does this **lyric poem** convey toward warfare, especially civil warfare?

Applying Meanings

The United States was heavily involved in the Vietnam War. What are your feelings about the war, based on your studies and your conversations with older Americans or with Vietnamese refugees in the U.S.?

Creative Writing Response

Writing a Poem.   Write a short, free-verse poem called "Thoughts of X," in which X is some time or place that you miss. You may use the place you wrote about in the Writer's Response (see page 276) or choose another place or time.

Critical Writing Response

Comparing Viewpoints.   Like "Thoughts of Hanoi," Hwang Sun-won's "Cranes" (see page 270) was written at a time of civil warfare in the author's homeland. In a brief essay, compare and contrast the thoughts, feelings, and actions of the speaker in "Thoughts of Hanoi" and the protagonist in "Cranes." Focus on the physical and emotional effects of warfare in general and civil warfare in particular. Before you begin, you may find it helpful to list your ideas on a chart like the one below.

	"Thoughts of Hanoi"	"Cranes"
Feeling toward the "enemy"		
Thoughts about war		
Actions		
Writer's tone		

Zhang Jie
b. 1937, People's Republic of China

Isolde Ohlbaum

In the early 1980s, the American writer Annie Dillard documented in her book *Encounters with Chinese Writers* a heated exchange between Zhang Jie (jan' jyē') and the American beat poet Allen Ginsberg. Although Zhang is a small, seemingly fragile woman, and Ginsberg is a large, imposing man, Zhang was not afraid to speak her mind. "Mr. Ginsberg! you should not think only of yourself!" she exclaimed. "You must live and work so as to fulfill your obligations! Have your goals firmly in your mind. You should not take drugs! Think of your responsibility to society!" Such outspokenness and conviction are characteristic of Zhang's novels and short stories, which have caused controversy in China and won praise abroad.

Zhang's concern with social responsibility stems in part from the circumstances of her childhood. Raised in the Chinese capital of Beijing (bā'jing') (formerly Peking), Zhang grew up in dire poverty after her father abandoned the family a few months after her birth. She observed that in China at that time, her father had no binding or legal responsibility to his family.

Feeling that women had more rights under China's new Communist government, Zhang joined the Communist Party as a young woman and supported government policy even when it meant compromising her own desires. She had hoped, for example, to study literature in college. Instead, she studied economics, which the new government felt was of more use to society. Later she was among the many men and women who left their homes to work in factories or on farms in the hopes of improving China's shaky economy.

Speaking of her early life, Zhang recalls that she was "like a darting dragonfly, with no goals in life and no substantial pursuits. Only through literature did I discover myself." Zhang was not able to begin her writing career, however, until the Cultural Revolution ended and more moderate leaders came to power. In 1978 she won a nationwide award for her story "The Music of the Forests." Three years later her novel *Leaden Wings* won China's Mao Dun Literary Prize.

Reader's Guide

LOVE MUST NOT BE FORGOTTEN

Background

In 1949, the Communists established the People's Republic of China under their military hero Mao Zedong (also spelled Mao Tse-tung). The new Communist regime instituted drastic social and economic changes and became increasingly oppressive. During Mao's Cultural Revolution, many moderate political figures were removed from power, imprisoned, and sometimes executed. China's writers were also silenced.

After Mao's death in 1976 China came under more moderate leadership. Encouraged by the new spirit of openness, many writers emerged and began writing of past injustices and the need for future reforms. Zhang Jie won fame for writing of the continued inequality between the sexes despite government claims to the contrary. During the 1980s the government again became more repressive and in 1989 ordered a military crackdown on prodemocracy demonstrators in Beijing's Tiananmen Square. Few writers were allowed to publish within China, and those lucky enough to escape went to live abroad.

Among Chinese readers Zhang Jie enjoys huge popularity, despite much controversy over her 1979 story ''Love Must Not Be Forgotten,'' reprinted here. This story suggests that, for all the changes effected by the Communists, Chinese women still face centuries-old social pressures to marry and subordinate themselves to their husbands and families.

Writer's Response

Although the United States has made progress toward equality between the sexes, do you think that there is still room for improvement? Think of examples that illustrate some of the inequalities that still exist today.

Literary Focus

A **flashback** is a scene in a movie, play, or story that interrupts the present action to show or tell what happened at an earlier time. Writers often use this device to develop a character or to give additional plot information. ''Love Must Not Be Forgotten'' uses several flashbacks to show the narrator's growing awareness of her mother's true situation and feelings.

LOVE MUST NOT BE FORGOTTEN

Zhang Jie

translated by

GLADYS YANG

In the opening paragraphs of "Love Must Not Be Forgotten," the narrator wonders if she should marry a certain man. As you read the story, decide what advice her mother would probably have given her about her dilemma.

HRW Photo by Darwin Chen

I am thirty, the same age as our People's Republic. For a republic thirty is still young. But a girl of thirty is virtually on the shelf.

Actually, I have a bona fide suitor. Have you seen the Greek sculptor Myron's *Discobolus?*[1] Qiao Lin[2] is the image of that discus thrower. Even the padded clothes he wears in winter fail to hide his fine physique. Bronzed, with clear-cut features, a broad forehead and large eyes, his appearance alone attracts most girls to him.

But I can't make up my mind to marry him. I'm not clear what attracts me to him, or him to me. I know people are gossiping behind my back, "Who does she think she is, to be so choosy?" To them, I'm a nobody playing hard to get. They take offense at such preposterous behavior.

Of course, I shouldn't be captious.[3] In a society where commercial production still exists, marriage, like most other transactions, is still a form of barter.

I have known Qiao Lin for nearly two years, yet still cannot fathom whether he keeps so quiet from aversion to talking or from having nothing to say. When, by way of a small intelligence test, I demand his opinion of this or that, he says "good" or "bad" like a child in kindergarten.

Once I asked, "Qiao Lin, why do you love me?" He thought the question over seriously for what seemed an age. I could see from his normally smooth but now wrinkled forehead that the little gray cells in his handsome head were hard at work cogitating. I felt ashamed to have put him on the spot.

Finally he raised his clear childlike eyes to tell me, "Because you're good!"

Loneliness flooded my heart. "Thank you, Qiao Lin!" I couldn't help wondering, if we were to marry, whether we could discharge our duties to each other as husband and wife. Maybe, because law and morality would have bound us together. But how tragic simply to comply with law and morality! Was there no stronger bond to link us?

When such thoughts cross my mind I have the strange sensation that instead of being a girl contemplating marriage I am an elderly social scientist.

Perhaps I worry too much. We can live like most married couples, bringing up children together, strictly true to each other according to the law. . . . Although living in the seventies of the twentieth century, people still consider marriage the way they did millennia ago, as a means of continuing the race, a form of barter or a business transaction in which love and marriage can be separated. Since this is the common practice, why shouldn't we follow suit?

But I still can't make up my mind. As a child, I remember, I often cried all night for no rhyme or reason, unable to sleep and disturbing the whole household. My old nurse, a shrewd though uneducated woman, said an ill wind had blown through my ear. I think this judgment showed prescience, because I still have that old weakness. I upset myself over things which really present no problem, upsetting other people at the same time. One's nature is hard to change.

I think of my mother, too. If she were alive, what would she say about my attitude to Qiao Lin and my uncertainty about marrying him? My thoughts constantly turn to her, not because she was such a strict mother that her ghost is still watching over me since her death. No, she was not just my mother but my closest friend. I loved her so

---

1. **Myron's *Discobolus:*** famous statue of a handsome athlete by this Greek sculptor of the fifth century B.C.
2. **Qiao Lin** (chyou′ lin′)
3. **captious** (kap′shəs): fault-finding; critical.

much that the thought of her leaving me makes my heart ache.

She never lectured me, just told me quietly in her deep, unwomanly voice about her successes and failures, so that I could learn from her experience. She had evidently not had many successes—her life was full of failures.

During her last days she followed me with her fine, expressive eyes, as if wondering how I would manage on my own and as if she had some important advice for me but hesitated to give it. She must have been worried by my naiveté and sloppy ways. She suddenly blurted out, "Shanshan, if you aren't sure what you want, don't rush into marriage—better live on your own!"

Other people might think this strange advice from a mother to her daughter, but to me it embodied her bitter experience. I don't think she underestimated me or my knowledge of life. She loved me and didn't want me to be unhappy.

"I don't want to marry, mother!" I said, not out of bashfulness or a show of coyness. I can't think why a girl should pretend to be coy. She had long since taught me about things not generally mentioned to girls.

"If you meet the right man, then marry him. Only if he's right for you!"

"I'm afraid no such man exists!"

"That's not true. But it's hard. The world is so vast, I'm afraid you may never meet him." Whether married or not was not what concerned her, but the quality of the marriage.

"Haven't you managed fine without a husband?"

"Who says so?"

"I think you've done fine."

"I had no choice. . . ." She broke off, lost in thought, her face wistful. Her wistful lined face reminded me of a withered flower I had pressed in a book.

"Why did you have no choice?"

"You ask too many questions," she parried, not ashamed to confide in me but afraid that I might reach the wrong conclusion. Besides, everyone treasures a secret to carry to the grave. Feeling a bit put out, I demanded bluntly, "Didn't you love my dad?"

"No, I never loved him."

"Did he love you?"

"No, he didn't."

"Then why get married?"

She paused, searching for the right words to explain this mystery, then answered bitterly, "When you're young you don't always know what you're looking for, what you need, and people may talk you into getting married. As you grow older and more experienced you find out your true needs. By then, though, you've done many foolish things for which you could kick yourself. You'd give anything to be able to make a fresh start and live more wisely. Those content with their lot will always be happy, they say, but I shall never enjoy that happiness." She added self-mockingly, "A wretched idealist, that's all I am."

Did I take after her? Did we both have genes which attracted ill winds?

"Why don't you marry again?"

"I'm afraid I'm still not sure what I really want." She was obviously unwilling to tell me the truth.

I cannot remember my father. He and Mother split up when I was very small. I just recall her telling me sheepishly that he was a fine handsome fellow. I could see she was ashamed of having judged by appearances and made a futile choice. She told me, "When I can't sleep at night, I force myself to sober up by recalling all those stupid blunders I made. Of course it's so distasteful that I often hide my face in the sheet for shame,

Chinese woman.

❓ *At what point does the narrative shift from the narrator's story to her mother's story?*

The Bettmann Archive

as if there were eyes watching me in the dark. But distasteful as it is, I take some pleasure in this form of atonement."

I was really sorry that she hadn't remarried. She was such a fascinating character, if she'd married a man she loved, what a happy household ours would surely have been. Though not beautiful, she had the simple charm of an ink landscape. She was a fine writer, too. Another author who knew her well used to say teasingly, "Just reading your works is enough to make anyone love you!"

She would retort, "If he knew that the object of his affection was a white-haired old crone, that would frighten him away." At her age, she must have known what she really wanted, so this was obviously an evasion. I say this because she had quirks which puzzled me.

For instance, whenever she left Beijing on a trip, she always took with her one of the twenty-seven volumes of Chekhov's stories published between 1950 and 1955.[4] She also warned me, "Don't touch these books. If you want to read Chekhov, read that set I bought you." There was no need to caution me. Having a set of my own, why should I touch hers? Besides, she'd told me this over and over again. Still she was on her guard. She seemed bewitched by those books.

So we had two sets of Chekhov's stories at home. Not just because we loved Chekhov, but to parry other people like me who loved Chekhov. Whenever anyone asked to borrow a volume, she would lend one of mine. Once, in her absence, a close friend took a volume from her set. When she found out, she was frantic, and at once took a volume of mine to exchange for it.

Ever since I can remember, those books were on her bookcase. Although I admire Chekhov as a great writer, I was puzzled by the way she never tired of reading him. Why, for over twenty years, had she had to read him every single day? Sometimes, when tired of writing, she poured herself a cup of strong tea and sat down in front of the bookcase, staring raptly at that set of books. If I went into her room then it flustered her, and she either spilt her tea or blushed like

---

4. **twenty-seven volumes of Chekhov's . . . 1955:** complete stories of Russian author Anton Chekhov, published in a Chinese edition in the 1950s.

a girl discovered with her lover.

I wondered: Has she fallen in love with Chekhov? She might have if he'd still been alive.

When her mind was wandering just before her death, her last words to me were: "That set . . ." She hadn't the strength to give it its complete title. But I knew what she meant. "And my diary . . . 'Love Must Not Be Forgotten'. . . . Cremate them with me."

I carried out her last instruction regarding the works of Chekhov, but couldn't bring myself to destroy her diary. I thought, if it could be published, it would surely prove the most moving thing she had written. But naturally publication was out of the question.

At first I imagined the entries were raw material she had jotted down. They read neither like stories, essays, a diary, or letters. But after reading the whole I formed a hazy impression, helped out by my imperfect memory. Thinking it over, I finally realized that this was no lifeless manuscript I was holding, but an anguished, loving heart. For over twenty years one man had occupied her heart, but he was not for her. She used these diaries as a substitute for him, a means of pouring out her feelings to him, day after day, year after year.

No wonder she had never considered any eligible proposals, had turned a deaf ear to idle talk whether well meant or malicious. Her heart was already full, to the exclusion of anybody else. "No lake can compare with the ocean, no cloud with those on Mount Wu."[5] Remembering those lines I often reflected sadly that few people in real life could love like this. No one would love me like this.

I learned that toward the end of the thirties, when this man was doing underground work for the Party in Shanghai,[6] an old worker had given his life to cover him, leaving behind a helpless wife and daughter. Out of a sense of duty, of gratitude to the dead, and deep class feeling, he had unhesitatingly married the daughter. When he saw the endless troubles of couples who had married for "love," he may have thought, "Thank Heaven, though I didn't marry for love, we get on well, able to help each other." For years, as man and wife they lived through hard times.

He must have been my mother's colleague. Had I ever met him? He couldn't have visited our home. Who was he?

In the spring of 1962, Mother took me to a concert. We went on foot, the theater being quite near. On the way a black limousine pulled up silently by the pavement. Out stepped an elderly man with white hair in a black serge tunic suit. What a striking shock of white hair! Strict, scrupulous, distinguished, transparently honest—that was my impression of him. The cold glint of his flashing eyes reminded me of lightning or swordplay. Only ardent love for a woman really deserving his love could fill cold eyes like those with tenderness.

He walked up to Mother and said, "How are you, Comrade Zhong Yu?[7] It's been a long time."

"How are you!" Mother's hand holding mine suddenly turned icy cold and trembled a little.

They stood face to face without looking at each other, each appearing upset, even

---

5. **Mount Wu:** one of a chain of picturesque mountains in eastern China.

6. **Party in Shanghai** (shang'hī'): that is, the Communist Party in the large eastern Chinese city of Shanghai.

7. **Zhong Yu** (jong'yoo')

Exterior gate of the Forbidden City in Beijing, China. *The Forbidden City was the dwelling of the Chinese Imperial family before the era of Communism.*

stern. Mother fixed her eyes on the trees by the roadside, not yet in leaf. He looked at me. "Such a big girl already. Good, fine—you take after your mother."

Instead of shaking hands with Mother, he shook hands with me. His hand was as icy as hers and trembling a little. As if transmitting an electric current, I felt a sudden shock. Snatching my hand away I cried, "There's nothing good about that!"

"Why not?" he asked with the surprised expression grown-ups always have when children speak out frankly.

I glanced at Mother's face. I did take after her, to my disappointment. "Because she's not beautiful!"

He laughed, then said teasingly, "Too bad that there should be a child who doesn't find her own mother beautiful. Do you remember in '53, when your mother was transferred to Beijing, she came to our ministry to report for duty? She left you outside on the veranda, but like a monkey you climbed all the stairs, peeped through the cracks in doors, and caught your finger in the door of my office. You sobbed so bitterly that I carried you off to find her."

"I don't remember that." I was annoyed at his harking back to a time when I was still in open-seat pants.

"Ah, we old people have better memories." He turned abruptly and remarked to Mother, "I've read that last story of yours. Frankly speaking, there's something not quite right about it. You shouldn't have condemned the heroine....There's nothing wrong with falling in love, as long as you don't spoil someone else's life.... In fact, the

Zhang Jie   **287**

hero might have loved her, too. Only for the sake of a third person's happiness, they had to renounce their love...."

A policeman came over to where the car was parked and ordered the driver to move on. When the driver made some excuse, the old man looked around. After a hasty "Goodbye" he strode back to the car and told the policeman, "Sorry. It's not his fault, it's mine...."

I found it amusing watching this old cadre[8] listening respectfully to the policeman's strictures. When I turned to Mother with a mischievous smile, she looked as upset as a first-form[9] primary schoolchild standing forlornly in front of the stern headmistress.[10] Anyone would have thought she was the one being lectured by the policeman. The car drove off, leaving a puff of smoke. Very soon even this smoke vanished with the wind, as if nothing at all had happened. But the incident stuck in my mind.

Analyzing it now, I realize he must have been the man whose strength of character won Mother's heart. That strength came from his firm political convictions, his narrow escapes from death in the revolution, his active brain, his drive at work, his well-cultivated mind. Besides, strange to say, he and Mother both liked the oboe. Yes, she must have worshiped him. She once told me that unless she worshiped a man, she couldn't love him even for one day.

But I could not tell whether he loved her or not. If not, why was there this entry in her diary?

"This is far too fine a present. But how did you know that Chekhov's my favorite writer?"
"You said so."
"I don't remember that."
"I remember. I heard you mention it when you were chatting with someone."

So he was the one who had given her the *Selected Stories of Chekhov*. For her that was tantamount to a love letter. Maybe this man, who didn't believe in love, realized by the time his hair was white that in his heart was something which could be called love. By the time he no longer had the right to love, he made the tragic discovery of this love for which he would have given his life. Or did it go deeper even than that?

This is all I remember about him.

Banner showing Chairman Mao, the leader of China's Communist revolution.

HRW Photo by Russell Dian

---

8. **old cadre** (ka'drē'): here, former member of a cadre, or small unified group; in this case, a group of underground rebels.

9. **first-form**: first-grade.

10. **headmistress**: female school principal.

How wretched Mother must have been, deprived of the man to whom she was devoted! To catch a glimpse of his car or the back of his head through its rear window, she carefully figured out which roads he would take to work and back. Whenever he made a speech, she sat at the back of the hall watching his face rendered hazy by cigarette smoke and poor lighting. Her eyes would brim with tears, but she swallowed them back. If a fit of coughing made him break off, she wondered anxiously why no one persuaded him to give up smoking. She was afraid he would get bronchitis again. Why was he so near yet so far?

He, to catch a glimpse of her, looked out of the car window every day straining his eyes to watch the streams of cyclists, afraid that she might have an accident. On the rare evenings on which he had no meetings, he would walk by a roundabout way to our neighborhood, to pass our compound gate. However busy, he would always make time to look in papers and journals for her work. His duty had always been clear to him, even in the most difficult times. But now confronted by this love he became a weakling, quite helpless. At his age it was laughable. Why should life play this trick on him?

Yet when they happened to meet at work, each tried to avoid the other, hurrying off with a nod. Even so, this would make Mother blind and deaf to everything around her. If she met a colleague named Wang[11] she would call him Guo[12] and mutter something unintelligible.

It was a cruel ordeal for her. She wrote:

---

11. **Wang:** common Chinese family name.
12. **Guo** (gwō): The names ''Wang'' and ''Guo'' are written with similar characters; because she is preoccupied, she confuses the two.

We agreed to forget each other. But I deceived you, I have never forgotten. I don't think you've forgotten either. We're just deceiving each other, hiding our misery. I haven't deceived you deliberately, though; I did my best to carry out our agreement. I often stay far away from Beijing, hoping time and distance will help me to forget you. But when I return, as the train pulls into the station, my head reels. I stand on the platform looking round intently, as if someone were waiting for me. Of course there is no one. I realize then that I have forgotten nothing. Everything is unchanged. My love is like a tree the roots of which strike deeper year after year—I have no way to uproot it.

At the end of every day, I feel as if I've forgotten something important. I may wake with a start from my dreams wondering what has happened. But nothing has happened. Nothing. Then it comes home to me that you are missing! So everything seems lacking, incomplete, and there is nothing to fill up the blank. We are nearing the ends of our lives, why should we be carried away by emotion like children? Why should life submit people to such ordeals, then unfold before you your lifelong dream? Because I started off blindly, I took the wrong turning, and now there are insuperable obstacles between me and my dream.

Yes, Mother never let me go to the station to meet her when she came back from a trip, preferring to stand alone on the platform and imagine that he had met her. Poor mother with her graying hair was as infatuated as a girl.

Not much space in the diary was devoted to their romance. Most entries dealt with trivia: why one of her articles had not come off; her fear that she had no real talent; the excellent play she missed by mistaking the time on the ticket; the drenching she got by going out for a stroll without her umbrella. In spirit they were together day and night, like a devoted married couple. In fact, they spent no more than twenty-four hours together in all. Yet in that time they experienced deeper happiness than some people in a whole lifetime. Shakespeare makes Juliet say, "I cannot sum up half my sum of wealth."[13] And probably that is how Mother felt.

He must have been killed in the Cultural Revolution. Perhaps because of the conditions then, that section of the diary is ambiguous and obscure. Mother had been so fiercely attacked for her writing, it amazed me that she went on keeping a diary. From some veiled allusions I gathered that he had questioned the theories advanced by that "theoretician" then at the height of favor and had told someone, "This is sheer Rightist[14] talk." It was clear from the tear-stained pages of Mother's diary that he had been harshly denounced; but the steadfast old man never knuckled under to the authorities. His last words were, "When I go to meet Marx,[15] I shall go on fighting my case!"

That must have been in the winter of 1969, because that was when Mother's hair turned white overnight, though she was not yet fifty. And she put on a black armband.[16] Her position then was extremely difficult. She was criticized for wearing this old-style mourning and ordered to say for whom she was in mourning.

"For whom are you wearing that, Mother?" I asked anxiously.

"For my lover." Not to frighten me she explained, "Someone you never knew."

"Shall I put one on too?" She patted my cheeks, as she had when I was a child. It was years since she had shown me such affection. I often felt that as she aged, especially during these last years of persecution, all tenderness had left her, or was concealed in her heart, so that she seemed like a man.

She smiled sadly and said, "No, you needn't wear one." Her eyes were as dry as if she had no more tears to shed. I longed to comfort her or do something to please her. But she said, "Off you go."

I felt an inexplicable dread, as if dear Mother had already half left me. I blurted out, "Mother!"

Quick to sense my desolation, she said gently, "Don't be afraid. Off you go. Leave me alone for a little."

I was right. She wrote:

> You have gone. Half my soul seems to have taken flight with you.
> I had no means of knowing what had become of you, much less of seeing you for the last time. I had no right to ask either, not being your wife or friend. . . . So we are torn apart. If only I could have borne that inhuman treatment for you, so that you could have lived on! You should have lived to see your name cleared and take up your work again, for the sake of those who loved you. I knew you could not be a counterrevolutionary. You were one of the finest men killed. That's why I love you—I am not afraid now to avow it.
> Snow is whirling down. Heavens, even God is such a hypocrite, he is using

---

13. **Shakespeare . . . wealth:** In *Romeo and Juliet* by William Shakespeare, Juliet makes this remark in describing her love for Romeo.

14. **Rightist:** in politics, conservative or reactionary; Chinese politics during the Cultural Revolution was dominated by Rightist Party members.

15. **Marx:** Karl Marx (1818–1883), German-born economic philosopher and father of modern socialism; a revered figure by Chinese and other Communists.

16. **black armband:** traditional sign of mourning in China and elsewhere.

HRW Photo by Darwin Chen

this whiteness to cover up your blood and the scandal of your murder.

I have never set store by my life. But now I keep wondering whether anything I say or do would make you contract your shaggy eyebrows in a frown. I must live a worthwhile life like you, and do some honest work for our country. Things can't go on like this—those criminals will get what's coming to them.

I used to walk alone along that small asphalt road, the only place where we once walked together, hearing my foot-steps in the silent night. . . . I always paced to and fro and lingered there, but never as wretchedly as now. Then, though you were not beside me, I knew you were still in this world and felt that you were keeping me company. Now I can hardly believe that you have gone.

At the end of the road I would retrace my steps, then walk along it again. Rounding the fence I always looked back, as if you were still standing there waving goodbye. We smiled faintly, like casual acquaintances, to conceal our un-dying love. That ordinary evening in early spring a chilly wind was blowing as we walked silently away from each other. You were wheezing a little be-cause of your chronic bronchitis. That upset me. I wanted to beg you to slow down, but somehow I couldn't. We both walked very fast, as if some important business were waiting for us. How we prized that single stroll we had together, but we were afraid we might lose control of ourselves and burst out with "I love you"—those three words which had tor-mented us for years. Probably no one else could believe that we never once even clasped hands!

No, Mother, I believe it. I am the only one able to see into your locked heart.

Ah, that little asphalt road, so haunted by bitter memories. We shouldn't overlook the most insignificant spots on earth. For who knows how much secret grief and joy they may hide. No wonder that when tired of writing, she would pace slowly along that little road behind our window. Sometimes at dawn after a sleepless night, sometimes on a moonless, windy evening. Even in win-ter during howling gales which hurled sand and pebbles against the window pane. . . . I thought this was one of her eccentricities, not knowing that she had gone to meet him in spirit.

She liked to stand by the window, too, staring at the small asphalt road. Once I thought from her expression that one of our closest friends must be coming to call. I hur-ried to the window. It was a late autumn evening. The cold wind was stripping dead leaves from the trees and blowing them down the small empty road.

She went on pouring out her heart to him in her diary as she had when he was alive.

Zhang Jie **291**

Right up to the day when the pen slipped from her fingers. Her last message was:

I am a materialist, yet I wish there were a Heaven. For then, I know, I would find you there waiting for me. I am going there to join you, to be together for eternity. We need never be parted again or keep at a distance for fear of spoiling someone else's life. Wait for me, dearest, I am coming—

I do not know how, on her deathbed, Mother could still love so ardently with all her heart. To me it seemed not love but a form of madness, a passion stronger than death. If undying love really exists, she reached its extreme. She obviously died happy, because she had known true love. She had no regrets.

Now these old people's ashes have mingled with the elements. But I know that no matter what form they may take, they still love each other. Though not bound together by earthly laws or morality, though they never once clasped hands, each possessed the other completely. Nothing could part them. Centuries to come, if one white cloud trails another, two grasses grow side by side, one wave splashes another, a breeze follows another ... believe me, that will be them.

Each time I read that diary, "Love Must Not Be Forgotten," I cannot hold back my tears. I often weep bitterly, as if I myself experienced their ill-fated love. If not a tragedy it was too laughable. No matter how beautiful or moving I find it, I have no wish to follow suit!

Thomas Hardy[17] wrote that "the call seldom produces the comer, the man to love rarely coincides with the hour for loving." I cannot judge them by conventional moral standards. What I deplore is that they did not wait for a "missing counterpart" to call them. If everyone could wait, instead of rushing into marriage, how many tragedies could be averted!

When we reach communism,[18] will there still be cases of marriage without love? Perhaps...since the world is so vast, two kindred spirits may never be able to answer each other's call. But how tragic! Could it be that by then we will have devised ways to escape such tragedies? But this is all conjecture.

Maybe after all we are accountable for these tragedies. Who knows? Should we take the responsibility for the old ideas handed down from the past? Because, if you choose not to marry, your behavior is considered a direct challenge to these ideas. You will be called neurotic, accused of having guilty secrets or having made political mistakes. You may be regarded as an eccentric who looks down on ordinary people, not respecting age-old customs—a heretic. In short, they will trump up endless vulgar and futile charges to ruin your reputation. Then you have to succumb to those ideas and marry regardless. But once you put the chains of an indifferent marriage around your neck, you will suffer for it for the rest of your life.

I long to shout: "Mind your own business! Let us wait patiently for our counterparts. Even waiting in vain is better than loveless marriage. To live single is not such a fearful disaster. I believe it may be a sign of a step forward in culture, education, and the quality of life."

---

17. **Thomas Hardy:** British author (1840–1928) whose fiction often challenged conventional morality and ideas about romantic love; his characters are often destroyed by love.

18. **When we reach communism:** when we reach a Communist ideal or perfect Communist state, as the teachings of communism say will one day happen.

First Thoughts

Did you find yourself sympathetic to the narrator's thoughts in the last paragraph? Explain why you agree or disagree with her point of view about marriage.

Identifying Facts

1. How old is the narrator, and why does she say she is virtually "on the shelf"? Who is Qiao Lin?

2. What is "Love Must Not Be Forgotten"? What private information does it reveal?

3. When did the mother's beloved die? What happened afterward?

Interpreting Meanings

1. What do the opening details reveal about the kind of person Qiao Lin is? Do you think the narrator will marry him? Why or why not?

2. What do the **flashbacks** involving the mother's true love reveal about the kind of person he was and the reasons the mother loved him?

3. Some readers feel that this story is very disjointed: It begins with the narrator's feelings about marriage but then veers off into a lengthy **flashback** about the narrator's mother and her love affair. Do you feel that the story is flawed and does not hold together, or do you think that it is a unified piece with a central theme? Explain your response.

Applying Meanings

Do the social pressures that affect the narrator and her mother exist in America today? Discuss.

Creative Writing Response

Writing a Diary Entry. Do you, like the narrator, feel that "If everyone could wait, instead of rushing into marriage, how many tragedies could be averted!"? Write your personal views about marriage, independence, or one of the other related ideas that Zhang Jie deals with in her story, as though you were writing a diary entry.

Language and Vocabulary

Wade-Giles and Pinyin Transliterations

Unlike English and many other **phonetic** languages written in an alphabet where letters represent sounds, Chinese is written in **characters** that represent ideas or meanings. These characters have many pronunciations, depending on the word's context and regional differences. This **ideographic** system has certain advantages: Chinese people who speak very different dialects can still understand each other by using the written characters. But Chinese can be extremely inaccessible to foreigners. For this reason, China's Communist government devised a way to use the Roman alphabet as an alternate way of writing Chinese. The system they developed, called **Pinyin**, came into standard use in the West in 1979 when the Chinese government asked English-language publications to adopt it.

Before 1979, however, the West had been using the **Wade-Giles** system to transliterate—that is, transfer into a different alphabet—Chinese words. Thus, while the names of recent Chinese writers like Zhang Jie (Chang Chieh in the Wade-Giles system) are more familiar under their Pinyin spellings, the names of earlier writers are better known by their Wade-Giles spellings. Except for Zhang Jie, the names of all Chinese writers in this book use Wade-Giles spellings. Consult a recent encyclopedia or another recent reference work to learn the Pinyin spellings of the following writers' names:

1. Li Po
2. Tu Fu
3. Chuang Tzu
4. Lao-tzu

LANGUAGE —AND— CULTURE

CONSCIENCE AND CONTROVERSY

Most of us think of writing, especially fiction writing, as a fairly benign process. We picture writers as a studious, slightly absent-minded breed for whom a brush with the law means, at worst, a parking ticket. But the reality for some writers has been far more harrowing. At different periods in history, writers the world over have come into conflict with repressive governments. Since the invention of the printing press, when the written word became widely available, down to the present day, there have been governments that have tried to block the writer's pen.

Aleksandr Solzhenitsyn (b. 1918)

Russian author Aleksandr Solzhenitsyn (sōl'zhə·nēt'sin) (see page 130) moved from obscurity as a high-school teacher to international renown as a writer after the publication of his first novel, *One Day in the Life of Ivan Denisovich* (1962). The novel, based on his own experiences, delivered a scathing condemnation of Soviet prison camps. Solzhenitsyn eventually became a thorn in the side of the Soviet government, which sought to quiet all forms of criticism. In spite of the obvious danger of writing inflammatory fiction under a regime of strict censorship, Solzhenitsyn was committed to his craft and his country. When he won the Nobel Prize for literature in 1970, he did not travel to Stockholm to claim the award, fearing that the Soviet government would not allow him to re-enter his country. Solzhenitsyn was finally deported in 1974. He now lives and writes in the U.S.

In spite of the Soviet Union's official view of Solzhenitsyn as a political threat, the author's writings go beyond the sphere of politics, reaching for what he feels are the higher truths of humanity. In his novel *Cancer Ward,* he wrote, ". . . it is not the task of the writer . . . to defend or criticize one or another form of government organization. The task of the writer is to select more universal and eternal questions, the secrets of the human heart and conscience . . . the laws of the history of mankind that were born in the depths of time immemorial and that will cease to exist only when the sun ceases to shine."

Federico García Lorca (1878–1936)

Some writers do not write about politics or governments at all, yet still make enemies of political and military leaders. Nowhere is this point more clearly made than in the life and death of the

Spanish poet and playwright Federico García Lorca (gär·sē'ə lôr'kä) (see page 94). García Lorca is among the best-loved Spanish-language poets of all time. Scholar Edith Helman writes, "Fervent in the love of his people, rooted in the Spanish earth, he inevitably expressed in his poetry . . . all the fears and hatred, frustration and longing of the Spaniards of his time and all times. When he voiced his own passionate love of freedom and impulse to revolt, he gave expression to the feelings of great numbers of inarticulate Spaniards who felt that he was speaking for them." In 1936, García Lorca found himself at the center of one of the great moral struggles of the twentieth century, the Spanish Civil War, which pitted the democratically elected Republic against Fascist forces backed by Hitler and Mussolini. García Lorca was already famous for his work in the theater, which he brought directly to farm workers in small Spanish villages. Early in the war, the Fascists, risking international condemnation, murdered the poet who so eloquently expressed the spirit of the Spanish people. The Fascists, lead by Franco, went on to win the war.

Ngũgĩ wa Thiong'o (b. 1938)

Even writers in nominally democratic countries have suffered imprisonment because of their words. By the 1970s, Kenyan author Ngũgĩ ('n·gōō'gē), the head of the Department of Literature at the University of Nairobi (Kenya's capital), had gained international acclaim as an author. But in 1977, Ngũgĩ was arrested. The cause of his arrest was never stated. Government officials—who had already banned a play that Ngũgĩ coauthored, *Ngaahika Ndeenda (I Will Marry When I Like)*—simply felt that his writings painted the regime in an unflattering light. Although he was never charged with any crime, Ngũgĩ remained in prison for over a year. Finally, mounting pressure by groups such as Amnesty International led to his release. He recorded his experience in his 1981 novel, *Detained*. Ngũgĩ continued to criticize the increasingly repressive Kenyan government. In 1982, hearing that he was soon to be arrested again, the author exiled himself and his family to England, where he lives, writes, and lectures today.

All of these authors hold one thing in common: their writings give a voice to thousands of voiceless people. And nothing worries tyrants more than citizens who, through the words of authors, can articulate their desires.

Schomburg Center for Research in Black Culture/New York Public Library

Kenyan writer Ngũgĩ wa Thiong'o.

WRITING ABOUT LITERATURE

Writing Answers to Essay Questions

The following strategies will help you write answers to the essay questions following each selection in this book.

1. Begin by reading the essay question carefully. Make sure you understand exactly what the question is asking you to do and note how much evidence it asks you to provide.

2. Identify the key verb in the question. It will help you pinpoint your assignment. Look for these key verbs:

- **Analyze (Examine).** To *analyze* something is to take it apart and see how it works. You might be asked to analyze one element of a work and explain its effect on other elements or the work as a whole. For example, you might be asked to analyze Gregor's reaction to finding himself an insect in Franz Kafka's *The Metamorphosis* (see page 20). Begin by identifying his reaction and then show how it affects his relationship with his employer, his relationship with his family, and his sense of self.

- **Compare/Contrast.** When you *compare*, you point out similarities; when you *contrast*, you point out differences. You might, for example, be asked to compare and contrast two short stories. The best way to organize information for your essay is to use a chart like this one, which shows you similarities and differences at a glance:

Vary the chart to suit the particular assignment. If you are asked to compare and contrast two poems, for example, you might use imagery, figures of speech, and tone as your points of discussion. If you are asked to compare and contrast two characters within a play, you might use personality, goals, and change. Once you have decided what points to discuss in your essay, decide on the order in which you will present your ideas. You can discuss all the elements of the first work and then all the elements of the second work (AABB order). Or you can discuss each element in turn (ABAB order), showing how it is similar or different in the two works.

- **Describe.** To *describe* means to paint a picture in words. For example, if you were asked to describe the scene at the entrance to Hell in Dante Alighieri's *Inferno*, you would try to convey its sights, sounds, and mood so that your readers can experience the scene. If you were asked to describe Eveline in James Joyce's story of the same name (see page 73), you would discuss what you know about her through direct and indirect characterization—how she looks, acts, speaks, feels, and affects others.

- **Discuss.** To *discuss* means to comment about something in a general way. For example, if you were asked to discuss the point of one of Jean de La Fontaine's fables you might summarize the fable and comment on its moral.

- **Evaluate.** To *evaluate* something is to judge how good or bad—or how effective or ineffective—it is. In thinking about your evaluation, start with your personal reaction to the work. (Did you like it or hate it? Did you find it fascinating or boring?). Next, refine this reaction into a more specific judgment. ("Even though the play was written in the nineteenth century, it still speaks to us today," or "This poem was too rambling to hold my interest.") In the body of your essay, state the reasons for your judgment, each reason examining an element of the work and each backed up with evidence from the work.

	Story A	Story B
Character		
Setting		
Plot		

- **Illustrate.** To *illustrate* means to provide examples to support an idea or statement. For example, you might be asked to illustrate the principles of Japanese haiku poetry. You would first define haiku and then show how several haiku poems fit this definition.

- **Interpret.** To *interpret* something means to explain its meaning and importance. For example, if you were asked to interpret a Shakespearean sonnet, you might explain each quatrain in turn then show how the final couplet summarizes or comments on the ideas in the quatrains. If you were asked to interpret a story's meaning, you would first identify the theme and then cite specific details from the work to support your interpretation.

- **Respond.** To *respond* is to give your personal reaction to something. If you were asked to respond to Barbara Kimenye's "The Pig," for example, you would state explicitly whether you liked or disliked it, how it made you feel, and what it made you think about. Be as specific as possible as you explain the reasons for your response.

3. Write a thesis statement in which you state the main idea of your essay. Include your thesis statement in the first paragraph, along with any additional sentences that help you catch the reader's attention.

4. Gather evidence to support this thesis statement. If you can use your book, look back over the work for examples and illustrations. For a closed-book essay, make notes on all the supporting details you can remember.

5. Write one paragraph for each main point. Include a topic sentence for each paragraph, and express your ideas as clearly as you can. Don't pad your answer with unrelated details or ideas.

6. End with a concluding paragraph. Summarize or restate your main points, and if you wish, give your personal response to the work. Try to end your essay with a "clincher sentence."

Writing and Revising an Essay ▪

You may be asked to choose your own topic for an essay on a specific work.

Prewriting

1. Choose a limited topic that you can cover adequately. If your assignment is an essay of four paragraphs, you can't possibly analyze all the characters in Ibsen's *A Doll's House*. But you do have room to analyze one character or the significance of the title. For ideas on the kinds of topics you might choose, review the list of key verbs on pages 296–297.

2. Write a thesis statement. Ask yourself, "What main idea about my topic do I want to discuss?" Then write one or two sentences that state this main idea. If you have trouble expressing your ideas in only one or two sentences, consider narrowing the topic.

3. List two or three main ideas that develop your thesis statement. Jot down the ideas that come to mind when you think about your thesis statement, and choose the strongest two or three. Then go back over the work to find specific points you may have overlooked. Don't rely simply on your memory.

4. Gather and arrange supporting evidence. Your essay should include quotations, specific details, and incidents from the literary work you are writing about—known as the **primary source**. You might also wish to refer to other works, letters, or interviews by the same writer. Finally, information from **secondary sources**—books, reviews, and critical essays about the work or the writer—may also provide supporting evidence for your ideas.

Before you begin writing, decide which evidence best supports your thesis statement. Then discard any weak or unrelated material. Once you've arranged your main ideas and evidence in the order that seems the most logical, you'll have an informal outline to work from.

Writing

Draft your essay following your outline and notes. Include evidence to support your thesis statement and the main idea of each paragraph. Structure your essay according to this plan:

I. INTRODUCTORY PARAGRAPH
  Catch the reader's interest.
  Tell what the essay will be about.
  Begin or end with the thesis statement.
II. BODY (Paragraphs 2, 3, etc.)
  Develop the thesis statement.
  Include a topic sentence and supporting evidence in each paragraph.
III. CONCLUDING PARAGRAPH
  Let the reader know that the essay is completed.
  Restate or summarize the thesis statement and main ideas.
  Include a personal response (optional).

Evaluating and Revising

Reread your first draft at least twice, checking once for content and once for style.

1. Content. Check to see that you've supported your thesis statement with at least two main ideas and that you've supported each main idea with sufficient evidence. If any part of your evidence appears weak or vague, go back over the work to find more convincing examples.

2. Style. To make your essay read smoothly, you may need to combine related sentences or break up long sentences into shorter ones. Cut unnecessary or repetitive words and phrases.

Proofreading and Publishing

The titles of poems, short stories, and essays should be enclosed in quotation marks; the titles of plays, novels, and other long works (such as epic poems) should be in italics. Sacred works like the Bible and the Koran and the individual books of these works are neither italicized nor placed in quotation marks. In handwriting and typing, italics are indicated by underlining.

Proofreader's Symbols

Symbol	Example	Meaning of Symbol
☰	''An honest thief''	Capitalize a lower-case letter.
/	''Wind And Water And Stone''	Change a capital letter to lower case.
∧	''Love Must Be Forgotten''	Insert a word.
∧	Lépold Sédar Senghor	Insert or change a letter.
⊙	2000 B.C	Insert a period.
⌃	''For Wei Pa In Retirement''	Insert a comma.
⌄	Petrarchs sonnets	Insert an apostrophe.
⌄ ⌄	Half a Day	Insert quotation marks.
underscore	from Kaffir Boy	Set in italics.
∼	Chrétein de Troyes	Change the order of letters.
∼	''Laments on the Dead War''	Change the order of words.
#	Guy deMaupassant	Insert space.
⌒	the nineteenth century	Close up space.
⌿	Isak Dinesen	Delete.
....	Isak Dinesen	Let it stand (stet).
⌢	Fyodor Dosstoevsky	Delete and close up space.
SP	''The 4 Ages''	Spell it out.
¶	In this story, Tolstoy	Indent to begin a new paragraph.

A Model Essay

The following essay is an interpretation of "The Two Brothers," by Leo Tolstoy. The essay shows the writer's revisions for a second draft.

TWO BROTHERS, TWO WAYS TO LIVE

To be content with what one has or to take a risk—what's [is] the best way to live? [Leo] Tolstoy deals with this question in his short parable ["]The 2 Brothers[."] [Although, ac] He seems to except both ways [approaches to life]. ~~He also seems to~~ favor the risk-taker. In the story, 2 brothers come across a stone with writing on it. The stone [message] declares that any one who goes into the forrest, crosses the river, siezes some bear cubs away from their mother and runs up the moun-tin [a] without looking back will find happiness in a house there. In other words, ~~there will be~~ a great reward [awaits] for one who takes a great risk.

The older brother, the cautous [cautious] one, raises many reasonable objections. The message might be a lie or a joke, or the brothers may have misunderstood it [he says]. They might get lost in the forrest or the river might be too wide to swim. The mother bear might kill the brothers! They might not be able to run up the mountain. And [Finally] even if all goes well, the older brother warns, [that] and they reach the house, "the happiness awaiting us there is not at all the sort of happiness we would want." Here are all the reasons why [in brief form] people do not take risks: they can't be [aren't] sure, there might be [what to do] danger, the result might not be worth the effort.

INTRODUCTORY PARAGRAPH
Catches the reader's interest. Presents thesis statement—the story's theme.

BODY
Begins to summarize the story.

States topic sentence.

Gives details to support topic sentence.

Quotes from story.

Interprets older brother's reaction.

adventurous   is willing to take the risks

The younger brother gives his reasons for going on. There

^he believes   feel

must be a reason for the message. He does not believe the

danger will be great, and if they don't try it, some one else will.

also   c

He points out that you can't suceed unless you try. Finally, he

says   is

said, he wouldn't want others to think he was afraid. He is a

casual

classic risk-taker. He is confident of the outcome, unconcerned

about the danger, and proud of his reputation.

the brothers   adages

Now they trade old sayings—and act on them. "A bird in the

says

hand is worth two in the bush" said the older brother, and set-

says

tles in. "Beneath a stone no water flows" said the younger

ing

brother. He sets out. He follows the instructions on the stone.

whose

At the top of the mountain he finds a city. The residents make

him their king. After ruling for 5 years, a stronger king defeats

him and he is banished and returns to his older brother.

brothers   their lives

So who made the best decision? Well, both are happy with

what has happened to them. The older brother says that he has

lived "Quietly and well" but the younger brother, while admit-

ting he has nothing now, beleives he has had wonderful experi-

^however^

ences. Tolstoy lets both brothers speak, but there is a hint that

he favors the younger brother. The younger brother is the one

eagerly   of the stone   also

who speaks first, accepting the challenge. And he is the one

who speaks last. "I shall always have something to remember,

while you have no memories at all," he says, and I can't help

States topic sentence.

Gives details to support topic sentence.

Interprets younger brother's reaction.

States topic sentence.

Supports topic sentence with quotations and details.

CONCLUDING PARAGRAPH

States topic sentence in question form.
Explains topic sentence.

Restates thesis statement.

Explains interpretation.

Quotes key passage in story.

Offers personal comment on interpretation.

agreeing with him. A quiet life can be rewarding, but the possi-

satisfying

bility of a big reward—and the chance for memories—tempts

vivid

me to aim as high as the younger brother.

Ends with clincher sentence.

Documenting Sources for a Research Paper

1. Parenthetical citations give brief information in parentheses immediately after a quotation or other reference. More detailed information about each source is given in the bibliography. This method of documenting sources is recommended by the Modern Language Association (MLA).

For a quotation from a prose passage by a writer who is identified in the text (page number):

Joyce ends the chapter with a beautiful image, "the tide . . . flowing in fast to the land with a low whisper of her waves, islanding a few last figures in distant pools" (173).

For a quotation by a writer whose name is not mentioned in the text (author's last name, page number):

In *Dubliners*, Joyce's collection of short stories, "[T]he recurrent situation is entrapment" (Levin, 5).

For a quotation from a play (act and scene, and line number if a poetic drama):

At this point Miranda rejoices, "O brave new world/That has such people in't!" (Act 5, Scene 1, lines 213–14).

For a quotation from a poem (line number):

In Paul Verlaine's "The Sky Is Just Beyond the Roof," the speaker asks, "Say, what have you done, you who are here, / With your lost youth?" (lines 15–16).

2. Footnotes are placed at the bottom of the page on which the reference appears. A raised number at the end of the reference within the essay indicates a footnote.[1] Footnotes are generally numbered consecutively within a work.

[1] Harry Levin, ed. *The Portable James Joyce* (New York: The Viking Press, 1965) p. 5.

[2] Frank O'Connor, *A Short History of Irish Literature* (New York: G.P. Putnam's Sons, 1967) p. 57.

Check a writing handbook, or ask your teacher for the style for footnoting poems, magazine articles, interviews, and books with more than one author.

3. End notes are identical to footnotes except that they are listed on a separate page entitled "Notes" at the end of a paper. End notes are numbered consecutively.

4. A Works Cited section should be included at the end of your essay. This is an alphabetical list of all of the print and nonprint sources you referenced in your essay. The list may include not only books but also magazine articles and videotapes. Entries in your **Works Cited** section are listed alphabetically by the author's last name. Here is a sample **Works Cited** section.

Works Cited

Alazraki, Jaime, ed. *Critical Essays on Jorge Luis Borges.* Boston: G. K. Hall & Company, 1987.

Paz, Octavio. "In Time's Labyrinth." *The New Republic* 3 November 1986: 30–35.

A HANDBOOK OF LITERARY TERMS

ALLEGORY   A story in which the characters, settings, and events stand for abstract or moral concepts. An allegory can be read on one level for its literal meaning and on another level for its symbolic, or allegorical, meaning. Leo Tolstoy's "How Much Land Does a Man Need?" is an example of an allegory. *See page* 59.

ALLITERATION   The repetition of consonant sounds in words that are close to one another. Alliteration occurs most often at the beginning of words, as in "broken bottle," but consonants within words may also alliterate, as in "always wide awake." The repetition of final consonant sounds in closely grouped words—as in *boasts and jests*—is called **consonance**. Poets may use alliteration and consonance to achieve special rhythmic and musical effects, to emphasize particular images and moods, or to give their poems greater unity. *See also* **Assonance**.

ALLUSION   A reference to a statement, person, place, event, or thing that is known from literature, history, religion, myth, politics, or some other field of knowledge. For example, the title of Anna Akhmatova's poem "Lot's Wife" (page 89) is an allusion to the Hebrew Bible story of the destruction of Sodom and Gomorrah. Allusions add depth of meaning to a work of literature by inviting comparisons. *See page* 174.

ANTAGONIST   *See* **Protagonist**.

ARGUMENT   *See* **Persuasion**.

ASSONANCE   The repetition of similar vowel sounds followed by different consonant sounds in words that are close together. For example, the long *a* sounds in "It's a great day for baseball" create assonance. Certain languages, such as Japanese, lend themselves to assonance. Like **alliteration**, assonance may be used in poetry to create special rhythmic and musical effects, to emphasize particular images or moods, or to achieve unity. *See page* 95. *See also* **Alliteration**.

ATMOSPHERE   The mood or feeling in a literary work. Atmosphere is usually created through descriptive details and evocative imagery. For example, a story set in a grimy factory town may create a gloomy atmosphere in which characters struggle against despair. *See page* 125. *See also* **Mood**.

AUTOBIOGRAPHY   An account of a person's own life. *Kaffir Boy* by Mark Mathabane is an autobiography about growing up under apartheid in South Africa. *See pages* 99, 230.

BIOGRAPHY   An account of a person's life written or told by another person. For example, Tacitus' historical account of imperial Rome, the *Annals* includes a biography of the emperor Nero.

CHARACTER   An individual in a story, play, or narrative poem. A character always has human traits, even if the character is an animal, such as the trickster Coyote in Native American tales, or a god or monster, such as Aphrodite and the giant Sinis in the Greek myth of Theseus. Most characters, however, are ordinary human beings, like Nora in Ibsen's *A Doll's House*.

   Characters can be classified as static or dynamic. A **static character** is one who does not change much in the course of a story. A **dynamic character**, on the other hand, changes in some important way as a result of the story's action. Characters can also be classified as flat or round. **Flat characters** have only one or two personality traits. They are one-dimensional—their personalities can be summed up by a single phrase. In contrast, **round characters** have more dimensions to their personalities—they are complex, solid, and multifaceted, like real people. *See page* 81. *See also* **Characterization**.

CHARACTERIZATION   The process by which the writer reveals the personality of a character. A writer can reveal a character in the following ways:

1. By telling us directly what the character is like: humble, ambitious, impetuous, easily manipulated, and so on
2. By describing how the character looks and dresses
3. By letting us hear the character speak
4. By revealing the character's private thoughts and feelings

5. By revealing the character's effect on other people—showing how other characters feel or behave toward the character
6. By showing the character's actions

The first method of revealing character is called **direct characterization**. When a writer uses this method, we do not have to figure out what a character's personality is like—the writer tells us directly. The other five methods of revealing a character are known as **indirect characterization**. When a writer uses these methods, we have to exercise our own judgment, putting clues together to figure out what a character is like—just as we do in real life when we are getting to know someone. *See also* **Character**.

CLIMAX   The point of greatest emotional intensity or suspense in a plot. The climax usually marks the moment toward the end of the plot when the conflict is decided one way or the other. Following the climax, the story is usually **resolved**. Long works, such as novels, may have more than one climactic moment, though usually the greatest climax occurs last. *See also* **Plot**.

CONFLICT   A struggle or clash between opposing characters, forces, or emotions. In an **external conflict**, a character struggles against some outside force: another character, society as a whole, or some natural force. An **internal conflict**, on the other hand, is a struggle between opposing needs, desires, or emotions within a single character. Many works, especially longer ones, contain both internal and external conflicts that are often interrelated. *See page* 269.

CONNOTATIONS   All the meanings, associations, or emotions that a word suggests. For example, an expensive restaurant might prefer to advertise its excellent ''cuisine'' rather than its excellent ''cooking.'' Both words have the same literal meaning, or **denotation**: ''prepared food.'' *Cuisine,* however, has connotations of elegance and sophistication, while *cooking* does not. The same restaurant would certainly not describe its food as ''great grub.''

Notice the difference between the following pairs of words: young/immature, ambitious/cutthroat, uninhibited/shameless, lenient/lax. In each pair, the second word carries unfavorable connotations that the first word does not.

DENOTATION   The literal, dictionary definition of a word. *See* **Connotations**.

DESCRIPTION   Writing that is intended to re-create a person, place, thing, event, or experience. Description uses **imagery**—language that appeals to the senses to show how something looks, sounds, smells, tastes, or feels to the touch.

DICTION   A writer's or speaker's choice of words. People use different types of words depending on the audience they're addressing, the subject they're discussing, and the effect they're trying to produce. For example, slang words that would be suitable in a casual conversation among friends (''Yo, Dude'') would be unsuitable at a presidential news conference. Similarly, the language a scientist would use in a scholarly article to describe a snowflake would be different from the language used by a poet.

Diction is an essential element of a writer's **style**. It may be, for instance, simple or ornate (big rooms/commodious chambers), general or specific (fish/fantailed goldfish), modern or old-fashioned (men's store/haberdashery). An important aspect of any writer's diction is the **connotation** that the words carry. *See page* 97.

DRAMA   A story that is written to be acted out in front of an audience. Drama is one of the major **genres**, or forms, of literature. The earliest dramas—from the Greek comedies and tragedies to the medieval European mystery, miracle, and morality plays—originally had a **sacred** or **ritual** function and were used in religious ceremonies or services. In medieval Japan, a very formal and stylized mode of drama known as **Noh** also developed from religious sources.

In Europe during the Renaissance and Enlightenment, playwrights such as William Shakespeare, Molière, and William Congreve created dramas in several forms—satires, historical plays, comedies, tragedies, and tragicomedies (which combined elements of both comedy and tragedy). In the late nineteenth century, the Norwegian playwright Henrik Ibsen helped influence the direction of much modern drama by creating such **Realist** plays as *A Doll's House*.

ELEGY   A poem that mourns the death of a person or laments something lost. Elegies may lament the passing of life and beauty, or they may be meditations on the nature of death. A type of

lyric poetry, an elegy is usually formal in language and structure, and solemn or even melancholy in **tone**. Modern examples include Margaret Atwood's "Elegy for the Giant Tortoises" and Aleksandr Solzhenitsyn's prose poem "A Journey Along the Oka". *See page* 183.

EPIPHANY **In a literary work, a moment of sudden insight or revelation that a character experiences.** The word *epiphany* comes from the Greek and can be translated as "manifestation" or "showing forth." The term has religious meanings that have been transferred to literature. James Joyce gave the word its literary meaning in an early draft of his novel *A Portrait of the Artist as a Young Man*. In his story "Eveline" for example, the title character's epiphany comes when she realizes she is unable to board the ship with the sailor. *See page* 74.

ESSAY **A short piece of nonfiction prose that examines a single subject from a limited point of view.** There are two major types of essays. **Formal essays** are usually serious and impersonal in tone. Because they are written to inform or persuade, they are expected to be factual, logical, and tightly organized. **Informal essays** (also called **personal essays**) generally reveal much about the personalities and feelings of their authors. They tend to be conversational in tone, and many, such as Santha Rama Rau's "By Any Other Name" are autobiographical in nature. *See page* 252.

EXISTENTIALISM **A modern European movement in philosophy, religion, and art that asserts "existence precedes essence," that is, that the universe and everything in it exists but has no meaning, and that people supply meaning through their actions.** Some existentialists such as Albert Camus emphasize that each person is free to make moral choices that define and give meaning to his or her life. Through their choices and actions, human beings are responsible for what they make of themselves and their lives. *See pages* 11, 111, 123.

FALLING ACTION *See* **Dramatic Structure.**

FANTASY **A work that takes place in an unreal world and features incredible characters.** Much **science fiction** is fantasy. *See pages* 12, 38.

FICTION *See* **Nonfiction.**

FIGURE OF SPEECH **A word or phrase that** describes one thing in terms of another and is not meant to be understood on a literal level. Figures of speech (sometimes called **figurative language**) always involve some sort of imaginative comparison between seemingly unlike things. The most common figures of speech are the **simile** (a heart like a comforting fire), the **metaphor** (the dark cloak of night), and **personification** (angry winds shouting through the canyon). *See pages* 15, 161. *See also* **Hyperbole, Metaphor, Onomatopoeia, Personification, Simile, Symbol, Understatement**.

FLASHBACK **A scene in a narrative work that interrupts the present action of the plot to "flash backward" and tell what happened at an earlier time.** The flashback is one of the **conventions** of Homer's *Iliad* and *Odyssey* that became a standard feature of many later epics.

FORESHADOWING **Clues that hint at what is going to happen later in the plot.** Foreshadowing arouses the reader's curiosity and builds up **suspense**. In "Life Is Sweet at Kumansenu" for example, Abioseh Nicol includes details in his initial description of Meji to foreshadow the story's surprise ending. *See page* 201.

FRAME STORY **A story that serves to bind together several different narratives.** Both *The Thousand and One Nights* and Boccaccio's *Decameron* use frame stories as a device for unifying various shorter stories.

FREE VERSE **Poetry that has no regular meter or rhyme scheme.** Free verse usually relies instead on the natural rhythms of ordinary speech. Poets writing in free verse may use **alliteration**, **internal rhyme**, **onomatopoeia**, **repetition**, or other devices to achieve their effects. They may also place great emphasis on **imagery**. *See pages* 10, 95.

GENRE **The category to which a literary work belongs.** Examples of genres include **drama**, the **epic**, the **novel**, the **short story**, and **lyric poetry**.

IAMBIC PENTAMETER **A line of poetry made up of five iambs.** An **iamb** is a metrical **foot**, or unit of measure, consisting of an unstressed syllable followed by a stressed syllable ($\smile$ $'$). The word *preferred,* for example, is made up of one iamb. Pentameter is derived from the Greek words *penta* ("five") and *meter* ("measure"). **Sonnets**

and **blank verse** use iambic pentameter. It is by far the most common verse line in English poetry because of its similarity to the natural rhythms of the English language. Here are two lines of iambic pentameter from Shakespeare's *The Tempest*:

> His mother was a witch, and one so strong
> That could control the moon, make flows and
> ebbs

See also **Meter.**

IMAGERY   Language that appeals to the senses. Most images are visual—that is, they appeal to the sense of sight. But imagery can also appeal to the reader's senses of hearing, touch, taste, or smell. While imagery is an element in all types of writing that involve **description**, it is especially important in poetry. Writers and poets often use **figures of speech** to create vivid images. *See page 197.*

IRONY   A contrast or discrepancy between expectations and reality—between what is said and what is really meant, between what is expected and what really happens, or between what appears to be true and what is really true. Irony in literature falls into three major categories:

1. Verbal irony occurs when a writer or speaker says one thing but really means the opposite. If you tell a friend who shows up an hour late for an appointment that "you just love being kept waiting in the rain," you are using verbal irony.

2. Situational irony occurs when what actually happens is the opposite of what is expected or appropriate. An example of situational irony takes place in Greek mythology when Zeus falls in love with a mortal woman named Semele. Zeus promises to give Semele anything she wants. To his dismay, she begs to see him in his true form as the Lord of Heaven. Zeus reluctantly agrees, and the brilliant splendor of the god burns her to death.

3. Dramatic irony occurs when the audience or the reader knows something important that a character in a play or story does not know. Dramatic irony can heighten a comic effect or generate **suspense**. In *Oedipus Rex* for example, when the Corinthian messenger tells Oedipus that the King of Corinth has died of natural causes, Oedipus believes he has been released from the prophecy that says he will murder his father. The audience, however, knows that the truth has yet to come to light. *See pages* 148, 210.

LYRIC POETRY   Songlike poetry that focuses on expressing private emotions or thoughts. Most lyric poems are short, and they usually imply rather than directly state a single strong emotion. The term *lyric* comes from the ancient Greece, where lyric poems, such as those by Sappho (Unit Four), were recited to the accompaniment of a stringed instrument called a lyre. Today lyric poets still try to make their poems melodious, but they rely only on the musical effects they can create with words (such as **rhyme**, **rhythm**, **alliteration**, and **onomatopoeia**). *See pages* 156, 276.

MAGICAL REALISM   A twentieth-century literary style that combines incredible events with realistic details and relates them all in a matter-of-fact tone. Magical realism originated in Latin America, where authors such as Gabriel García Márquez (Unit Eleven) drew on elements of **surrealism** and local **folklore** to create a style that was both timeless and innovative. *See pages* 12, 174.

METAPHOR   A figure of speech that makes a comparison between two seemingly unlike things without using the connective words *like, as, than,* or *resembles*. A **direct metaphor** states that one thing is another, such as "the stars are icy diamonds." ("Stars like icy diamonds" is a **simile**.) Often metaphors are **implied**: "Against her black formal gown, she wore a constellation of diamonds" implies a comparison between diamonds and stars and between the black gown and a night sky.

- An **extended metaphor** is a metaphor that is developed over several lines of writing or even through an entire poem or paragraph. Marie de France uses an extended metaphor that compares the love of Tristan and Iseult to a honeysuckle in "Chevrefoil" (Unit Eight).
- A type of **cliché**, a **dead metaphor** is a metaphor that has become so common that we no longer even notice that it is a figure of speech. Our everyday language is filled with dead metaphors, such as "the pinnacle of success," "a tower of strength," and "the root of the problem."
- A **mixed metaphor** is the inconsistent mixture of two or more metaphors. Mixed metaphors are usually unintentional and often conjure up ludi-

crous images: ''Those snakes in the grass pulled the rug out from under us.'' *See page* 161.

METER A generally regular pattern of stressed and unstressed syllables in poetry. Meter is measured in units called feet. A **foot** consists of one stressed syllable and usually one or more unstressed syllables. The standard feet used in English poetry are the **iamb** (as in convínce), the **trochee** (as in bórrŏw), the **anapest** (as in cŏntrădíct), the **dactyl** (as in áccŭrăte), and the **spondee** (as in séaweéd). In meters such as **iambic pentameter**—which consists of five iambs per line—other feet may be substituted occasionally. Such variations prevent the meter from sounding sing-song and monotonous.

When we want to indicate the metrical pattern of a poem, we mark the stressed syllables with the symbol ′ and the unstressed syllables with the symbol ˘. Indicating the metrical pattern of a poem in this way is called **scanning** the poem, or **scansion**. Here, for example, is a passage from *The Tempest* with the scansion marked. Note how Shakespeare varies the basic iambic pentameter by substituting an anapest for one of the feet in the second line and by adding an extra unstressed syllable at the end of the third line.

This blue-eyed hag was hither brought with child
And here was left by the sailors. Thou, my slave,
As thou reportst thyself, wast then her servant
See page 95. *See also* **Blank Verse, Iambic Pentameter**.

MODERNISM A broad trend in literature and the other arts, from approximately 1890 to 1940, that reflected many artists' concern over society's loss of traditional values. In general, modernist writers sought new forms to reflect the fragmentation and uncertainty that they felt characterized modern life. Many modernist poets, for example, rejected traditional meter in favor of **free verse**. Novelists such as James Joyce employed a new technique called **stream of consciousness** to record the jagged monologue of their characters' thoughts. *See pages* 9, 168.

MOTIF In literature, a word, character, object, image, metaphor, or idea that recurs in a work or in several works. The rose is a motif that has reccurred throughout centuries of love poetry.

In the *Prose Edda* contest is a recurring motif. A literary motif always bears an important relationship to the theme of the work. *See page* 59. *See also* **Symbol**.

MOTIVATION The reasons that compel a character to act as he or she does. A character's motivations fuel the plot of a story and set it into motion.

MYTH An anonymous, traditional story that explains a belief, a custom, or a mysterious natural phenomenon. Most myths are related to religion in some way, and almost all of them involve the exploits of gods and heroes. Every culture has its own mythology, including **origin myths**, which explain how things came to be.

NARRATIVE Any work of literature, written or oral, that tells a story. Narrative literature may be fictional (such as fairy tales and short stories) or nonfictional (such as autobiographies and histories); it may be prose, such as *The Metamorphosis* or poetry, such as the *Iliad*. Narrative is distinguished from drama, which acts out, rather than tells, a story.

NARRATOR The person or character who tells a story. *See* **Point of View**.

NATURALISM A radical offshoot of Realism that arose in France in the 1870s. Naturalist writers, led by Émile Zola, considered free will an illusion and often showed their characters as helpless victims of heredity, fate, and their environment.

NONFICTION Prose writing that narrates real events. Nonfiction is distinguished from **fiction**—writing that is basically imaginative rather than factually true. Popular forms of nonfiction are **autobiography**, **biography**, and the **essay**. Other forms of nonfiction include newspaper articles, historical and scientific writing, and even personal diaries and letters.

NOVEL A long fictional prose narrative, usually of more than fifty thousand words. In general, the novel uses the same basic literary elements as the short story: **plot**, **character**, **setting**, **theme**, and **point of view**. The novel's length usually permits these elements to be more fully developed than they are in the short story. However, this is not always true of the modern novel. Some are basically character studies, with only the barest plot structures. Others reveal little about their characters and concentrate instead on setting or **tone** or even on language itself.

Although some early prose narratives resemble the novel in form, the novel as a distinct literary genre is widely considered to have emerged in Japan around A.D. 1000 with Lady Murasaki Shikibu's *Tale of Genji* and in Europe with the publication of Miguel de Cervantes' *Don Quixote* in 1605.

ONOMATOPOEIA The use of a word whose sound imitates or suggests its meaning. Many familiar words, such as *clap, squish, snort,* and *whine,* are examples of onomatopoeia. In poetry, onomatopoeia can reinforce meaning while creating evocative and musical effects. *See page 95.*

PARADOX An apparent contradiction that is actually true. For example, to say that "she killed him with kindness" is a paradox. The statement challenges us to find an underlying truth that resolves the apparent contradiction. *See page 279 See also* **Oxymoron**.

PARALLELISM The repetition of words, phrases, or sentences that have the same grammatical structure or that restate a similar idea. Also called **parallel structure**, parallelism is used frequently in literature that is meant to be read aloud, such as poetry and speeches, because it helps make the literature memorable. In much biblical writing, such as the Book of Psalms (Unit Three), the rhythm of parallelism helps to unify ideas, emphasize images, and heighten the emotional effect of the words. **Structural parallelism** (repetition of a word or an entire sentence pattern), **restatement** (repetition of an idea using different words), and **antithesis** (the balancing of contrasting ideas) are some of the ways writers achieve the effect of parallelism.

PERSONIFICATION A kind of metaphor in which a nonhuman thing or quality is talked about as if it were human. For example, the familiar figure of a blindfolded woman holding a sword and a pair of scales is a personification of justice. The names of many everyday objects, such as the "hands of a clock," and many ordinary expressions, such "an angry sky," involve personification. In poetry, personification invites the reader to view the world as if natural and inanimate objects possess the same feelings, qualities, and

souls that people do. Li Ch'ing-chao's "Peonies" provides a fine example of personification. *See page* 170.

PERSUASION Writing that tries to convince the reader or listener to think or act in a certain way. Examples of persuasion include political speeches, editorials, and advertisements, as well as many **essays** and longer works of literature. Persuasion may appeal to both the emotions and the intellect. When it appeals primarily to reason rather than to emotion, it is called **argument**.

PLOT The series of related events that make up a narrative, such as a story, novel, or epic. The plot is the underlying structure of a narrative. Most plots are built on these "bare bones": A **basic situation**, or **exposition**, introduces the characters, setting, and, usually, the narrative's major **conflict**. Out of this basic situation, **complications** develop, intensifying the conflict. **Suspense** mounts to a **climax**—the most exciting or tense part of the plot. At the climax, the outcome of the conflict is determined. Finally, all the problems or mysteries of the plot are unraveled in the **resolution**, or **dénouement**. Longer narrative works, such as novels, plays, or epics, often contain **subplots**, or minor plots interwoven with the main plot.

POETRY A kind of rhythmic, compressed language that uses figures of speech and imagery designed to appeal to our emotions and imaginations. Most of the world's poetry falls into three major types: **lyric poetry**, the **ballad**, and the **epic**. Some specialized types of poetry, however, such as the **haiku** of Japan, defy these broad categorizations. Though poetry is one of the oldest forms of human expression, it is extremely difficult to define. The English Romantic poet William Wordsworth called it "the spontaneous overflow of powerful feelings," and the Japanese scholar Kamo Mabuchi claimed that it provides "without explanation the reasons governing order and disorder in the world." *See page* 156.

POINT OF VIEW The vantage point from which a writer tells a story. There are three main points of view: **omniscient**, **first-person**, and **limited third-person**.

1. In the **omniscient** (or "all-knowing") **point of view**, the person telling the story—the **narrator**—knows everything that's going on in the story.

This omniscient narrator is outside the story, a godlike observer who can tell us what all the characters are thinking and feeling, as well as what is happening anywhere in the story. For example, in ''The Rat Trap'' by Selma Lagerlöf, the narrator enters into the thoughts and secrets of every character.

2. In the **first-person point of view**, the narrator is a character in the story. Using the pronoun *I*, this narrator tells us his or her own experiences but cannot reveal with certainty any other character's private thoughts. When we read a story in the first person, we hear and see only what the narrator hears and sees. We may have to be skeptical and interpret what this narrator says because a first-person narrator may or may not be objective, honest, or perceptive. The short story ''Borges and Myself'' uses a first-person narrator.

3. In the **limited third-person point of view**, the narrator is outside the story—like an omniscient narrator—but tells the story from the vantage point of only one character. The narrator goes where this chosen character goes and reveals this character's thoughts. The reader learns the events of the narrative through the perceptions of the chosen character. Hwang Sun-won's ''Cranes'' is an example of a story told from the limited third-person point of view. *See page* 63.

PROSE POETRY Poetry written in prose form, but using poetic devices such as rhythm, imagery, and figurative language to express a single strong emotion or idea. This form of lyric poetry developed in the nineteenth century in France and was popularized by Charles Baudelaire and Arthur Rimbaud. *See page* 131.

PROTAGONIST The main character in a work of fiction, drama, or narrative poetry. The protagonist is the character whose conflict sets the plot in motion. (The character or force that struggles against or blocks the protagonist is called the **antagonist**.) Most protagonists are **rounded, dynamic characters** who change in some important way by the end of the story. Whatever the protagonist's weaknesses, we usually identify with his or her conflict and care about how it is resolved. *See also* **Character**.

REALISM In literature and art, the attempt to depict people and things as they are, with-out idealization. Although realistic description has long been a tool of writers the world over, Realism as a movement developed during the mid-nineteenth century as a reaction against Romanticism. Realist writers believed fiction and drama should truthfully depict the harsh, gritty reality of everyday life without beautifying, sentimentalizing, or romanticizing it. Gustave Flaubert, Henrik Ibsen, and Anton Chekhov are considered Realist writers. *See also* **Naturalism**.

RESOLUTION *See* **Plot**.

RHYME The repetition of accented vowel sounds and all sounds following them in words that are close together in a poem. ''Lark'' and ''shark'' rhyme, as do ''follow'' and ''hollow.'' The most common type of rhyme, **end rhymes**, occurs at the ends of lines. **Internal rhymes** occur within lines.

When words sound similar but do not rhyme exactly, they are called **approximate rhymes** (or **half rhymes**, **slant rhymes**, or **imperfect rhymes**). ''Lark'' and ''lurk'' are approximate rhymes, as are ''follow'' and ''halo.''

The pattern of end rhymes in a poem is called its **rhyme scheme**. A rhyme scheme is indicated by assigning each new end rhyme a different letter of the alphabet. Many traditional forms of poems, such as the **Italian sonnet** and the Persian **rubá'i**, follow strict rhyme schemes. For example, most English translations of the rubá'i follow the rhyme scheme *aaba,* as the following example from Edward FitzGerald's translation of Omar Khayyám's *Rubáiyát* illustrates:

A Book of Verses underneath the Bough,	*a*
A Jug of Wine, a Loaf of Bread—and Thou	*a*
Beside me singing in the Wilderness—	*b*
Oh, Wilderness were Paradise now!	*a*

See pages 90, 95.

RHYTHM The alternation of stressed and unstressed syllables in language. Rhythm occurs naturally in all forms of spoken and written language. The most obvious kind of rhythm is produced by **meter**, the regular pattern of stressed and unstressed syllables found in some poetry. But writers can also create less structured rhythms by using different kinds of **repetition** (such as **rhyme**, **alliteration**, **assonance**, **parallelism**, and **refrains**), or by balancing long and short words, phrases, or lines. Such rhythms are common in

free verse. *See pages* 95. *See also* **Free Verse, Meter.**

SATIRE   A kind of writing that ridicules human weakness, vices, or folly in order to bring about social reform. Satires often try to persuade the reader to do or believe something by showing the opposite view as absurd or—even more forcefully—vicious and inhumane. To achieve their purpose, satirists may use **exaggeration** (such as **hyperbole**), **irony, parody,** and **wit.** Voltaire uses all these techniques in his scathing satire of European Rationalism, *Candide. See page* 138.

SCIENCE FICTION   A form of fantasy writing in which scientific facts, assumptions, or hypotheses form the basis of adventures in the future, on other planets, in other dimensions of space or time, or under new variants of scientific laws. Although science fiction is usually set in the future, writers often use it to comment, in the form of **satire**, on the present. *See pages* 12, 138.

SETTING   The time and place of a story, play, or narrative poem. Usually the setting is established early in a narrative through descriptive details and **imagery**. Longer works may have more than one setting. For example, Voltaire's *Candide* begins in Europe but moves to South America and other parts of the globe.

Setting is often closely linked to the **mood** of a literary work. For example, the exotic island setting of *The Tempest* contributes to the play's mood of isolation, imprisonment, and supernatural mystery. Setting may also reveal **character** by showing whether a character is in harmony with a particular place or in **conflict** with it. In "Life Is Sweet at Kumansenu" for example, the mother Bola accepts and ultimately gains consolation from the traditions of her village. Finally, setting may suggest a story's **theme**. In "Eveline" for example, the main character must make a decision between remaining in the paralyzing setting of Dublin and escaping overseas with a sailor. *See pages* 180–181. *See also* **Atmosphere**.

SHORT STORY   A short fictional prose narrative. Although some ancient prose narratives such as the Book of Ruth, resemble modern short stories, as a distinct **genre** the short story developed in the nineteenth century. Short stories are more limited than **novels**, usually having only one major **character, plot, setting,** and **theme.** The short story is usually built on a plot that consists of a **basic situation** or **exposition, conflict, complications, climax,** and **resolution**. However, many modern short stories concentrate less on "what happens" and more on revealing a character or evoking a vivid emotional effect.

SIMILE   A figure of speech that makes a comparison between two seemingly unlike things by using a connective word such as *like, as, than,* or *resembles.* "A full moon like an accusing face," "hail hard as B-B pellets," "an actor's hand opening more gracefully than a blossom," and "clouds resembling stuffed animals" are all examples of similes.

Like an extended metaphor, an **extended simile** is developed over several lines of writing or even through an entire poem or paragraph. An **epic** or **Homeric simile** is an elaborately extended simile that relates heroic events to simple, everyday events. Homer used many such similes in his epic poems, the *Iliad* (Unit Four) and the *Odyssey*. *See page* 161. *See also* **Figure of Speech, Metaphor.**

SPEAKER   In a poem, the voice that addresses us. The speaker may be the poet or may be a **persona**, a character whose voice and concerns do not necessarily reflect those of the poet.

STANZA   A group of lines in a poem that form a single unit. A stanza in a poem is something like a paragraph in prose: It often expresses a unit of thought. A stanza may consist of one line or any number of lines beyond that. Stanzas are usually named for the number of lines they contain or for the meter and rhyme scheme that they follow. A **couplet**, for example, consists of two lines, a **tercet** of three lines, and a **quatrain** of four lines. The typical **ballad stanza** is a quatrain with the rhyme scheme *abcb* and an **iambic meter** with four stresses in the first and third lines and three stresses in the second and fourth lines. *See pages* 90, 92.

STREAM OF CONSCIOUSNESS   A modern writing style that tries to depict the random flow of thoughts, emotions, memories, and associations rushing through a character's mind. The writings of both the Irish novelist James Joyce and the English novelist Virginia Woolf employ stream-of-consciousness technique. *See page* 74.

STYLE   The way a writer expresses his or her thoughts through language. Style may best be described as *how* an author writes rather then *what* he or she writes. **Diction**, **tone**, **figures of speech**—every choice a writer makes in deciding how to communicate his or her ideas contributes to style. Style is usually viewed separately from content, and it is often what leads critics to classify certain works as "great."

SURREALISM   A twentieth-century literary and artistic movement that sought to break down the barriers between rational and irrational thoughts and situations. Influenced by the theories of Sigmund Freud and using dreamlike imagery, surrealist writers and artists sought to portray the workings of the unconscious mind. Leading figures in the Surrealist movement, which flourished in the 1920s and 1930s, include André Breton, Guillaume Appolinaire, and Salvador Dalí. *See page* 21.

SUSPENSE   The uncertainty or anxiety a reader feels about what will happen next in a story. Any kind of writing that has an effective plot involves some degree of suspense. *See also* **Plot**.

SYMBOL   A person, place, thing, or event that stands both for itself and for something beyond itself. Many symbols have become widely recognized: A lion is a symbol of majesty and power; a dove is a symbol of peace. These symbols are sometimes called **public symbols**. But writers often invent new, personal symbols, whose meaning is revealed in a work of poetry or prose. In Maupassant's short story "The Jewels" for example, Madame Lantin's jewelry becomes a symbol for the deceptive nature of appearances. *See page* 21. *See also* **Allegory**.

SYMBOLISM   A literary movement that began in France during the late nineteenth century and emphasized the use of highly personal symbols to suggest ideas, emotions, and moods. The French Symbolists believed that emotions are fleeting, individual, and essentially inexpressible—and that therefore the poet is forced to *suggest* meaning rather than express it.

The leading Symbolists, such as Paul Verlaine and Arthur Rimbaud, were reacting against **Realism** and **Naturalism** and became important influences on the **Surrealist** movement of the twentieth century. *See page* 89. *See also* **Naturalism, Realism, Surrealism**.

THEME   The central idea or insight of a work of literature. A theme is not the same as the subject of a work, which can usually be expressed in a word or two: old age, ambition, love. The theme is the idea the writer wishes to convey about the subject—the writer's view of the world or revelation about human nature. In "Life Is Sweet at Kumansenu" for example, Abioseh Nicol's subject is love, but his theme is that love endures despite repeated disappointment and death and ultimately makes life sweet and worth living.

While some stories, poems, and plays have themes that are **directly stated**, most themes are **implied**. It is up to the reader to piece together all the clues the writer has provided about the work's total meaning. Two of the most important clues to consider are how the main character has changed and how the conflict has been resolved. In addition, long works such as novels and plays may have more than one theme. *See pages* 242, 260, 298.

TONE   The attitude a writer takes toward the reader, a subject, or a character. Tone is conveyed through the writer's choice of words and descriptions of **characters** and **setting**. Tone can usually be described with an adjective, such as amused, angry, indifferent, or sarcastic.

UNDERSTATEMENT   A figure of speech that consists of saying less than what is really meant, or saying something with less force than is appropriate. Understatement is the opposite of **hyperbole**, or **overstatement**, and is a form of **irony**. To say, "It is a bit wet out there" after coming in from a torrential downpour is to use understatement. Understatement can be used to create a kind of deadpan humor, and it can contribute to an overall satiric tone, as in Cervantes' *Don Quixote*.

GRAMMAR, USAGE, AND MECHANICS:
A Reference Guide

Note to Students

As you write and revise formal essays and papers on topics in literature, you may want to review points of grammar, usage, capitalization, punctuation, and spelling. This reference section provides rules and examples that you will find helpful in your writing.

Problems of Agreement

Agreement of Subject and Verb

1. **A verb should agree with its subject in number. Singular subjects take singular verbs. Plural subjects take plural verbs.**

    He watches movies. [The singular verb *watches* agrees with the singular subject *he*.]
    They watch movies. [The plural verb *watch* agrees with the plural subject *they*.]

    Like single-word verbs, verb phrases also agree with their subjects. However, in a verb phrase, only the first auxiliary (helping) verb changes its form to agree with a singular or plural subject.

    The **train was arriving** late.
    Two **trains were arriving** late.

2. **The number of the subject is not changed by a phrase following the subject.**

    This **bag** of marbles **is** full. [*Bag* is the subject, not *marbles*.]
    These **marbles** of glass **are** blue. [*Marbles* is the subject, not *glass*.]

3. **Compound prepositions such as *together with*, *in addition to*, *as well as*, and *along with* following the subject do not affect the number of the subject.**

    Sara, along with Elena, **is going** on the trip. [The subject of the sentence is singular because it names one person, *Sara*. Therefore, the predicate of the sentence uses the singular auxiliary verb form *is*.]

4. **The following indefinite pronouns are singular: *each*, *either*, *neither*, *one*, *everyone*, *everybody*, *no one*, *nobody*, *anyone*, *anybody*, *someone*, *somebody*.**

    Each of the dessert-chefs **bakes** pastry. [*Each one* bakes.]
    Neither of the pastries **is** an éclair. [*Neither one* is an éclair.]

5. **The following indefinite pronouns are plural: *several*, *few*, *both*, *many*.**

    Several of these trails **are** dangerous for hikers who are inexperienced.

6. **The indefinite pronouns *some*, *all*, *most*, *any*, and *none* may be either singular or plural. These pronouns are singular when they refer to a singular word and plural when they refer to a plural word.**

    Some of the writing **is** scary. [*Some* refers to the singular noun *writing*.]
    Some of the words **are** descriptive. [*Some* refers to the plural noun *words*.]

7. **A compound subject contains two or more nouns or pronouns that are the subject of the same verb. Compound subjects joined by the word *and* are usually plural in form and therefore take a plural verb.**

    Dante, **Boccaccio**, and **Calvino are** great writers in the Italian language. [Three people *are* writers.]

8. **Compound subjects that name only one person or thing take a singular verb.**

    My **best friend and constant companion is** Kara Kern. [One person is my best friend and constant companion.]

9. **Singular subjects joined by the words *or* or *nor* take a singular verb.**

    Either **Carlos** or **Tony bikes** to school. [*Either* Carlos bikes *or* Tony bikes, not both.]

10. **When a singular subject and a plural subject are joined by *or* or *nor*, the verb agrees with the subject nearer the verb.**

Neither the producers nor the **director was** present at the screening.

Neither the director nor the **producers were** present at the screening.

Other Problems in Subject-Verb Agreement

11. **The contractions *don't* and *doesn't* must agree with their subjects.**

With the singular subjects *I* and *you* and with plural subjects, use the contraction *don't* (*do not*).

I **don't** speak.   They **don't** tell.
We **don't** care.   These **don't** work.

With all other singular subjects, use the singular *doesn't* (*does not*).

She **doesn't** study.   This **doesn't** move.
It **doesn't** run well.   Donna **doesn't** work here.

12. *Collective nouns* **are singular in form, but they name a group of persons or things. Use a plural verb with a singular collective noun when you are referring to the individual parts or members of the group acting separately. Use a singular verb when you refer to the group acting together as a unit.**

army	club	fleet	jury
assembly	committee	flock	panel
audience	faculty	group	swarm
class	family	herd	team

The family **have** sat down for their dinner. [*Family* is thought of as a group of individuals.]

The family **has** its meals mostly at home. [*Family* is thought of as a single unit.]

Be sure that any pronoun referring to the collective noun agrees with the noun (*their* in the first example above, *its* in the second).

13. **A verb agrees with its subject, not with its predicate nominative, the noun or pronoun complement that refers to the same person or thing as the subject.**

$\quad$S$\qquad\qquad$PN
Cavities are my biggest problem.

$\qquad\qquad$S$\qquad$PN
My biggest **problem is** cavities.

14. **Contractions such as *here's*, *where's*, *how's*, and *what's* include the verb *is*. Do not use one of these contractions unless a singular subject follows it.**

There **are** [not *There's*] **mice** on the counter!

15. **A word or a phrase stating a weight, a measurement, or an amount of money or time is usually considered one item and takes a singular verb.**

Five dollars is all I can spend.
One quarter of the grain **was** sold at the market.

Sometimes, however, the amount is thought

of as individual pieces or parts. If so, a plural verb is used.

> **Ten** of the pages **were** missing.
> **Two thirds** of the apples **taste** sour.

16. **The title of a work of art, literature, or music, even when plural in form, takes a singular verb.**

> *Dubliners* contains "Eveline," one of my favorite short stories. [one collection]

17. ***Every*** **or** ***many a*** **before a subject calls for a singular verb.**

> Almost **every** member **was** tired.
> **Many a** student **enjoys** poetry.

18. **A few nouns that look plural in form take singular verbs.**

> The **news is** on at six and ten o'clock.
> **Physics was** Willis's best subject.

Some nouns that end in *-s* take a plural verb even though they refer to a single item.

> The **pliers are** in the toolbox.
> Your **pants are** very stylish.

Agreement of Pronoun and Antecedent

1. **A pronoun should agree with its antecedent in number and gender.**

A pronoun usually refers to a noun or another pronoun that comes before it. The word that a pronoun refers to is called its **antecedent**. A few singular personal pronouns have forms that indicate the gender of the antecedent. *He, him,* and *his* are masculine; *she, her,* and *hers* are feminine; *it* and *its* are neuter.

> **Sei Shōnagon** kept **her** journal in private.
> **Elie Wiesel** wrote **his** memoirs years after the war.

2. **When the antecedent of a personal pronoun is another kind of pronoun, look in a phrase following the antecedent to determine gender.**

> **Each** of the **girls** reads **her** own newspaper.
> **One** of the **boys** cooks **his** own dinner.

3. **When the antecedent may be either masculine or feminine, use both the masculine and the feminine forms.**

> **Every one** of the passengers sat in **his or her** assigned seat.

4. **Use a singular pronoun to refer to** *each, either, neither, one, everyone, everybody, no one, nobody, anyone, anybody, someone,* **or** *somebody.*

> **Every** boy in the bus fastened **his** seatbelt.
> **Each** student has **his or her** own locker.

When the meaning of *everyone* and *everybody* is clearly plural, use the plural pronoun.

> **Everyone** talked to **their** [not *his or her*] parents.

5. **Two or more singular antecedents joined by** *or* **or** *nor* **should be referred to by a singular pronoun.**

> Neither **Palmira nor Alicia** fixed **herself** any dinner.

6. **Two or more antecedents joined by** *and* **should be referred to by a plural pronoun.**

> **Tia and Reg** grew **their** own vegetables.

7. **The number of a relative pronoun is determined by the number of its antecedent.**

> **Everyone who** comes to the party will have a good time. [The relative pronoun *who* refers to the singular pronoun *everyone* and thus takes the singular verb form *comes*.]
> **All who** come will have a good time. [*Who* refers to the plural pronoun *all* and thus takes the plural verb form *come*.]

Tips for Writers

Sentences with two or more singular antecedents joined by *or* or *nor* can sound awkward if the antecedents are of different genders. If a sentence sounds awkward, revise it to avoid the problem.

AWKWARD:	**Nelson** or **Liz** will bring **his** or **her** records.
REVISED:	**Nelson** will bring **his** records, or **Liz** will bring **hers**.

Using Pronouns Correctly

Nominative and Objective Uses

Case

Case is the form of a noun or pronoun that shows its use in a sentence. In English, there are three cases: *nominative*, *objective*, and *possessive*.

Choosing the correct case form for a noun is no problem, because the form remains the same in the nominative and objective cases.

> The **professor** [nominative] carpools with another **professor** [objective].

Only in the possessive case does a noun change its form, usually by adding an apostrophe and *s*.

> My **father's** [possessive] workshop is cluttered with gardening tools and broken appliances.
> **I** [nominative] forgot to mail **my** [possessive] application to **her** [objective] yesterday.

The Case Forms of Personal Pronouns

Here are the case forms of personal pronouns. Notice that all personal pronouns, except *you* and *it*, have different nominative and objective forms.

PERSONAL PRONOUNS

SINGULAR

Nominative Case	Objective Case	Possessive Case
I	me	my, mine
you	you	your, yours
he, she, it	him, her, it	his, her, hers, its

PLURAL

Nominative Case	Objective Case	Possessive Case
we	us	our, ours
you	you	your, yours
they	them	their, theirs

The Nominative Case

1. **The *subject* of a verb is in the nominative case.**

> **He** was excited that **they** had come. [*He* is the subject of *was*; *they* is the subject of *had come*.]

2. **A *predicate nominative* is in the nominative case.**

A pronoun used as a predicate nominative always follows a form of the verb *be* or a verb phrase ending in *be* or *been*.

> It is **he**.
> That could be **she**.

The Objective Case

3. **The *direct object* of a verb is in the objective case.**

A *direct object* is a noun or pronoun that receives the action of the verb or shows the result of the action.

> The lesson of La Fontaine's fable impressed **him** and **me**. [*The lesson* is the subject of the verb *impressed*. The lesson impressed *whom*? The answer is *him and me*.]

4. **The *indirect object* of the verb is in the objective case.**

An *indirect object* is a noun or pronoun that tells to whom or for whom something is done. Pronouns used as indirect objects are in the objective case: *me, him, her, us, them*.

> Prospero's magic cloak gave **him** many powers.
> Sei Shōnagon's writing brought **her** much delight.

5. **The *object of a preposition* is in the objective case.**

A prepositional phrase begins with a preposition and ends with a noun or pronoun, which is the *object of the preposition*. A pronoun used as an object of a preposition must be in the objective case.

> Jared sat behind **us**.

Errors often occur when the object of a preposition is compound. You can usually figure out the correct pronouns by trying each one separately in the prepositional phrase.

> Mike raced ahead of him and I. [*Mike raced ahead of him* is correct, but *Mike raced ahead of I* is incorrect. The correct forms of the pronouns are *him* and *me*: Mike raced ahead of **him** and **me**.]

Tips for Writers

Some mistakes in usage are more common than others. In speech, for example, people often incorrectly use the pronoun *me* in a compound subject.

INCORRECT: Faith and **me** built a bookcase.
CORRECT: Faith and **I** built a bookcase.

6. **In an infinitive clause, both the subject and object of the infinitive are in the objective case.**

> My baby sister wanted **me to carry her**. [*Me* is the subject of *to carry*. *Her* is the object of *to carry*. The entire infinitive clause is the direct object of *wanted*.]

Many people use incorrect pronoun forms with the preposition *between*. You have probably heard phrases such as *between you and I* and *between you and he*. These phrases are incorrect. The pronouns are objects of a preposition and should be in the objective case. The correct phrases are *between you and me* and *between you and him*.

Special Pronoun Problems

Using Who and Whom Correctly

7. ***Who* is used as a subject or predicate nominative, and *whom* is used as an object.**

NOMINATIVE	OBJECTIVE
who	whom
whoever	whomever

In spoken English, the use of *whom* is becoming less common. In fact, when you are speaking, you may correctly begin any question with *who*, regardless of the grammar of the sentence. In written English, however, you should make a distinction between *who* and *whom*.

8. **The use of *who* or *whom* in a subordinate clause depends on how the pronoun functions in the clause.**

When you choose between *who(ever)* or *whom(ever)* in a subordinate clause, follow these steps:

STEP 1:   Find the subordinate clause.

STEP 2:   Decide how the pronoun is used in the clause—as subject, predicate nominative, object of the verb, or object of a preposition.

STEP 3:   Determine the case of the pronoun according to the rules of standard English.

STEP 4:   Select the correct form of the pronoun.

(*Whoever, Whomever*) I choose will lead the group.

STEP 1:   The subordinate clause is (*whoever, whomever) I choose.*

STEP 2:   In this clause, the subject is *I,* the verb is *choose,* and the pronoun is the direct object of the verb *choose; I choose (whoever, whomever).*

STEP 3:   The direct object of a verb is in the objective case.

STEP 4:   The objective form is *whomever.*

ANSWER: **Whomever** I choose will lead the group.

Remember that no words outside the subordinate clause affect the case of the pronoun. In this example, the entire clause is used as the subject of *will lead,* the verb in the main clause. The pronoun *whomever* is used as the direct object (objective case) within its clause.

Frequently, in subordinate clauses *whom* is omitted because it is understood.

> The person [whom] he asked is Joyce.
> The person [whom] she talked to is from the Australian outback.

9. **Pronouns used as *appositives* are in the same case as the word to which they refer.**

An *appositive* is a noun or pronoun that follows another noun or pronoun to identify or explain it.

> The members, **he, she,** and **I,** each read a different part. [Since *members* is the subject of the sentence, the pronouns in apposition with it (*he, she, I*) must be in the nominative case.]

10. **Use the possessive case of a noun or pronoun before a gerund. Do not confuse the gerund form with the present participle, also an *-ing* form of the verb, which is used as an adjective.**

> The panel applauded **my dancing**. [The gerund *dancing* is the object of the verb *applauded*. The possessive form *my* modifies the gerund.]
> Can you see **me dancing** a ballet with a professional troupe? [Here the participle *dancing* modifies *me,* the object of *see.*]

The Pronoun in an Incomplete Construction

11. **When *than* and *as* introduce an incomplete construction, use the form of the pronoun that you would use if the construction were completed.**

    Notice how pronouns change the meaning of sentences with incomplete constructions.

    > Vicky likes Paula better than **I.**
    > Vicky likes Paula better than **me.**

    In the first sentence, the nominative case pronoun *I* is the subject of an understood verb: *Vicky likes Paula better than I* [*like Paula*]. In the second sentence, the objective case pronoun *me* is the object of the under-

stood verb: *Vicky likes Paula better than* [*Vicky likes*] *me.*

Using Modifiers Correctly

1. **Adjectives and adverbs are modifiers; that is, they state qualities of other parts of speech. Adjectives modify nouns and pronouns. Adverbs modify verbs, adjectives, and other adverbs.**

ripe apple	**juicy** peaches	[adjectives]
talk **softly**	jump **well**	[adverbs]

2. **Use adjectives to compare one noun with another noun that has the same quality.**

    > That apple is **riper** than this one.
    > This peach is **juicier** than that one.

3. **Use adverbs to make comparisons between verbs.**

    > I shoveled the snow slowly, but Phoebe shoveled even **more slowly**.

4. **There are three degrees of comparison: *positive, comparative,* and *superlative*.**

POSITIVE	COMPARATIVE	SUPERLATIVE
cool	cooler	coolest
wet	wetter	wettest
tasty	tastier	tastiest
helpful	more helpful	most helpful
slowly	more slowly	most slowly
good	better	best
bad	worse	worst

5. **Avoid double comparisons.**

    A **double comparison** is incorrect because it contains both *-er* and *more* or *-est* and *most*.

    > This is the **dullest** [not *most dullest*] movie I've ever seen.

6. **Be sure your comparisons are clear.**

    > The snowfall here this year was as much as the Rockies. [This sentence incorrectly compares snowfall to mountains.]
    > The snowfall here this year was as much as it was in the Rockies. [This sentence correctly compares the snowfall in two different places.]

Tips for Writers

In writing papers about literary topics, you will often need to compare and contrast two or more literary works or specific aspects of them, such as character, plot, or setting. Comparisons, accurately expressed, can help you to make distinct points about works of literature. For example, you may wish to show that the characters in one novel are "more carefully developed" than in another or that the plot of one novel is "less complex" than that of another.

Misplaced Modifiers

7. **A misplaced modifier is a phrase or clause that sounds awkward because it modifies the wrong word(s). Modifying phrases should be placed as near as possible to the words they modify.**

    MISPLACED: I was awarded a scholarship after four years of study yesterday.
    CORRECTED: Yesterday, I was awarded a scholarship after four years of study.

8. **Place an adjective or adverb clause as near as possible to the word it modifies.**

    MISPLACED: I carried the box from school, which weighed thirty pounds.
    CORRECTED: From school, I carried the box, **which weighed thirty pounds**.

The Rules for Capitalization

First Words

1. **Capitalize the first word in every sentence.**

    Each room of the house seemed to have its own color theme. In one room there was a host of blues—pale, slate, and midnight. In yet another we found only orange and yellow tones.

    Traditionally, the first word of a line of poetry is capitalized.

    Water, water, everywhere,
    And all the boards did shrink;

    Water, water, everywhere,
    Nor any drop to drink.

    —from ''The Rime of the Ancient Mariner,''
    Samuel Taylor Coleridge

Some writers do not follow these practices. When you are quoting, be sure to use capital letters exactly as they are used in the source of the quotation.

Pronoun *I*

2. **Capitalize the pronoun *I*.**

    Lani and I always walk to school.

Proper Nouns and Proper Adjectives

3. **Capitalize proper nouns and proper adjectives.**

    Common nouns name general people, places, or things. A **proper noun** names a particular person, place, or thing. **Proper adjectives** are formed from proper nouns.

    Common nouns are not capitalized unless they begin a sentence or a direct quotation or are included in a title (see page 319). Proper nouns are always capitalized.

    COMMON NOUNS: a philosopher, a country, a ruler
    PROPER NOUNS: Plato, France, Queen Elizabeth
    PROPER ADJECTIVES: Platonic ideas, French bread, Elizabethan drama

    Some proper names consist of more than one word. In these names, short prepositions (generally, fewer than five letters) and articles are not capitalized.

    Joan of Arc
    American Federation of Labor
    Alexander the Great

    To find out whether a noun should be capitalized, check in a dictionary. The dictionary will tell you if a word should always be capitalized or if it should be capitalized only in certain uses.

Names of People

4. **Capitalize the names of people.**

    GIVEN NAMES: Len, Beth
    SURNAMES: Andretti, Schwartz

Geographical Names

5. Capitalize geographical names.

> TOWNS, CITIES: Los Angeles, Beijing, Madrid
> COUNTIES, TOWNSHIPS: Nassau County, Township of Soweto
> STATES: Missouri, Nebraska, Connecticut, Oregon
> REGIONS: the North, the Northwest, Continental Divide

Words such as *north, west,* and *southeast* are *not* capitalized when they indicate direction, unless they begin a sentence.

> west of here, heading northeast

> COUNTRIES: the United States; Scotland, Australia
> CONTINENTS: North America, Europe, Asia, Antarctica
> ISLANDS: Ceylon, Madagascar, Hawaii
> MOUNTAINS: the Himalayas, Mount McKinley, the Urals
> BODIES OF WATER: Atlantic Ocean, Gulf of Mexico
> PARKS: Yellowstone National Park, Hyde Park
> ROADS, HIGHWAYS, STREETS: Route 45, Interstate 80, East Eleventh Street

In a hyphenated number, the second word begins with a small letter.

> Seventy-seventh Street

Organizations

6. Capitalize names of organizations, businesses, institutions, and government bodies.

> ORGANIZATIONS: American Medical Association, National Association for the Advancement of Colored People, United Nations

The word *party* is usually written without a capital letter when it follows a proper adjective: *Republican party, Democratic party, Communist party*

> BUSINESSES: General Electric, New York Telephone, Estelle's Auto Body
> INSTITUTIONS: Sloan-Kettering Hospital, Boston University, Crossroads High School

Do not capitalize words like *hotel, theater,* *college, high school,* and *post office* unless they begin a sentence or are part of a proper name.

> Howard University   a college course
> Trocadero Hotel   a hotel in Miami
> Shubert Theater   a theater in New York
> Seattle Post Office   a local post office
> Suffolk County Courthouse   the courthouse doors

> GOVERNMENT BODIES: Federal Bureau of Investigation, Congress, Department of Agriculture

Historical Events

7. Capitalize the names of historical events and periods, special events, and calendar items.

> HISTORICAL EVENTS AND PERIODS: French Revolution, Battle of Gettysburg, Vietnam War, Middle Ages, Great Depression
> SPECIAL EVENTS: Special Olympics, the U.S. Open
> CALENDAR ITEMS: Thursday, June, Chinese New Year

Nationalities and Races

8. Capitalize the names of nationalities, races, and peoples.

> African, Greek, Bantu, Chinese, Commanche, Korean

Brand Names

9. Capitalize the brand names of business products.

> Nylon, Skippy, Chrysler, Xerox

Do not capitalize the noun that often follows a brand name: *Skippy peanut butter.*

> ### Tips for Writers
> Do not capitalize the names of seasons unless they are personified or are part of the names of special events.
>
> "I saw old Autumn in the misty morn." [personification]
> Suzanne was voted Most Likely to Succeed in the annual Spring Election. [special event]

Particular Places, Things, Events

10. Capitalize the names of ships, planets, monuments, awards, and any other particular places, things, or events.

> SHIPS, TRAINS: the **U.S.S.** *Minnow*, the *Titanic*, the *Clipper*
> AIRCRAFT, SPACECRAFT, MISSILES: *Apollo 7*, *Challenger*, *Patriot*
> PLANETS, STARS: **S**aturn, **O**rion **N**ebula

Sun, moon and *earth* are not capitalized unless they begin a sentence or are listed with other heavenly bodies.

> MONUMENTS, MEMORIALS: **G**raceland, the **L**incoln **M**emorial
> BUILDINGS: **M**useum of **M**odern **A**rt, the Empire **S**tate **B**uilding
> AWARDS: **M**edal of **H**onor, **N**obel **P**rize, **P**alm d'**O**r

Specific Courses, Languages

11. Do *not* capitalize names of school subjects, except for languages and for course names followed by a number.

> Chris is taking **E**nglish, **h**istory and **t**yping. I'm taking **F**rench, **d**rama, **T**rigonometry II, and **E**nglish literature.

Do *not* capitalize the name of a class (*freshman, sophomore, junior, senior*) unless it is used as part of a proper noun.

> The sophomore class is going to win the **F**reshman-**S**ophomore game.

Titles of People

12. Capitalize the title of a person when it comes before a name.

> **P**resident **B**ush   **M**r. **C**ovello
> **D**r. **V**aldez   **M**s. **W**elch

Do not capitalize a title used alone or following a person's name, especially if the title is preceded by *a* or *the.*

> Julius Caesar wanted to be **e**mperor of Rome. The **g**overnor will present her speech at the groundbreaking ceremony.

13. Capitalize words showing family relation-

ship when used with a person's name but *not* when preceded by a possessive or article.

> Ramon's **g**randmother visited us last year.
> For Thanksgiving, we usually go to **A**unt **C**arlene and **U**ncle **M**ax's house.
> Does **C**ousin **E**d like your cat?
> But: My **c**ousin **E**d loves my dog.

Titles of Literary and Other Creative Works

14. Capitalize the first and last words and all important words in titles of books, periodicals, poems, stories, historical documents, movies, television programs, works of art, and musical compositions.

Unimportant words in a title are articles: *a, an, the*
short prepositions (fewer than five letters): *of, to, for, from*
coordinating conjunctions: *and, but, so, nor, or, yet, for*

> BOOKS: *The Tale of Genji, Madame Bovary, Things Fall Apart, The Name of the Rose*
> PERIODICALS: *Time, Life, Newsweek, Field and Stream*
> POEMS: "The World Is Too Much with Us," "The Golden Mean," "Jade Flower Palace"
> STORIES: "The Handsomest Drowned Man in the World," "The Jewels," "Cranes"
> HISTORICAL DOCUMENTS: Constitution, Declaration of Independence, Magna Carta
> TELEVISION PROGRAMS: *Murphy Brown, Nova, Murder She Wrote, Saturday Night Live*
> WORKS OF ART: *Odalisque, Waterlilies*
> MUSICAL COMPOSITIONS: *Aida*, "Can't Touch This," Mozart's *Requiem, The Magic Flute*

The words *a, an,* and *the* written before a title are capitalized only when they are the first word of a title.

> the *Chicago Sun Times, For Whom the Bell Tolls, The Diary of Anne Frank, The Red and the Black*

Before the names of magazines and newspapers, *a, an,* and *the* are usually not capitalized.

Religions

15. Capitalize names of religions and their

followers, holy celebrations, holy writings, and specific deities.

RELIGIONS AND FOLLOWERS: **C**atholicism, **Q**uaker, **J**ehovah's **W**itness, **H**indu, **P**rotestant, **J**ewish, **M**uslim, **M**ethodist, **B**uddhist, **A**nglican, **T**aoist, **P**resbyterian

HOLY DAYS AND SEASONS: **E**aster, **Y**om **K**ippur, **Q**uamsa, **P**assover, **C**hristmas, **R**amadan

HOLY WRITINGS: the **B**ible, the **T**almud, the **K**oran, the **V**edas, the **A**cts of the **A**postles

SPECIFIC DEITIES: **A**llah, **G**od, **B**rahma, **J**ehovah, **B**uddha

The word *god* is not capitalized when it refers to the gods of ancient mythology.

Zeus was the father of all **g**ods.
The **g**oddess Athena was thought to be all-wise.
The Greek **g**od Hermes was the messenger of the **g**ods; in Roman mythology, he is known as Mercury.

Punctuation

End Marks

End marks—*periods, question marks,* and *exclamation points*—are used to indicate the purpose of a sentence.

1. Use a period to end a statement (*or declarative sentence*).

Your father is here.
The child wanted to know where the toy was.

Notice in the second example that a declarative sentence containing an indirect question is followed by a period.

2. Use a question mark to end a question (*or interrogative sentence*).

Should we buy these?
Is it time yet?

A direct question may have the same word order as a declarative sentence. Since it is a question, however, it is followed by a question mark.

She was a nice person?

3. Use a period or exclamation point to end an imperative sentence.

When an imperative sentence makes a request, it is generally followed by a period.

Tips for Writers

Be sure to distinguish between a declarative sentence that contains an indirect question and an interrogative sentence, which asks a direct question.

INDIRECT QUESTION: Al asked what road he should take to get to the beach.
DIRECT QUESTION: Al asked, ''What road should I take to get to the beach?''

Please run fast.
Bring me a pen.

4. Use an exclamation point to end an exclamation.

Excellent! What a great job!
Oops!

Sometimes declarative, interrogative, and imperative sentences show such strong feeling that they are more like exclamations than statements, questions, or requests. If so, an exclamation point should be used instead of a period or question mark.

The house is on fire!
Won't you leave!
Don't break that!

5. Use a period after an abbreviation.

PERSONAL NAMES: D. H. Lawrence, N. K. Sandars
TITLES USED WITH NAMES: Mr., Ms., Mrs., Dr.
STATES: Fla., Mo., Pa., Ala.
TIME OF DAY: A.M., P.M.
YEARS: B.C., A.D.
ADDRESSES: Ave., St., Blvd.
ORGANIZATIONS AND COMPANIES: Co., Corp., Inc.
UNITS OF MEASURE: lb., oz., in., ft., yd., mi.

Abbreviations for government agencies and international organizations and some other frequently used abbreviations are written without periods. Abbreviations in the metric system are often written without the periods, especially in science books.

Commas

1. Use commas to separate two or more adjectives preceding a noun.

Tips for Writers

If an abbreviation comes at the end of a statement, do not use an additional period as an end mark. However, use a question mark or an exclamation point if one is needed.

> Please tell me when it's 2 P.M.
> Does she work for Rowe, Inc.?

> We explored the **hot, damp, smelly attic.**

When the last adjective in a series is thought of as part of the noun, the comma before the adjective is omitted.

> We washed the **small, round glass windows.**

You can use two tests to determine whether two adjectives should be separated by a comma:

TEST 1: Insert the word *and* between the adjectives. If *and* fits sensibly between the adjectives, use a comma. In the first example sentence, *and* can be logically inserted: *hot and damp attic.* In the second sentence, *and* sounds logical between the first two adjectives (*small and round*) but not between the second and third (*round and glass*).

TEST 2: Change the order of the adjectives. If the order of the adjectives can be reversed sensibly, use a comma. *Round, small glass windows* makes sense, but *glass, small round windows* does not.

2. **Use commas before *and*, *but*, *or*, *nor*, *for*, *so*, and *yet* when they join independent clauses.**

> **Howard stubbed his toe,** and **he screamed.**
> **María gets up early,** yet **she is always late.**

Do not be misled by compound verbs, which often make a sentence look as though it contains two independent clauses.

> COMPOUND SENTENCE: **Jean cut the vegetables,** and **Malcolm made the salad.** [two independent clauses]
> SIMPLE SENTENCE: **John Milton outlined** the poem and **wrote** it. [one subject with a compound verb]

In the following correctly punctuated compound sentence, notice that independent clauses appear on both sides of the coordinating conjunction.

> **He wrote poetry,** and **he loved to act.**

3. **Use commas to set off nonessential clauses and nonessential participial phrases.**

A *nonessential* (or *nonrestrictive*) clause or participial phrase adds information that is not necessary to the main idea in the sentence. Omitting such a clause or phrase will not change the basic meaning of the sentence.

> NONESSENTIAL CLAUSE: The letter**, which is not stamped,** cannot be mailed.
> NONESSENTIAL PHRASE: William Black**, an accomplished artist,** illustrated many of his own poems.

When a clause or phrase is necessary to the meaning of a sentence—that is, when it tells *which ones*—the clause or phrase is *essential* (or *restrictive*), and commas are *not* used. Notice how the meaning of each sentence below changes when the essential clause or phrase is omitted.

> ESSENTIAL CLAUSE: Only students **who are taller than five feet eight inches** may try out for the basketball team.
> ESSENTIAL CLAUSE: The poster **that I want** has a green border.

An adjective clause beginning with *that* is usually essential.

> ESSENTIAL PHRASE: The most famous speech **made by Dr. Martin Luther King, Jr.,** began "I have a dream. . . ."

4. **Use a comma after introductory words such as *well*, *yes*, *no*, and *why* when they begin a sentence.**

> **Yes,** my hair is natural.
> **Well,** it's always been this color.

5. **Use a comma after an introductory participial phrase.**

> **Resting in the shade of the tree,** I felt cooler.
> **Disappointed with the film,** Tia left the theater.

6. Use a comma after a series of introductory prepositional phrases.

> **Toward the end of the speech,** we started clapping.
> **By the end of the night,** we were all tired.

A short introductory prepositional phrase does not require a comma unless the comma is necessary to make the meaning clear.

> **With my car** I can get to work faster.
> **With my car,** driving is a pleasure. [The comma is necessary to avoid reading *car driving*.]

7. Use a comma after an introductory adverb clause.

> **When you get home,** give me a call.
> **After you figure it out,** tell me what to do.

8. Use commas to set off elements that interrupt the sentence.

> He is, **in fact,** my best friend.
> My brother, **of course,** scored the winning run.

If an "interrupter" comes at the beginning or at the end of a sentence, only one comma is needed.

> **After all,** he is an expert.

9. Use commas to set off appositives and appositive phrases.

> The Minters, **our neighbors,** were invited to the picnic.

When an appositive has no modifiers and is closely related to the word preceding it, it should not be set off by commas.

> The Polish composer **Chopin** is her favorite.
> We **students** took a poll.

10. Use commas to set off words used in direct address.

> **Corey,** you need a new coat.
> I need to ask your advice, **Ms. Kim.**

11. Use commas to set off parenthetical expressions.

> **Strictly speaking,** I don't like it.
> Yesterday, **I believe,** was her birthday.

A contrasting expression introduced by *not* is parenthetical and must be set off by commas.

> I'm sure it was Ferdowsi, **not Saadi,** who wrote the *Shahname*.

12. Use a comma to separate items in dates and addresses.

> My friend traveled to **Paris, France,** on **Sunday, July 14, 1991.**
> I mailed the letter to **29 West Orange Road, Teaneck, NJ 07631,** on **May 19, 1991.**

Notice that no comma separates the month and day (*May 19*) or the house number and street name (*29 West Orange Road*) because each is considered one item. Also, the ZIP code is not separated from the name of the state by a comma: *Teaneck, NJ 07631*.

13. Use a comma after the salutation of a friendly letter and after the closing of any letter.

> Dear Mr. Kilgannon,
> Yours truly,

14. Use a comma after a name followed by an abbreviation such as *Jr.*, *Sr.*, and *M.D.*

> Johnny Chin, **M.D.**
> John F. Kennedy, **Jr.**

Semicolons

1. Use a semicolon between independent clauses in a sentence if they are not joined by *and*, *but*, *or*, *nor*, *for*, *so*, or *yet*.

Notice in the following examples that the semicolon replaces the comma and the conjunction joining the independent clauses.

> First I filled the tub, **and** then I took a bath.
> **First I filled the tub;** then I took a bath.

A semicolon can be used between two closely related independent clauses.

> Phoebe baked the bread. Then she set the table.
> **Phoebe baked the bread;** then she set the table.

2. Use a semicolon between independent clauses joined by conjunctive adverbs or transitional expressions.

> Gabe was tired; **however,** he couldn't fall asleep.

I made several dishes; **in addition,** several friends brought appetizers.

When conjunctive adverbs and transitional expressions appear *within* one of the clauses and not *between* clauses, they are usually punctuated as interrupters (set off by commas). The two clauses are still separated by a semicolon.

We tried to see all the Seurat paintings; the museum, **however,** closed before we could do so.

3. Use a semicolon (rather than a comma) to separate independent clauses joined by a coordinating conjunction when there are commas within the clauses.

CONFUSING: Broccoli, peppers, and lettuce are vegetables, and nectarines, peaches, and bananas are fruits.

CLEAR: Broccoli, peppers, and lettuce are vegetables; nectarines, peaches, and bananas are fruits.

4. Use a semicolon between items in a series if the items contain commas.

He visited **Brussels, Belgium; Naples, Italy; Bombay, India; and Bangkok, Thailand,** on his trip.

Auditions will be held **Tuesday, July 16; Wednesday, July 17; and Thursday, July 18.**

Colons

1. Use a colon before a list of items, especially after expressions like *the following* and *as follows.*

You will visit **the following cities:** London, Athens, and Cairo.

Other colors are **as follows:** green, yellow, blue, and white.

If a noun is followed by a list of appositives, then the colon is used to make the meaning of the sentence clear.

On the menu there were three choices: French, Italian, or blue cheese dressing.

Do *not* use a colon before a list that follows a verb or a preposition.

INCORRECT: Additional sports include: table ten-

nis, badminton, croquet, and horseshoes.

CORRECT: Additional sports include table tennis, badminton, croquet, and horseshoes.

2. Use a colon before a long, formal statement or quotation.

Alfred North Whitehead wrote: ''Intelligence is quickness to apprehend as distinct from ability, which is capacity to act wisely on the thing apprehended.''

3. Use a colon between the hour and the minute.

4:08 A.M.   9:14 P.M.

4. Use a colon between chapter and verse when referring to passages from the Bible.

Psalms 110:2   Genesis 2:3

5. Use a colon between volume and issue number or between volume and page number of a periodical.

Life 58:4 [volume and issue number]
Life 58:102 [volume and page number]

6. Use a colon after the salutation of a business letter.

Dear Dr. Adell: To Whom It May Concern:

Italics

When writing or typing, indicate italics by underlining. If your composition were to be printed, the underlined words would be set in italics. For example, if you type:

Anton Chekhov wrote The Cherry Orchard.

the sentence would be printed like this:

Anton Chekhov wrote *The Cherry Orchard.*

If you use a personal computer, you can probably set words in italics yourself.

1. Use italics (underlining) for titles of books, plays, films, newspapers, periodicals, works of art, long musical compositions, long poems, television programs, ships, aircraft, and so on.

BOOKS: *Love in the Time of Cholera, Divine Comedy*
PLAYS: *The Misanthrope, Oedipus Rex*

FILMS: *Casablanca, Alien*
PERIODICALS: *Discover,* the *New Statesman*
WORKS OF ART: *Starry Night, Nightwatch*
LONG MUSICAL COMPOSITIONS: *Aida,*
The 1812 Overture
TELEVISION SERIES: *The Wonder Years, Master-*
piece Theater
SHIPS: *Titanic, Andrea Doria*
AIRCRAFT, SPACECRAFT: *Luna 7, Saturn 2, Hin-*
denburg

The words *a, an,* and *the* written before a title are italicized only when they are part of the title. Before the names of newspapers and magazines, however, they are not italicized, even if they are capitalized on the front page of the newspaper or on the cover of the magazine.

Holst composed **The Planets**.
I read the **Boston Phoenix** and **People**.

Magazine articles, chapter headings, and titles of short poems, short stories, short musical compositions, and individual episodes of TV shows should be placed in quotation marks, not italicized, when referred to in a composition. See the following section.

2. **Use italics (underlining) for foreign words and for words, letters, and figures referred to as such.**

The word **hullabaloo** comes from Scottish.
The **5** on my test looks like an **8**.

Quotation Marks

1. **Use quotation marks to enclose a direct quotation—a person's exact words.**

Cynthia asked, **"How long is the movie?"**
"It's two hours," I answered.

2. **Begin a direct quotation with a capital letter.**

When he was finished raking the yard, Mack said, **"L**et's cook out."
Amy said, **"A**bout ten minutes." [Although this quotation is not a sentence, it is Amy's complete remark.]

If the direct quotation is a fragment of the original quotation, it may begin with a small letter.

When Shakespeare's Miranda first lays eyes on Ferdinand, she remarks that **"n**othing ill can dwell in such a temple." [The quotation is only a phrase from Miranda's sentence.]

3. **When a quoted sentence is divided into two parts by an interrupting expression, begin the second part with a small letter.**

"Before yesterday," she said, "**t**here were trees here."

If the second part of a quotation is a new sentence, a period (not a comma) follows the interrupting expression; and the second part begins with a capital letter.

"The game already started," May said. "**L**et's go to the movies, instead."

An interrupting expression is not a part of a quotation and therefore should never be inside quotation marks.

INCORRECT: "If he doesn't come, he said, we won't have enough people."
CORRECT: **"If he doesn't come,"** he said, **"we won't have enough people."**

When two or more sentences by the same speaker are quoted together, use only one set of quotation marks.

Wanda said, **"Yesterday seemed warmer than today. I wonder what the temperature is?"**

Tips for Writers

Do not use quotation marks for *indirect quotations.*

DIRECT QUOTATIONS: Sasha said, "I've already read that book."
She asked him, "Have you ever been to Memphis?"
INDIRECT QUOTATIONS: Sasha said that he'd already read that book.
She asked him if he'd ever been to Memphis.

4. **Set off a direct quotation from the rest of the sentence by commas or by a question mark or an exclamation point.**

Mr. Rosenfeld said, "Please come back and visit us soon," as he dropped me off at my house.
Grace asked, "Have you been able to locate Sur-

inam?'' as she opened the oversized atlas on her desk.

5. Place commas and periods inside closing quotation marks.

> ''I haven't read the book,'' said Janine, ''but I saw the movie.''
> ''Mushrooms,'' a poem by Margaret Atwood, presents vivid images.

6. Place semicolons and colons outside closing quotation marks.

> Father's advice was, ''Always be polite''; I wonder if his father told him that, too.
> Choose one of the following ''specials of the day'': pot roast, chicken, or pasta salad.

7. If the quotation is a question or an exclamation, place question marks and exclamation points inside the closing quotation marks. Otherwise, place them outside.

> ''Are we there yet?'' I asked, hoping for the best.
> What is the meaning of ''censer''?

8. When you write dialogue (a conversation), begin a new paragraph every time the speaker changes.

> ''I won't go through with it,'' said Adam softly.
> ''Well, then,'' Alice said, ''I guess I'll have to do it alone.''
> ''Yes,'' he said. ''You will.''

9. When a quoted passage consists of more than one paragraph, put quotation marks at the beginning of each paragraph and at the end of the entire passage. Do not put quotation marks after any paragraph but the last.

> ''Today,'' the reporter said, ''several buildings were burned to the ground in Waco, Texas.
> ''Police are ruling the fires accidental, and are still searching for the cause of the blaze. Eyewitnesses speculate that it may have been caused by a gas leak.''

10. Use single quotation marks to enclose a quotation within a quotation.

> Vernon said, ''I saw Run DMC live, singing 'Rockbox.' ''

> Michael asked, ''Who said 'Go West, young man'?''

11. Use quotation marks to enclose titles of articles, short stories, essays, poems, songs, individual episodes of TV shows, chapters, and other parts of books or periodicals.

> I'm going to read Flannery O'Connor's short story ''A Good Man Is Hard to Find.''
> He likes the song ''My Way.''

Italicize the title of a poem long enough to be published in a separate volume. Such poems are usually divided into titled or numbered sections, such as cantos, parts, or books. Long musical compositions include operas, symphonies, ballets, oratorios, and concertos.

> When I read *Thurber's Carnival*, I wanted to read ''The Scotty Who Knew Too Much,'' too.
> I read ''Canto 6'' of the *Divine Comedy* by the Italian poet Dante.

Apostrophes

With the Possessive Case

1. Add an apostrophe and an *s* to form the possessive case of a singular noun. The *possessive* of a noun or pronoun shows ownership or relationship.

> an **editor's** opinion   **Francine's** book

2. Add only an apostrophe to a proper name ending in an *s*-sound if the name has two or more syllables or if the addition of *'s* would make the name awkward to pronounce.

> **Ms. Rodriguez'** wallet   **Wallace Stevens'** poetry

3. Add only an apostrophe to form the possessive case of a plural noun ending in *s*.

> **countries'** populations   **dentists'** bills

Although most plural nouns end in *s*, some are irregular. To form the possessive case of a plural noun that does not end in *s*, add an apostrophe and an *s*.

children's toys   **women's** careers

Do not use an apostrophe to form the *plural* of a noun. Remember that the apostrophe shows ownership or relationship.

Three **runners** [not **runners'**] wore sneakers.
Three **runners'** [not **runner's**] sneakers were white.

4. **Do not use an apostrophe with a possessive personal pronoun.**

My, your, her, its, our, and *their* are used before a noun. *Mine, yours, hers, ours,* and *theirs,* on the other hand, are never used before a noun; they are used as subjects, complements, or objects in sentences. *His* may be used in either way.

I saw **your** jacket. I saw a jacket of **yours**.
That is **her** baby. That baby is **hers**.

The possessive form of *who* is *whose,* not *who's.* Similarly, the possessive forms for *it* and *they* are *its* and *their,* not *it's* or *they're.*

5. **Add an apostrophe and an *s* to form the possessive case of an indefinite pronoun.**

anyone**'s** guess   neither**'s** book

6. **For possessives of compound words, names of organizations and businesses, and words showing joint possession, make only the last word possessive in form.**

COMPOUND WORDS:
someone else's problem
state legislature's decision
ORGANIZATIONS:
World Wildlife Conservation's plea
Greenpeace's funding
BUSINESS:
Con Edison's workers
JOINT POSSESSION:
Matt and Julie**'s** story had the fewest characters and the most dialogue. [The story belongs to both Matt and Julie.]

When one of the words showing joint possession is a pronoun, both words should be possessive in form.

Eddie's and my surfboards were in desperate need of wax. [not *Eddie and my surfboards*]
Alex's and my relationship has improved since we began to write to each other.

7. **When two or more persons possess something individually, make each of their names possessive in form.**

Mrs. Mackay's and **Mrs. Stone's** husbands both work in the local post office. [the husbands of two different women]
Bill's and **Leon's backpacks** have reflective strips attached to them. [individual, not joint, possession]

With Contractions

8. **Use an apostrophe to show where letters or numbers have been omitted in a contraction.**

| who is / who's | I am / I'm |
| 1991 / '91 | you are / you're |

EXCEPTIONS:
| will not / won't | shall not / shan't |

9. **To prevent confusion, use an apostrophe and an *s* to form the plurals of lowercase letters, some uppercase letters, numerals, and some words referred to as words.**

My daughter is learning her ABC**'s**.
Good writers dot their *i*'**s** and cross their *t*'**s**.

Hyphens

1. **Use a hyphen in some compound nouns.**

brand-new   great-grandmother   mother-in-law

2. **Use a hyphen to divide a word at the end of a line.**

One of my favorite words is the noun **an-thology**.

Divide an already hyphenated word only at a hyphen.

Yesterday at the fair he went on the **merry-go-round**.

Do not divide a word so that one letter stands alone.

The young couple rented a new **apart-ment** [not a-partment].

A dictionary will indicate the best place to divide a word.

3. Use a hyphen with compound numbers from *twenty-one* to *ninety-nine* and with fractions used as adjectives.

> twenty-four degrees
> one-third gallon [but *one third* of the paint]

4. Use a hyphen with the prefixes *ex-*, *self-*, *all-*, and with the suffix *-elect*, and with all prefixes before a proper noun or proper adjective.

> **mid-**September, **self-**taught, President-**elect**

Dashes

Use a dash to indicate an abrupt break in thought or speech or an unfinished statement or question.

Many words and phrases are used parenthetically; that is, they break into the main thought of a sentence. Most parenthetical elements are set off by commas or parentheses.

> The general, **I believe,** is a brilliant strategist.
> Radishes, **however,** do not agree with me.

Sometimes these elements demand a stronger emphasis. In such instances, a dash is used.

> She had only one desire—to flee, flee from the dull life she led—but it was too late.
> The real culprit, you see—ah, but that information must remain a secret for the moment.

Parentheses

Use parentheses to enclose material that is added to a sentence but is not considered of major importance.

> During World War I **(from 1914 to 1918)**, the airplane came into prominence in military strategy.

Punctuation marks are used within parentheses when the parenthetical matter is a full sentence. However, a punctuation mark is not placed within parentheses if the mark belongs to the sentence as a whole.

> Mark your answers clearly. (Do not use ink.)
> Senator Albert Gore (Democrat, Tennessee) has made several speeches on that subject.
> The graph shows the changes clearly (see Figure 3).

Spelling

Tips for Writers

Here are five tips for improving your spelling.
1. To learn the spelling of a word, pronounce it, study it, and write it.
2. Use a dictionary.
3. Spell by syllables.
4. Proofread for careless spelling errors.
5. Keep a spelling notebook.

Words with *ie* and *ei*

1. **Write *ie* when the sound is long *e*, except after *c*.**

> achieve   niece   ceiling   reprieve
> conceit   thief   siege   fiend

2. **Write *ei* when the sound is not long *e*.**

> neighbor   weigh   freight
> reign   heinous   height
>
> EXCEPTIONS: friend, conscience, financier, seize

Words with *-cede*, *-ceed*, and *-sede*.

3. **Only one English word ends in *-sede*: supersede; only three words end in *-ceed*: exceed, proceed, and succeed; all other words with this sound end in *-cede*.**

> precede   recede   secede
> intercede   concede   accede

Adding Prefixes

4. **When a prefix is added to a word, the spelling of the original word itself remains the same.**

> dis + satisfy = **dis**satisfy   im + mature = **im**mature

Adding Suffixes

5. **When the suffix *-ness* or *-ly* is added to a word, the spelling of the original word remains the same.**

> casual + ly = casual**ly**   habitual + ly = habitual**ly**

EXCEPTIONS:

1. Words ending in *y* usually change the *y* to *i* before *-ness* and *-ly: empty / emptiness; busy / busily*
2. *True, due,* and *whole* drop the final *e* before *-ly: truly, duly, wholly*

Most one-syllable adjectives ending in *y do* follow rule 5: *sly / slyness; dry / dryly.*

6. Drop the final silent *e* before adding a suffix that begins with a vowel.

> care + ing = caring   sense + ible = sensible

EXCEPTIONS:

1. Keep the final silent *e* in words ending in *ce* or *ge* before a suffix that begins with *a* or *o: manageable, courageous*
2. To avoid confusion with other words, keep the final silent *e* in some words:
   dye + ing = dyeing [not dying]
   singe + ing = singeing [not singing]

7. Keep the final silent *e* before adding a suffix that begins with a consonant.

> nine + ty = ninety   definite + ly = definitely

EXCEPTIONS:
true + ly = truly   judge + ment = judgment

8. When a word ends in *y* preceded by a consonant, change the *y* to *i* before any suffix except one beginning with *i*.

> accompany + ment = accompaniment
> plenty + ful = plentiful

EXCEPTIONS:

1. Some one-syllable words:
   shy + ness = shyness
   sky + ward = skyward
2. *lady* and *baby* with suffixes:
   ladylike   ladyship   babyhood

9. When a word ends in *y* preceded by a vowel, simply add the suffix.

> buoy + ant = buoyant   joy + ful = joyful

EXCEPTIONS:
day + ly = daily   pay + ed = paid

Doubling Final Consonants

10. When a word ends in a consonant, double

the final consonant before a suffix that begins with a vowel only if the word: (1) has only one syllable or is accented on the last syllable, and (2) ends in a single consonant preceded by a single vowel.

> swim + ing = swimming
> repel + ent = repellent

Otherwise, simply add the suffix.

> wink + ed = winked
> insist + ence = insistence

Plurals of Nouns

11. To form the plurals of most English nouns, add *s*.

> violin / violins   night / nights

12. To form the plurals of other nouns, follow these rules.

If the noun ends in *s, x, z, ch,* or *sh,* add *es.*

> dress / dresses   fox / foxes   match / matches

If the noun ends in *y* preceded by a consonant, change the *y* to *i* and *es.*

> cry / cries   theory / theories   ruby / rubies

EXCEPTION: The plurals of proper nouns: the *Murphys,* the *Rileys.*

If the noun ends in *y* preceded by a vowel, add *s.*

> monkey / monkeys   buoy / buoys

For some nouns ending in *f* or *fe,* change the *f* to *v* and add *s* or *es.*

Noticing how the plural is pronounced will help you remember whether to change the *f* to *v.*

> kerchief / kerchiefs   safe / safes   knife / knives

If the noun ends in *o* preceded by a consonant, add *es.*

> potato / potatoes   hero / heroes
> tomato / tomatoes

If the noun ends in *o* preceded by a vowel, add *s.*

> patio / patios   radio / radios   tattoo / tattoos

Nouns for musical terms that end in *o* preceded by a consonant form the plural by adding only *s*.

> soprano / soprano**s**   solo / solo**s**
> piano / piano**s**

A number of nouns that end in *o* preceded by a consonant have two plural forms.

> tornado / tornado**s** *or* tornado**es**
> zero / zero**s** *or* zero**es**

The best way to handle plurals of words ending in *o* preceded by a consonant is to check their spelling in a dictionary. The plurals of some nouns are irregular.

> tooth / teeth   man / men   mouse / mice

Some nouns have the same form in both the singular and the plural.

> deer   moose   salmon   Swiss

Plurals of Common Nouns

13. If a compound noun is written as one word, form the plural by adding *s* or *es*.

> cupful / cupful**s**   leftover / leftover**s**
> eyelash / eyelash**es**

If a compound noun is hyphenated or written as two words, make the main noun plural. The *main noun* is the noun that is modified.

> mother-in-law / mother**s**-in-law
> notary public / notari**es** public

> EXCEPTIONS: drive-in / drive-in**s**
> lean-to / lean-to**s**

Plurals of Latin and Greek Loan Words

14. Some nouns borrowed from Latin and Greek form the plural as in the original language.

> nucleus / nucl**ei**   crisis / cris**es**   datum / dat**a**

A few Latin and Greek loan words have two plural forms.

> vortex / vort**ices** *or* vort**exes**
> gymnasium / gymnasi**a** *or* gymnasium**s**

Check a dictionary to find the preferred spelling of such plurals.

Plurals of Numbers, Letters, Symbols, and Words Used as Words

15. To form the plurals of numerals, most capital letters, symbols, and words used as words, add an *s*.

> Change the *N***s** to *V***s**.

To prevent confusion, use an apostrophe and an *s* to form the plurals of lowercase letters, certain capital letters, and some words used as words.

> Your *r*'**s** look like *z*'**s**.

The plurals of decades and centuries may be formed by adding an *s* or an apostrophe and an *s* (*'s*).

> During the **1900's** (*or* **1900s**) many new inventions appeared.

Spelling Numbers

16. Always spell out a number that begins a sentence.

> **Two thousand two hundred** cows are kept on this farm.

17. Within a sentence, spell out numbers that can be written in one word or two words; use numerals for other numbers.

> Over the weekend we drove **seven hundred miles**.
> He has a collection of **325** different butterflies.

18. Spell out numbers used to indicate order.

> I placed **third** [not 3rd] in the tournament.

> EXCEPTION: Use numerals for dates when you include the name of the month. Always use numerals for years.

> School ends on June **3** [not 3rd]. [Writing *the third of June* is also correct.]
> In **1945**, Ricardo came from Italy to the United States.

GLOSSARY

The glossary below is an alphabetical list of words found in the selections in this book. Use this glossary just as you use a dictionary—to find out the meanings of unfamiliar words. (A few technical, foreign, or obscure words in this book are not listed here, but instead are defined for you in the footnotes or glosses that accompany each selection.)

Many words in the English language have more than one meaning. This glossary gives the meanings that apply to the words as they are used in the selections of this book. Words closely associated in form and meaning are usually listed together as one entry (for example, *invert* and *inverted*), and the definition is given for the first form.

The following abbreviations are used:

adj., adjective	**n.**, noun	**v.**, verb
adv., adverb	**pl.**, plural form	

Unless a word is very simple to pronounce, its pronunciation is given in parentheses. A guide to the pronunciation symbols appears at the bottom of each right-hand glossary page.

For more information about words in this glossary, or about words not listed here, consult a dictionary.

▼ A ▼

abase (ə·bās') **v.** To humble, humiliate, degrade.

abdicate (ab'di·kāt') **v.** To formally withdraw from an office or position.

abhor (ab·hôr') **v.** To draw back in hatred or disgust.

abjure (ab·joor') **v.** To reject; renounce; give up.

abode (ə·bōd') **n.** Home; dwelling place.

abominable (ə·bäm'ə·nə·bəl) **adj.** Hateful; repulsive.

abound (ə·bound') **v.** To be abundant; exist in plentiful amounts.

abstain (ab·stān') **v.** To do without voluntarily.

abstemious (ab·stē'mē·əs) **adj.** Moderate; temperate.

abyss (ə·bis') **n. 1.** The void or chaos which existed before the world's creation. **2.** A bottomless pit.

accomplice (ə·käm'plis) **n.** A partner in a criminal act.

accord **v.** To give or bestow upon.

accouterments (ə·kōōt'ər·mənts) **n., pl.** Equipment issued to a soldier, excluding clothes and weapons.

acquit (ə·kwit') **v.** To clear someone of a charge or accusation.—**acquittal** **n.**

adept (ə·dept') **adj.** Highly skilled, expert. **n.** (ad'ept') an expert.

adjacent (ə·jā'sənt) **adj.** Next to; near.

admonition (ad·mə·nish'ən) **n.** A warning or scolding.

adorn (ə·dôrn') **v.** To decorate.

adversary (ad'vər·ser'·ē) **n.** An opponent; enemy.

adverse (ad·vurs') **adj. 1.** Moving or working in an opposite direction. **2.** Unfavorable; harmful.

advocate (ad'və·kit) **n.** A person who speaks in another's cause.

aesthetic (es·thet'ik) **adj.** Relating to what is tasteful or beautiful in art, nature, and the like.—**aesthetically** **adv.**

affable (af'ə·bəl) **adj.** Easy to talk to; approachable; good-natured.

afflict (ə·flikt') **v.** To inflict pain or suffering upon.

afford (ə·fôrd') **v. 1.** To be able to pay for. **2.** To give.

affront (ə·frunt') **n.** An open or intentional offense or insult.

aggrieved (ə·grēvd') **adj.** Offended; wrongly treated; injured in legal rights.

alight **v.** To dismount; descend.

allay (ə·lā') **v.** To relieve (fears, for example); pacify; calm.

allot (ə·lät') **v.** To distribute or apportion by random chance.

allusion (ə·lōō'zhən) **n.** An indirect reference; casual mention.

aloof (ə·lōōf') **adj.** Cool and distant; reserved.

amble (am'bəl) **v.** To walk in an unhurried, leisurely fashion.

amiable (ā'mē·ə·bəl) **adj.** Friendly or good-natured.

ample (am'pəl) **adj. 1.** Adequate. **2.** More than enough.

anarchy (an'ər·kē) **n. 1.** Political disorder; chaos. **2.** Breakdown of government.

ancestral (an·ses'trəl) **adj.** Coming from an ancestor or forefather.

anguish (ang'gwish) **n.** Great pain and suffering because of loss, worry, or grief.

animated (an'i·māt·id) **adj.** Lively; spirited.

annex (ə·neks') **v.** To add on or attach, especially to a larger thing.

anticipate (an·tis'ə·pāt') **v.** To expect.

apparition (ap·ə·rish′ən) *n.* A strange figure, like a ghost, that appears suddenly.

appeal *v.* To make an earnest request.

appease (ə·pēz′) *v.* To pacify or quiet by giving what is demanded.

apprehension (ap′rē·hen′shən) *n.* A sudden anxious expectation; dread.

approbation (ap′rə·bā′shən) *n.* Official approval.

arable (ar′ə·bəl) *adj.* Able to be plowed so as to produce crops.

ardor (är′dər) *n.* Passion.

arduous (är′jōō·əs) *adj.* That which requires great care or effort.

arid (ar′id) *adj.* Dry; wasted and lifeless.

arrest (ə·rest′) *v.* To stop or check the progress or course of.

arrogant (ar′ə·gənt) *adj.* Being unjustifiably proud; haughty.

asinine (as′ə·nīn) *adj.* Like an ass; stupid; silly; stubborn. —**asininely** *adv.*

assail (ə·sāl′) *v.* To attack with physical violence; assault.

assent (ə·sent′) *v.* To agree.

assert (ə·surt′) *v.* To declare. —**assert oneself:** To insist on attention or one's rights.

assiduous (ə·sij′ōō·əs) *adj.* Performed with careful and persistent attention.

assuage (ə·swāj′) *v.* To lessen, calm, or ease.

atone (ə·tōn′) *v.* To make amends for.

augury (ô′gyōō·rē) *n.* Telling of the future from omens.

auspicious (ôs′pish·əs) *adj.* Of good omen; favorable.

avert (ə·vurt′) *v.* **1.** To turn away. **2.** To prevent. —**aversion** *n.*

avid (av′id) *adj.* **1.** Eager; enthusiastic. **2.** Characterized by a very strong desire or craving.

avowal (ə·vou′əl) *n.* An open acknowledgment or admission.

▼ **B** ▼

babel (bā′bəl) *n.* Tumult; confusion.

baleful (bāl′fəl) *adj.* Of evil or harmful appearance or effect. —**balefully** *adv.*

ballast (bal′əst) *n.* Anything heavy carried in the hold of a ship to improve stability.

banal (bā′nəl) *adj.* Unoriginal; stale; commonplace.

barren (ber′ən) *adj.* Sterile; unproductive; empty.

beguile (bē·gīl′) *v.* To deceive.

bemuse (bē·myōōz′) *v.* To bewilder or confuse.

benevolent (bə·nev′ə·lənt) *adj.* Desiring to do good; kindly.

bereave (bē·rēv′) *v.* To deprive of something or someone.

bid *v.* To command.

blandishment (blan′dish·mənt) *n.* A flattering remark, intended to coax or persuade.

blasphemy (blas′fə·mē′) *n.* Any act, writing, or speech showing disrespect or irreverence for God or sacred things.

bode *v.* To predict, usually that which is evil.

boon *n.* Blessing; benefit.

boor *n.* A clumsy, ill-mannered person.

bounty *n.* **1.** Reward. **2.** Generosity.

brandish *v.* To wield in an exultant manner.

brood *v.* To contemplate in a troubled way.

▼ **C** ▼

cajole (kə·jōl′) *v.* To coax with insincere flattery.

calamitous (kə·lam′ə·təs) *adj.* Causing an extreme misfortune; disastrous.

caldron (kôl′drən) *n.* A large vat or boiler.

candid (kan′did) *adj.* Honest; straightforward.

candor (kan′dər) *n.* **1.** Honesty and frankness in expression. **2.** A fair and unbiased attitude.

capacity (kə·pas′i·tē) *n.* Ability or talent.

capricious (kə·prish′əs, -prē′shəs) *adj.* Tending to change suddenly and impulsively; flighty.

captivate (kap′tə·vāt′) *v.* To fascinate; hold the attention of.

censure (sen′shər) *v.* To condemn severely.

chide *v.* To scold mildly.

chivalry (shiv′əl·rē) *n.* The qualities of a knight: courage, honor, and willingness to help the weak and protect women.

chronicle (krän′i·kəl) *n.* A chronologically arranged historical record.

civic (siv′ik) *adj.* Of or having to do with a city, citizens, or citizenship.

clairvoyant (kler·voi′ənt) *adj.* Able to perceive things

---

fat, āpe, cär; ten, ēven; is, bīte; gō, hôrn, tōol, look; oil, out; up, fʉr; get; joy; yet; chin; she; thin, then; zh, leisure; ng, ring; ə for *a* in *ago*; *e* in *agent*; *i* in *sanity*; *o* in *comply*; *u* in *focus*; ' as in *able* (ā′b'l).

that are beyond the range of the senses.

clamber (klam′bər) *v.* To climb clumsily, especially with all fours.

clan *n.* A tribal division; extended family.

clandestine (klan·des′tin) *adj.* Kept hidden or secret because unlawful or evil.

clemency (klem′ən·sē) *n.* Mercy toward an enemy or offender.

coagulate (kō·ag′yōō·lāt′) *v.* To thicken; solidify.

coddle *v.* To treat a weak person tenderly.

cogitate (käj′ə·tāt′) *v.* To ponder carefully or think deeply about.

colossus (kə·läs′əs) *n.* Anything great in size or importance.

comely (kum′lē) *adj.* 1. Pleasing or attractive in appearance. 2. Seemly, decorous, proper.

commandeer (käm′ən·dir′) *v.* To seize.

commend (kə·mend′) *v.* 1. To praise. 2. To recommend. 3. To entrust.

commiserate (kə·miz′ər·āt′) *v.* To feel pity or sympathy for.

commission (kə·mish′ən) *n.* Money paid to a salesperson or agent, usually a percentage of a sale's proceeds.

communal (käm·yōō′nəl) *adj.* Held in common; shared by all.

compatriot (kəm·pā′trē·ət) *n.* A fellow citizen or countryman.

compensation (käm′pen·sā′shən) *n.* Anything given in exchange for, especially payment for damage or loss.

complacent (kəm·plās′ənt) *adj.* Overly contented or self-satisfied.

comprise (kəm·prīz′) *v.* To consist of; be composed of.

compunction (kəm·punk′shən) *n.* Remorse; feeling of guilty uneasiness.

concede (kən·sēd′) *v.* 1. To grant a privilege. 2. To admit that something is true.

conceivable (kən·sēv′ə·bəl) *adj.* Able to be imagined or believed. —**conceivably** *adv.*

conciliatory (kən·sil′e·ə·tôr′ē) *adj.* That which placates or soothes the anger of.

condescend (kän′di·send′) *v.* To deal with a person as if he or she were of inferior status.

conducive (kən·dōōs′iv) *adj.* That contributes.

confer (kən·fur′) *v.* 1. To give or bestow. 2. To consult together.

conflagration (kän′flə·grā′shən) *n.* A large, destructive fire.

conjecture (kən·jek′chər) *n.* A guess.

conjugal (kän′jə·gəl) *adj.* Of or relating to marriage or the marital relation.

consecrate (kän′si·krāt′) *v.* To set apart as holy and sacred.

consign (kən·sīn′) *v.* To assign to an unfavorable, objectionable position or place; relegate.

console (kən·sōl′) *v.* To comfort; ease the grief or sadness of. —**consolation** *n.*

conspicuous (kən·spik′yōō·əs) *adj.* Attracting attention because of an unusual quality or qualities; noticeable. —**conspicuously** *adv.*

conspiracy (kən·spir′ə·sē) *n.* A secret plan to do a foul deed.

consternation (kän′stər·nā′shən) *n.* Strong shock or fear that makes a person feel bewildered or helpless.

constitutional (kän′stə·tōō′shə·nəl) *adj.* Basic to the make-up of a person or thing.

consume (kən·sōōm′) *v.* To destroy; burn.

contaminate (kən·tam′ə·nāt′) *v.* To corrupt or defile.

contemplate (kän′təm·plāt′) *v.* 1. To look at with focused and thoughtful attention. 2. To ponder deeply. —**contemplation** *n.*

contemptuous (kən·temp′chōō·əs) *adj.* Regarding another as mean or unworthy; scornful. —**contemptuously** *adv.*

contentious (kən·ten′shəs) *adj.* Argumentative; quarrelsome.

contrive *v.* (kən·triv′) To bring about; manage.

converse (kən·vurs′) *v.* To speak with informally.

conviction (kən·vik′shən) *n.* 1. A deeply held belief. 2. A judgment of guilt by a court of law.

convulse (kən·vuls′) *v.* To cause to tremble or shake, as with pain or laughter.

corpulent (kôr′pyōō·lənt) *adj.* Obese; excessively fat.

corrosive (kə·rōs′iv) *adj.* Causing to wear away or be eaten away.

cosmopolitan (käz′mə·päl′ə·tən) *adj.* 1. Common to or representative of all or much of the world. 2. Worldly or broad-minded in views or habits.

counsel (koun′səl) *n.* Advice.

courier (koor′ē·ər) *n.* A messenger.

courtier (kôrt′ē·ər) *n.* An attendant in a court of royalty.

covenant (kuv′ə·nənt) *n.* A solemn agreement or contract in which two or more parties promise to do or refrain from doing some specific thing.

covert (kuv´ərt, *often, as adj.,* kō´vərt) *n.* A hiding place. *adj.* Covered over; secret; disguised.

cower (kou´ər) *v.* To hunch down or shrink from, as with fear.

credulous (krej´oo·ləs) *adj.* Believing too easily.

creed *n.* **1.** A formal statement or expression of religious faith. **2.** A statement of beliefs or principles on any subject.

crestfallen (krest´fôl´ən) *adj.* Depressed; dejected.

crux *n.* The crucial or critical point.

curate (kyoo´rit; -rāt) *n.* A member of the clergy.

curt *adj.* Rudely brief.

▼ D ▼

dalliance (dal´yəns) *n.* Flirting.

debacle (di·bä´kəl) *n.* A sudden and complete failure or defeat.

decrepit (dē·krep´it) *adj.* Weak or worn out by old age or long use.

defile (dē·fīl´) *v.* To profane; show disrespect and contempt.

deft *adj.* Skillful and quick.

deign (dān) *v.* To perform some action, despite believing it to be beneath one's dignity.

dejected (di·jek´tid) *adj.* Depressed; downcast. **—dejectedly** *adv.*

deluge (del´yooj´) *n.* A great flood.

delusion (di·loo´zhən) *n.* A false belief; wrong notion.

denounce (di·nouns´) *v.* **1.** To inform against. **2.** To publicly censure or condemn.

deploy (dē·ploi´) *v.* To position forces systematically over an area.

depraved (dē·prāvd´, di-) *adj.* Morally corrupt; utterly wicked.

desolate (des´ə·lit) *adj.* Uninhabited; forlorn.

despicable (des´pi·kə·bəl; də·spik´ə-) *adj.* Contemptible; vile; low.

destine (des´tin) *v.* To predetermine; insure or intend by fate.

destitute (des´tə·toot´) *adj.* **1.** Extremely poor. **2.** (with **of**) Totally lacking.

deteriorate (dē·tir´ē·ə·rāt´) *v.* To become or cause to be worse.

detest (dē·test´) *v.* To hate. **—detestable** *adj.*

dexterous (deks´tər·əs; -trəs) *adj.* Being skillful in using the body or mind. **—dexterously** *adv.*

dictate (dik´tāt´) *n.* A guiding principle; something required by authority.

dictum *n.* A formal pronouncement or statement.

diffuse (di·fyoos´) *adj.* Spread out.

digression (di·gresh´ən) *n.* A temporary turning aside from the main subject.

diligence (dil´ə·jəns) *n.* Careful, hard work.

din *n.* Loud, chaotic noise.

dire *adj.* Dreadful; awful.

discern (di·zurn´; -surn´) *v.* To perceive and recognize differences.

discomfiture (dis·kum´fi·chər) *n.* Frustration.

disconcert (disk´ən·surt´) *v.* To upset, fluster, or embarrass.

disconsolate (dis·kän´sə·lit) *adj.* Inconsolable; terribly unhappy.

discordant (dis·kôrd´ʼnt) *adj.* Not in agreement; conflicting.

disdain (dis·dān´) *n.* Scorn felt for someone considered inferior.

disheveled (di·shev´əld) *adj.* Untidy; in disorder.

disjointed (dis·joint´id) *adj.* Lacking unity; disconnected.

disown (dis·ōn´) *v.* To refuse to accept as one's own.

disparage (di·spar´ij) *v.* To speak of in a belittling way.

dispel (di·spel´) *v.* To scatter; disperse.

dispense (di·spens´) *v.* To exempt. **—dispense with** *v.* To eliminate.

disperse (di·spurs´) *v.* To break up and scatter; distribute widely.

disposed (dis·pōzd´) *adj.* Inclined; possessing a certain demeanor or tendency.

dispute (di·spyoot´) *v.* To argue; quarrel.

dissimulate (di·sim´yoo·lat´) *v.* To conceal (one's feelings, for example) by pretense.

dissipated (dis´ə·pāt´id) *adj.* Spent or wasted by excessive pleasure-seeking, especially drinking and gambling.

dissolution (dis´ə·loo´shən) *n.* Death; dissolving.

dissuade (di·swād´) *v.* To advise or persuade against

---

fat, āpe, cär; ten, ēven; is, bīte; gō, hôrn, tool; look; oil, out; up, fur; get; joy; yet; chin; she; thin, then; zh, leisure; ng, ring; ə for a in *ago*; e in *agent*; i in *sanity*; o in *comply*; u in *focus*; ´ as in *able* (ā´b'l).

an action. —**dissuasion** *n.*

distend (dis·tend′) *v.* **1.** To extend or stretch out. **2.** To be or cause to become swollen.

diversified (də·vər′sə·fīd′) *adj.* Varied.

divination (div′ə·nā′shən) *n.* Foretelling the future by means of omens or magic.

divinity (də·vin′ə·tē) *n.* Quality of being like God or a god; a god or deity.

docile (däs′əl) *adj.* Easily managed or controlled; submissive.

doctrine (däk′trən) *n.* The body of beliefs or principles of a religion, political party, and the like.

dominion (də·min′yən) *n.* Sovereignty; power to control or rule.

dumb *adj.* Silent; mute.

duplicity (dōō·plis′ə·tē) *n.* A deception based on hypocritical actions; deceitfulness.

▼ **E** ▼

ebb *v.* To weaken or decline.

edict (ē′dikt′) *n.* A decree; a publicly proclaimed order.

edify (ed′i·fī′) *v.* To instruct so as to improve morally.

efface (ə·fās′) *v.* To erase.

egocentric (ē′gō·sen′trik) *adj.* Self-centered.

elated *adj.* Very happy.

elude (e·lōōd′) *v.* To evade or escape from by cleverness or quickness.

eminence (em′i·nəns) *n.* **1.** An elevated thing or place, as a mountain. **2.** Greatness.

emphatic (em·fat′ik) *adj.* Expressed with force or stress. —**emphatically** *adv.*

emulate (em′yōō·lāt′) *v.* To imitate in order to equal or surpass.

endow (en·dou′) *v.* **1.** To give some quality to. **2.** To give money or property which will provide additional income.

engender (en·jen′dər) *v.* To cause to be; produce.

enjoin (en·join′) *v.* To command someone to do or refrain from doing something.

enmity (en′mə·tē) *n.* Hostility.

ensue (en·sōō′) *v.* To follow immediately, as an event.

enterprise (ent′ər·prīz′) *n.* An undertaking.

entreat (en·trēt′) *v.* To ask sincerely and urgently; beg.

equanimity (ek′wə·nim′ə·tē) *n.* The ability to maintain composure and calmness.

eschew (es·chōō′) *v.* To stay away from; avoid.

estrange (e·strānj′) *v.* **1.** To keep apart or separate. **2.** To make hostile or unfriendly.

etiquette (et′i·kit) *n.* Established rules of behavior in society or a profession.

evasion (ē·vā′zhən) *n.* The act of evading (a consequence or responsibility, for example) through deception or cleverness.

evoke *v.* To draw forth a mental image or reaction. —**evocation** *n.*

exasperate (eg·zas′pər·āt′) *v.* To annoy; try the patience of.

excel (ek·sel′) *v.* To be better than others.

excursion (eks·kur′zhən) *n.* A short trip taken for pleasure.

execration (ek′si·krā′shən) *n.* The act of cursing or speaking abusively of a person or thing.

executor (ek′si·kyōōt·ər) *n.* A person who carries out some action.

exhilarate (eg·zil′ə·rāt′) *v.* To make lively; stimulate.

exorcise (eks′ôr·sīz′) *v.* To drive out an evil spirit by a religious or magic ritual. —**exorcist** *n.*

expanse (ek·spans′) *n.* A wide, open area.

expedient (ek·spē′dē·ənt) *n.* A thing useful to achieve an end.

extirpate (ek′stər·pāt′) *v.* To destroy; exterminate; uproot.

extort (eks·tôrt′) *v.* To get money or goods by threats or violence.

exude (eg·zyōōd′; -zōōd′) *v.* To ooze.

exult (eg·zult′) *v.* To be very happy; to feel joyful and triumphant.

▼ **F** ▼

faction (fak′shən) *n.* A split within an organization or country; internal conflict.

fallow *adj.* Plowed but not cultivated or planted.

falsification (fôl′sə·fi·kā′shən) *n.* A false or misleading statement.

falter (fôl′tər) *v.* To weaken or waver.

fastidious (fas·tid′ē·əs) *adj.* Overly particular and critical. —**fastidiously** *adv.*

fatuous (fach′ōō·əs) *adj.* Contentedly stupid; foolish.

feign (fān) *v.* To pretend.

felicity (fə·lis′i·tē) *n.* Joy; gladness.

fervent (fur′vənt) *adj.* Very warm or intense in feeling.

fervor (fur′vər) *n.* Strong, warm feeling.

filial (fil′ē·əl) *adj.* Of, referring to, or appropriate for one's children.

flaccid (flak′sid; flas′id) *adj.* Flabby; hanging loosely.

flail *v.* To beat with a stick or whip.

flaunt (flônt) *v.* To make a showy, impudent display; show off.

flout *v.* To scoff or jeer at; scorn.

forbear (fôr'bər') *v.* [past tense, *forbore*] To refrain from; to be patient.

foreboding (fôr·bōd'ing) *n.* A prediction or feeling that something harmful will take place; apprehension.

forestall (fôr·stôl') *v.* To prevent or delay by taking action ahead of time.

forfeit (fôr'fit) *v.* To lose, give up, or be deprived of because of some crime or failure.

forge *v.* To make a metal object by heating and hammering.

forlorn (fôr·lôrn') *adj.* Deserted; miserable; hopeless.

formidable (fôr'mə·də·bəl) *adj.* Producing fear or horror.

forswear *v.* (fôr·swer') To promise abstinence from; pledge to give up.

fortitude (fôr'tə·tōod') *n.* The strength to bear misfortune or pain with patience.

foster *v.* To bring up or raise with care.

fraternal (frə·turn'əl) *adj.* Brotherly.

frivolity (fri·väl'ə·tē') *n.* Lack of seriousness or sense; silliness.

furtive (fur'tiv) *adj.* Secretive; done in a stealthy or sneaky way.

futile (fyōot'l) *adj.* Useless; hopeless.

▼ G ▼

gall (gôl) *n.* 1. Feeling of bitterness. 2. Irritation, annoyance.

gambol (gam'bəl) *v.* To frolic; to play animatedly.

gaunt (gônt) *adj.* Lean and bony; emaciated; scrawny.

gentility (jen·til'i·tē) *n.* 1. The quality of being refined and polite. 2. The condition of being born into the upper classes.

glade *n.* An open area or space, especially in the woods.

glut *n.* Excessive fullness.

goad *v.* To urge on.

grapple (grap'əl) *v.* To struggle in hand-to-hand combat.

grizzled (griz'əld) *adj.* Gray, especially in reference to hair.

grueling (grōo'əl·ing) *adj.* Exhausting; very difficult.

guile (gīl) *n.* Deceitfulness and craftiness; cunning.

guise (gīz) *n.* 1. Manner or way of dressing. 2. Deceiving or false appearance.

gyration (jī·rā'shən) *n.* The act of moving in a circular or spiral path around a central axis or point.

▼ H ▼

haggard (hag'ərd) *adj.* Gaunt, having a wasted, wild look.

haggle *v.* To argue about the price of.

hapless (hap'lis) *adj.* Unlucky.

harry *v.* 1. To disturb or worry; harass. 2. To force or prod.

havoc (hav'ek) *n.* Vast destruction or ruin.

hectic (hek'tik) *adj.* Happening in a confused or excited rush.

heedless (hēd'lis) *adj.* Paying no attention.

homage (häm'ij; äm'-) *n.* Something given or done to show respect.

homily (häm'ə·lē) *n.* A sermon, especially on a religious or biblical subject.

hovel (huv'əl) *n.* A small, impoverished dwelling or hut.

hover (huv'ər) *v.* To float or remain suspended in the air; wait close by, especially in an annoying way.

▼ I ▼

icon (ī'kän) *n.* A picture or image, regarded as sacred, of a religious figure.

ignoble (ig·nō'bəl) *adj.* Not noble; common or low.

immaculate (im·mak'yōo·lit) *adj.* 1. Spotlessly clean. 2. Flawless. 3. Pure; innocent.

imminent (im'ə·nənt) *adj.* Likely to happen very soon.

immutable (im·myōot'ə·bəl) *adj.* Unchangeable.

impartial (im·pär'shəl) *adj.* Unbiased; not favoring either side in a dispute or contest.

impassive (im·pas'iv) *adj.* Displaying no emotion; calm.

impediment (im·ped'ə·mənt) *n.* Hindrance.

impel (im·pel') *v.* To propel; drive forward.

impend (im·pend') *v.* To be about to occur; to loom.

impenetrable (im·pen'i·trə·bəl) *adj.* Not capable of being passed through; dense.

---

fat, āpe, cär; ten, ēven; is, bīte; gō, hôrn, tōol, look; oil, out; up, fur; get; joy; yet; chin; she; thin, then; zh, leisure; ng, ring; ə for *a* in *ago; e* in *agent; i* in *sanity; o* in *comply; u* in *focus;* ' as in *able* (ā'b'l).

imperceptible (im′pər·sep′tə·bəl) *adj.* Not easily sensed.—**imperceptibly** *adv.*

imperial (im·pir′ē·əl) *adj.* **1.** Of or relating to an empire. **2.** Majestic.

imperious (im·pir′ē·əs) *adj.* Bossy; arrogant; domineering.

impervious (im·pur′vē·əs) *adj.* Incapable of being attacked.

implacable (im·plā′kə·bəl; -plak′-) *adj.* Not capable of being pacified or quieted.

implore (im·plôr′) *v.* To beg or plead for.

impotent (im′pə·tənt) *adj.* Powerless, ineffective. —**impotently** *adv.*

impregnable (im·preg′nə·bəl) *adj.* Not capable of being penetrated or entered by force.

improvise (im′prə·viz′) *v.* To make or do with the materials at hand in order to fill a pressing need.

impudent (im′pyoo·dənt) *adj.* Disrespectfully bold; brazen. —**impudently** *adv.*

impulsive (im·pul′siv) *adj.* Acting or likely to act without forethought or plan. —**impulsively** *adv.*

incantation (in′kan·tā′shən) *n.* The recitation of magical words to cast a spell or perform magic.

incarnate (in·kär′nit; -nāt) *adj.* Appearing as a recognizable, living example; personified.

incendiary (in·sen′dē·er′ē) *adj.* Related to the deliberate destruction of property by fire.

incense (in·sens′) *v.* To make very angry; enrage.

incessant (in·ses′ənt) *adj.* Unending; continuing or repeating endlessly. —**incessantly** *adv.*

incomprehensible (in′käm·prē·hen′sə·bəl) *adj.* Not understandable.

incongruous (in·kän′groo·əs) *adj.* Inconsistent with expectations; lacking harmony or compatibility.

incredulous (in·krej′oo·ləs) *adj.* Disbelieving or unwilling to believe; skeptical.

indefatigable (in′di·fat′i·gə·bəl) *adj.* Untiring.

indifferent (in·dif′ər·ənt) *adj.* Having or displaying no preference, bias or interest.

indignation (in′dig·nā′shən) *n.* Anger felt in reaction to unfairness.

indiscretion (in′di·skresh′ən) *n.* An unwise or careless act or comment.

indispensable (in′di·spen′sə·bəl) *adj.* Of key importance; necessary.

indisposition (in′dis·pə·zish′ən) *n.* Unwellness or slight sickness.

indulgence (in·dul′jəns) *n.* **1.** The act of giving way to another's or one's own desires. **2.** Something given as a favor.

inert (in·urt′) *adj.* Characterized by mental or physical inactivity or slowness.

inextricable (in·eks′tri·kə·bəl) *adj.* Incapable of being set free or disentangled from.

infallible (in·fal′ə·bəl) *adj.* Incapable of error; reliable.

infamy (in′fə·mē) *n.* Shameful or wicked reputation.

infatuation (in·fach·oo·ā′·shən) *n.* An unreasoning or shallow love, affection, or attachment.

infer (in·fur′) *v.* To draw a conclusion from evidence or an assumption.

infuse (in·fyooz′) *v.* To put; fill. —**infused** *adj.*

ingenious (in·jēn′yəs) *adj.* Demonstrating creativity or resourcefulness.—**ingenuity** *n.*

ingrate (in′grāt) *n.* An ungrateful person.

inherent (in·hir′ənt) *adj.* Existing as an essential or natural part of the whole.

iniquity (i·nik′wi·tē) *n.* Wickedness; sinfulness; wrongdoing.

initiate (i·nish′ē·āt′) *v.* To introduce or instruct.

initiative (i·nish′ə·tiv) *n.* **1.** Responsibility for taking the first step in and following through with a project or plan. **2.** Ability to think or act for oneself, without needing encouragement or urging.

inordinate (in·ôr′də·nit) *adj.* Lacking restraint; excessive.

insensible (in·sen′sə·bəl) *adj.* Lacking sensation or consciousness; unaware.

insignificant (in′sig·nif′i·kənt) *adj.* Unimportant; of no meaning or consequence.

insolent (in′sə·lənt) *adj.* Disrespectful; rude; arrogant.

insouciant (in·soo′sē·ənt) *adj.* Calmly indifferent; carefree. —**insouciance** *n.*

instigation (in′stə·gā′shən) *n.* An urging on to some evil act.

insular (in′sə·lər) *adj.* **1.** Isolated. **2.** Narrow-minded.

insuperable (in·soo′pər·ə·bəl) *adj.* Incapable of being overcome.

intensive (in·ten′siv) *adj.* Thorough; deep; concentrated. —**intensively** *adv.*

intent (in·tent′) *adj.* Directed or fixed. —**intent on** or **upon** *adj.* Having the attention fixed; strongly directed.

intercede (in′tər·sēd′) *v.* To make an appeal on behalf of another or others. —**intercession** *n.*

interlude (in′tər·lood′) *n.* Entertainment between the acts of a play.

interminable (in·tur'mi·nə·bəl) *adj.* That which continues, or seems to continue, without end.

intermittent (in'tər·mit''nt) *adj.* Ending and beginning again at intervals.

intervene (in'tər·vēn') *v.* **1.** To occur between two points in time. **2.** To come between.

intimate (in'tə·mət) *adj.* **1.** Innermost or personal **2.** Closely acquainted; very familiar.

intimation (in'tə·mā'shən) *n.* A hint; subtle implication.

intolerable (in·täl'ər·ə·bəl) *adj.* Unbearable; too painful or severe to be endured.

intrepid (in·trep'id) *adj.* Not afraid; courageous.

intricate (in'tri·kit) *adj.* Elaborately detailed; complex.

intrigue (in·trēg'; *for n., also* in'trēg) *v.* **1.** To plot or scheme in a secret manner. **2.** To interest greatly. *n.* A secret plot or scheme.

invariable (in·ver'ē·ə·bəl) *adj.* Never changing; constant.

invert (in·vurt') *v.* To place upside down. —**inverted** *adj.*

inveterate (in·vet'ər·it) *adj.* Long-lasting; long-standing; habitual.

invoke *v.* To call on God or a god for assistance.

irreparable (ir·rep'ə·rə·bəl) *adj.* Not able to be repaired.

issue (ish'ōō; -yōō) *n.* Children; offspring.

▼ **J** ▼

jeopardy (jep'ərd·dē) *n.* Intense danger or peril.

joust *n.* A fight between two mounted knights wielding lances.

jubilation (jōō'bə·lā'shən) *n.* Triumphant joyfulness.

judicious (jōō·dish'əs) *adj.* Showing good judgment; wise and cautious.

justification (jus'tə·fi·kā'shən) *n.* A fact or argument that shows that someone is right or has acted reasonably.

juxtapose (juks'tə·pōz') *v.* To place one thing or idea close to or side by side with another.

▼ **K** ▼

kindred (kin'drid) *n.* Family; kinfolk.

knight-errant (nīt er''nt) *n.* A knight looking for ad-

ventures that will allow him to correct injustices or show his strength and skill.

knoll (nōl) *n.* Small hill.

▼ **L** ▼

laborious (lə·bôr'ē·əs) *adj.* Involving intensive work; difficult.

labyrinth (lab'ə·rinth') *n.* An complex network of winding passageways; maze.

lamentation (lam'ən·tā'shən) *n.* An outward show of grief; wailing or crying.

legitimate (lə·jit'ə·mət) *adj.* **1.** Born to married parents. **2.** Legal; lawful.

lineage (lin'ē·ij) *n.* Direct descent from an ancestor.

loath (lōth, lō*th*) *adj.* Reluctant.

loin *n.* [usually plural] The hips or the lower abdomen of the body, regarded as the source of strength and procreative power.

loll *v.* To lounge about.

lop *v.* To remove by chopping off.

lout *n.* An awkward, foolish person; oaf.

lucid (lōō'sid) *adj.* Easily understood.

lumber (lum'bər) *v.* To move about in a clumsy, noisy manner.

▼ **M** ▼

magnanimous (mag·nan'ə·məs) *adj.* Noble-spirited; generous. —**magnanimity** *n.*

malice (mal'is) *n.* Active ill will; desire to deliberately harm another; spite. —**malicious** *adj.*

malignant (mə·lig'nənt) *adj.* Very evil or dangerous.

manifest (man'ə·fest') *v.* To become apparent; show.

manifold (man'ə·fōld') *adj.* Many and diverse.

mannerism (man'ər·iz''m) *n.* A unique feature of behavior, speech, and so on, that has become habitual.

martyr (märt'ər) *n.* **1.** A person who prefers to suffer or die rather than deny his or her principles or beliefs. **2.** A person who undergoes immense pain or suffering for a long time.

materialize (mə·tir'ē·əl·īz') *v.* To appear suddenly, in concrete form.

mean *adj.* Of little value; inferior.

mediocre (mē'dē·ō'kər) *adj.* **1.** Average; ordinary **2.** Of inferior quality.

---

fat, āpe, cär; ten, ēven; is, bīte; gō, hôrn, tōol, look; oil, out; up, fur; get; joy; yet; chin; she; thin, *th*en; zh, leisure; ng, ring; ə for *a* in *ago; e* in *agent; i* in *sanity; o* in *comply; u* in *focus;* ' as in *able* (ā'b'l).

meditation (med′ə·tā′shən) *n.* Solemn reflection on spiritual matters.

melancholy (mel′ən·käl′ē) *n.* Depression; gloominess; sadness.

metaphysics (met·ə·fiz′iks) *n.* A branch of philosophy dealing with the nature of being and reality.

mete *v.* To distribute or dole out; usually with *out*.

meticulous (mə·tik′yōō·ləs) *adj.* Very careful or finicky about details.

minister (min′is·tər) *n.* A person or thing serving as the agent of some higher power.

mire *n.* An area of deep mud or slush.

misalliance (mis·ə·lī′əns) *n.* A bad partnership; a marriage of incompatible partners.

misgiving (mis·giv′ing) *n.* An unsettling feeling of fear or doubt.

monotony (mə·nät′′n·ē) *n.* Boring sameness.

morose (mə·rōs′) *adj.* Gloomy; in a bad or sullen mood.

mortify (môrt′ə·fī′) *v.* To arouse great shame or humiliation.

mundane (mun′dān′) *adj.* Of the world; ordinary, day-to-day.

muster *v.* To gather or bring together.

mutiny (myōōt′′n·ē) *n.* A revolt, as by soldiers or sailors, against their officers. —**mutinous** *adj.*

▼ N ▼

nascent (nas′ənt; nās′-) *adj.* Coming into existence; in the process of being born.

nativity (nə·tiv′ə·tē) *n.* Birth and, particularly, the circumstances surrounding a birth.

nimble *adj.* Moving about in a quick or light manner.—**nimbly** *adv.*

nocturnal (näk·tur′nəl) *adj.* Of or occurring during the night.

nonplus (nän′plus′) *v.* To puzzle or bewilder into a state of inaction.

novice (näv′is) *n.* A beginner; amateur; newcomer.

nuptial (nup′shəl) *n.* A wedding.

nurture (nur′chər) *v.* To care for, especially by feeding or protecting.

▼ O ▼

obdurate (äb′door·ət) *adj.* 1. Lacking sympathy. 2. Stubborn. —**obduracy** *n.*

oblation (ə·blā′shən) *n.* 1. Gift of or offering to God or a god. 2. The bread and wine of the Eucharist.

oblige (ə·blīj′) *v.* 1. To cause to do something by moral, legal, or physical force. 2. To perform a favor.

oblivion (ə·bliv′ē·ən) *n.* The state of complete forgetfulness.

obscurity (əb·skyoor′ə·tē) *n.* Inconspicuousness; lack of fame.

obsess (əb·ses′) *v.* To haunt in mind or preoccupy to an extreme degree.

obsolete (äb′sə·lēt′) *adj.* 1. Outdated. 2. No longer used.

obstinate (äb′stə·nət) *adj.* Very stubborn.

obtuse (äb·tōos′) *adj.* Slow to comprehend; dull-witted. —**obtuseness** *n.*

odious (ō′dē·əs) *adj.* Hateful; disgusting.

ogre (ō′gər) *n.* A monster or giant who eats people.

ominous (äm′ə·nəs) *adj.* Seeming to threaten evil or misfortune; sinister.

omnipotent (äm·nip′ə·tənt) *adj.* All-powerful.

oratory (ôr′ə·tôr′ē) *n.* Public speaking, especially in a traditional manner.

▼ P ▼

pacify (pas′ə·fī′) *v.* To make calm; to appease or make quiet.

painstaking (pānz′tāk′ing) *adj.* Taking great pains or care. —**painstakingly** *adv.*

pallid (pal′id) *adj.* Pale in color or complexion.

palpable (pal′pə·bəl) *adj.* Plainly evident to the senses.

palpitate (pal′pə·tāt′) *v.* To beat more rapidly than normal, usually referring to the heart.

paltry (pôl′trē) *adj.* Trivial; having little or no worth.

pandemonium (pan′də·mō′nē·əm) *n.* Any scene of chaotic noise or confusion.

pander *v.* To act in a way that helps satisfy the base desires or exploits the weakness of another.

paragon (par′ə·gän′) *n.* Something that is a model or example of perfection.

paternal (pə·tur′nəl) *adj.* Of or referring to the father's side of a family; fatherly.

pathos (pā′thäs′) *n.* The quality in something experienced or observed that moves one to feelings of pity or sorrow.

patriarch (pā′trē·ärk) *n.* 1. An elderly and honored man. 2. A man regarded as the father or founder of a family or institution.

patronize (pā′trən·īz′) *v.* To be helpful to or supportive of someone but treat as an inferior. —**patronizingly** *adv.*

pedant (ped′′nt) *n.* A teacher who places undue emphasis on minor details or rules rather than on genuine learning.

peer *n.* A person who is the equal of another.

peevish (pē'vish) *adj.* Difficult to please; easily irritated. —**peevishly** *adv.* —**peevishness** *n.*

pelt *n.* The coat or skin of a fur-bearing animal. *v.* To throw things at.

penitent (pen'i·tent) *adj.* Feeling sorry or regretful for having done wrong.

pensive *adj.* (pen'siv) Thoughtful; considering sad or serious matters.

perfidious (pər·fid'ē·əs) *adj.* Acting in betrayal of trust; treacherous.

peril (per'əl) *n.* Danger.

periphery (pə·rif'ər·ē) *n.* Outer parts or boundary, especially of a rounded object.

perish (per'ish) *v.* 1. To be destroyed, obliterated, or ruined. 2. To die suddenly and violently.

perplexed (pər·plekst') *adj.* Puzzled; confused.

persecution (pur'sə·kyōō'shən) *n.* The state of being cruelly oppressed or mistreated.

perseverance (pur'sə·vir'əns) *n.* Persistent, patient effort.

pervade (pər·vād') *v.* To exist widely.

perverse (pər·vurs') *adj.* Stubbornly persisting in error.

pestilence (pes'tə·ləns) *n.* Any disease, especially one of epidemic proportions, as bubonic plague.

pestilential (pes'tə·len'shəl) *adj.* 1. Of, causing, or likely to cause infection. 2. Deadly to a wide population.

petition (pə·tish'ən) *v.* To ask for sincerely or formally.

petrify (pe'tri·fī') *v.* To paralyze with fear.

phantasm (fan'taz'em) *n.* A ghost, specter; a vision of something that has no physical reality.

piety (pī'ə·tē) *n.* Loyalty (to God, parents, or country, for example).

pilgrimage (pil'grim·ij) *n.* 1. A trip undertaken by a pilgrim, especially to a holy place. 2. A long journey.

pitiable (pit'ē·ə·bəl) *adj.* Arousing or deserving compassion, sometimes mixed with scorn.

plunder (plun'dər) *v.* To steal, especially during a time of war.

ponder (pän'dər) *v.* To consider deeply and carefully.

ponderous (pän'dər·əs) *adj.* Heavy or massive.

portent (pôr'tent) *n.* Something that foretells or predicts a coming event, often of an unfortunate nature; an omen.

postulate (päs'chə·lāt') *v.* To assume, as the basis of an argument, the truth of something unproven or unprovable; claim.

practicable (prak'ti·kə·bəl) *adj.* That which can be accomplished or put into practice.

precarious (pri·ker'ē·əs) *adj.* Dependent upon uncertain circumstances or persons.

precedent (pres'ə·dənt) *n.* A case that may serve as an example for a later one.

precept (prē'sept) *n.* A command or direction for action or behavior.

precinct (prē'sinkt') *n.* A district of a city; neighborhood.

precipice (pres'i·pis) *n.* A high, steep cliff.

precipitate (prē·sip'ə·tit) *adj.* Acting or happening very hastily. —**precipitately** *adv.*

precursor (prē·kur'sər) *n.* A person or thing that comes before another; forerunner.

predatory (pred'ə·tôr'ē) *adj.* Living by hunting and feeding on other animals.

preeminent (prē·em'ə·nənt) *adj.* Very fine; surpassing all others.

preliminaries (prē·lim'ə·ner'ēs) *n., pl.* Procedures or steps leading up to main part or action.

premonition (prem'ə·nish'ən) *n.* A feeling that something unfortunate is going to happen.

preoccupied (prē·äk'yə·pīd') *adj.* Wholly absorbed with one's thoughts; engrossed. —**preoccupation** *n.*

prescience (presh'əns) *n.* Knowledge of a thing or event before it exists or takes place.

presumption (prē·zump'shən) *n.* 1. An overstepping of proper limits. 2. A supposing.

pretension (prē·ten'shən) *n.* 1. A claim to nobility or some other distinction. 2. An extravagant and unjustified outward show; pretentiousness.

prevaricate (pri·var'i·kāt') *v.* To avoid the truth; lie.

primal (prī'məl) *adj.* 1. Original. 2. Of chief importance.

---

fat, āpe, cär; ten, ēven; is, bīte; gō, hôrn, tōōl, look; oil, out; up, fur; get; joy; yet; chin; she; thin, then; zh, leisure; ng, ring; ə for *a* in *ago*; *e* in *agent*; *i* in *sanity*; *o* in *comply*; *u* in *focus*; ' as in *able* (ā'b'l).

primordial (prī·môr′dē·əl) *adj.* Existing or occurring from the world's beginning.

pristine (pris′tēn′) *adj.* **1.** Original. **2.** Unspoiled.

procure (prō·kyoōr′) *v.* To obtain or make happen by an effort; secure.

prodigal (präd′i·gəl) *adj.* Carelessly wasteful.

prodigy (präd′ə·jē) *n.* A person of amazing ability. —**prodigious** *adj.*

profound (prō·found′) *adj.* **1.** Deeply felt. **2.** Having great intellectual depth.

profuse (prō·fyoōs′) *adj.* Abundant; pouring out in excess. —**profusely** *adv.*

promontory (präm′ən·tôr·ē) *n.* A high ridge of land that overlooks a body of water.

propaganda (präp′ə·gan′də) *n.* The widespread promotion of the ideas or practices of a particular group or party intended to gain support for one's own cause or to damage another's.

propitiate (prō·pish′ē·āt′) *v.* To appease or pacify.

prostrate (präs′trāt′) *adj.* Lying face down.

protract (prō·trakt′) *v.* To prolong; lengthen.

protrude (prō·troōd′) *v.* To jut out.

provincial (prə·vin′shəl) *adj.* **1.** Narrowminded; unsophisticated. **2.** From a province, especially a rural one.

prowess (prou′is) *adj.* Bravery; courage.

prudent (proōd′′nt) *adj.* Careful; cautious.

punctual (punk′choō·əl) *adj.* Timely; prompt. —**punctually** *adv.*

purge (pʉrj) *v.* To cleanse of impurities; to clear away or out.

▼ **Q** ▼

quandary (kwän′drē) *n.* A state of perplexity or confusion; dilemma.

quarter (kwôrt′ər) *n.* **1.** A particular district or neighborhood. **2.** Lodgings. **3.** Mercy granted to a surrendering enemy.

quaver (kwā′vər) *v.* To shake or quiver.

quibble (kwib′əl) *v.* To evade the truth of a point by focusing on a petty detail.

quicken (kwik′ən) *v.* To become revived.

▼ **R** ▼

rampart (ram′pärt′, -pərt) *n.* An embankment of earth, usually supporting a wall, that encircles a castle or fort for defense against attack.

rapture (rap′chər) *n.* A joyous, almost ecstatic condition or feeling.

ratify (rat′ə·fī) *v.* To confirm; make valid or legal.

ravage (rav′ij) *v.* To ruin; destroy.

raze *v.* To lay level with the ground; destroy.

realm (relm) *n.* Kingdom; province; region.

rebuke (ri·byoōk′) *v.* To reprimand or scold.

reckoning (rek′ən·ing) *n.* **1.** The settlement or accounting of rewards or punishments for an action. **2.** Counting or calculation.

recompense (rek′əm·pens′) *v.* To pay for; compensate.

reconciliation (rek′ən·sil′ē·ā′shən) *n.* A settling of a quarrel; restoration of harmony.

recriminate (ri·krim′ə·nāt′) *v.* To meet the charges of an accuser by accusing him or her of wrongdoing. —**recrimination** *n.*

rectify (rek′tə·fī′) *v.* To amend, correct, or make right.

redemption (ri·demp′shən) *n.* A deliverance from sin and its punishments.

redouble (rē·dub′əl) *v.* To double, as in size or degree.

reflect (ri·flekt′) *v.* To contemplate seriously; ponder. —**reflection** *n.*

relent (ri·lent′) *v.* To yield.

relic (rel′ik) *n.* **1.** A thing of the past, saved for its historic interest. **2.** *pl.* Those fragments surviving from the past.

relinquish (ri·ling′kwish) *v.* To abandon claim to; let go of; yield.

rend *v.* [past tense *rent*] To rip up or tear apart violently.

render *v.* To represent or reproduce in words, pictures, or performance.

renounce (ri·nouns′) *v.* To purposefully give up a claim, right, way of living, and so forth; to repudiate or disown.

renown (ri·noun′) *n.* Illustrious reputation; great fame.

repast (ri·past′) *n.* A meal; feast.

replenish (ri·plen′ish) *v.* To refill or make complete again; to renew the supply.

reprehensible (rep′ri·hen′sə·bəl) *adj.* Deserving of criticism or blame.

repress (ri·pres′) *v.* To hold back, restrain or curb. —**repression** *n.*

reprimand (rep′rə·mand) *n.* A severe scolding, especially by someone in authority.

reproach (ri·prōch′) *v.* To scold, reprimand, or censure, especially in a way that produces shame.

reprobation (rep′rə·bā′·shən) *n.* Disapproval, condemnation, rejection.

reprove (ri·proov′) **v.** To scold or censure.

repulse (ri·puls′) **v. 1.** To repel or drive back; reject. **2.** To be disgusting to. —**repulsive adj.; repulsion n.**

reputed (ri·pyoot′id) **adj.** Recognized or supposed to be so.

requite (ri·kwīt′) **v. 1.** To repay or reward. **2.** [*Archaic*] To do something in return.

residue (rez′·ə·doo′) **n.** Left-over portion; remainder.

resin (rez′ən) **n.** A semisolid, sticky substance given off by some plants and trees.

resolute (rez′ə·loot′) **adj.** Having a decided purpose; determined.

resolve (ri·zälv′) **v.** To determine or decide; settle on.

respite (res′pit) **n.** A temporary period of rest or relief.

resplendent (ri·splen′dənt) **adj.** With much splendor; dazzling; shining brilliantly.

retaliate (ri·tal′ē·āt′) **v.** To do something to get revenge for an injury or evil. —**retaliation n.**

retinue (ret′′n·yoo′) **n.** A group of assistants and servants who follow an important person.

retort v. To reply in a quick, sharp manner.

revel (rev′əl) **v.** To be festive in a noisy manner.

reverberate (ri·vur′bə·rāt′) **v.** To resound; continue in a series of echoes.

revere (ri·vēr′) **v.** To have great respect and love for.

reverie (rev′ər·ē) **n.** Daydreaming; state of being lost in thought or imagining, especially of pleasant things.

revile (ri·vīl′) **v.** To verbally abuse someone.

rhetoric (ret′ər·ik) **n. 1.** Language intended to persuade. **2.** Showy, elaborate language that is lacking in clarity and sincerity.

rile v. To prod into action by upsetting; irritate.

rout n. An utter and overpowering defeat.

ruse (rooz) **n.** A trick.

▼ S ▼

sacrilege (sak′rə·lij) **n.** The act of taking, using, violating, or treating disrespectfully something which is consecrated to God or religion.

sage n. A person greatly respected for wisdom and judgment.

salutation (sal·yoo·tā′shən) **n.** A greeting.

sanctify (sank′te·fī′) **v.** To make or set apart as holy.

sanction (sank′shən) **n.** Official approval given for an action.

sap v. To empty, drain, or exhaust; weaken.

scourge (skurj) **n.** A punishment; a cause of severe trouble or suffering.

scrupulous (skroo′pyə·ləs) **adj.** Giving careful attention to what is right or proper.

scrutinize (skroot′′n·īz′) **v.** To examine or inspect carefully and closely.

seduce (si·doos′) **v.** To persuade into wrongdoing or disloyalty.

sensuous (sen′shoo·əs) **adj.** Perceived by the senses, especially with pleasure or enjoyment.

sepulcher (sep′əl·kər) **n.** A vault, chamber, or grave for the dead.

sequence (sē′kwens) **n.** The following of one thing after another in some logical order.

serenity (sə·ren′ə·tē) **n.** Calmness; composure; tranquility.

sever (sev′ər) **v. 1.** To cut off by force. **2.** To separate; divide.

sheaf n. A quantity of cut stalks of grain, and the like, bundled together.

sheer adj. Very steep.

shroud v. 1. To wrap a corpse in burial cloth. **2.** To hide or conceal.

siege (sēj) **n.** The besetting of a fortified place by an army to compel surrender.

sinewy (sin′yoo·ē) **adj. 1.** Strong; powerful. **2.** Marked by good muscular development.

sinister (sin′is·tər) **adj.** Ominous; indicating lurking evil or harm.

slake v. 1. Satisfy; quench. **2.** To cause a fire to die out.

slough (sluf) **v.** To get rid of or throw off.

sluice (sloos) **n.** A gate or valve used in opening or closing an artificial passage for water.

sojourn (sō′jurn) **v.** To stop and dwell in a place temporarily.

solder (säd′ər) **v.** To join (metal pieces) with a melted metal compound.

solicitous (sə·lis′ə·təs) **adj.** Showing care or attention; anxiously willing. —**solicitously adv.**

---

fat, āpe, cär; ten, ēven; is, bīte; gō, hôrn, tool, look; oil; out; up, fur; get; joy; yet; chin; she; thin, then; zh, leisure; ng, ring; ə for a in *ago*; e in *agent*; i in *sanity*; o in *comply*; u in *focus*; ′ as in *able* (ā′b'l).

soliloquy (sə·lil'ə·kwē) *n.* **1.** The act of talking to oneself. **2.** Lines in a play used to reveal a character's thoughts to the audience.

somber (säm'bər) *adj.* **1.** Dark and dismal. **2.** Melancholy; depressed.

sonorous (sə·nôr'əs; sän'ər-) *adj.* Quality of sound which is full, deep, and resonant.

sordid (sôr'did) *adj.* **1.** Dirty; squalid. **2.** Dishonorable or ignoble; mean or petty.

sovereignty (säv'rən·tē) *n.* **1.** Supreme political power or authority. **2.** Supremacy in power or position.

spit *n.* A thin, pointed rod used to hold meat over a fire.

spoils *n., pl.* Goods and land captured in war; booty.

squander (skwän'dər) *v.* To spend wastefully or extravagantly.

stamina (stam'ə·nə) *n.* Endurance; ability to stand fatigue.

statute (stach'ōot) *n.* A law or established rule.

steadfast (sted'fast') *adj.* Firmly established; unchanging; steady.

stealthy (stel'thē) *adj.* Intentionally secretive or sly. **—stealthily** *adv.*

stifling (stī'fling) *adj.* Suffocating; oppressively lacking in fresh air.

stoic (stō'ik) *adj.* Showing no emotion; indifferent.

stratagem (strat'ə·jəm) *n.* A trick or plan to fool an enemy.

stricture (strik'chər) *n.* **1.** A condition that limits, restrains, or restricts. **2.** Harsh criticism.

stupefy (stōo'pə·fī') *v.* To deprive of sensibility; stun.

stupendous (stōo·pen'dəs) *adj.* Amazing; astonishing in magnitude or scope.

stupor (stōo'pər) *n.* Condition in which there is a partial or complete loss of sensibility, as from shock.

suave (swäv) *adj.* Smoothly pleasant and polite. **—suavely** *adv.*

subdue (sub·dōo') *v.* **1.** To conquer. **2.** To bring wild land into a cultivated state.

submissive (sub·mis'iv) *adj.* Being obedient and yielding without resistance. **—submission** *n.*

subside (səb·sīd') *v.* **1.** To descend; move to a lower level. **2.** To become tranquil, less intense.

substantiate (səb·stan'shē·āt') *v.* To establish the existence or truth of; prove.

subtle (sut'·əl) *adj.* **1.** Able to see fine distinctions. **2.** Mentally acute; clever. **—subtly** *adv.*

suckle *v.* **1.** To nurse. **2.** To bring up or rear.

suffice (sə·fīs') *v.* To meet or satisfy a need; to be sufficient.

sumptuous (sump'chōo·əs) *adj.* Expensive; lavish; luxurious.

superficial (sōo'pər·fish'əl) *adj.* **1.** Concerned only with the obvious; not profound; shallow. **2.** Lying on or affecting only the surface.

superfluous (sə·pur'flōo·əs) *adj.* **1.** Not necessary or needed. **2.** More than is needed.

supplant (sə·plant') *v.* To replace, especially through force, trickery, or treachery.

supplication (sup'lə·kā'shən) *n.* A humble prayer or request to a deity or superior.

surety (shoor'ə·tē) *n.* Guarantee.

surpass (sər·pas') *v.* To excel; outdo all others.

surreptitious (sur·əp·tish'əs) *adj.* Secretive. **—surreptitiously** *adj.*

sway *n.* Influence; clout; dominant control.

syntax (sin'taks) *n.* The arrangement, organization, and relationship of words in a sentence.

▼ **T** ▼

taciturn (tas'ə·turn') *adj.* Usually silent; not fond of talking.

tantamount (tan'tə·mount') *adj.* Equivalent in value, meaning, or effect.

tarry *v.* To stay in a place, especially in expectation; delay; linger.

temper *v.* To bring steel to the required degree of strength and toughness by heating and sudden cooling.

temperate (tem'pər·it) *adj.* Moderate; self-restrained.

tempestuous (tem·pes'chōo·əs) *adj.* Like a storm with high winds and heavy rain; violent.

temporal (tem'pə·rəl) *adj.* **1.** Worldly; not eternal. **2.** Of, pertaining to, or limited by, time.

tenet (ten'it) *n.* Any principle or creed held to be true, especially by some organization.

tenuous (ten'yōo·əs) *adj.* **1.** Not dense, as the atmosphere at a high altitude. **2.** Insubstantial; fragile; inadequate.

tepid (tep'id) *adj.* Lukewarm.

terminate (tur'mə·nāt) *v.* To end.

theological (thē'ə·läj'i·kəl) *adj.* Having to do with the study of God.

throng *n.* A multitude of people crowded together.

thwart (thwôrt) *v.* To hinder; block.

timorous (tim'ər·es) *adj.* Fearful; timid. **—timorously** *adv.*

torrid (tôr'id) *adj.* **1.** Very hot, especially with reference to climate. **2.** Extremely passionate.

tortuous (tôr'chōō·əs) *adj.* Winding; crooked; not straight.

transact (tran·zakt') *v.* To carry on or conduct, especially business —**transaction** *n.*

transgress (trans·gres') *v.* To go beyond the limits set by laws, commandments, and so forth. —**transgression** *n.*

traverse (trə·vʉrs') *v.* To move across.

tribute (trib'yōōt) *n.* Money paid to one nation's sovereign by another, as a tax, payment for protection, and so on.

tumult (tōō'mult') *n.* Noisy commotion and uproar; violent disturbance.

turmoil (tʉr'moil) *n.* Disturbed activity; violent agitation.

▼ **U** ▼

unassailable (un'ə·sāl'ə·bəl) *adj.* Unable to be successfully attacked or challenged.

unassuming (un'ə·sōō'ming) *adj.* Modest.

unconditional (un·kən·dish'ən·əl) *adj.* Absolute; without exceptions or reservations.

undermine (un'dər·mīn') *v.* **1.** To wear away the foundations of. **2.** To cause to weaken by craft or stealth.

underpin (un'dər·pin') *v.* To prop up or support from underneath.

undeterred (un·dē·tʉrd') *adj.* Not kept from action by fear or doubt.

undulate (un'dyōō·lāt) *v.* To move in a wavelike manner.

unremitting (un'ri·mit'ing) *adj.* Persistent; persevering; not stopping. —**unremittingly** *adv.*

unshriven (un·shriv'ən) *adj.* Without forgiveness of sin through confession.

unwonted (un·wän'tid) *adj.* Uncommon; unaccustomed; unusual.

upbraid (up·brād') *v.* To scold or rebuke strongly.

usurp (yōō·zʉrp') *v.* To take power unlawfully.

▼ **V** ▼

valiant (val'yənt) *adj.* Brave.

valor (val'ər) *n.* Bravery.

vanguard (van'gärd) *n.* The leading part of an army.

vanquish (vang'kwish) *v.* To conquer.

vehement (ve'ə·ment) *adj.* With great passion —**vehemently** *adv.*

venerate (ven'ər·āt') *v.* To look upon with reverence.

vent *v.* To express feelings.

veracious (və·rā'shəs) *adj.* **1.** Telling the truth; honest. **2.** Characterized by truth and accuracy.

vermin (vʉr'mən) *n. pl.* Various insects regarded as pests.

versatile (vʉr'sə·təl) *adj.* Able to do many things.

vex *v.* To irritate; annoy. —**vexation** *n.*

vicissitudes (vi·sis'ə·tōōdz') *n. pl.* Unpredictable and irregular changes in fortune, life, and so on; ups and downs.

vile *adj.* Very bad; evil; wicked; low.

vindictive (vin·dik'tiv) *adj.* Tending to seek revenge; retaliatory. —**vindictiveness** *n.*

vivacity (vi·vas'ə·tē) *n.* Liveliness; spiritedness.

void *n.* That which is empty; vacuum. *adj.* Empty; vacant.

voluminous (və·lōōm'ə·nəs) *adj.* **1.** Filling, or capable of filling, volumes. **2.** Of great quantity.

vulnerable (vul'nər·ə·bəl) *adj.* Easily attacked, tempted, or damaged.

▼ **W** ▼

wake *n.* A watch over a dead body before burial.

wane *v.* To grow smaller gradually, said of the moon's face, after it has been fully lighted.

wanton (wän'tən) *adj.* Willfully and intentionally malicious.

wax *v.* To grow larger gradually, said of the lighted portion of the moon's face, until the full moon is visible.

wisp *n.* A slender, filmy fragment or strand.

wrangle (rang'gəl) *v.* To dispute or quarrel angrily and noisily; brawl.

wrathful (rath'fəl) *adj.* Extremely angry.

wrest (rest) *v.* To snatch or wrench forcibly.

writhe (rīth) *v.* To twist and turn in pain.

▼ **Z** ▼

zenith (zē'nith) *n.* **1.** The summit; peak. **2.** That point in the sky directly overhead.

---

fat, āpe, cär; ten, ēven; is, bīte; gō, hôrn, tōōl, look; oil, out; up, fʉr; get; joy; yet; chin; she; thin, *th*en; zh, leisure; ng, ring; ə for *a* in *ago*; *e* in *agent*; *i* in *sanity*; *o* in *comply*; *u* in *focus*; ' as in *able* (ā'b'l).